AF715076

International Investment Law and the Pandemic

Nijhoff International Investment Law Series

Series Editors

Prof. Eric De Brabandere (*Leiden University*)
Prof. Tarcisio Gazzini (*University of Padua*)
Prof. Stephan W. Schill (*University of Amsterdam*)
Prof. Attila Tanzi (*University of Bologna*)

Editorial Board

Andrea K. Bjorklund (McGill University) – Juan Pablo Bohoslavsky (UNCTAD and Universidad Nacional de Rio Negro [Argentina]) – Chester Brown (University of Sydney) – Patrick Dumberry (University of Ottawa) – Michael Ewing- Chow (National University of Singapore) – Susan D. Franck (American University) – Ursula Kriebaum (University of Vienna) – Makane Mbengue (University of Geneva) – Catherine A. Rogers (Penn State Law) – Christian Tams (University of Glasgow) – Andreas Ziegler (University of Lausanne)

VOLUME 26

The titles published in this series are listed at *brill.com/iils*

International Investment Law and the Pandemic

Edited by

Antonino Alì, Sondra Faccio, Marco Pertile

BRILL | NIJHOFF

LEIDEN | BOSTON

Cover image: © 2024 Artists Rights Society (ARS), New York / VG Bild-Kunst, Bonn. The Montreal Museum of Fine Arts.

Library of Congress Cataloging-in-Publication Data

Names: Alì, Antonino, editor. | Faccio, Sondra, editor. | Pertile, Marco, editor.
Title: International investment law and the pandemic / edited by Antonino Alì, Sondra Faccio, and Marco Pertile.
Description: Leiden ; Boston : Brill, 2025. | Series: Nijhoff international investment law series | Includes bibliographical references and index. | Summary: "At the dawn of the most serious and challenging global health emergency of contemporary times, the investment regime, with its Investor-State Dispute Settlement (ISDS) mechanism, was already facing its own 'crisis'. In 2019, the number of treaty terminations were exceeding the number of new treaties entering into force, with the Energy Charter Treaty experiencing a veritable exodus. The ISDS was undergoing a reform, which aimed to dismantle the system based on ad hoc arbitration in favour of a multilateral court. States began to enact laws to review FDI in strategic sectors, concerned that foreign investors could undermine national security. Some commentators argued that the investment regime, and ISDS in particular, was 'shrinking', or even 'dead'.
Identifiers: LCCN 2024040266 | ISBN 9789004711198 (hardback) | ISBN 9789004711204 (ebook)
Subjects: LCSH: Investments, Foreign (International law) | Investments, Foreign–Law and legislation. | COVID-19 Pandemic, 2020-
Classification: LCC K3830.I5845 2025 | DDC 346/.092–dc23/eng/20240828
LC record available at https://lccn.loc.gov/2024040266

Typeface for the Latin, Greek, and Cyrillic scripts: "Brill". See and download: brill.com/brill-typeface.

ISSN 2351-9542
ISBN 978-90-04-71119-8 (hardback)
ISBN 978-90-04-71120-4 (e-book)
DOI 10.1163/9789004711204

Copyright 2025 by Koninklijke Brill BV, Leiden, The Netherlands.
Koninklijke Brill BV incorporates the imprints Brill, Brill Nijhoff, Brill Schöningh, Brill Fink, Brill mentis, Brill Wageningen Academic, Vandenhoeck & Ruprecht, Böhlau and V&R unipress.
All rights reserved. No part of this publication may be reproduced, translated, stored in a retrieval system, or transmitted in any form or by any means, electronic, mechanical, photocopying, recording or otherwise, without prior written permission from the publisher. Requests for re-use and/or translations must be addressed to Koninklijke Brill BV via brill.com or copyright.com.

This book is printed on acid-free paper and produced in a sustainable manner.

Contents

Notes on Editors

Antonino Alì

is Associate Professor of International Law at the Faculty of Law and at the School of International Studies of the University of Trento (Italy). He previously held positions as an Assistant Professor of International Law at the University of Milan (2002–2005) and the University of Geneva (1999). His most recent research activity focuses on the relationship between national security and both International and European law. As of February 2024, he serves as a member of the 'Core Group for Assessment and Strategic Analysis on the Exercise of Special Powers' within the Department for Administrative Coordination at the Presidency of the Council of Ministers of Italy.

Sondra Faccio

is Associate Professor of International Law at the School of International Studies and the School of Law of the University of Trento (Italy). She is an attorney at law, admitted to the Bar of Verona (Italy). She has been a visiting scholar at the University of Cincinnati College of Law (2023), Ernst Mach Scholar at Vienna University-Faculty of Law (2012–2013), and visiting PhD student at Columbia Law School (2010–2011). Her fields of expertise are International investment law and arbitration, conflict of laws.

Marco Pertile

is Professor of International Law at the School of Law and the School of International Studies of the University of Trento (Italy). Since 2018, he has been teaching a course on Human Rights and Natural Resources at PSIA – Sciences Po in Paris. Previously, he was Visiting Professor (2012–2017) and Marie Curie Fellow (2010–2012) at the Graduate Institute of International and Development Studies in Geneva, Lecturer at the Geneva Academy of International Humanitarian Law and Human Rights (2011), Visiting Professional at the International Criminal Court (2006) and Visiting Researcher at the Max Planck Institute in Heidelberg (2003). He's co-Director of the Journal QIL – Questions of International Law.

Notes on Contributors

Pia Acconci

is a Professor of International Law at the University of Teramo. She holds a PhD in International Economic Law. She has an extensive teaching and lecturing portfolio, covering topics on investment and health protection at various universities and international conferences. Acconci's extensive publications focus on the intersection of international and EU law. She actively participates in and leads research and study groups, notably as co-coordinator of the SIDI Interest Group on 'International and EU Health Law' since June 2016 and as a member of the ILA Committee on 'Global Health Law' since 2015. In addition, she was the academic coordinator of the Jean Monnet module on EU investment law from September 2018 to February 2023.

David Collins

is a Professor of International Economic Law at City, University of London specializing in law of the WTO and international investment law with a particular focus on digital trade and services. He is Co-Editor in Chief of the journal International Trade Law & Regulation and Series Editor for Routledge's Insights on International Economic Law. He is admitted as a Solicitor in England & Wales and Called to the Bars of Ontario and New York.

Tarcisio Gazzini

is Professor of International Law at the University of Padova. He has also taught at the Universities of Glasgow and VU Amsterdam. Between 2014 and 2017 he co-directed a research project financed by the Swiss National Science Foundation on Foreign Investment in Africa: Gaining Development Momentum. He's the author of Interpretation of Investment International Treaties (Hart, 2016) and a founding member of the book series International Investment Law (Brill).

Marco Grantaliano

is an associate at the Brussels office of Gianni & Origoni. He graduated from the University of Rome – La Sapienza and the College of Europe (Bruges), with an LLM in European Law and Economic Analysis. He was legal and economic consultant at the Italian Ministry of Economic Development. He joined Gianni & Origoni's Antitrust and Regulatory team in 2021. He specializes in EU and Italian competition law, with a focus on State aid control and foreign direct investment control, and routinely collaborates with universities in Italy and abroad to assist, teach, and research on EU law and competition law matters.

Silvina González Napolitano
is Professor of Public International Law at the University of Buenos Aires and University Torcuato Di Tella. As an expert in the Ministry of Foreign Affairs of Argentina she has participated in the negotiation of several investment treaties. She also acts as arbitrator in investment arbitration. In the past, she worked in the Argentine Treasury Attorney General's Office, first as counsel and then as Director of the National Directorate of International Affairs and Controversies, where she represented Argentina in about 50 investment arbitrations.

Gian Maria Farnelli
is Associate Professor of International Law at the Department of Legal Studies, University of Bologna. He has been counsel and research assistant for Italy in inter-state disputes and research assistant to arbitrators in investor-state disputes. He has been a member of the Italian delegation during the Intergovernmental Conference on the negotiation of the Agreement on biological diversity of areas beyond national jurisdiction. His publications, in Italian and English, address issues of law of the sea, environmental law, State immunity, investment law and the law of international adjudication.

Jens Hillebrand Pohl
is an Adjunct Professor at Maastricht University and the United Nations University. An experienced attorney, having practiced before U.S. federal and state courts in New York and for EU institutions, Jens holds an LL.M. from Harvard Law School and a MSc in Economics and Business from Stockholm School of Economics, and is pursuing two PhDs in law and political science at Maastricht University and Tampere University, respectively. He is the founding series editor of Springer Studies in Law & Geoeconomics and a former article editor of the Harvard International Law Journal.

Avidan Kent
PhD (Cantab) is an Associate Professor in Law, the Law School's Director of Research, and the Founder and Convenor of UEA's International Law Research Group. He has written/edited books, reports, journal articles and chapters on a varied list of topics, including Environmental Law, International Economic Law, International Tribunals, Public Participation and Climate-Induced

Migration. He has written reports/papers for IGOs, governments, think tanks and one museum.

Yulia Levashova
is an Associate Professor at Nyenrode Business University in the Netherlands and a director of the dispute prevention program at the Asia Pacific FDI Network. Her specialization is international investment arbitration, commercial arbitration, Corporate Social Responsibility (CSR) and due diligence. Levashova is also an independent practitioner who serves as an arbitrator and provides legal consultancy to the Dutch government and international organizations, e.g., UNECE and UNCTAD.

Sebastián Mantilla Blanco
is an Assistant Professor of International Economic Law at The Fletcher School of Law & Diplomacy (Tufts University). Previously, he was a Post-Doctoral Researcher at the University of Bonn in Germany, a Post-Doctoral Global Fellow at New York University (Spring 2023), and an Independent Counsel at Zuleta Abogados (Colombia). He was also a Visiting Professor at the School of Law and Political Sciences of the Universidad de la Sabana in Colombia. He holds a Doctorate in Law (Dr. Iur.) as well as an LL.M. from the University of Bonn, and a law degree from the Pontificia Universidad Javeriana in Bogotá (Colombia).

Ksenia Polonskaya
is a faculty member at Carleton University. Her research focuses on international law, legal theory, and international investment arbitration. She is a convener of the Interest Group on Feminism and International Law with the European Society of International Law (ESIL).

Francesco Salerno
is a practicing competition lawyer with a PhD from the London School of Economics. Francesco Maria has several years of experience advising clients on foreign direct investment matters before the European Commission and the Courts in Luxembourg. He has published several articles on independent regulatory authorities, competition law and regulation in network industries and he has published with Lexology the chapter on FDI in Italy.

Jamie Trinidad KC
is a Fellow and Director of Studies in Law at Wolfson College, Cambridge, and a Fellow of the Lauterpacht Centre for International Law. He is also a practising barrister.

Valentina Vadi
is an Adjunct Professor in International Law at the School of Political Sciences of the University of Florence and a Research Fellow at the Department of Political Science, Law, and International Studies of the University of Padua. She was formerly a Professor in International Economic Law at Lancaster University (2015–2021). She is the author of several monographs and more than a hundred articles in peer-reviewed journals in the field of international economic law.

Mikael Wigell
is Research Director at the Finnish Institute of International Affairs. He is also Adjunct Professor at Tampere University and Expert Member of the World Economic Forum. He earned his PhD at the London School of Economics and he has been a Visiting Fellow at the Changing Character of War Centre, Oxford University. His latest book is as editor of Geo-economics and Power Politics in the 21st Century: The Revival of Economic Statecraft (Routledge, 2018; 2020).

Niccolò Zugliani
is a postdoctoral Research Fellow at Bocconi University and an Adjunct Professor at the University of Milan. He holds a PhD from the University of Verona and an LLM from the University of Vienna. He has been visiting PhD candidate at the Grotius Centre for International Legal Studies, at the University of Ottawa, and at the Amsterdam Center for International Law. He has published on issues of public international law, international economic law and jurisdiction of domestic courts.

Introduction

Antonino Alì, Sondra Faccio, and Marco Pertile

At the dawn of the most serious and challenging global health emergency of contemporary times, the investment regime, with its Investor-State Dispute Settlement (ISDS) mechanism, was already facing its own 'crisis'. In 2019, the number of treaty terminations were exceeding the number of new treaties entering into force, with the Energy Charter Treaty experiencing a veritable exodus.[1] The ISDS was undergoing a reform, which aimed to dismantle the system based on ad hoc arbitration in favour of a multilateral court.[2] States began to enact laws to review FDI in strategic sectors, concerned that foreign investors could undermine national security.[3] Some commentators argued that the investment regime, and ISDS in particular, was 'shrinking', or even 'dead'.[4]

Despite this, three years after the World Health Organization (WHO) declared the novel coronavirus (2019-nCoV) a public health emergency of international concern, the number of ISDS claims has continued to rise,[5] even

1 Center for International Environmental Law (CIEL), International Institute for Sustainable Investment (IISD) and ClienthEarth, 'Investor-State Dispute Settlement (ISDS) Mechanisms and the Right to a Clean, Healthy, and Sustainable Environment. Joint Submission from IISD, CIEL and ClientEarth on the Call for Inputs from the UN Special Rapporteur on Human Rights and the Environment' (2023) <www.iisd.org/publications/brief/iisd-ciel-clientearth-isds-sustainable-enivronment-submission-2023> accessed 5 October 2023; UNCTAD, 'The Changing IIA Landscape: New Treaties and Recent Policy Developments' (2020) IIA Issues Note No 1 <https://investmentpolicy.unctad.org/publications/1230/the-changing-iia-landscape-new-treaties-and-recent-policy-developments>, accessed 5 October 2023.

2 As to the ISDS reform, see the webpage of the United Nations Commission on International Trade Law (UNCITRAL), Working Group III: Investor-State Dispute Settlement Reform <https://uncitral.un.org/en/working_groups/3/investor-state> accessed 5 October 2023.

3 For example, Regulation (EU) 2019/452 of the European Parliament and of the Council of 19 March 2019 Establishing a Framework for the Screening of Foreign Direct Investments into the Union [2019] OJ L079I/1.

4 CIEL, IISD and ClientEarth (n 1) 3; Douglas Thomson, 'EU Says "ISDS is Dead" ahead of Japan Trade Deal' (Global Arbitration Review, 6 July 2017) <https://globalarbitrationreview.com/article/eu-says-isds-dead-ahead-of-japan-trade-deal> accessed 5 October 2023.

5 At least 68 ISDS cases were initiated under international investment agreements (IIAs) in 2021, compared to 68 know cases in 2020 and 55 in 2019. See, UNCTAD, 'Facts on Investor-State Arbitrations in 2021: With a Special Focus on Tax-related ISDS Cases' (2022) IIA Issues Note No 1 <https://investmentpolicy.unctad.org/publications/1266/facts-on-investor-state-arbitrations-in-2021-with-a-special-focus-on-tax-related-isds-cases> accessed 5 October 2023; UNCTAD, 'Investor-State Dispute Settlement Cases: Facts and Figures 2020' (2021) IIA

© KONINKLIJKE BRILL BV, LEIDEN, 2025 | DOI:10.1163/9789004711204_002

though only a few of them relate to measures taken by states during the pandemic.[6] States have continued to negotiate a new generation of investment treaties, including provisions aimed at limiting the discretion of arbitral tribunals and avoiding excessive restrictions on states' regulatory powers for health purposes.[7] Overall, screening measures have not deterred FDI flows.[8]

However, it is undeniable that the pandemic has influenced the changes already underway and has also questioned the capacity of the system to respond to unexpected challenges. Crucial issues include the screening of FDI in strategic sectors, states' room to maneuver in adopting public policy measures, and the conduct of arbitral proceedings, including the use of experts and scientific knowledge.

In this regard, the book embraces two different but interrelated perspectives. Firstly, it questions reforms, concerning both arbitral proceedings and investment treaties, in light of the needs exposed by the pandemic. It also aims to understand whether such needs influenced the screening mechanisms. Secondly, it investigates the resilience of international investment law and arbitration focusing on the challenges posed by the pandemic. Indeed, it is submitted that, regardless of the ongoing reforms, the current regime may already feature legal tools that allow for appropriate reaction capacity.

More specifically, the book is divided into four parts: the first part dwells on the reform of the ISDS mechanism and investment treaties; the second focuses on the investment screening and the adoption of legal instruments to address security or public order risks; the third investigates the application of old and new generation of investment treaty standards, as well as treaty and customary law defences; the last part assesses the use of scientific data and knowledge in investment arbitration.

Issues Note No 4 <https://investmentpolicy.unctad.org/publications/1256/investor-state-dispute-settlement-cases-facts-and-figures-2020#:~:text=In%202020%2C%20at%20least%2068,by%20the%20end%20of%202020.> accessed 5 October 2023; UNCTAD 'Investor-State Dispute Settlement Cases Pass the 1,000 Mark: Cases and Outcomes in 2019' (2020) IIA Issues Note No 2 <https://investmentpolicy.unctad.org/publications/1231/investor-state-dispute-settlement-cases-pass-the-1-000-mark-cases-and-outcomes-in-2019> accessed 5 October 2023.

6 *VINCI Highways SAS and VINCI Concessions SAS v. Republic of Peru*, ICSID Case No ARB/21/60; *ADP International SA and Vinci Airports SAS. v. Republic of Chile*, ICSID Case No ARB/21/40. Some cases indirectly involve COVID-related measures, e.g., *Cyrus Capital Partners, LP and Contrarian Capital Management, LLC v. United Mexican States*, ICSID Case No. ARB/23/33.

7 See Chapters 1, 2, 8, 9, 11, 12.

8 Report from the Commission to the European Parliament and the Council, Second Annual Report on the screening of foreign direct investments into the Union, (2022) COM(2022)433 final, 2.

With reference to the first part, the scholarly debate has shown that one of the main criticisms of the international investment law regime relates to arbitral control over the exercise of public authority by host states. As such, investment treaties are perceived as unduly restricting the freedom of states to purse economic, social, health or environmental policies. Therefore, since the first decade of the new century, a new generation of investment treaties has been negotiated by states to address public concerns and avoid excessive restrictions on their regulatory powers. Criticism has also targeted the ISDS mechanism, which at the time of the pandemic was in the process of being reformed under the auspices of the UNCITRAL.

Acconci (Chapter 1) illustrates this trend and relates it to the issues that have arisen in past health-related investment arbitration cases, such as patent protection and access to essential medicines, and control over harmful goods such as tobacco. The author argues that the competition between the protection of public health and the protection of investments under different regulatory tools has emerged as a common feature within international investment arbitration. Existing international legal instruments, including the new generation of investment treaties, do not, however, fully succeed in striking a fair balance between them. The author thus pleads for the adoption of a new multilateral wide-ranging investment treaty.

Gazzini and Vadi (Chapter 2) focus specifically on investment treaty practice during and after the COVID pandemic, assessing how the challenges faced by states during the pandemic have led them to rethink their investment treaties. The chapter examines clauses that limit the scope of certain substantive provisions, such as those on indirect expropriation, and exceptions that states may invoke to justify or excuse a conduct otherwise contrary to treaty obligations. The authors argue that the COVID pandemic has not only made the reform of investment agreements more urgent than ever, but also demonstrated the need to amend treaties with a view to safeguarding public health without undermining the protection of investors and the enjoyment of intellectual property rights.

Polonskaya (Chapter 3) examines the impact of the pandemic on the ISDS reform and the administration of arbitral proceedings. She shows that different actors – *i.e.*, states, investors, international organizations, and tribunals – have responded to the challenges posed by the pandemic adopting solutions of a procedural and technical nature, which may foster coordination and contribute to the reform of the ISDS mechanism.

The second part of the book illustrates the impact of the pandemic on investment screening and on the adoption of mechanisms to address risks to security and public order.

Domestic screening of foreign investment, often on national security grounds, had already intensified before the pandemic, in parallel with geo-economic rivalry between states. Indeed, over the past decade, FDI has increasingly been used by states as an instrument of economic statecraft. Screening and restrictive measures have been introduced to limit the influence of foreign investors in strategic areas and to exert pressure on certain states by curbing investors' incoming and outgoing activities.

Taking a broad view of the global scenario, Pohl and Wigell (Chapter 4) describe governments' concerns about geo-economic rivalry and associated risks, showing that they have shaped the way states deal with FDI. The authors also discuss how the existing international legal frameworks may face a changing landscape. Considering the impact of the recent pandemic on states' perceptions of geo-economic risks, they draw out the future implications for international investment law and policy.

Alì (Chapter 5) examines how the COVID pandemic has led to a significant re-evaluation of global FDI screening processes. In the short term, heightened concerns about foreign acquisition of critical health care and medical technology assets have resulted in a tighter regulatory framework for screening FDI in the health sector. The pandemic has had long-term consequences, including shifts in supply chains which have led governments to consider economic resilience and supply chain stability alongside traditional security concerns in assessing their national interest. In addition, the economic downturn caused by the pandemic has made certain industries more vulnerable to foreign takeovers, prompting governments to expand their mechanisms for monitoring and regulating foreign direct investment. As a result, the chapter describes the interplay of immediate and enduring factors shaping FDI screening practices in the post-COVID world.

Salerno and Grantaliano (Chapter 6) focus on the screening framework adopted by the European Union (Regulation (EU) No. 2019/452) and analyse data on screening activities during the pandemic in three selected EU jurisdictions, namely France, Italy, and Germany. The authors show that although enforcement of FDI screening mechanisms increased significantly between 2020 and 2022, the increase cannot be directly attributable to the pandemic. According to the authors, other factors, reflecting the geo-economic rivalry described by Pohl and Wigell, were already in place well before the COVID crisis and influenced the rise of investment screening in the years 2020–2022.

The third part of the book proceeds to illustrate the application of treaty standards and potential defences by states in investment disputes involving governments' policies adopted to tackle the pandemic and, more broadly, health and environmental emergencies. In this context, the number of cases in which investors have challenged COVID-related measures is limited and their outcome is still unknown.[9] Therefore, the chapters draw on past arbitral practice to trace the possible evolution of the interpretation and application of treaty standards in cases involving public health, safety, and environmental measures.

Mantilla Blanco (Chapter 7) focuses on the full protection and security standard and considers the potential of the standard in the context of COVID-related measures. Based on past arbitral decisions, the author discusses the extent to which the COVID pandemic fits into the categories of risk covered by the full protection and security standard and examines states' responses to the pandemic through the prism of due diligence. The author argues that scientific knowledge can be a central element in the assessment of the full protection and security standard in cases involving health and environmental issues. He suggests that the Agreement on the Application of Sanitary and Phytosanitary Measures under WTO law may provide a valuable framework for the use of scientific evidence in the review of pandemic-related measures by arbitrators.

Levashova (Chapter 8) captures recent developments in the application of the fair and equitable treatment standard and the right to regulate, in order to identify the main points of reference for arbitral tribunals in the context of possible direct and indirect COVID-related claims, or any claims arising from states' emergency measures. The author discusses the 'list of requirements' elaborated by arbitral tribunals for the assessment of legitimate expectations, including the legitimate objective of the state to serve the public interest. She concludes by advocating the adoption of a structured reasoning by arbitrators based on the application of the first prong of the proportionality test (the review of the measure's suitability), combined with the duty to defer to the state authorities' margin of appreciation.

Zugliani (Chapter 9) approaches the analysis of indirect expropriation considering the provisions of the new generation of treaties aimed at safeguarding the states' regulatory powers and discusses the application of the 'police powers doctrine' in the context of COVID-related regulatory measures. The author concludes that, despite states' and arbitrators' effort to establish some 'point of references' in the assessment of indirect expropriation, international investment proceedings remain highly unpredictable, and a finding of a regulatory expropriation will mostly depend on the specific circumstances of each case.

Two closely related chapters then follow: Collins (Chapter 10) and González Napolitano (Chapter 11) deal with the defences of states under customary law and investment treaties, respectively.

---

9 See the cases mentioned in (n 6).

Collins focuses on the customary defences of states, in particular *force majeure*, distress, and necessity. He observes that necessity appears to be the best option for host states to argue in cases involving COVID-related measures, but problems may arise for respondents in attempting to demonstrate their necessary lack of contribution to the circumstances of the immanent peril and in proving that the measures were proportionate and/or reasonable to the threat. According to the author, the success of customary international law defences is likely to depend on whether the various measures taken by states are seen as effective or counterproductive, which in the context of the COVID pandemic has been undoubtedly a matter of much controversy around the world.

González Napolitano reviews a number of arbitral awards, in which defences relating to the right to health, the environment or safety have been invoked on the basis of treaty provisions on exceptions or non-precluded measures. She discusses the approach taken by tribunals in these cases, with a view to determining the scope of states' action to protect health in future cases involving pandemic-related measures, the defences available to them in the event of claims by affected investors, and the likelihood of success of their defences in the light of previous tribunals' decisions. The author notes that despite the efforts of states to draft more precise provisions on the right to regulate and exceptions in new-generation treaties, these provisions still lend themselves to multiple interpretations by investment tribunals. New treaties should thus contain even more precise guidelines to distinguish the scope, limits, and effect of the state's regulatory power, both in general and in emergency situations.

The final part of the book deals with the use of scientific data and knowledge in investment arbitration. Science-intensive legal issues in investment arbitration increasingly require arbitrators to engage with scientific and technical knowledge when assessing claims. So far, the use of science has played a major role only in relation to some environmental, public health and energy disputes, but it is expected to become a key aspect of future investment disputes involving pandemic-related measures and climate change policies. In these proceedings, scientific evidence will be key and international guidelines together with recommendations and technical documents from specialized agencies (such as the WHO) may become an important point of reference for adjudicators, not only to understand the factual background of the dispute, but also to assess the legitimacy and reasonableness of the measure at issue. In addition, the introduction of science into the proceedings through *amici curiae* briefs and/or party and tribunal experts and the rules governing their use, will become pivotal to the effective management of investment arbitration proceedings and the quality of their outcomes.

Against this backdrop, Faccio (Chapter 12) illustrates whether, and to what extent, scientific knowledge and information have been used by arbitrators in the past and how they are expected to be used in the future in assessing states' regulatory measures. According to the author, science is expected to play a growing and influential role in investment arbitration, extending beyond pandemics to encompass environmental and energy matters. Science may be relevant in assessing whether a genuine risk exists, whether the measures taken by the state are in good faith and appropriate in light of the risk, and whether their application is reasonable. In the opinion of the author, general standards and guidelines elaborated by international organizations or NGOS can ensure that all countries have equal access to scientific information when adopting regulatory measures.

Kent and Trinidad (Chapter 13) discuss public participation in investment arbitration and how *amici curiae* can provide valuable public health-related knowledge in ISDS proceedings. Drawing on the broader practice of *amicus* interventions in public health-related ISDS proceedings, the authors discuss what lessons can be learned to address future pandemics.

Farnelli (Chapter 14) reviews the current procedural framework for the use of experts in investment arbitration. The author observes that the assessment of scientific and technical facts – through experts – has played and will continue to play an (increasingly) important role in investment arbitration, especially in relation to health and environmental disputes. However, the importance of experts has not yet been matched by a corresponding development in the procedural rules governing their use in investment arbitration. In this regard, he argues that direct regulation by relevant ISDS institutions providing guidelines for the use of tribunal-appointed experts may be a wise solution for dealing with highly technical and specialized medical and environmental issues.

CHAPTER 1

Public Emergencies and Investment Law before the Pandemic: Past Emergencies and Lessons Learned

Pia Acconci

1 Introductory Remarks

The COVID-19 pandemic has been an extraordinary global emergency presenting significant challenges both from economic and social standpoints. Developments arising from such an emergency are still uncertain from an international and EU law perspective.

This chapter illustrates how investment arbitral tribunals have assessed competing public and private interests in cases involving health measures before the COVID-19 pandemic, notably the AIDS, malaria and tuberculosis emergencies that occurred in least-developed countries during the 1990s, the worldwide tobacco consumption emergency,[1] and the Argentinian crisis at the beginning of the current Millennium. These three pre-COVID-19 emergencies occurred at a time when a revaluation of the conventional pro-investor framework of international investment treaties was about to start. This analysis may help understanding the impact of the COVID-19 pandemic on the international investment legal framework and its ongoing revision.

As it is known, since the middle of the last century,[2] international investment law has expanded through the conclusion of thousands of international treaties, primarily bilateral in nature. Under their traditional framework, investment treaties do not provide for the protection of public health and/or other non-economic interests, such as the environment and/or cultural heritage, as they have been designed with the specific objective of promoting

1 At the time of the negotiation and conclusion of the Framework Convention on Tobacco Control (FCTC), the World Health Organization (WHO) pointed out tobacco consumption was an epidemic and a global problem. This is still its view, as it can be inferred from WHO, 'WHO Report on the Global Tobacco Epidemic, 2021' (2021) <https://iris.who.int/bitstream/handle/10665/343287/9789240032095-eng.pdf?sequence=1> accessed 28 August 2023.

2 The first bilateral investment treaty was the Germany-Pakistan BIT (signed 25 November 1959, entered into force 28 April 1962).

© KONINKLIJKE BRILL BV, LEIDEN, 2025 | DOI:10.1163/9789004711204_003

and protecting foreign investments.[3] Such treaties include provisions on non-discriminatory treatment, fair and equitable treatment, expropriation and the settlement of disputes between a national investor of one state-party and of another state-party through direct arbitration. This recurring legal framework is evident in numerous bilateral investment treaties and investment chapters in free trade agreements.

Until the beginning of this Millennium, the lack of specific provisions for the protection of public health in international investment treaties was not a subject of considerable discussion, in light of regulatory diversification typical of international law. This diversification has traditionally kept the international regulatory protection of economic and non-economic interests separate. In addition, the number of arbitral proceedings arising from the application of such treaties was relatively small. Treaty-based arbitral tribunals were established mainly because of acts of expropriation justified by economic reasons.

Things have changed since then. The number of cases has increased dramatically, leading to an ongoing debate on the legitimacy of international investment law, in terms of reasonableness, proportionality and democratic principles.[4] Disputes arising from domestic non-discriminatory regulatory measures implemented to pursue public interest objectives have become common features in investment arbitration. Foreign investors have activated treaty protections alleging that such measures amounted to a breach of the fair

3 This is mainly due to their original design, which aimed to facilitating and protecting investments made by a national of one contracting party, commonly an economic advanced state, in the territory of another contracting party, usually a developing country, on the assumption that relevant flows of investments abroad had a typical pattern, from the north to the south of the world.

4 See, among others, Barnali Choudhury, 'Recapturing Public Power: Is Investment Arbitration's Engagement of the Public Interest Contributing to the Democratic Deficit?' (2008) 41 Vand J Transnatl L 775; Benedict Kingsbury and Stephan Schill, 'Public Law Concepts to Balance Investors' Rights with State Regulatory Actions in the Public Interest – the Concept of Proportionality' in Stephan Schill (ed) *International Investment Law and Comparative Public Law* (OUP 2010) 75; Gus van Harten, 'Investment Treaty Arbitration, Procedural Fairness, and the Rule of Law' in Stephan Schill (ed) *International Investment Law and Comparative Public Law* (OUP 2010) 627; Jason Webb Yackee, 'Toward a Minimalist System of International Investment Law?' (2008–2009) 32 Suffolk Transnational Law Review 303; Nida Mahmood, 'Democratizing Investment Laws: Ensuring 'Minimum Standards' for Host States' (2013) 14 Journal of World Investment & Trade 79; Lorenzo Cotula, 'Democraticising International Investment Law' (IIED 2015) <www.iied.org/sites/default/files/pdfs/migrate/12577IIED.pdf> accessed 28 August 2023; Barnali Choudhury, 'International Investment Law and Non-Economic Issues' (2020) 53 *Vanderbilt Journal of Transnational Law* 1; Jeswald J Salacuse, *The Law of Investment Treaties* (3rd edn, OUP 2021).

and equitable treatment standard[5] and/or to a form of indirect expropriation.[6] According to claimants, these measures had to comply with the requirements for lawful expropriation as laid down in the applicable international investment treaty. Consequently, a state could only implement a health-related domestic regulatory measure in a non-discriminatory manner and upon payment of adequate, effective, and prompt compensation, even if such a measure was the outcome of the exercise of regulatory powers for the safeguard of a public interest.[7]

As a result, some economically advanced states, like Canada, the United States, the Netherlands, and Italy, along with some emerging states, such as India, have started to focus on the revision of the typical pro-investor approach of their international investment treaties by negotiating the inclusion of safeguards and/or other special provisions for the protection of non-economic

5 States have included fair and equitable treatment clauses in their investment treaties, mostly bilateral, to balance conflicting interests: those of foreign investors and those of host states through the establishment of mutual relations based on reasonableness, proportionality and fairness. Arbitral case-law shows that the effective interpretation and application of these treatment causes have become an autonomous reason for disputes. Specifically, various arbitral tribunals have considered, and sometimes upheld, claims of foreign investors for compensation of their alleged legitimate expectations arising from treaty fair and equitable treatment clauses as to the stability, in terms of invariability, of a host state's domestic law. See, among the others, the following early cases *Metalclad Corporation v. The United Mexican States*, ICSID Case No. ARB(AF)/97/1, Award (30 August 2000) para 99; *Tecnicas Medioambientales Tecmed S.A. v. Mexico*, ICSID Case No. ARB(AF)/00/2, Award (29 May 2003) para 154; *Azurix Corp. v. The Argentine Republic*, ICSID Case No. ARB/01/12, Award (14 July 2006).

6 See, among the others, the following early cases *Antoine Geotz and Others v. Burundi*, ICSID Case No. ARB/95/3, Award (10 February 1999); *Pope & Talbot, Inc. v. Canada*, UNCITRAL, Interim Award (26 June 2000); *CME Czech Republic B.V. Investments v. The Czech Republic*, UNCITRAL, Partial Award (13 September 2001). See Sondra Faccio, *Indirect Expropriation in International Investment Law. Between State Regulatory Powers and Investor Protection* (Editoriale Scientifica 2020).

7 As to arbitral cases related to public health, see, in particular, *Chemtura Corporation v. Government of Canada*, UNCITRAL, Award (2 August 2010); *LG&E Energy Corp., LG&E Capital Corp., and LG&E International, Inc .v. Argentine Republic*, ICSID Case No. ARB/02/1, Decision on Liability (3 October 2006); *Compañía de Aguas del Aconquija S.A. and Vivendi Universal S.A. v. Argentina*, ICSID Case No. ARB/97/3, Award (15 August 2007); *Les Laboratoires Servier, S.A.S., Biofarma, S.A.S., Arts et Techniques du Progres S.A.S. v. Republic of Poland*, UNCITRAL, PCA Award (14 February 2012); *Apotex Holdings Inc. and Apotex Inc. v. The United States*, ICSID Case No. ARB(AF)/12/1, Award (25 August 2014); *Eli Lilly and Company v. Canada*, UNCITRAL, Final Award (16 March 2017).

interests.[8] The European Commission has contributed to this trend, after the Lisbon Treaty entered into force in 2009, which included foreign direct investments as part of EU exclusive competence on common commercial policy. Since then, the European Commission has negotiated and/or concluded international treaties which not only provide for safeguards and exceptions, but also for specific provisions and/or clauses on sustainable development and a host State's 'right to regulate' for public interests. One important example of a mega-regional economic agreement between the European Union member states and Canada is the 2016 Comprehensive Economic and Trade Agreement (CETA).[9]

2 The Issue of Access to Essential Drugs and Increasing Foreign Investments in the Pharmaceutical Sector

Access to essential drugs by people of least-developed countries has become an international issue with the entry into force of the Trade-Related Aspects of Intellectual Property Rights (TRIPS) Agreement in 1995. The TRIPS Agreement establishes minimum standards of protection and enforcement that each government has to guarantee to the intellectual property held by nationals of fellow WTO members. As epidemics of diseases such as AIDS, malaria and tuberculosis in least developed countries have underscored, the protection of intellectual property may conflict with the need to grant affordable access to essential drugs. Affordable access to essential drugs can make the difference in terms of deaths and economic burden on domestic healthcare services, as such countries lack local pharmaceutical manufacturing capacity.

Even before the TRIPS Agreement took force in 1995, various strategies were employed by both industrialised WTO members, such as Canada, and developing WTO members, like India, to circumvent pharmaceutical patents and keep the price of essential drugs low.[10] For example, compulsory licensing, which

---

8 See, in particular, the Model BIT published by the United States in 2012, India in 2015, the Belgium-Luxembourg Economic Union (BLEU) and the Netherlands in 2019, Italy in 2020 and Canada in 2021.

9 EU-Canada Comprehensive Economic and Trade Agreement (signed 30 October 2016, provisionally in force 21 September 2017) (CETA). Updates and information about CETA are available on the website of the European Commission.

10 Before the entry into force of the TRIPS Agreement in 1995, the most common methods used to circumvent pharmaceutical patents were four. First, states denied product patents, that is provided only for patents concerning process, but not products, within their national law systems. Second, they provided for flexibility as regards protecting

can be defined as an 'authorization granted by a government to a party other than the holder of a patent on an invention to use that invention without the consent of the patent holder', allows for the production of a generic equivalent drug without the consent of the patent holder.[11] Conversely, voluntary licensing is usually provided via an arrangement between the patent holder and the generic producer. Article 31 of the TRIPS Agreement provides for compulsory licensing, but under strict conditions. Article 31, letter (f), establishes that compulsory licensing must be granted 'predominantly for the supply of the domestic market of the member authorizing such use', apart from national emergencies or compulsory licensing granted to react to anti-competitive

pharmaceutical patents, by allowing a Bolar exception. This means that a company is allowed to do tests and/or trials on patented drugs of another company, without the permission of the patent holder, in order to gain regulatory approval before the expiry of a patent and put its generic version on the market as soon as the patent expires. Third, states authorized importation of a patented drug without the permission of the patent holder. Under this method, parallel importers buy at a low price in one state and import (it) into another state whose home market has a higher price for the drug. This method is commonly known as parallel importation and it is based on the exploitation of the differences in prices fixed by a patent holder in the markets of different states. Such differences can be considerable. Parallel importation becomes a public issue if the importing state's patent law provides that the rights of the patent holder have been exhausted when its patent has been placed on the market in another state with its consent. Thus, the patent holder cannot exercise its rights in the importing state to prevent parallel importation. Fourth, a state public body or agency granted permission to copy a patented drug to meet local needs before the patent expired and without the authorization of the patent holder. Methods numbers one and fourth allowed companies, that wished to make a copy of a patented drug, to do it legally. Since 1995, the recourse to such methods, in particular to numbers one and four, has become more difficult. The TRIPS Agreement does not regulate the resort to a Bolar exception or to parallel importation. This implies that such practices are, in principle, permitted. Article 6 of the TRIPS Agreement is relevant, as this provides that '[f]or the purposes of dispute settlement under this Agreement, subject to the provisions of articles 3 and 4 nothing in this Agreement shall be used to address the issue of the exhaustion of intellectual property rights'. Articles 3 and 4 deal with national and most-favoured-nation treatments. See, among the others, Pia Acconci, 'The Implementation of the Patent Regulation of the TRIPS Agreement and the Protection of Non-trade Values. Have Continuous Negotiations Become the Mechanism for Balancing Them?' in Aldo Ligustro, Giorgio Sacerdoti (eds), Liber Amicorum *in Honour of Paolo Picone. New Trends in International Economic Law* (Editoriale Scientifica 2011) 803; Ping Xiong, 'Pharmaceutical Patents in the TRIPS Agreement and the Right to Health. Can These Rights Be Reconciled?' (2012) 36 UWAL Rev 115; Kimberly Bagdis, 'The Whole Is Greater than the Sum of Its Parts: A Holistic Approach to TRIPS' (2021) 36 Temp Intl & Comp L 197.

11 See WIPO, *Intellectual Property Handbook: Policy, Law and Use* (WIPO Publication 2004) 34–40.

practices. This means that states lacking local pharmaceutical manufacturing capacity, for example least-developed states, cannot import from states which are specialised in the generic production of some essential drugs, like Brazil and India.[12] There have been some attempts to not implement the TRIPS Agreement, particularly article 31, letter f). After years of discussion within and outside the WTO, such a provision was eventually amended.[13] This example concerning generic drugs and compulsory licensing under the TRIPS Agreement shows how international and national responses to a humanitarian issue, such as access to essential drugs at affordable price by people of least-developed states, can be impacted by international rules protecting economic interests, like pharmaceutical patents.

Not only international treaty rules on trade, but also those on investment are relevant, as intellectual property rights are often included in the lists of possible protected investments under the applicable treaties.[14] In this regard, it is worth mentioning that a few states have revised their international investment

12 Some attempts not to apply article 31, letter f, of the TRIPS Agreement were successful, like that of South Africa at the end of nineties of the last century. Its government attempted to promote generic production of drugs through law. In 1998, a coalition of multinational pharmaceutical companies went to the High Court of Pretoria to object to this attempt. However, the same coalition retired its claim under pressure from NGOs and international public outcry in 2001. WTO Members have agreed on a political and regulatory solution in order to also allow compulsory licensing for exportation from a Member specialized in the production of generic, that is affordable, essential drugs to a least developed Member in need to satisfy its people requests without having adequate domestic capacity.

13 The new text runs as follows 'the obligations of an exporting Member under article 31, letter f), shall not apply with respect to the grant by it of a compulsory license to the extent necessary for the purposes of production of a pharmaceutical product(s) and its export to an eligible importing Member(s).' This amendment was adopted in 2005 and entered into force in 2017. This is not the best solution needed, but its existence along with other similar mechanisms are still bargaining tools for least developed countries, among others, to promote voluntary licensing.

14 Although there is no absolute definition of investment, a typical open-ended definition reads as follows: '[t]he term "investment" means every kind of asset established or acquired by an investor of one Contracting Party in the territory of the other Contracting Party in accordance with the laws and regulations of the latter and shall include particularly, but not exclusively: a) movable and immovable property as well as any other rights in rem, such as mortgages, liens, and pledges; [...]; c) claims to money which have been used to create an economic value or claims to any performance having an economic value; d) intellectual property rights, such as copyrights, patents, industrial designs or models, trade or service marks, trade names, technical processes, know-how and goodwill, as well as other similar rights recognized by the laws of the Contracting Parties'. Italy-Lebanon BIT (signed 7 November 1997, entered into force 9 February 2000) art 1.

treaties to exclude compulsory licensing from the scope of the provisions on regulatory expropriations,[15] although no dispute between a host state and a foreign investor concerning compulsory licensing has been brought before an investment arbitral tribunal so far. Other disputes concerning foreign investments in the pharmaceutical sector have nonetheless been referred to treaty-based arbitration.[16]

For example, access to essential drugs is indirectly at the root of the case *Eli Lilly and Company v. Canada,* brought before an UNCITRAL arbitral tribunal established in accordance with the 1992 North America Free Trade Agreement (NAFTA).[17] According to the claimant, a US corporation, the denial by Canadian courts, including the Supreme Court, of the claimant's patent on two main components of drugs – 'atomoxetine' and 'olanzapine' –, amounted to a breach of the standards of treatment provided for in the NAFTA. In the claimant's opinion, Canada had breached, amongst others, its obligation under article 1105 of the Treaty to accord fair and equitable treatment. The claim was based on the claimant's alleged 'legitimate expectations' under such a provision. The tribunal did not uphold the investor's claim.[18] Two points can be made in relation to this case. First, the objections made by Canada, the respondent State, were in line with its traditional favourable approach towards the production of generic pharmaceutical products. Indeed, Canada has traditionally implemented and interpreted applicable international trade rules with a certain degree of flexibility with a view to granting the maximum possible access to essential drugs, rather than absolute protection of the patent holder's exclusive rights.[19] Second, a relevant number of third parties submitted reports and/

15 For instance, disputes arising from a domestic regulatory act establishing compulsory licensing are outside the field of application of any treaty concluded by India in accordance with its 2015 Model BIT. This means that such disputes cannot be settled through arbitration. See also, among others, the Myanmar-Singapore BIT (signed 24 September 2019, not in force) art 6.5; Brazil-India BIT (signed 25 January 2020, not in force) art 3.6, letter c); Bahrain-Japan BIT (signed 23 June 2022, not in force) art 11.6.

16 See Sébastien Manciaux, 'Big Pharma and Investment Arbitration' (2021) 4 Vietnamese J of L Sciences 88.

17 *Eli Lilly and Company v. The Government of Canada*, UNCITRAL, ICSID Case No. UNCT/14/2, Notice of Arbitration (12 September 2013).

18 ibid, Award (16 March 2017) paras 387, 430, 441–442. The judgments of Canadian courts had been issued over a period of six years, specifically from 2002 to 2008.

19 In particular, Canadian domestic legislation allows to resort to the so-called 'Bolar exception', that is the experimental use exception in relation to the regulatory approval of medicines. Under this 'exception' a third party can use a patented invention for such an approval, without the consent of the patent's holder. See Viviana Munoz Tellez, 'Bolar Exception' in Carlos M Correa and Reto M Hilty (eds), *Access to Medicines and Vaccines* (Springer Link 2021).

or briefs as *amici curiae* to the arbitral tribunal to show the heterogeneity of interests at the root of the dispute. In particular, *amici*'s briefs underlined two conflicting needs: on the one hand, the need of patent holders as private investors to rely on the protection of their exclusive rights and, on the other, the need of affordable pharmaceutical products worldwide.[20]

Other issues concerning pharmaceutical products have arisen from the application of international investment treaties. One concerned whether or not the application for a new marketing authorization for a drug or for a renewal of an existing authorization could be qualified as an investment under the applicable international investment treaty. In *Les Laboratoires Servier, S.A.S., Biofarma, S.A.S., Arts et Techniques du Progres S.A.S. v. Poland,* the state refused to renew the claimant's marketing authorization for a few of its drugs. The investor, a multinational pharmaceutical company based in France, brought a claim against Poland under the 1990 France – Poland BIT. The arbitral tribunal upheld the claim based on the BIT and decided that Poland's refusal to renew the authorization amounted to an indirect expropriation without compensation.[21] This decision was based on an extensive interpretation of the definition of investment provided in the applicable treaty, as the tribunal considered the marketing authorisation – the 'right' to sell – within such a definition, although the economic activity at stake – selling – was not an investment itself. The tribunal decided that the denial of such an authorization amounted to expropriation.[22] Under this decision, the production and selling of pharmaceutical products abroad is an investment like any other. In contrast, the arbitral tribunal in the *Apotex I* and *Apotex II* cases, which involved a claim against the United States, came to the opposite conclusion. This tribunal declined its jurisdiction by deciding that a marketing authorization application was a commercial activity, rather than an investment under such a Treaty.[23] The tribunal relied on the definition of investment in the NAFTA, which includes an exhaustive list of relevant economic activities, whereas the majority of international investment treaties include a non-exhaustive list in this respect.

---

20 See, among others, *Eli Lilly* (n 17) Amicus Curiae Submission of Intellectual Property Law Professors (23 February 2016) submitted by dr Burcu Kilic, professor Brook K Baker, professor Cynthia Ho and Mr Yaniv Heled; by a group of intellectual property law professors; and by the Canadian Generic Pharmaceutical Association.

21 *Les Laboratoires Servier, S.A.S., Biofarma, S.A.S., Arts et Techniques du Progres S.A.S. v. Poland,* UNCITRAL, PCA Award (14 February 2012). Many parts of this award are redacted.

22 ibid paras 575, 642–645.

23 *Apotex Holdings Inc. and Apotex Inc. v. The United States,* ICSID Case No. ARB(AF)/12/1, Award (25 August 2014) paras 243–246.

Keeping in mind that several cases related to the pharmaceutical sector have been amicably settled or discontinued, while others remain unpublished, the aforementioned examples show the heterogeneous nature of investment disputes within this sector. Consequently, a case-by-case approach is also expected to prevail in future decisions because of the variety of treaty definitions of investment, their typical open-ended languages, and differences in the approach of arbitrators.

3 Tobacco Control as a Health Issue within International Investment Law

The implementation of the Framework Convention on Tobacco Control (FCTC), that was concluded within the World Health Organization (WHO) on 21 May 2003 and entered into force on 27 February 2005, is another relevant example of competing economic and non-economic concerns (i.e. health concerns) before the COVID-19 pandemic.[24]

Following the entry into force of the FCTC, a few WHO member states chose to adopt plain packaging legislations. In two investment treaty-based arbitral proceedings, Philip Morris claimed that these legislations amounted to indirect expropriations as trademarks were an investment under the applicable investment treaties.[25]

The arbitral tribunals, which were convened in response to Phillip Morris' claims against Australia and Uruguay, did not render decisions in favour of the prioritization of the protection of public health over the protection of foreign investors. Nevertheless, they did not rule in favour of the claimants.

The arbitral tribunal established by the Permanent Court of Arbitration on request of Philip Morris Asia Ltd. against Australia, in accordance with the Arbitration Rules of the UNCITRAL, did not deal with the legitimacy of the 2011 Australia's Plain Packaging Legislation, under the 1993 bilateral investment treaty between Hong Kong and Australia. The tribunal declined its jurisdiction based on its determination that 'the commencement of treaty-based investor-State arbitration constitutes an abuse of right (or abuse of process) when an

24 The WHO Framework Convention is the only international convention that has been concluded in accordance with the WHO Constitution. Its article 19 provides for the adoption of international conventions by the WHO Assembly.

25 See *Philip Morris Asia Ltd. v. Australia*, UNCITRAL Award on Jurisdiction and Admissibility (17 December 2015), and *Philip Morris Brands SARL, Philip Morris Product S.A. and Abal Hermanos S.A. v. Uruguay*, ICSID Case No. ARB/10/7 Award (8 July 2016).

investor has changed its corporate structure to gain the protection of an investment treaty at a point in time where a dispute was foreseeable'.[26]

An ICSID arbitral tribunal was convened in response to the request made by several subsidiaries of Philip Morris International Inc., namely Philip Morris Brands SARL, Philip Morris Product S.A. and Abal Hermanos S.A., against Uruguay. The tribunal's primary focus was to determine the legitimacy of the domestic measures on tobacco control, as regulated by the 1988 bilateral investment treaty between Switzerland and Uruguay. The tribunal considered such measures as domestic health-related regulatory measures and concluded that they were the outcome of the exercise of the host State's 'police powers'.[27] Specifically, the tribunal underlined that '[p]rotecting public health has since long been recognized as an essential manifestation of the State's police power'.[28] During the proceedings, Uruguay had in effect maintained that its 'regulations were applied in a non-discriminatory manner to all tobacco companies, and they amounted to a reasonable, good faith exercise of Uruguay's sovereign prerogatives'.[29] The tribunal upheld this view, by stressing that '[t]he Challenged Measures were taken by Uruguay with a view to protect public health in fulfilment of its national and international obligations'.[30] In his

26 *Philip Morris v. Australia* (n 25) para 389. As to the position of the claimant, see particularly paras 265–266, 281 ff. In particular, the tribunal concluded that Philip Morris, the parent company, did not hold a relevant decision-making power over the local subsidiary, Philip Morris Asia Ltd. Philip Morris had taken the control after the restructuration of this subsidiary. According to the claimant, the enactment of the 'Plain Packaging' Legislation was not expected. See ibid paras 389–397. Conversely, according to the Tribunal, 'the adoption of the Plain Packaging Measures was foreseeable well before the Claimant's decision to restructure was taken (let alone implemented)' ibid paras 390–391, 566–569. As to Australia's view, see ibid para 393.

27 *Philip Morris v. Uruguay* (n 25) para 287.

28 ibid para 291. The tribunal, inter alia, specifies that 'the Challenged Measures were a valid exercise by Uruguay of its police powers for the protection of public health. As such, they cannot constitute an expropriation of the Claimants' investment. For this reason also, the Claimants' claim regarding the expropriation of their investment must be rejected' ibid para 307.

29 ibid para 13, 216–221. Paragraph 216 clarifies that '[i]t is Uruguay's submission that preserving and protecting public health is a quintessential manifestation of police power, which is in turn an essential element of a State's permanent sovereignty. Uruguay has the right to exercise its inherent sovereign power to protect public health without incurring international responsibility generally (either for alleged expropriation or breach of other standards of treatment).'

30 ibid para 306. According to the tribunal, the domestic regulatory measures taken by Uruguay were not 'arbitrary and unnecessary' but rather were potentially 'effective means to protecting public health'. The tribunal also stresses that 'the incidence of smoking in Uruguay has declined, notably among young smokers [...] and that these were public

concurring and dissenting opinion, arbitrator Gary Born also acknowledges Uruguay's regulatory sovereignty 'to regulate in the interests of public health and safety in the future'. He underlines that the arbitral award 'makes clear that Uruguay possesses broad and unquestioned sovereign powers to protect the health of its population, both in the context of tobacco regulation and otherwise' and that '[n]othing in the BIT prevents Uruguay from exercising these powers'.[31] The WHO, which intervened as *amicus curiae*, emphasised that 'tobacco consumption and the exposure to tobacco smoke cause death, disease and disability' in light of unequivocal scientific evidence and the domestic regulatory measure at stake was the domestic implementing legislation of the WHO FCTC.[32] As it will discussed further in Chapter 12, the *Philip Morris v. Uruguay* case is important, because of the participation of the World Health Organization and the use by the arbitral tribunal of the WHO FCTC as an 'evidence-based treaty'. In other cases, however, scientific uncertainty is much more common. For example, anti-COVID-19 domestic regulatory measures were not based on international 'evidence-based' instruments, by contrast there was a sharp debate on their scientific foundations and states did not follow the WHO International Health Regulations. As a matter of fact, the lack of preparedness in terms of national response and prevention capacity was due to low implementation of these Regulations.

4 Relevant Arbitral Investment Treaty-Based Cases against Argentina

Because of its emergency laws adopted in the between 2001 and 2002, a great number of arbitral tribunals were established on the basis of international investment agreements against Argentina, to decide whether or not such laws

---

health measures which were directed to this end and were capable of contributing to its achievement.' ibid paras 307, 391. In this connection, the tribunal referred to the position of the Organization of Economic and Development Cooperation (OECD), as its membership is still mainly composed of home states of foreign investors, other investment treaty-based arbitral cases, international customary law, a few general principles, like proportionality and good faith, beyond the letter of the law, that is beyond the letter of the applicable international investment agreement, certain international treaties, such as the 2014 Free Trade Area Agreement between the European Union and Singapore, the reports submitted to the tribunal by the World Health Organization and by the Pan-American Health Organization as *amici curiae*. See ibid para 391.

31 See ibid, Concurring and Dissenting Opinion Co-Arbitrator Gary Born (8 July 2016) paras 90, 197.

32 See ibid, Written Submission (Amicus Curiae Brief) by the WHO and the Secretariat of the Tobacco Control Convention (28 January 2015).

required compensation in accordance with the applicable treaties. Argentina submitted a few counterclaims to show that its financial crisis had brought about both economic and social instability, amongst others in terms of worsening health conditions in its territory[33] and, thus, its laws were justified under necessity in light of international customary law, applicable international investment agreements and/or under relevant international conventions on human rights protection, such as the 1966 International Covenant on Economic, Social and Cultural Rights.[34] According to Argentina, conflicting international obligations were at stake in these cases and its choice to sacrifice the protection of foreign investments was justified for the safeguard of economic and social human rights of its people.

Arbitral tribunals have reached different conclusions regarding the significance of the serious social crisis in Argentina. Some arbitral tribunals accepted Argentina's arguments, whilst others dismissed them. For example, the ICSID arbitral tribunal in the case of *LG&E v. Argentina* established that Argentina's financial crisis had adversely affected the quality of domestic healthcare services and hindered local people's universal access to essential drugs.[35] The tribunal concluded that 'Argentina's enactment of the Emergency Law was a necessary and legitimate measure on the part of the Argentine Government',[36]

33 See, in particular, Jayson J Falcone, 'Argentina's Plight – An Unusual Temporary Solution to a Sovereign Debt Crisis' (2003–2004) Suffolk Transnational Law Review 357; Jörn Axel Kämmerer, 'Argentine Debt Crisis' (2014) *Max Planck Encyclopedia of Public International Law* <https://opil.ouplaw.com/display/10.1093/law:epil/9780199231690/law-9780199231690-e1818> accessed 28 August 2023.

34 See, among others, *Suez, Sociedad General de Aguas de Barcelona S.A. and Vivendi Universal S.A. v. Argentina*, ICSID Case No. ARB/03/19, and *AGW Group v. Argentina*, UNCITRAL, Decision on jurisdiction (30 July 2010) para 262 where the tribunal specifies that 'Argentina is subject to both international obligations, *i.e.* human rights *and* treaty obligation, and must respect both of them equally. Under the circumstances of these cases, Argentina's human rights obligations and its investment treaty obligations are not inconsistent, contradictory, or mutually exclusive. Thus, as discussed above, Argentina could have respected both types of obligations'; *SAUR v. Argentina*, ICSID Case No. ARB/04/4, Decision on jurisdiction and liability (6 June 2012) paras 328–332; *EDF v. Argentina*, ICSID Case No. ARB/03/23, Award (11 June 2012) paras 909–914, where the tribunal denies that Argentina's conduct could be justified by international *jus cogens* concerning 'basic human rights such as life, health, personal integrity and education, which were directly threatened by the socio-economic crisis suffered by Argentina'. See also Urbaser S.A. and Consorcio de Aguas Bilbao Bizkaia, Bilbao Biskaia Ur Partzuergoa v. The Argentine Republic, ICSID Case No. ARB/07/26, Award (8 December 2016) para 1200. See also Chapters 10 and 11.

35 *LG&E* (n 7) paras 234, 238.

36 ibid para 240.

but only with regard to a specific period of time, that is from 1 December 2001 to 26 April 2003.[37]

In the *Azurix v. Argentina* case, by contrast, the tribunal dismissed Argentina's counterclaim, by stating, inter alia, that '[t]he Tribunal understands that governments have to be vigilant and protect the public health of their citizens but the statements and actions of the provincial authorities contributed to the crisis rather than assisted in solving it'.[38]

In the *Compañía de Aguas del Aconquija S.A. and Vivendi Universal S.A. v. Argentina* case, Argentina referred to the need of protecting health several times to justify its breach of its concession contracts with the claimants.[39] According to Argentina, one specific reason was that the claimants had undermined local public health, by providing polluted potable water, that is a possible vector of infectious diseases, particularly cholera.[40] The tribunal rejected Argentina's argument, by deciding that the local population had not suffered harm as a result of the occasional deterioration in water quality, and stated that Argentina's reaction was indeed 'irresponsible, unreasonable and disproportionate' in breach of Article 3 of the investment treaty.[41]

5 Concluding Remarks

Competition among public and private interests protected by distinct regulatory instruments has emerged as a common feature within international investment arbitration. These interests often reflect divergent priorities. Traditional international investment treaties are investor-oriented. They reflect the clear choice of the contracting states to prioritize investment protection. Since the beginning of this century, the traditional balance among various interests has started to be challenged by a few local communities, representatives of civil society and respondent states within investment arbitral proceedings. This

37 ibid para 245. See also *Sempra Energy International Corp. v. Argentina*, ICSID Case No. ARB/02/16, Award (28 September 2017) para 332. For further information on my view on the relevance of investment arbitral cases against Argentina in relation to health protection, see Pia Acconci, *Tutela della salute e diritto internazionale* (CEDAM 2011) 421–428.

38 See *Azurix* (n 5) para 144. As to Argentina's claim concerning the connection between public health and 'the quality and quantity of drinkable water', ibid para 129. As to the claimant's reply, see ibid para 132–136.

39 *Vivendi* (n 7). As to the claim of the respondent State to justify its conduct for 'legitimate public welfare objectives', see ibid paras 6.5.14., 6.7.4., 6.8.6.

40 ibid para 6.4.8.

41 ibid paras 4.12.4, 7.6.2.

has led to conflicts of interests, among others, between health protection and the protection of investment and of intellectual property rights, in relation to investments in the pharmaceutical sector, the control over harmful goods, like tobacco products, and serious political and social emergencies.

As a consequence of early cases, economic advanced and emerging states have chosen to ensure the protection of certain non-economic interests, like public health, within international investment treaties by revising their applicable international treaties through the injection of specific provisions for the safeguard of a few recurrent non-investment interests and concerns, as exceptions and safeguards, and of clauses on a host State's 'right to regulate' for legitimate public purposes.[42]

Subsequent arbitral proceedings show that, in complex cases arising from conflict of heterogeneous interests, a few arbitral tribunals have accepted the relevance of the protection of non-investment concerns, admitted third party participation, such as briefs from *amici curiae*[43] and experts, and referred to international standards and/or general principles, like proportionality and good faith, and special interpretative methods. As a consequence, transparency and openness have increased, although the relevance of a few non-investment interests and concerns has been accepted on a case-by-case basis and cannot be forecast in advance because of the state margin of appreciation, as well as the discretion of arbitrators.

The interaction between a state's margin of appreciation and the discretionary powers of arbitrators has been a subject of debate and dissatisfaction due to the inconsistency of treaty practice. A couple of questions, in particular, remain unanswered. Should arbitrators conform to strict legalism, demonstrating deference to the literal interpretation of the law, particularly the specific international treaties upon which their jurisdiction is based? Under this approach, the regulatory autonomy of states at an international law level is paramount, and non-investment concerns cannot be safeguarded within treaty-based arbitral proceedings if no exceptions and/or specific clauses are provided in the applicable treaty. Or should arbitrators fill the regulatory gaps through a pro-active approach on request of respondent states? If arbitrators act as law-makers, without specific provisions in treaties, arbitral tribunals might become a tool of governance by extending the applicable rules to the merits through the importation into the international legal framework on investment

42 As examples see the texts of Model BIT (n 7).

43 To this end, ICSID amended its Arbitration Rules in 2006. See ICSID, 'Arbitration Rules', in ICSID, *ICSID Convention, Regulations and Rules* (2022) 88, arts 32, 37 <https://icsid.worldbank.org/rules-regulations/convention> accessed 23 August 2023.

of international rules related to other sectors, such as human rights and the environment, whether the respondent state requests it or not. In this respect, arbitral tribunals might facilitate systemic interpretation of investment treaties in conformity with article 31 (3), letter c, of the 1969 Vienna Convention on the Law of Treaties. This would enhance their discretionary powers through interpretative methods like the 'standard of review' which is used within judiciary and administrative proceedings in Canada and the United States.[44] On the other hand, the need to overcome legal diversification through interpretation might arise on request of a claimant investor. For instance, this might occur in relation to a claim to challenge compulsory licensing as a breach of the fair and equitable treatment standard in light of alleged legitimate expectations and/or as an indirect expropriation. This would be a claim to obtain compensation in accordance with the applicable international investment treaty. However, one must acknowledge that the prospects of success of this claim are significantly reduced after the revision and the conclusion of a number of international investment agreements which ensure the host state's exercise of regulatory powers to safeguard non-investment interests, such as health. These regulatory innovations might be an appropriate legal basis for states' defences. On the contrary, claimants might require arbitrators to import into the applicable law international provisions of the TRIPS Agreement on patent waiver, that, at article 31-*bis* (2), provide for the state's obligation to pay 'adequate remuneration' to the affected patent owner, in order to show that the respondent state did not comply with such rules.[45] In addition, domestic law

44 The choice of the relevant standard is one open issue. The standard of review can be deferential, objective, for instance if it is based on scientific knowledge and data, and reasonable. There is an ongoing debate on the recourse to the 'standard of review' method within treaty-based investment arbitral proceedings. See, in particular, William Burke-White and Andreas von Staden, 'The Need for Public Law Standards of Review in Investor-State Arbitrations' in Stephan Schill (ed), *International Investment Law and Comparative Public Law* (OUP 2010) 689; Caroline Henckels, 'Indirect Expropriation and the Right to Regulate: Revisiting Proportionality Analysis and the Standard of Review in Investor-State Arbitration' (2012) J Intl Econ L 223, 238; Anna T Katselas, 'Do Investment Treaties Prescribe a Deferential Standard of Review' (2012) 34 Mich J Intl L 87; Niccolò Zugliani, 'A Role for Precedent in the Determination of the Standard of Review Applicable by Investment Arbitral Tribunals? A Case Study of ECT-based Energy Disputes Against Spain' (2022) 2 The Italian Rev of Int and Comparative L 370.

45 A few international investment treaties refer to article 31 of the TRIPS Agreement as a legality test. See, for instance, the Singapore-Myanmar BIT (n 15) art 6.5; 2020 Regional Comprehensive Economic Partnership Agreement among ASEAN, Australia, China, Japan, New Zealand and the Republic of Korea (signed 15 November 2020, entered into force 1 January 2022) art 10.6 letters b), i).

and contracts might become relevant as an integrating framework. This could make assessing and interpreting the applicable law more difficult with arbitral proceedings taking longer.

In conclusion, the proliferation of international treaties has resulted in legal diversification which poses challenges in mitigating conflicts of interest, preventing disputes between host states and foreign investors, and determining the applicable law and appropriate interpretative methods by arbitrators. Hence, a fruitful interaction between health protection and international investment law cannot be taken for granted. This is the main lesson learned from public health emergencies before the COVID-19 pandemic. What can be expected for the future? The COVID-19 pandemic has shown that large-scale manufacturing capacity, technology transfer and global supply chains are essential for global health security. Foreign private investments are needed to this end, especially in least-developed countries. International treaties can encourage such innovative foreign investments in the health sector, through special clauses and safeguards, as additional defences for host states. However, this would bring about further legal diversification. Against this backdrop, the negotiation of a multilateral wide-ranging investment treaty is even more desirable, although unlikely because of recurrent political divergences and social differences among states.[46]

---

46 See Federico Ortino, 'The Social Dimension of International Investment Agreements: Drafting A New BIT/MIT Model?' (2005) 7 Intl L FORUM du Droit International 243; Loukas Mistelis and Giammarco Rao, 'Multilateral Principles in a Bilateral World' (2021) 1 The Italian Rev of Int and Comparative L 59. See Pia Acconci, 'The Integration of Non-investment Concerns as an Opportunity for the Modernization of International Investment Law: Is a Multilateral Approach Desirable?' in Giorgio Sacerdoti and others (eds), *General Interests of Host States in International Investment Law* (CUP 2014) 165.

CHAPTER 2

The Impact of the Pandemic on the Reform of Investment Treaty Standards

Tarcisio Gazzini and Valentina Vadi

1 Introduction*

The development of international investment law has not followed a clear trajectory but rather occurred through a series of minor, historically contingent, and at times accidental steps.[1] Yet, investment treaties concluded roughly between 1990 and 2010 are similar in their basic structure. They favoured investors to the point that as a rule they imposed obligations on states only.[2] They were also largely silent on the use of regulatory powers by states to pursue public interest.

The need to recalibrate those treaties and the perceived shortcomings of investment arbitration have triggered a debate on the reform of the investment treaty regime and, more importantly, various initiatives by states. While some states prefer protecting foreign investments through domestic legislation[3] others have reconsidered their investment treaties[4] and model bilateral investment treaty (BIT).[5] The recent COVID-19 pandemic has not only made such reform more compelling and timelier than ever but also demonstrated the need to include treaty provisions on the safeguard of public health without

* Tarcisio Gazzini authored the introduction, Sections 2–4 and 7; Valentina Vadi Sections 5–6 and the conclusions.

1 Joost Pauwelyn, 'At the Edge of Chaos? Foreign Investment Law as a Complex Adaptive System. How it Emerged and how it can be Reformed' (2014) 29 ICSID Rev 371, 374.

2 As admitted by the Tribunal in *Spyridon Roussalis v. Romania*, ICSID Case No. ARB/06/1, Award (7 December 2011) para 871.

3 See, in particular, Protection of Investment Act 2015 (South Africa).

4 For two interesting examples, see EU-Canada Comprehensive Economic and Trade Agreement (signed 30 October 2016, provisionally in force 21 September 2017) (CETA); ECOWAS Common Investment Code (signed 22 December 2019, entered into force 22 December 2019) (ECOWIC).

5 Indian Model BIT (2015) <https://edit.wti.org/document/show/d0eac9a8-2de6-44a8-9e9f-2986b8817aa9>.

© KONINKLIJKE BRILL BV, LEIDEN, 2025 | DOI:10.1163/9789004711204_004

unduly undermining the protection of investors and the enjoyment of intellectual property rights.

This chapter examines the impact of the pandemic on the reform of investment treaties. It focuses on the clauses limiting the scope of application of specific substantive rules (scope limitations), and the exceptions providing defences to justify or excuse conduct otherwise contrary to treaty obligations (affirmative defences).[6] It aims to assess how the problems and challenges encountered by states during the pandemic have led them to reconsider their investment treaties. Part 2 investigates investment treaty practice during and after the COVID-19 pandemic while Parts 3 and 4 focus, respectively, on standards of treatment and general provisions and exceptions. Parts 5 and 6 scrutinize public health-related provisions and the issues related to patents, compulsory licensing, and parallel imports. Finally, Part 7 explores the investment treaty provisions concerning technology transfer.

2 Investment Treaty Practice during and in the Aftermath of the COVID-19 Pandemic

The World Health Organization (WHO) declared COVID-19 a Public Health Emergency of International Concern on 30 January 2020 and then characterized it as a pandemic on 11 March 2020.[7] On 5 May 2023, it acknowledged the end of the global health emergency.[8] According to the United Nations Conference on Trade and Development (UNCTAD), since the outbreak of the pandemic, states and International Organizations have concluded 55 investment treaties and, precisely, 22 bilateral investment treaties (BITS), of which 7 have entered into force, and 33 treaties with investment provisions (TIPS), of which 17 have entered into force.[9]

---

6 On the distinction, see Caroline Henckels, 'Scope Limitation or Affirmative Defence? The Purpose and Role of Investment Treaty Exception Clauses' in Lorand Bartels and Federica Paddeu (eds), *Exceptions in International Law* (OUP, 2020) 363. For a more articulated taxonomy, see Jorge E Viñuales, 'Seven Ways of Escaping a Rule: Of Exceptions and Their Avatars in International Law' in Lorand Bartels and Federica Paddeu, ibid 65.

7 See WHO, International Health Regulations (3rd edn, 2005).

8 Jamie Gumbrecht, Jacqueline Howard and Deidre McPhillips, 'WHO says COVID-19 is no Longer a Global Health Emergency' CNN(5 May 2023) <https://edition.cnn.com/2023/05/05/health/who-ends-covid-health-emergency/index.html#:~:text=The%20World%20Health%20Organization%20declares,Covid%2D19%20global%20health%20emergency.&text> accessed 30 October 2023.

9 UNCTAD, 'International Investment Agreements Navigator'<https://investmentpolicy.unctad.org/international-investment-agreements> accessed 27 May 2023. Unless

A perusal of those treaties immediately triggers two observations. On the one hand, BITs have lost the popularity they used to enjoy a couple of decades ago, whereas regionalism is still on the rise.[10] On the other hand, more than half of the TIPs concluded in the period under consideration have limited investment content either because they focus on trade and trade-related issues or – as in the case of several agreements concluded by the United Kingdom – they mirror the agreements concluded by the European Union (EU) before Brexit.

This analysis, therefore, relates to investment agreements providing for a substantial and in several cases quite sophisticated treatment of foreign investment. Unfortunately, the UNCTAD database is incomplete in two respects: it does not provide all investment agreements and when it does it is not always possible to retrieve their authentic text(s). Even with these significant limitations, the available treaties offer some interesting elements.

3 Standards of Treatment

Treaties concluded during and after the pandemic confirm a clear trend in recent investment treaty practice, namely the significant compression of contingent and non-contingent standards of treatment of foreign investors. Contingent standards rely on comparisons and include the national treatment (NT) and the most favored national treatment (MFN) provisions.[11] Such provisions are ubiquitous in international investment treaties. Treaties concluded during and after the pandemic often require consideration for *legitimate public welfare objectives*[12] when assessing the likeness of given investments with their domestic or foreign comparators. Such likeness serves as a benchmark to apply the MFN and NT standards. For example, the Regional Comprehensive Economic Partnership between the Association of Southeast Asian Nations (ASEAN) and Australia, China, India,

---

differently indicated, all treaties and model BITs referred to in this chapter are available at UNCTAD website <https://investmentpolicy.unctad.org/international-investment-agreements/model-agreements> accessed 30 October 2023.

10 UNCTAD, 'The Rise of Regionalism in International Investment Policymaking: Consolidation or Complexity?' (2013) 3 IIA Issues Note <https://unctad.org/system/files/official-document/webdiaepcb2013d8_en.pdf> accessed 30 October 2023.

11 See however DRC-Rwanda BIT (signed 26 June 2021, not in force) art 4 on MFN and art 4, para 6 on NT.

12 Pacific Alliance-Singapore FTA (signed 26 January 2022, not in force) arts 8.5.4, 8.6.4; Indonesia-Korea FTA (signed 18 December 2020, entered into force 1 January 2023) arts 7.4, 7.5, footnote 17.

Japan, Korea, and New Zealand (RCEP) provides that 'whether the treatment is accorded in 'like circumstances' under this Article depends on the totality of the circumstances, including whether the relevant treatment distinguishes between investors or investments on the basis of legitimate public welfare objectives.'[13]

Moving to non-contingent (or absolute) standards of treatment, investment agreements concluded during or after the pandemic offer various approaches to the fair and equitable treatment (FET) standard and its cognate minimum standard of treatment (MST). Some of them reproduce the traditional and rather rudimentary FET or MST clause. The BIT between Japan and Georgia, for instance, imposes the obligation upon the host state to 'accord to investments of investors of the other Contracting Party fair and equitable treatment and full protection and security in accordance with customary international law'.[14]

Several other treaties confirm the tendency already evident in investment treaty practice before the pandemic to significantly squeeze FET clauses.[15] States normally agree on a positive list of measures, often characterized by a rather high threshold of gravity, that constitute breaches of the standard. The BIT between Hungary and Kyrgyzstan, for instance, lists several measures as breaching the FET standard including:

> a) denial of justice in criminal, civil or administrative proceedings; or
> b) fundamental breach of due process, including a fundamental breach of transparency and obstacles to effective access to justice, in judicial and administrative proceedings; or
> c) manifest arbitrariness; or
> d) targeted discrimination on manifestly wrongful grounds, such as gender, race or religious belief; or
> e) harassment, coercion, abuse of power or similar bad faith conduct.[16]

---

13 Regional Comprehensive Economic Partnership (2020) between ASEAN (Association of South-East Asian Nations) and Australia, China, Japan, Korea, and New Zealand (RCEP) (signed 15 November 2020, entered into force 1 January 2021) art 10.3, footnote 17, art 10.4, footnote 19.

14 Japan-Georgia BIT (signed 29 January 2021, entered into force 23 July 2021) art 4. See also Japan-Bahrein BIT (signed 26 June 2022, not in force) art 5.

15 See, for instance, CETA (n 4) art 8.10.

16 Hungary-Kyrgyzstan BIT (signed 29 September 2021, entered into force 10 April 2022) arts 2 (2), 2(3). See also the Hungary-Oman BIT (signed 2 February 2022, entered into force 24 October 2022) arts 3(2), 3(3); Colombia-Spain BIT (signed 19 September 2021, not in force) arts 7(1), 7(2).

The treaties concluded during the pandemic also witnessed the growing preference for the minimum standard of treatment as opposed to the traditional FET standard. The minimum standard of treatment is tied to customary international law. An annex often further clarifies the content of such minimum standard.[17] The standard originally developed within the North American Free Trade Agreement (NAFTA) and rapidly spread beyond North America. With some drafting differences, the content of the clause includes 'the obligation not to deny justice in criminal, civil, or administrative adjudicatory proceedings in accordance with the principle of due process embodied in the principal legal systems of the world'.[18]

However, it is with regard to the provisions on expropriation and, more precisely, indirect expropriation, that the treaties under discussion are more sophisticated and, in some cases, innovative than earlier treaties. Some treaties recall the expropriation provision in treaties such as CETA. They thus provide that: 'non-discriminatory regulatory actions by a Party that are designed and applied to protect legitimate public welfare objectives, such as public health, [FN omitted] safety, and the environment, do not constitute indirect expropriations, except in rare circumstances'.[19]

Other treaty provisions confirm that regulatory actions designed and applied to protect legitimate public welfare objectives, including public health, can be considered indirect expropriation only in rare circumstances (or exceptional circumstances).[20] Some further elucidate that those actions must be 'extremely severe or disproportionate in light of its purpose or effect',[21] or 'manifestly excessive' compared with the objective they pursue.[22] In both cases, the provision introduces a very high presumption against qualifying state actions as indirect expropriation. Consequently, tribunals must show the utmost deference to the regulatory powers of the host state when assessing the context, non-discriminatory nature, objectives, proportions, and effects of the relevant actions.

---

17 See, for instance, Australia-United Kingdom FTA(signed 17 December 2021, not in force) art 13(7) and Annex 13A.

18 ibid art 13(7)(2)(a). See also RCEP(n 13) art 10(5); Indonesia-Korea FTA (n 12) art 7(6); Pacific Alliance-Singapore FTA (n 12) art 8(7); Turkey-Uruguay BIT (signed 23 April 2022, not in force) art 4(1)(2); Angola-Turkey BIT (signed 27 July 2021, not in force) art 3(2)(3); Israel-Korea FTA (signed 12 May 2021, not in force) art 45(1)(2).

19 Australia-United Kingdom FTA(n 17) Annex 13B (Expropriation); Switzerland-Indonesia BIT (signed 24 May 2022, not in force) Annex A; Israel-Korea FTA (n 18) Annex 9A.

20 Colombia-Spain BIT (n 16) art 11(5).

21 Israeli-Korea FTA (n 18) Annex 9A (Expropriation) art 3(b).

22 Switzerland-Indonesia BIT (n 19) Annex A (Expropriation) art 3(b).

More innovative and drastic provisions compared to the previous ones are contained in a third group of treaties. They exclude that non-discriminatory regulatory actions designed and applied to achieve legitimate public welfare objectives, including public health, may constitute indirect expropriation.[23] Here the protection of the regulatory powers of the host state is enhanced by a largely self-judging provision that leaves tribunals only the power to double-check the purpose of these actions as well as the good faith and non-discrimination.

Finally, some BITs, like the BIT between India and Brazil, cover only direct expropriation, described as expropriation through formal transfer of title or outright seizure.[24] The exclusion of indirect expropriation from the scope of the treaty is reiterated by an explicit provision ruling out the qualification as expropriation of non-discriminatory regulatory measures designed and applied to protect legitimate public interest or public purpose objectives.[25]

4 General Provisions and Exceptions

A few of the treaties under discussion contain a general provision obliging the parties not to relax labour, environmental, and health standards. This obligation appears either in the preamble[26] or in the main text of the treaties.[27] Such provision is by no means new as it can be found in several investment treaties concluded before the pandemic. The obligation aims at once to reaffirm the state regulatory powers to pursue legitimate public interests and avoid a normative race to the bottom to attract foreign investments.

Indeed, one of the main features of the recent investment treaty practice is the growing insistence on the host state's right to regulate. Traditionally, investment treaties were not only manifestly unbalanced as a matter of content, but also silent on the exercise of regulatory powers. Already before the pandemic, states worried that the adoption of regulatory measures to protect the public

23 RCEP (n 13) Annex 10B (Expropriation) art 4; Pacific Alliance-Singapore FTA (n 12) Annex C.3(b); Indonesia-Korea BIT (n 12) Annex 9A (Expropriation); Hungary-Oman BIT (n 16) 6(4).

24 India-Brazil BIT (signed 25 January 2020, not in force) art 6.3.

25 ibid art 6.4.

26 Switzerland-Indonesia BIT (n 19).

27 Hungary-Kyrgyzstan BIT (n 16) art 3(1).Article 2(7) further provides that a Party can request consultation if it considers that the other Party is encouraging investment by lowering domestic environmental, labour or occupational health and safety legislation. See also India-Brazil BIT (n 24) art 22.2; Colombia-Spain BIT (n 16) art 16.

interest could expose them to claims by affected investors. They thus translated this concern into increasingly sophisticated treaty provisions. The trend has been confirmed and magnified during and in the aftermath of the pandemic in two ways.

On the one hand, some treaties refer to an unqualified right to regulate. For instance, the Free Trade Agreement (FTA) between the United Kingdom and New Zealand recognizes 'the right of each Party to regulate in order to achieve legitimate public policy objectives, such as the protection of public health, safety, and the environment'.[28]

Most treaties include specific provisions on the exercise of regulatory powers, sometimes in combination with a reference to an unqualified right to regulate with different levels of deference. From this perspective, the measures adopted by the host state are qualified as:

> measures necessary to achieve legitimate policy objectives, such as the protection of public health, safety, environment and social or consumer protection;[29]
>
> [measures the Host State] considers appropriate to ensure that investment activity in its territory is undertaken in a manner sensitive to environmental, health, or other regulatory objectives;[30] and
>
> reasonable measures to achieve legitimate public policy objectives, such as security public policy objectives, such as security, sustainable development, social security, privacy, data privacy, data protection, the promotion or protection of cultural diversity, human rights, health human rights, health, education, social services, consumers, natural resources or the environment.[31]

On the other hand, other treaties contain provisions modelled after Article XX of the General Agreement on Tariffs and Trade (GATT).[32] Those provisions

---

28 UK-New Zealand FTA (signed 28 February 2022, not in force) art 14.1. See also Switzerland-Indonesia BIT (n 19) art 12(1), as well as the preambles of the Brazil-India BIT (n 24) and of the Colombia-Spain BIT (n 16).

29 Hungary-Oman BIT (n 16) art 3(1); Hungary-United Arab Emirates BIT (signed 15 July 2021, entered into force 10 April 2022) art 3(1).

30 UK-New Zealand FTA (n 28) art14(18)(1). See also Venezuela-Colombia BIT (signed 3 February 2023, not in force) art 14(a).

31 Colombia-Spain BIT (n 16) art 14(1).

32 General Agreement on Tariffs and Trade 1994 (adopted 15 April 1994, entered into force 1 January 1995) 1867 UNTS 190; Marrakesh Agreement Establishing the World Trade Organization, Annex 1A (adopted 15 April 1994, entered into force 1 January 1995) 1867 UNTS 187, 33 ILM 1153 (1994).

include a chapeau, excluding from its scope arbitrary or discriminatory measures as well as disguised restrictions, and a series of subject matters. As explained by the WTO adjudicatory bodies, measures adopted under Article XX are scrutinized through a two-tiered analysis: provisional justification by characterizing the measure under any of the subject matters and appraisal of the same measure under the chapeau.[33]

The investment provisions of this category, like those in the first category, require various levels of deference to the state powers and, accordingly, expand or reduce the extent of arbitral review. These tribunals pay low deference in ascertaining whether measures are 'necessary' to protect certain interests and values. They pay high deference in assessing whether given measures are 'designed and applied' to achieve other regulatory objectives. The following examples are illustrative:

> Nothing in this Treaty shall be construed to prevent the adoption or enforcement by a Party of measures of general applicability applied on a non-discriminatory basis that are necessary to:
> a) protect public morals or maintaining public order;
> b) protect human, animal or plant life or health;
> c) ensure compliance with law(s) and regulations that are not inconsistent with the provisions of this Treaty;
> d) protect and conserve the environment, including all living and non-living natural resources; ore) protect national treasures or monuments of artistic, cultural, historic or archaeological value.[34]

> Nothing in this Treaty shall be construed to prevent the adoption or enforcement by a Party of measures designed and applied to achieve any of the
> (a) public morals and safety;
> (b) human life or health, (c) national security;

33 WTO, *United States – Standards for Reformulated and Conventional Gasoline, Report of the Appellate Body* (29 April 1999) WT/DS2/AB/R, 22. As to the order of the two determinations, see WTO, *United States – Section 337 of the Tariff Act of 1930, Report of the Panel* (7 November 1989) L/6439 – 36S/345, para 5.9; and WTO, *United States – Shrimp, Report of the Appellate Body* (October 1998) WT/DS58/AB/R12, para 120. According to Lorand Bartels, Federica Paddeu, 'Introduction' in Lorand Bartels and Federica Paddeu(n 6) 1, 5, however, 'there is no necessary logic to the order of analysis.'

34 Brazil-India BIT (n 24) art 23(1). See also, for similar provisions, Japan-Bahrein BIT (n 14) art 18(1)(a); Switzerland-Indonesia BIT (n 19) art 41.

(d) living and non-living exhaustible natural resources; and
(e) the environment.[35]

Interestingly, in line with WTO jurisprudence,[36] the BIT between Brazil and India clarifies that to determine whether any given measure is 'necessary', account must be taken on whether any less restrictive alternative reasonable measures were available to the host state. Two variants deserve to be noticed. Hungary and Oman have adopted a minimalist version of Article XXGATT and agreed that their BIT

> shall not affect the right of the Contracting Parties to regulate in a non-discriminatory manner within their Territories through measures necessary to achieve legitimate policy objectives, such as the protection of public health, safety, environment and social or consumer protection.[37]

The BIT between India and Brazil, in turn, incorporates the chapeau at the end of exceptions provision, which reads:

> Nothing in this Treaty shall be construed to prevent a Party from adopting, maintaining or enforcing any measure it deems appropriate to ensure that investment activity in its territory is undertaken in a manner according to labor, environmental and health law of that Party, provided that this measure is not applied in a manner which would constitute a means of arbitrary or unjustifiable discrimination or a disguised restriction.[38]

It is worth noting that the provisions belonging to the categories sketched above are sometimes applied in combination with each other. In other words, they are building blocks states may use to reduce their exposure to, and build a protective wall against, claims brought by investors. Therefore, the host state can invoke more than one of these provisions in order to dodge treaty violations and the consequent responsibility.

In the case of the BIT between India and Brazil, for instance, the host state confronted with measures adopted in the context of a pandemic can invoke the right to regulate generally recognized in the preamble, and, more importantly,

---

35 DRC-Rwanda BIT (n 11) art 26 (1) (authors translation).
36 See, for instance, *United States – Section 337 of the Tariff Act of 1930* (n 33) para 5.26.
37 Hungary-Oman BIT (n 16) art 3.
38 India-Brazil BIT (n 24).

Article 22, allowing it to adopt the measures *it deems appropriate* to ensure that investments are undertaken in accordance with its health law as well as Article 23, permitting the adoption of measures *necessary* to protect human health.

5 Public Health

In analysing the development of international investment law during and after the pandemic, a key question is whether, and if so to what extent, states have inserted public health considerations in investment treaties concluded since 2020. The scrutiny of the fifty-plus investment treaties concluded during and after the pandemic reveals that public health has taken up more and more space in these treaties, especially with regard to the regulatory measures states can adopt to tackle the emergency.[39] Nonetheless, states have not inserted revolutionary changes in their treaties, preferring an incremental approach. Accordingly, public health-related clauses already used in the past have multiplied expanding their scope. Before examining the breadth and reach of these new provisions, this section briefly reviews how early investment treaties governed public health considerations and explores new trends and developments.

In the past, reference to public health used to be minimal in international economic law. For instance, Treaties of Friendship, Commerce, and Navigation (FCN treaties) allowed limiting the admission of nationals or goods of the other party necessary to maintain public health.[40] Many such treaties prohibited the imposition of 'duties or charges on account of [...] quarantine'.[41] Decades later, the Protocol to the very first BIT – the one between Germany and Pakistan – excluded that measures taken for reasons of public health could be considered as discriminatory and, therefore, contrary to Article 2 of the treaty.[42] Nonetheless, most investment treaties concluded between 1959 and

39 See Vincent Beyer and Hamed El-Kady, 'Accelerating Substantive International Investment Agreements Reform: Policy Perspectives in Times of a Global Pandemic' in YuliaLevashova and Pascale AccaouiLorfing (eds), *Balancing the Protection of Foreign Investors and States Responses in the Post-Pandemic World* (Kluwer 2022) Chapter 9.

40 See, for instance, the US-Japan Treaty of Friendship, Commerce and Navigation (signed 2 April 1953, entered into force 30 October 1953) art I.3.

41 Treaty of Amity and Commerce Between United Mexican States and the Emperor of Japan (signed 30 November 1888, entered into force 29 January 1889) art VI; Treaty of Commerce and Navigation Between the United States and the Ottoman Empire (signed 25 February 1862, entered into force 5 June 1862) art IX.

42 Germany-Pakistan BIT (signed 25 November 1959, entered into force 28 April 1962).

2010 did not generally refer to public health.[43] International investment agreements' lack of reference or limited reference to public health considerations did not necessarily entail arbitral tribunals' lack of deference to state actions to pursue the public interest. Arbitral tribunals may show attention to state efforts to advance the public interest even when international investment agreements include no reference to or only make passing mention of public health issues. Yet, the task of striking the right balance between private and public interests was entrusted to arbitrators. Some tribunals showed high deference to measures adopted for protecting public health,[44] while others preferred to focus on the treaty text.[45]

This uncertainty has prompted states to gradually restate their right to regulate and their need to defend fundamental interests and values, including public health. Moreover, they have adopted a wide variety of measures to protect public health that could affect international trade and foreign investments.[46] For instance, the 2012 United States Model BIT includes no less than seven references to health in its preamble. It also contains various provisions relating to performance requirements, investment and labor, indirect expropriation, and the possibility for arbitral tribunals to request expert opinions on factual issues concerning health, safety, or other scientific matters.[47] Similarly, the 2015 Norwegian Model BIT includes extensive reference to public health in its preamble, acknowledges the right to regulate, and prohibits discrimination, unlawful expropriation, performance requirements, and lowering of standards.[48] The preamble to the 2017 Colombia Model BIT reaffirms the right of states to 'regulate the investments made' to protect 'legitimate public welfare objectives,' including human rights and the environment.[49] Human rights

---

43 Freya Baetens, 'Protecting Foreign Investment and Public Health Through Arbitral Balancing and Treaty Design' 71 ICLQ (2022) 139, 157.

44 *Chemtura Corporation v. Government of Canada*, UNCITRAL, Award (2 August 2010); *Methanex Corporation v. United States of America*, UNCITRAL, Final Award of the Tribunal on Jurisdiction and Merits (3 August 2005).

45 *S.D. Myers, Inc. v. Government of Canada*, UNCITRAL, Award (13 November 2000).

46 See Valentina Vadi, *Public Health in International Investment Law and Arbitration* (Routledge 2013) 26–27.

47 US Model BIT (2012), preamble, art 8 (performance requirements), art 12 (Investment and Environment), art 13 (Investment and Labor), art 32 (Expert Reports), Annex B (Expropriation) <https://ustr.gov/sites/default/files/BIT%20text%20for%20ACIEP%20Meeting.pdf> accessed 30 May 2023. See also Chapters 12 and 14.

48 Norwegian Model BIT (2015), preamble, arts 3, 6, 8, 11, 12 <https://edit.wti.org/document/show/3b8bd5cf-2a4e-438c-a8cf-21ebdc1cce91> accessed 30 May 2023.

49 Colombia Model BIT (2017), preamble <https://edit.wti.org/document/show/cdde4cbc-6572-4cad-8c39-8c3413009e52?textBlockId=363fc8ea-efef-428c-a00f-9003fd471cde&page=2> accessed 30 May 2023.

include the right to life, the right to health, and the right to an adequate standard of living.[50] These treaty reforms have been paralleled by growing domestic regulation in the public health field in the past decades.[51]

With regard to treaties concluded during or after the pandemic, some investment treaties mention public health in their preambles, stating that the parties seek to advance economic cooperation without jeopardizing the objective of public health protection.[52] While it is generally held that preambles do not contain binding obligations, they are not merely symbolic. They can influence the interpretation of treaties as they explain the treaty philosophy, object, and purpose and establish a dialogue between the treaty makers and the arbitrators. Although they do not have binding force, preambles may refer to treaties, customary international law, or general principles of law, which are binding sources of law.[53] By referring to the need to protect public health and human rights in their preambles, treaty-makers implicitly remind arbitrators that international treaties, customary law norms, and general principles of law require the protection of public health and human rights.[54] Some of these norms, such as the prohibition of scientific or medical experimentation without free, prior, or informed consent, also have peremptory status.[55] Therefore, arbitrators can deduce several important norms for the protection of public health from treaty preambles and these can influence their interpretation of the treaty text.[56] Preambles can infuse investment treaties with public health considerations. While not imposing new obligations on the parties to an agreement, this approach recognizes

---

50 International Covenant on Economic, Social, and Cultural Rights (adopted 16 December 1966, entered into force 3 January 1976) 999 UNTS 171, arts 11, 12; International Covenant on Civil and Political Rights (adopted 16 December 1966, entered into force 23 March 1976) 999 UNTS 171 (ICCPR), art 2.

51 For a seminal study, see Lawrence O Gostin, *Public Health Law – Power, Duty, Restraint* (University of California Press 2008).

52 See the preambles of the Japan-Morocco BIT (signed 8 January 2020, entered into force 23 April 2022); Hungary-Kyrgyzstan BIT (n 27); Venezuela-Colombia BIT (n 30); San Marino-Hungary BIT (signed 21 September 2022, not in force); Japan-Bahrain BIT (signed 23 June 2022, not in force); Turkey-Uruguay BIT (n 18); Angola-Turkey BIT (signed 27 July 2021, not in force). See also the Agreement Establishing the African Continental Free Trade Area (signed 21 March 2018, entered into force 1 January 2021) (AfCFTA).

53 DRC-Rwanda BIT (n 11) preamble (referring to international labor law and human rights).

54 On global health law, see e.g. Allyn L Taylor, 'Global Health Law: International Law and Public Health Policy' (2017) International Encyclopedia of Public Health 268–281.

55 See ICCPR (n 50) art 4.

56 For a similar argument in a different legal context, see Nikolaos A Papadopoulos, 'Revisiting the Preamble of the European Social Charter: Paper Tiger or Blessing in Disguise?' (2022) 22 HRL Rev 1.

the potential for investment to affect public health and strives to prevent downward pressure on public health protection in investment liberalization.

In addition to these preambular statements, the most recent investment treaties also include specific provisions relating to health. Some of those treaties include a general clause consenting to appropriate measures to ensure that investment activity is undertaken with consideration for health concerns.[57] Stronger treaty terms emphasize the linkage between public health and the state's right to regulate.[58]

Some investment treaties also clarify that non-discriminatory regulations designed and applied to protect public health do not constitute indirect expropriation.[59] Regulatory actions to protect public health include measures concerning 'the regulation, pricing and supply of, and reimbursement for, pharmaceuticals (including biological products), diagnostics, vaccines, medical devices, gene therapies and technologies, health-related aids and appliances, and blood and blood-related products'.[60] While some treaties, such as the Australia–UK FTA and the Indonesia–Switzerland BIT, admit that even such regulations 'in rare circumstances' can amount to indirect expropriation,[61] most recent treaties do not add such qualifiers.[62] This qualification may engender confusion if treaties do not specify what these rare circumstances are. In this regard, the BIT between Indonesia and Switzerland clarifies the meaning of the uncommon situations that can transform a state measure into an indirect taking. Such rare circumstances refer to those situations in which 'the impact of an action … is so serious as to make them appear manifestly excessive in respect to the objective pursued.'[63]

Other treaties include a general exception for protecting public health.[64] General exceptions concerning public health are variously articulated but generally provide that nothing in a given agreement shall be interpreted to prevent a party from adopting any non-discriminatory measure necessary to

57 See, for instance, AUKFTA (n 17) art 13.17.

58 See, for instance, the San Marino-Hungary BIT (n 52) art 3; Indonesia-Switzerland BIT (n 19) art 12(1); Turkey-Uruguay BIT (n 18) Preamble. See also CETA (n 4) art 8.9.

59 Turkey-Uruguay BIT (n 18) Annex 1.

60 AUKFTA (n 17) Annex 13 B (Expropriation), footnote 25.

61 Indonesia-Switzerland BIT (n 19) Annex A, Expropriation, 3(b); AUKFTA (n 17) Annex 13B Expropriation.

62 See also Venezuela-Colombia BIT (n 30) art 7c; San Marino-Hungary BIT (n 52) art 6c.

63 Indonesia-Switzerland BIT (n 19) Annex A, Expropriation.

64 See, for instance, Japan-Morocco BIT (n 52) art 21; San Marino-Hungary BIT (n 52) art 16.8; Indonesia-Switzerland BIT (n 19) art 41.

protect human, animal, or plant life or health.[65] From a public health perspective, introducing public health considerations as an exception to investment or trade rules contradicts the alleged importance of public health. Traditionally, exceptions are read narrowly and only operate in limited cases, where the risk to public health is so grave that the host state has no choice but to adopt a given regulatory measure. Moreover, the implementation and operation of such a clause very much depends on the specific circumstances of the case, the arguments presented by the parties, and the composition of the arbitral tribunal.[66]

One of the most innovative and interesting provisions concerning public health appears in the 2021 African, Caribbean, and Pacific (ACP) – EU Partnership Agreement.[67] Although the provision is not included in the investment chapter, it can influence the interpretation of the same. Article 29 of the Partnership Agreement acknowledges that 'health is central to people's lives and a key indicator of sustainable development.' Accordingly, the parties 'reaffirm their commitment to protecting and promoting the highest attainable standard of physical and mental health for all' and 'strengthen national health systems'.[68] The provision also emphasizes states' promotion of 'universal health coverage, equitable and universal access to comprehensive and quality healthcare services and access to safe, effective, quality and affordable essential medicines and vaccines.'[69] Particular attention is paid to the 'integration of reproductive health into national strategies and programs.'[70] Finally, the Agreement requires states to 'cooperate to prevent and address communicable diseases' and global health crises by, among other things, 'support[ing] research and development, and the deployment of vaccines, diagnostics and medicines.'

Finally, the 2023 Investment Protocol to the African Continental Free Trade Area (AfCFTA)[71] contains what can be considered the most advanced protection

65 See, for instance, Turkey-Uruguay BIT (n 18) art 7.

66 See, for instance, *Eco Oro Minerals Corp v. Republic of Colombia*, ICSID Case No. ARB/16/41, Decision on Jurisdiction, Liability and Directions on Quantum (9 September 2021).

67 African, Caribbean, and Pacific (ACP)-EU Partnership Agreement, Negotiated Agreement text initialed by EU OACPS chief negotiators (15 April 21) <https://international-partnerships.ec.europa.eu/policies/european-development-policy/acp-eu-partnership_en> accessed 30 October 2023.

68 ibid arts 29(1), 29(2).

69 ibid art 29(3).

70 ibid art 29(5).

71 African Continental Free Trade Area (signed 21 March 2018, entered into force 30 May 2019) (AfCFTA); Draft AfCFTA Protocol on Investment (2023) <https://www.bilaterals.org/IMG/pdf/en_-_draft_protocol_of_the_afcfta_on_investment.pdf> accessed 24.02.2024.

of pandemics to date. Following the Declaration on the Risk of Investor-State Dispute Settlement with Respect to COVID-19 Pandemic Related Measures, adopted by the African Union on 24 November 2020,[72] Article 27 of the Protocol contains a comprehensive provision on the regulation of foreign investment from the standpoint of public health and more specifically pandemics. It reads:

> 1. Each State Party has the right to determine its public health policies and priorities, to establish its own levels of domestic public health protection, and to adopt or modify its relevant laws and measures in the context of epidemics, pandemics and other public health emergencies *in accordance with its international commitments*.
> 2. Each State Party shall, in accordance with national laws and regulations, promote and facilitate investments in the public health sector and the subsectors and related industries, including medical equipment, pharmaceuticals especially for chronic diseases, vaccines and Intensive Care Units requirements.
> 3. State Parties shall cooperate to identify relevant investment policies and measures to address epidemics, pandemics and other public health emergencies in accordance with the decisions and declarations of the African Union.[73]

Article 27 of the Protocol reaffirms the State's right – and often also the duty under domestic[74] and international law – to regulate as an expression of sovereignty[75] and recognizes that the exercise of regulatory powers must conform to the state's international commitments.[76] Although Article 27 of the Protocol is not groundbreaking, it is central to the whole treaty and in particular the

---

72 See Makane M Mbengue, 'Narratives of Solidarity in Times of Crisis Tales from Africa' in Makane M Mbengue and Jean d'Aspremont (eds), *Crisis Narratives in International Law* (Brill 2022) 65–68.

73 Draft AfCFTA Protocol on Investment (n 71) art 27 (emphasis added).

74 In *Urbaser S.A. and Consorcio de Aguas Bilbao Bizkaia, Bilbao Biskaia Ur Partzuergoa* v. *Argentina*, ICSID Case No. ARB/07/26, Award (8 December 2016) para 622, for instance, the Tribunal stressed the responsibilities incumbent upon the Respondent under the Constitution to ensure public health and access to water.

75 The Preamble refers to the inherent right of States Parties to regulate in their territories and to introduce measures in order to achieve their national public policy objectives, promote sustainable development and protect public health.

76 In this regard, it is reminiscent of environmental provisions such as BLEU (Belgium-Luxembourg Economic Union)-Colombia BIT (signed 4 February 2009, not in force) art VII(1).

provisions on contingent standards and expropriation. According to Articles 13 and 15 of the Protocol, measures *designed and applied* to protect public health cannot amount to a violation, respectively, of the national treatment standard and the most-favoured nation standard. The two provisions are self-judging insofar as the measures *designed and applied* – and not necessary – to protect public health fall within their scope. Crucially, Article 20 of the Protocol expressly prevents the qualification as indirect expropriation of non-discriminatory regulatory actions *designed* to protect public health. Once more, deference to the State is almost complete. When combined, these clauses provide States with an effective shield against claims concerning regulatory measures. As long as their measures are neither discriminatory nor arbitrary, States can confidently fulfill their obligations under the Protocol and their responsibilities under domestic and general international law.

6 Patents, Compulsory Licensing, and Parallel Imports

The most recent investment treaties contain sophisticated provisions relating to patents, compulsory licenses, and parallel imports. Investment treaties generally offer a broad definition of investment comprising intellectual property.[77] The policy justification for protecting intellectual property through investment treaties is that they induce foreign direct investment (FDI) in the research and development (R&D) of new products, stimulating local inventive activities and encouraging technology transfer into the country. Investment treaties generally do not include detailed regulation of intellectual property; the implicit point of reference is the Agreement on Trade-Related Aspects of Intellectual Property Rights (TRIPS Agreement) which provides for minimum standards of treatment. Instead, FTAs often contain a chapter dedicated to intellectual property (that confirms or strengthens the TRIPS standards of protection).[78]

The pandemic triggered a massive global demand for medicines, vaccines, and health technologies to respond to COVID-19 like diagnostics, ventilators,

77 Valentina Vadi, 'Towards a New Dialectics – Pharmaceutical Patents, Public Health, and Foreign Direct Investments' (2015) 5 New York J of Intellectual Property and Entertainment L 1.

78 Peter-Tobias Stoll, 'Hybrid International Intellectual Property Protection: Coherence, Governance and Balance' in Henning Grosse Ruse-Khan and Axel Metzger (eds), *Intellectual Property Ordering beyond Borders* (CUP 2022) 96–118.

and personal protective equipment.[79] Although states scaled up their manufacturing capacity, most countries did not have sufficient production to cover the growing demand for medical products and technologies.[80] Moreover, existing production capacities did not match domestic demand for IP-protected diagnostics, treatment, or vaccines.

Therefore, developing and industrialized countries enacted regulations recognizing the pandemic as a health emergency and facilitating the grant of non-voluntary licenses and other flexibilities to use existing technologies. These regulatory instruments did not identify specific intellectual property rights. Instead, they enabled authorities to authorize a government entity or third party to use IP-protected technology to address the health emergency. This approach facilitated ongoing R&D efforts by granting rapid access to IP-protected technologies. For instance, in Germany, legislation enabled the Federal Ministry for Health to authorize using patent-protected inventions to ensure the supply of diagnostics, medicines, and personal protective equipment for the public interest and national security.[81] Israel similarly issued a government-use license for importing a COVID-19 treatment.[82] Bolivia notified the TRIPS Council that it needed 15 million doses of COVID-19 vaccines and signed an agreement with a Canadian generic manufacturer to import the generic version of COVID-19 vaccines.[83]

Compulsory licensing is a regulatory tool that allows governments to temporarily authorise the production of a patented invention without the patent owner's consent for public policy reasons. While compulsory licenses generally provide some remuneration for the patent holder, this is usually a fraction of the sum the patent holder would get through voluntary licensing.[84]

79 WTO, WIPO, and WHO, *Promoting Access to Medical Technologies and Innovation Intersections between Public Health, Intellectual Property, and Trade* (WTO, WIPO, and WHO, 2nd edn 2021) 4–5.

80 ibid 7.

81 ibid. 8.

82 ibid.

83 ibid 9.

84 Yousuf A Vawda, 'Compulsory Licenses and Government Use: Challenges and Opportunities' in Carlos M Correa and Reto M Hilty (eds), *Access to Medicines and Vaccines* (Springer 2022) 73, 77 (reporting that in the sixties, the US government was able to procure cheaper generic medicines at less than 1% of their list price). Other studies report that the price reductions after compulsory licenses range from 6.7% to 98%. See Eduardo Urias and Shyama V Ramani, 'Access to Medicines after TRIPS: Is Compulsory Licensing an Effective Mechanism to Lower Drug Prices? A Review of the Existing Evidence' (2020) 3J Int Bus Policy, 367–84. But see Eric M Solovy and Deepak Raju, 'The UNDP/WHO Remuneration Guidelines: A Proposed Formula for Inadequate Remuneration for

Compulsory licensing is one of the flexibilities on patent protection included in most domestic intellectual property systems and permitted under the TRIPS Agreement.[85] As WTO members experienced difficulties in reconciling patent protection with access to essential medicines, the 2001 Doha Declaration on the TRIPS Agreement and Public Health clarified the meaning of this flexibility stating that each WTO member has the right to grant compulsory licenses, the freedom to determine the grounds for granting such licenses and what constitutes a national emergency or other circumstances of extreme urgency. It also restated that the TRIPS Agreement 'can and should be interpreted in a manner supportive of WTO Members' right to protect public health and, in particular, to promote access for all.'[86] The 2003 waiver and the TRIPS Amendment have relaxed some requirements for issuing compulsory licenses, allowing developing countries that lack pharmaceutical manufacturing capacity to import medicines under such licenses.[87] More recently, the WTO Ministerial Decision on 17 June 2022 on the TRIPS Agreement in the context of the COVID-19 pandemic has reaffirmed the WTO members' right to issue compulsory licenses for producing COVID vaccines.[88] The decision will last five years, with the possibility of future extension.

In turn, parallel trade occurs when a product covered by intellectual property rights has been placed in a first market by the patent holder and then imported into a second market without the patent holder's permission.[89] As parallel trade tends to force price convergence across markets, it increases economic welfare by permitting consumers in importing countries to benefit from

---

Compulsory Licensing in Violation of the TRIPSAgreement' (2021) 16 JIPLP,1192–1202 (arguing that adequate compensation requires payment of the full market value).

85 Agreement on Trade-Related Aspects of Intellectual Property Rights (TRIPS Agreement), Marrakesh Agreement Establishing the World Trade Organization (adopted 15 April 1994, entered into force 1 January 1995) Annex 1C, 1869 UNTS 299, 33 ILM 1197, art 31.

86 WTO, Declaration on the TRIPS Agreement and Public Health, IV Ministerial Conference, Doha (20 November 2001) WT/MIN(01)/DEC/W/2, para 5.

87 Decision on Implementation of Paragraph 6 of the Doha Declaration on the TRIPS Agreement and Public Health (30 August 2003) WT/L/540; Amendment of the TRIPS Agreement (signed 8 December 2005, entered into force 23 January 2017) WT/L/641(enabling developing and least-developed countries to have access to medicines. Exporting countries can grant compulsory licenses to generic producers for exporting medicines to countries lacking production capacity.)

88 WTO, Ministerial Decision on the TRIPS Agreement, Adopted 17 June 2022 (22 June 2022) WT/MIN(22)/30, WT/L/1141.

89 From a legal perspective, parallel imports are based on the principle of *international exhaustion*. Once sold the patent owner has no rights regarding the additional commercialization of the product.

lower prices realized by more efficient producers in exporting countries. Thus, parallel trade can be a crucial tool for developing countries to get medicines and vaccines by importing them from other countries where they are available at lower prices. The TRIPS Agreement does not set a standard for parallel trade but leaves it to the regulatory autonomy of member states.[90] The WTO Ministerial Decision of 17 June 2022 on the TRIPS Agreement in the context of the COVID-19 pandemic waives the TRIPS requirement that a compulsory license of vaccine technology be predominantly for the supply of the domestic market.[91] However, it mandates reasonable efforts to prevent parallel imports.

Regulatory measures such as compulsory licenses and parallel trade cannot be regarded as instances of *direct expropriation*. Indeed, the patent holder maintains ownership of the property and the possibility to commercialize the pharmaceutical product although non-exclusively. However, the question may arise as to whether measures such as compulsory licenses and parallel imports can effectively offset the foreign investor's enjoyment of intellectual property and thus constitute *indirect expropriation*.

Under Chapter 9 of the 2021 Israel – Republic of Korea FTA, the provisions on expropriation 'shall not apply to the issuance of compulsory licenses granted in relation to intellectual property rights in accordance with the TRIPS Agreement, or to the revocation, limitation, or creation of intellectual property rights, to the extent that such issuance, revocation, limitation, or creation is consistent with … the TRIPS Agreement'.[92] Almost identical provisions appear in other recent investment treaties.[93] More interestingly, the BIT between India and Brazil excludes compulsory licensing from the scope of protection of the treaty: '[t]his Treaty shall not apply to the issuance of compulsory licenses granted in relation to intellectual property rights, or to the revocation, limitation or creation of intellectual property rights, to the extent that such issuance, revocation, limitation or creation is consistent with the international obligations of Parties under the WTO Agreement.'[94] To clarify the content of the

90 TRIPS Agreement (n 85) 6.

91 ibid art 31(f).

92 Israel-Republic of Korea FTA (signed 12 May 2021, not in force) art 9.7.

93 See e.g. RCEP (n 13) art 10.13.4: Expropriation; Pacific Alliance-Singapore FTA (n 12) art 8.13.5; UK-New Zealand FTA (n 28) art 14.4(5); Switzerland-Indonesia BIT (n19) art 7(6); Italian Model BIT (2022) <https://investmentpolicy.unctad.org/international-investment-agreements/treaty-files/6438/download> art 9.5.

94 Brazil-India BIT (signed 25 January 2020, not in force) art 3.6.c.

TRIPS Agreement, some investment treaties also refer to the Doha Declaration, the 2003 Waiver, and the 2017 Amendment.[95]

The conditions for lawfully granting a compulsory license are listed in Article 31 of the TRIPS Agreement as clarified by the Doha Declaration, the TRIPS Amendment, and the 2022 Ministerial Decision on the TRIPS Agreement in the context of the COVID-19 pandemic. As long as these requirements are fulfilled (and they include adequate remuneration), no violation of intellectual property occurs. In remunerating the patent holder, states may consider 'the humanitarian and not-for-profit purpose of specific vaccine distribution programs aimed at providing equitable access to COVID-19 vaccines' and 'existing good practices in instances of national emergencies, pandemics or similar circumstances.'[96] If no breach of intellectual property occurs, no international responsibility arises. At the WTO, the 2022 Ministerial Decision clarifies that WTO cannot challenge any measure taken in conformity with the Decision. The text of the TRIPS Agreement seems to confirm this reading by not considering compulsory licenses as limited exceptions but as 'other uses without authorization of the patent holder.'[97]

After examining the most recent investment treaty provisions, one may wonder whether these are entirely new and/or should be considered essential for enabling an appropriate balance between private and public interests. The provisions of the new treaties tend to reflect the state-of-art in treaty drafting with respect to compulsory licensing. Earlier treaties already excluded that compulsory licenses could amount to indirect expropriation.[98] The 2018 Comprehensive and Progressive Agreement for Trans-Pacific Partnership (CPTPP), for example, excludes claims of alleged unlawful expropriation and prohibited performance requirements based upon the issuance of a compulsory license as long as the compulsory license complies with Article 31 TRIPS Agreement and the CPTPP's intellectual property Chapter 5.[99] Other treaties, such as the 2018 United States-Mexico-Canada Agreement (USMCA),

---

95 See, for instance, EU-UK Trade and Cooperation Agreement (signed 30 December 2020, entered into force 1 May 2021) Title V Intellectual Property, Section IV Patents, art 250.

96 WTO, Ministerial Decision on the TRIPS Agreement (n 88) para 3(d).

97 Vadi (n 46) 78.

98 US Model BIT (n 47) art 6.5.

99 Comprehensive and Progressive Agreement for Trans-Pacific Partnership (CPTPP) between Australia, Brunei Darussalam, Canada, Chile, Japan, Malaysia, Mexico, Peru, New Zealand, Singapore and Vietnam (signed 8 March 2018, entered into force 30 December 2018 for Australia, Canada, Japan, Mexico, New Zealand and Singapore,14 January 2019 for Vietnam, 19 September 2021 for Peru, 29 November 2022 for Malaysia and 21 February 2023 for Chile).

recognised the flexibilities afforded in the 2001 Declaration on TRIPS and Public Health, thus reaffirming the states' right to issue compulsory licensing of patented medicines and lowering their costs.[100] Similarly, the 2017 CETA expressly recognised the importance of the Doha Declaration on the TRIPS Agreement and Public Health, the subsequent waiver, and Amendment: '[i]n interpreting and implementing the rights and obligations under this chapter, the Parties shall ensure consistency with [the Doha] Declaration. The Parties shall contribute to the implementation of and respect the Decision of the WTO General Council of 30 August 2003 on Paragraph 6 of the Doha Declaration, as well as the Protocol amending the TRIPS Agreement, done at Geneva on 6 December 2005.'[101]

Are these provisions in new investment treaties essential to distinguish compulsory licenses and similar flexibilities from indirect expropriation before arbitral tribunals? In theory, without such clauses, the police powers' doctrine and contextual, purposive, and evolutionary interpretation criteria can and should inform arbitral tribunals' reasoning. Given the varying economic, social, and cultural conditions of states, arbitral tribunals should recognize some margin of appreciation to states in addressing public health emergencies.[102] The WTO Doha Declaration, the Amendment, and the 2022 Decision should provide arbitrators with a roadmap to reach an appropriate balance between private and public interests. As noted by an arbitrator, 'tribunals must be sensitive to the difficulties of government decision-making in the face of legitimate objectives that pull in different directions'.[103] Some states have even justified their measures to protect public health using the language of state security. In practice, however, it remains unclear how arbitral tribunals would concretely balance the private and public interests at stake. Fears of expensive investor-state arbitration and resulting compensation can lead the state to a 'regulatory chill.' Instead, the introduction of such clauses can assuage states' concerns. Such clauses clarify the existing intellectual property law and strengthen states' inherent right to protect public health.

100 United States-Mexico-Canada Agreement (signed 1 October 2018, into force 1 July 2020) (USMCA) art 20.A.6.

101 CETA (n 4) art 20.3.

102 Valentina Vadi and Lukasz Gruszczynski, 'Standards of Review in International Investment Law and Arbitration: Multilevel Governance and the Commonweal' (2013) 16 J Intl Econ L 613.

103 *Eco Oro Minerals Corp.* v. *Colombia*, ICSID Case No.ARB/16/41, Decision on Jurisdiction, Liability and Directions on Quantum, Partial Dissent of Professor Philippe Sands QC (9 September 2021) para 28.

7 Technology Transfer

In times of emergency, compulsory licensing provides, at least in potential terms, a formidable means to tackle public health crises and pandemics in particular. Yet, in the long term, the capacity of developing countries to prevent and manage those crises may depend to a large extent on investments in the pharmaceutical sector[104] and the transfer of technology.[105]

While pharmaceutical companies are the main source of technologies,[106] they are not obliged to transfer them. Compelling them to disclose technology information through administrative procedures could amount to indirect expropriation. Additionally, forced transfer of technology is included in the list of performance requirements and as such expressly prohibited by many investment treaties, including those concluded during the pandemic.[107] Foreign ownership restrictions, on the contrary, are generally considered consistent with the international commitments of states. According to the Western states, 'the private sector [cannot be forced] to transfer its technologies. Incentives can therefore only take the form of encouragement, promotion and facilitation of projects which are part of a global and comprehensive approach to development'.[108]

Yet, the protection of investors' intellectual property has caused significant tension and contrasts, especially between Western countries and China, which have culminated in a dispute brought by the United States against China before the WTO. The authority for the Panel lapsed on 9 July 2021 following several suspensions at the request of the applicant.[109] In literature, it has

104 United Nations Economic and Social Commission for Asia and the Pacific, 'Foreign Direct Investment and Policies in the Health Sector in Asia and the Pacific 2022/2023' (2023) <https://repository.unescap.org/handle/20.500.12870/4921> accessed 30 October 2023, (noting that the 'COVID-19 pandemic has exposed the cracks in the current health sector. From 2019 to 2020, investment in the health-care sector dropped by 45 per cent and continued to decline in 2021 to 34 per cent in the first three quarters of 2022'.)

105 See Andrea Andrenelli, Julien Gourdon, and EvdokiaMoïse, International Technology Transfer Policies (2019) 222 OECD Trade Policy Papers <www.oecd-ilibrary.org/trade/international-technology-transfer-policies_7103eabf-en> accessed 30 October 2023.

106 EU, Reflection Paper on TT to DC and LDCs (14 February 2003) WT/WGTTT/W/5, para 54. Likewise, see the OECD, *Guidelines for Multinational Enterprises* (OECD Publishing 2011) 55.

107 See, for instance the UK-New Zealand FTA (n 28) art 14.8(1)(g).

108 See, for instance the position of the EU, 'Intervention at the TRIPs Council Regular Session' (28 February 2018) <www.eeas.europa.eu/node/40516_en> accessed 30 October 2023.

109 *China – Certain Measures Concerning the Protection of Intellectual Property Rights*, DS542.

been argued that the current legal framework is porous, inadequate, or even unfair.[110]

However, voluntary technology transfer remains crucial to reduce the 'technological gap' between industrialised and developing countries and enhance the competitiveness of the latter, by facilitating the diversification of their economy, reducing their economic vulnerability, and boosting their sustainable development.[111] Increasing transfer of technology has been a traditional objective of developing countries even more urgent and compelling in the public health sector, as demonstrated by the recent COVID-19 pandemic.[112] In the public health sector, the problems commonly faced by those states may include lack of facilities and infrastructure; inadequate distribution systems for essential medicines; lack of human resources; and the absence of legislative and governance frameworks for managing the provision of services and for ensuring accountability.[113]

For developing countries and least developed countries (LDCs) with little or no research capacity, the question is how to access these technologies and use them to achieve sustainable development.[114] Technology transfer may be pursued through several channels, including 'encouraging the adoption of concrete voluntary measures of technology transfer in the context of sustainability standards, corporate social responsibility (CSR), and responsible business conduct'.[115] It can take multiple forms and have an important beneficial impact on education, training, management, and technological skills.[116] In a broad

110 See, in particular, Julia Ya Qin, 'Forced Technology Transfer and the US-China Trade War: Implications for International Economic Law' (2019) 22 J Intl Econ L 743 (suggesting 'a country-classification system capable of differentiating among countries with different levels of economic and technological development'.) See also Qian Yin, 'Forced Technology Transfer Performance Requirement in International Investment Agreements. A Chinese Perspective' (2022) 17 Journal of Intellectual Property Law & Practice, 114.

111 See UNCTAD, 'Draft International Code of Conduct on the Transfer of Technology' (5 June 1985) UN Doc TD/CODE TOT/47; EU, 'Reflection Paper on TT to DC and LDCs' (14 February 2003) WT/WGTTT/W/5, paras 4, 5.

112 See, for instance, Ellen T Hoen, 'Protecting Public Health through Technology Transfer: The Unfulfilled Promise of the TRIPS Agreement' (2022) 24 Health and Human Rights J 211.

113 WHO, 'Advancing the Right to Health: The Vital Role of Law' (2017) <https://apps.who.int/iris/bitstream/handle/10665/252815/9789241511384-eng.pdf> accessed 30 October 2023.

114 EU (n 111) para 4.

115 UNCTAD, *LDCs Report 2021. The LDCs in the Post-COVID World: Learning from 50 Years of Experience* (UNCTAD 2021) 134.

116 As pointed out by the EU (n 108), '[t]he acquisition by LDCs of a sound and viable technological base does not indeed depend solely on the provision of technology or equipment,

perspective, transfer of technology can enhance the enjoyment of human rights and environmental protection, most prominently in the context of climate change policies.[117]

It is worth recalling that under Article 66(2) of the TRIPS Agreement

> [d]eveloped country Members shall provide incentives to enterprises and institutions in their territories for the purpose of promoting and encouraging technology transfer to least-developed country Members in order to enable them to create a sound and viable technological base.[118]

In the Annex to the TRIPS Agreement, Members specifically recognised 'the desirability of promoting the transfer of technology and capacity building in the pharmaceutical sector in order to overcome the problem faced by Members with insufficient or no manufacturing capacities in the pharmaceutical sector'.[119] Transfer of technology can integrate and complete compulsory licensing under Article 31 TRIPS, which is designed to allow eligible Members to use the subject matter of a patent without the consent of the patent holder to tackle emergencies.[120]

The pivotal role investors can play in enhancing technology transfer to boost the sustainable development of the host state can be found in investment treaties concluded by African organisations.[121] ECOWIC is probably the

---

but also on acquisition of know-how, management and production skills, improved access to knowledge sources as well as on adaptation to local economic conditions'.

117 See, in particular, Stephen Humphreys, 'Perspective: Technology Transfer and Human Rights: Joining Up the Dots' (2009) 9 Sustainable Development Law & Policy 2; International Council on Human Rights Policy, 'Beyond Technology Transfer: Protecting Human Rights in a Climate-Constrained World' in Joshua D Sarnoff (ed), *Research Handbook on Intellectual Property and Climate Change* (Elgar 2016) 126; Dalindyebo B Shabalala, 'Climate Change, Human Rights, and Technology Transfer Normative Challenges and Technical Opportunities' in Molly K Land and Jay D Aronson (eds), *New Technologies for Human Rights Law and Practice* (CUP 2018) 46.

118 See Siva Thambisetty and others, 'Addressing Vaccine Inequity during the COVID-19 Pandemic: The TRIPS Intellectual Property Waiver Proposal and Beyond' (2022) 82 CLJ 384; James Bacchus, *An Unnecessary Proposal A WTO Waiver of Intellectual Property Rights for COVID-19 Vaccines*, Cato Institute, 78 Free Trade Bulletin <www.jstor.org/stable/resrep27669> accessed 20 October 2023.

119 WTO, 'Annex to the TRIPS Agreement' (8 December 2005) WT/L/641, 4.

120 See WTO, 'Draft Ministerial Decision on the TRIPS Agreement' (17 July 2022) WT/MIN(22)/W15/Rev.2.

121 See, in particular, Common Market for Eastern and Southern Africa (signed 5 November 1993, entered into force 8 December 1994) (COMESA) art 100; Treaty Establishing the

most sophisticated agreement when it comes to the transfer of technology.[122] While fully respecting relevant WTO and WIPO disciplines,[123] it reiterates in Article 49 that states can provide incentives for promoting and encouraging the transfer of technology. Investors, in turn, are encouraged to adopt practices that permit the transfer and rapid diffusion of technologies and know-how. Importantly, it expressly states that '[m]ember States and investors shall provide, on request and on mutually agreed terms and conditions, technical and financial cooperation in favour of requesting Party'.[124]

Despite these significant precedents, investment treaties concluded during the pandemic are almost silent on the promotion of technology transfer. A notable exception is the preamble of the Rwanda-Congo BIT, which recognizes 'l'importante contribution que les investissements peuvent apporter au développement durable des Parties, notamment la réduction de la pauvreté, l'augmentation de la capacité de production, la croissance économique, le transfert de technologie et la promotion des droits de l'homme et du développement humain'.[125]

8 Conclusions

In the most recent international investment treaties, the pendulum has swung from the traditional approach focusing, primarily if not exclusively, on protecting foreign investors' rights, to an increasingly sophisticated protection of state sovereignty. Historically, investment treaties did not intend to restrain state regulatory powers but remained silent on those powers, thus leaving arbitral tribunals to balance of private and public interests. Given the uncertainty raised by conflicting arbitral awards and diverging approaches, states have gradually reaffirmed their right to take measures in the public interest and developed a variety of provisions recalibrating the content of investment treaties.[126] The pandemic has accelerated such reform.

East African Community (EAC) (signed 30 November 1999, entered into force 7 July 2000) art 80. See also Draft Pan-African Investment Code (31 December 2016) <https://au.int/sites/default/files/documents/32844-doc-draft_pan-africaninvestment_code_december_2016_en.pdf> accessed 30 October 2023.

122 ECOWIC (n 4) art 49.

123 ibid.

124 ibid.

125 Rwanda-Congo BIT (n 11) Preamble.

126 José E Alvarez, 'The Return of the State' (2011) 20 Minnesota J Intl L 268.

In reforming their treaties, states have used an incremental rather than revolutionary approach. On the one hand, they have reconsidered the content of investment treaties, mainly by significantly narrowing the scope and reducing the reach of investment treaty standards. For instance, the newest treaties exclude the qualification of non-discriminatory measures adopted by the state as indirect expropriation or confine it to rare exceptions.[127] On the other hand, states have increasingly referred to the right to regulate to protect the public interest by using multiple overlapping and possibly not mutually exclusive exceptions.

The pandemic has made such reform even more urgent and led states to take a range of policy measures to cope with the lack of facilities and infrastructure, the inadequate production and distribution of essential medicines, and the lack of human resources. To shield such measures from the scrutiny of international tribunals, states have adopted the 2022 WTO Decision on the TRIPS Agreement and gradually reformed the language of their new investment treaties.[128] The WTO Decision affirms that 'Members shall not challenge any measures taken in conformity with this decision'.[129] Therefore, compulsory licensing should not be the object of specific disputes. The Decision also waives the need 'to make efforts to obtain an authorization from the right holder' under Article 31(b) of the TRIPS Agreement and the requirement that compulsory licenses 'be predominantly to supply its domestic market' under Article 31(f). Several recent investment treaties regard compulsory licenses as flexibilities that do not amount to indirect expropriation.[130]

Technology transfer has eventually found its way into at least one investment treaty signed between developing countries. Voluntary technology transfer is part and parcel of international intellectual property law and there is no need to restate the obvious. This is not to say that technology transfer is not important. From a long-term perspective, reducing the technological gap between developed and developing states is imperative to increase the latter's capacity to prevent and manage public health crises. How to better reward investors for this kind of transfer while

127 See further Chapters 1, 8, 9, 11, 12.

128 WHO, Advancing the Right to Health: The Vital Role of Law (2017) <https://apps.who.int/iris/bitstream/handle/10665/252815/9789241511384-eng.pdf> accessed 30 October 2023.

129 WTO,Ministerial Decision on the TRIPS Agreement (n 88).

130 Jean Paul Roekaert, 'Investment Treaty Arbitration and the TRIPS Patent Waiver: Indirect Expropriation Analysis of COVID-19 Vaccine Patents' (2023) 46 Hastings Intl & Comp L Rev 59.

upholding their intellectual property rights in order to support research and development initiatives remains an open question.

The provisions of the new treaties tend to reflect the state-of-art in treaty drafting. The main difference between the newest treaties and the earlier ones lies in the growing number of safeguards, exceptions, and statements reaffirming the state right to regulate. In theory, in the absence of such provisions, the police powers doctrine and contextual, purposive, and evolutionary interpretation criteria can and should inform arbitral tribunals' reasoning. Given the varying economic, social, and cultural conditions of states, arbitral tribunals should recognize some margin of appreciation to states in addressing issues of public concern. At the end of the day, IIAs are not intended to promote regulatory harmonization among parties.

In practice, however, such clauses can assuage states' concerns by reaffirming the state's right to regulate in general and its duties under general international law, including international human rights law. Accordingly, the reform process of investment treaties is well underway and has demonstrated the capacity of states to take full advantage of the essentially bilateral or regional nature of the current legal framework. The different provisions recently inserted in those treaties and read in the broader context of general international law could provide a roadmap for governments and arbitral tribunals alike to reach an appropriate balance between private and public interests.

CHAPTER 3

The Impact of the Pandemic on the ISDS Reform

Ksenia Polonskaya

1 Introduction*

International investment dispute settlement (ISDS) is at the stage of ongoing reform.[1] The reform resulted from multiple legitimacy criticisms mounted against the ISDS mechanism in the past decade, a phenomenon also known as the 'backlash'.[2] To improve the credibility of ISDS, governments, non-governmental organizations, and arbitration institutions participate in the multilateral reform process under the umbrella of the UNCITRAL.[3] In 2020, amidst the reform efforts, the World Health Organization (WHO) declared COVID-19 to be a pandemic[4] and some world leaders even compared combating COVID to a war.[5] The spread of COVID-19 resulted in a serious crisis worldwide. In my view, it is helpful to look at the COVID-19 crisis, and more generally at any crisis (including but not limited to COVID-19), from a managerial perspective, i.e., to understand how the decision-makers meet the challenges and what consequences arise from their actions.[6]

In this light, I will consider the following questions: how did the COVID-19 measures impact the ISDS reform? What lessons for the reform process can we

* This chapter draws on research supported by the Social Sciences and Humanities Research Council.

1 Anthea Roberts and Taylor St John, 'Complex Designers and Emergent Design: Reforming the Investment Treaty System' (2022) 116 AJIL 96.

2 Michael Waibel (ed), *The Backlash Against Investment Arbitration: Perceptions and Reality* (Kluwer 2010).

3 UN, 'UNCITRAL Working Group III' <https://uncitral.un.org/en/working_groups/3/investor-state> accessed 2 April 2023.

4 WHO, 'Coronavirus Disease (COVID-19) Pandemic' <www.who.int/europe/emergencies/situations/covid-19> accessed 2 April 2023.

5 Alexandre Lemarié and Cédric Pietralunga, 'Nous Sommes en Guerre: Face au Coronavirus, Emmanuel Macron Sonne la 'Mobilisation Générale' *Le Monde* (Paris, 17 Mach 2020) <www.lemonde.fr/politique/article/2020/03/17/nous-sommes-en-guerre-face-au-coronavirus-emmanuel-macron-sonne-la-mobilisation-generale_6033338_823448.html> accessed 2 April 2023.

6 Iain Scobbie, 'Crisis? What Damned Crisis?' in Makane Moïse Mbengue and Jean D'Aspremont (eds), *Crisis Narratives in International Law* (Brill 2021) 22.

© KONINKLIJKE BRILL BV, LEIDEN, 2025 | DOI:10.1163/9789004711204_005

learn from the arbitral practice during the pandemic? I will examine the impact of the pandemic on the ISDS reform and analyse the arbitral practice to draw some lessons from the adjudicatory experiences.[7] Furthermore, I will examine how different participants of the international investment regime, including but not limited to states, investors, international organizations, and tribunals, have responded to the pandemic in the context of the ongoing ISDS reform.

In this chapter, I will show that the pandemic-related measures have impacted the ISDS reform efforts. In particular, governments, arbitral institutions, and tribunals alike adopted different responses to the pandemic. These responses can be characterized (1) as reactive rather than proactive, and (2) by their *ad hoc* nature. For example, Canada adopted a Policy Statement on Foreign Investment Review and COVID-19, which announced 'enhanced scrutiny' of 'foreign direct investments of any value [...] in Canadian businesses that are related to public health or involved in the supply of critical goods and services to Canadians or to the Government'.[8] As observed in Chapter 5, the European Union (EU) introduced a Guidance to Member states urging them to 'make full use' of existing FDI screening mechanisms 'to take fully into account the risks to critical health infrastructures, supply of critical inputs, and other critical sectors'.[9]

In the UNCITRAL context, the participating governments, in collaboration with the ICSID Centre, continued their work on the Code of Conduct, amongst other issues. As it will be discussed in section 3, some non-governmental organizations have also developed proposals on how to reform ISDS, short of abandoning it. In addition, governments have continued to refine their IIAs. For instance, the government of Canada recently released the 2021 Model Bilateral Investment Treaty (BIT) that incorporates a Code of Conduct for arbitrators.[10] The Italian Model BIT of 2022 includes the provisions on corporate social responsibility and responsible business conduct as well as references to the 2019 International Labour Organization (ILO) Centenary Declaration for the Future of Work.[11]

7 ICSID, 'Code of Conduct for Adjudicators in International Investment Disputes' <https://icsid.worldbank.org/resources/code-of-conduct> accessed 2 April 2023.
8 UNCTAD, 'Investment Policy Responses to the COVID-19 Pandemic' 8 <https://unctad.org/system/files/official-document/diaepcbinf2020d3_en.pdf> accessed 2 April 2023.
9 ibid.
10 Charles-Emmanuel Côté, 'The New Canadian Model Investment Treaty: A Quiet Evolution' (2022) 337 Columbia FDI Perspectives No 337 <https://ccsi.columbia.edu/sites/default/files/content/docs/fdi%20perspectives/No%20337%20-%20C%C3%B4t%C3%A9%20-%20FINAL.pdf> accessed 2 April 2023.
11 Italian Model BIT (2022) <https://investmentpolicy.unctad.org/international-investment-agreements/treaty-files/6438/download> arts 19, 22.

The arbitration institutions also joined the chorus.[12] Some institutions issued a joint statement that signalled their commitment to contribute 'to stability and foreseeability in a highly unstable environment, including by ensuring that pending cases may continue and that parties may have their cases heard without undue delay'.[13] The ICSID Secretariat also adopted a range of measures to deal with COVID-19. For instance, the Centre shifted to remote working arrangements.[14] In addition, the International Chamber of Commerce (ICC) issued a Guidance Note on Possible Measures Aimed at Mitigating the Effects of the COVID-19 Pandemic.[15] The document overviews the procedural tools available to the parties and provides further guidance on administering the proceedings through teleconferencing. The ICC specified that tribunals had a 'duty to conduct the arbitration in an expeditious and cost-effective manner'.[16] Accordingly, the tribunals must 'fulfil' this duty and run the hearing virtually whenever necessary.[17] However, when tribunals proceed with the virtual hearings, they must ensure that the parties retain their procedural rights, such as having an equal opportunity to present their case before the tribunal.[18]

In this context, this chapter first examines how the pandemic impacted the activities of the Working Group under the auspices of the UNCITRAL and whether COVID-19 generated any additional issues for the Working Group to consider. Second, it examines the proposals outside the activities of the Working Group that pertain to COVID-19 and the ISDS reform. Third, it scrutinises the arbitral practice to identify the issues that some tribunals faced in the context of the pandemic. Finally, the chapter further analyses whether and to what extent the practical solutions implemented during the pandemic may

12 Freshfields, 'Latest Arbitral Rules Reforms' <www.freshfields.com/en-gb/our-thinking/campaigns/international-arbitration-in-2021/latest-arbitral-rules-reforms/> accessed 2 April 2023.

13 ICC, 'Joint Statement: Arbitration and COVID-19' (17 April 2020) <https://iccwbo.org/content/uploads/sites/3/2020/04/covid19-joint-statement.pdf> accessed 13 December 2022.

14 ICSID, 'Hearings and Sessions Held in ICSID Cases from March to December (2019 v 2020)' (20 December 2020) <https://icsid.worldbank.org/news-and-events/news-releases/hearings-and-sessions-held-icsid-cases-march-december-2019-vs-2020> accessed 13 December 2022.

15 ICC, 'ICC Guidance Note on Possible Measures Aimed at Mitigating the Effects of the COVID-19 Pandemic' (9 April 2020) <https://iccwbo.org/publication/icc-guidance-note-on-possible-measures-aimed-at-mitigating-the-effects-of-the-covid-19-pandemic/> accessed 13 December 2022.

16 ibid para 25.

17 ibid.

18 ibid para 28.

contribute to the reform of the ISDS mechanism and lead to improved coordination between states.

2 Ongoing Reform Efforts and Reform Proposals in Light of COVID-19

While the COVID-19 pandemic is now officially behind us, global emergencies could strike again in the future. In this context, it is necessary to review the proposals generated during the pandemic to have a better understanding of the possible solutions to future emergencies.[19] This section examines the ongoing ISDS reform under the umbrella of the UNCITRAL and overviews the reform proposals made outside of the UNCITRAL framework; the purpose is to understand how the COVID-19 pandemic influenced the reform process and highlight the lessons learned.

2.1 *Adjusting to the Pandemic: UNCITRAL Working Group III*

This subsection examines how UNCITRAL, its Secretariat, and Working Group III modified their procedures and activities in the context of the pandemic. Specifically, it analyses the decisions of the Working Group on administering the sessions and maintaining the reform progress.

The member states of The United Nations Commission on International Trade Law (the Commission) were swift to react by adjusting the activities of the Working Groups in response to the pandemic. For example, under the ordinary procedure, the Chair of the Working Group and the Rapporteur must be re-elected every four years.[20] However, given that Working Group III functioned in a hybrid format and not all delegations could attend the deliberations in person, the Group decided not to run the elections.[21] Accordingly, the Chairperson of the Working Group III and the Rapporteur continued to serve in their respective capacities.[22]

19 WHO, 'Statement on the Fifteenth Meeting of the IHR (2005) Emergency Committee on the COVID-19 Pandemic' (5 May 2023) <www.who.int/news/item/05-05-2023-statement-on-the-fifteenth-meeting-of-the-international-health-regulations-(2005)-emergency-committee-regarding-the-coronavirus-disease-(covid-19)-pandemic> accessed 23 September 2023.

20 UNCITRAL, 'Decisions Adopted by States Members of UNCITRAL in August 2020 in Accordance With the Procedure for Taking Decisions of UNCITRAL During the Coronavirus Disease 2019 (COVID-19) Pandemic' (28 August 2020), A/CN.9/1038, para 3.

21 UNCITRAL, 'Letter From the Chairperson of the Working Group III' (1 September 2020), <https://uncitral.un.org/sites/uncitral.un.org/files/media-documents/uncitral/en/280422_letter_from_chair_of_wg_iii_1.pdf> accessed 13 November 2022.

22 These were Shane Spellisey of Canada and Ms. Natalie Yu-Lin Morris-Sharma of Singapore.

Under the proposal of the Chair of UNCITRAL, the participant-states adopted a few changes to facilitate the activities of the Working Groups. Specifically, they proclaimed that the values of 'transparency, inclusiveness, flexibility, effectiveness and equality' are guiding the activities of the Working Groups, including Working Group III.[23] To reinforce these values, they adopted several adjustments to the undertakings of the Working Group. First, there was a possibility to engage in the sessions remotely. Here the participant-states expressed an understanding that the possibility of remote engagement can enhance equality among the participants and improve the accessibility of the sessions, especially for the regions most impacted by the COVID-related restrictions.[24]

Second, the Chairs of the Working Group committed to 'ensuring an inclusive and transparent approach [...] to accommodate remote participation'.[25] The members accounted for the possibility of technical disruptions and difficulties for the delegations. The principle of inclusive participation embraced the necessity to enable all delegates to participate on 'equal footing' to the extent possible. As Daria Davitti and others have aptly explained, COVID-19 revealed and exacerbated existing inequalities.[26] This observation equally applies to the reform context, for example, in terms of who has access to the necessary technical equipment to participate in the debates.

Third, the member states adjusted the approach to the ordinary decision-making procedure across the working groups. Accordingly, each group's Chairperson and Rapporteur had to 'prepare a summary reflecting the deliberations and any conclusions reach[ed] in the session'.[27] In addition, to enable equal participation of the delegates who joined the sessions remotely, the chairpersons were required to prepare 'a provisional agenda for each session in consultation with the UNCITRAL members states' and 'circulate it for comment'.[28]

In the Special Letter, the Chairperson of the Group signalled the commitment to maintain the momentum of the talks despite the challenges posed by the pandemic.[29] In particular, the Chair encouraged the delegates to take

---

23 UNCITRAL, 'Decisions Adopted by States' (n 20) 2.

24 ibid para 1.

25 ibid para 2.

26 Daria Davitti and others, 'COVID-19 and the Precarity of International Investment Law' (6 May 2020), <https://medium.com/iel-collective/covid-19-and-the-precarity-of-international-investment-law-c9fc254b3878> accessed 13 December 2022.

27 UNCITRAL, 'Decisions Adopted by States' (n 20).

28 ibid para 5.

29 UNCITRAL, 'Letter From the Chairperson' (n 21).

advantage of making the written submissions to 'facilitate the discussions'.[30] Following the recommendations made by the Commission, Working Group III made some adjustments to the ordinary procedures, allowing remote participation to ensure inclusivity in deliberations. Given the circumstances of the pandemic, specifically the travelling restrictions, this step was necessary to ensure wider participation. Arguably, as with any remote participation, there was a risk that the participants who engaged in the sessions remotely would miss an opportunity to participate in informal interactions.

Session 39 of the Working Group was the very first session that ran in the hybrid format, and not without some technical difficulties.[31] For instance, the delegate from Brazil raised concerns over the complications in connecting to the platform. In his view, it was problematic in light of the accessibility mandate, especially if the Working Group made substantive progress in the deliberations and some delegates could not join the process due to technical disruptions.[32] In response, the Secretariat committed to resolving the issues of access in an expedient manner.[33] Given the adjusted rules of procedure, either the Chair or the Rapporteur had to be present during the online session to provide a possibility to draft the summary of the issues discussed at the session.[34]

During the session, the Chair also emphasized the importance of the discussion on capacity building and the possibility of connecting the agenda of the 39th session with the deliberations on the advisory centre.[35] Given the Commission's and the Group's emphasis on capacity building, in the future, it might be helpful to consider whether the Commission can enable remote participation for the delegations in the aftermath of the pandemic. Furthermore, it will be helpful to reflect on embedding the option of remote participation for the advisory centre.

Accordingly, the values of 'transparency, inclusiveness, flexibility, effectiveness and equality' have guided the activities of the Working Group amidst the pandemic. To pursue these values more effectively, the Group may wish to develop guidelines based on the practical lessons learned from the

30 UNCITRAL, 'Decisions Adopted by States' (n 20) 2.

31 UNCITRAL, 'Working Group III (ISDS Reform), 39th Session' (5 October 2020) 94:00 <https://conferences.unite.un.org/carbonweb/public/uncitral/speakerslog/ad732ba5-7c55-47c5-94d7-fa394c58af10> accessed 2 April 2023.

32 ibid 71:23–71:25.

33 ibid 74:16.

34 ibid 25:00–25:14.

35 ibid 51:46.

deliberations process during the pandemic to inform the decision-making in the future if another global emergency arises.

2.2 *Proposals to Address the Pandemic-Related Concerns*

This subsection explores the proposals and responses of the participants of the investment law regime, outside the UNCITRAL context. In this section, I cover the proposals by the International Institute for Sustainable Development (IISD) and the Columbia Centre on Sustainable Development (CCSD).

IISD made two propositions.[36] First, it suggested that states could withdraw their consent to ISDS. In its analysis, IISD considered a contractual model of consent withdrawal. According to this model, the state can withdraw its consent to arbitrate so far as an investor did not accept it by filing a claim.[37] For instance, in *AES v. Kazakhstan*, the tribunal faced a question whether the Government of Kazakhstan can revoke a consent to ICSID by repealing its national law where it was expressed.[38] It also had to examine potential conditions of such revocation.[39] The tribunal explained two possible approaches to the issue.[40]

The first approach follows the model in contract law on offer and acceptance.[41] Under this approach, the government can change its national laws without any constraints.[42] Accordingly, if the government decides to repeal the law that incorporates its consent to arbitrate and the investor did not take advantage of it by filing a claim, consent would no longer be valid.[43] The second approach is based on public international law reasoning with respect to unilateral declarations. Under this model, the state 'does not have complete freedom to retract a unilateral commitment'.[44] The tribunal concluded that the question on the effects of repealed legislation upon state's consent could not 'be answered in general terms' and required it to be 'case-specific'.[45] The

36 Nathalie Bernasconi-Osterwalder and Sarah Brewin Nyaguthii Maina, 'Commentary: Protecting Against Investor–State Claims Amidst COVID-19: A Call to Action For Governments' (2020) <www.iisd.org/system/files/publications/investor-state-claims-covid-19.pdf> accessed 13 December 2022.

37 ibid 8.

38 *AES v. Kazakhstan*, ICSID Case No. ARB/10/16, Award (1 November 2013) para 207.

39 ibid.

40 ibid para 208.

41 ibid para 208(i).

42 ibid.

43 ibid.

44 ibid para 208(ii).

45 ibid para 216.

tribunal further noted that it would not apply the first approach based on the contractual model.[46] Instead, it would examine 'the specific instrument at stake and the scope and nature of the consent given therein'.[47] In the circumstances of the *AES* case, a national law repealed by Kazakhstan explicitly 'provided' 'an assurance' that the government would not 'unilaterally withdraw' investors' rights.[48] Accordingly, this law raised 'specific expectations' upon which investors relied.[49] Given this context, the tribunal ruled that Kazakhstan could not revoke its consent to arbitrate unilaterally by repealing its domestic law.[50] Thus, while the realisation of the IISD's proposition is possible in principle, it can be a subject to multiple challenges and requires a more detailed assessment.

The second IISD's proposition focused on a possibility to suspend the application of ISDS; and develop a joint interpretation that would clarify that states acted 'in necessity and therefore cannot be found in breach of their investment treaty obligations for COVID-related measures'.[51] The IISD's concern is that in emergency circumstances, it would be difficult for states to defend their regulatory measures in ISDS.[52] Indeed, the doctrine of necessity requires 'the act of the state *be the only way* for the [s]tate to safeguard an essential interest against a grave and imminent peril'.[53] As it will be illustrated in Chapters 10 and 11, the tribunals previously applied this approach to the doctrine of necessity during the saga of cases against Argentina.[54] The contradictory arbitral interpretations in these cases contributed to the backlash against international investment law (IIL).

Such joint-interpretation (as proposed by IISD) could result in the situation where states label the regulatory measures that impact on investments to be COVID-related without it necessarily being the case.[55] IISD notes that if the states attempt to disguise intentionally wrongful acts' as 'COVID-related measures', these attempts can be reviewed under the state-to-state dispute settlement.[56] This approach presumes that states will be willing to exercise

46 ibid para 219.
47 ibid.
48 ibid para 220.
49 ibid para 221.
50 ibid.
51 Bernasconi-Osterwalder and Brewin (n 36) 8.
52 ibid.
53 ibid 5 (emphasis added).
54 *National Grid plc v. Argentine*, UNCITRAL, Award (3 November 2008) paras 83–102.
55 Bernasconi-Osterwalder and Brewin (n 36) 8.
56 ibid.

diplomatic protection and act in the interests of their investors. Historical evidence shows that it might not necessarily be the case.[57] For instance, in the *Barcelona Traction* case, Canada (where the Barcelona Traction company was incorporated) did not exercise its diplomatic protection and did not support a claim to the International Court of Justice (ICJ).[58]

Martin Gronemann and Markus Krajewski also find a proposition that states should themselves classify regulatory measures (even if adverse to investments) as COVID-related to be problematic.[59] The reason is that the governments will not have any objective criteria to classify the measures and as a result, such determinations can become self-judging. The concerns expressed by Gronemann and Krajewski are undoubtedly well-founded. For instance, in the World Trade Organization (WTO) and the International Tribunal for the Law of the Sea (ITLOS) context, some governments expansively applied the notions of national security and military activity to curb the jurisdiction of the international dispute settlement bodies.[60] One example is Russia's defence in *Russia-Measures Concerning Traffic in Transit.* In these proceedings, Russia contended before the Dispute Settlement Body (DSB) of the WTO that the definition of national security was self-judging.[61] The panel ultimately adopted a contrary position.[62] The problem with the self-judging approach is that it leaves too much discretion to the governments without much oversight.

IISD was not alone in its proposals to curtail possible claims. For example, the CCSD proposed to establish 'an immediate moratorium on all arbitration claims by private corporations against governments'.[63] It further specified that all arbitration claims that target anti-pandemic regulatory measures should be permanently restricted.[64] This proposal is far-reaching especially since CCSD did not offer any particulars on how it could be framed. Arguably, the moratorium on the ISDS claims could be envisaged as a modification of a relevant

57 *Barcelona Traction, Light and Power Company, Limited (Belgium v. Spain)* [1970] ICJ Rep 3, 9.

58 ibid.

59 ibid.

60 E.g., *Case Concerning the Detention of Three Ukrainian Naval Vessels (Ukraine v. Russian Federation)*, (Provisional Measures, Order of 25 May 2019) ITLOS Reports 2019, para 8.1.

61 WTO, *Russia – Measures Concerning Traffic in Transit* (5 April 2019) WT/DS512/R, para 7.26.

62 ibid.

63 CCSI, 'Call for ISDS Moratorium During COVID-19 Crisis and Response' (6 May 2020)<https://ccsi.columbia.edu/content/call-isds-moratorium-during-covid-19-crisis-and-response> accessed 2 April 2023.

64 ibid.

investment treaty. In this case, the VCLT rules on modification (Part IV) would apply.[65] The CCSD proposal, however, did not elaborate on such a possibility.

The proposals by IISD and CCSD are thought provocative yet require greater attention to details on how their recommendations can be carried out. However, they are useful to keep in mind for two reasons. First, these proposals focus on the need to coordinate a response to global emergency, such as a pandemic. Second, they recommend ex ante guidance on how to respond to the pandemic in the investment context in anticipation of the possible investment claims.

3 COVID-19 in the Arbitral Practice: Lessons for the Reform Process

During the COVID-19 pandemic, tribunals and parties encountered new challenges in the arbitral proceedings. This section examines how the tribunals responded to the pandemic-induced challenges. In addition, it investigates whether the arbitral practice can inform current and future reform efforts. The analysis of the arbitral practice shows that arbitrators examined COVID-19-related issues in three contexts. First, the tribunals reviewed the possibility of delaying or suspending the ongoing proceedings. Second, they considered the stay of enforcement of the arbitral awards. Third, the tribunals dealt with the substantive investment standards while adopting an *ad hoc* approach to legal interpretation in response to the pandemic-related concerns. This section further suggests that the ISDS participants may wish to develop guiding principles in a coordinated manner to address global emergencies of the future.

First, the tribunals encountered multiple requests to suspend and delay the proceedings because of the COVID-19 pandemic. For example, in *AES v. Argentina*, the government of Argentina requested postponing the in-person hearing.[66] The tribunal refused the request. It opted for the virtual hearing instead.[67] To justify its decision, the tribunal cited its 'social responsibility concerns'.[68] In *Alicia Grace et al v. Mexico*, the tribunal dealt with a request to hold the hearings virtually yet chose to conduct the hearings in person.[69] The

65 *Vienna Convention on the Law of Treaties* (adopted 22 May 1969, entered into force 27 January 1980) 1155 UNTS 331 part iv.

66 *AES v. Argentine*, ICSID Case No. ARB/02/17, Decision on the Respondent's Proposal to Disqualify All Members of the Tribunal (6 April 2022) para 18.

67 ibid.

68 ibid.

69 *Alicia Grace v. Mexico*, ICSID Case No. UNCT/18/4, Procedural Order No 20: On the Format of the Hearing (18 February 2022).

tribunal maintained a possibility for the disputing parties to participate in the proceedings remotely if they (due to the pandemic measures) could not join in person.[70] In *Banco Bilbao v. Bolivia*, the tribunal also cited its 'social responsibility' to limit the spread of COVID-19 to justify holding virtual hearings.[71]

The tribunals have resolved the issues pertaining to the pandemic context hearings on a case-by-case basis. When the parties agreed to conduct the hearings in the videoconference format, the tribunals specified the minimal technical requirements for the proceedings, including the particulars of the applicable etiquette rules.[72] When the parties agreed on the virtual hearings, they also typically consented 'not to challenge the Tribunal's Award in any subsequent proceeding solely on the basis that the hearing was held virtually rather than in person'.[73] However, as the tribunal in *Gabriel Resources v. Romania* has noted, '[s]uch a stipulation, […] will not bar a Party from challenging an award based upon *the manner* in which a remote video proceeding was actually conducted'.[74] Accordingly, the parties still had a recourse to challenge the award to ensure procedural integrity of the ISDS process.

In some instances, the parties challenged the tribunals' assessment of the COVID-19-related risks. For example, Spain alleged that arbitrators failed to demonstrate the 'high moral character' required under the ICSID Convention when they had chosen to conduct the hearings virtually instead of in person.[75] The thrust of Spain's argument was that the arbitrators made 'misleading' and 'speculative statements'.[76] According to Spain, 'the Tribunal said that one of its arbitrators could not travel from Costa Rica to the Hague for a hearing at the end of the month because Costa Rica's borders were closed'; and (ii) the Tribunal 'said that one of the arbitrators could not travel' because 'it is unclear whether any facilities for travel will be available'.[77] Furthermore, Spain advanced an argument that the change of the hearing model from in-person

---

70 ibid para 3.

71 *Banco Bilbao Vizcaya Argentaria SA v. Estado Plurinacional de Bolivia*, ICSID Case No. ARB(AF)/18/5, Award (12 July 2022) para 72.

72 E.g., *Carrizosa v. Colombia*, ICSID Case No. ARB/18/5, Procedural Order No 3: Organization of the Hearing by Videoconference (24 September 2020) paras 2, 28–35; *Cortec Mining Kenya Limited v. Kenya*, ICSID Case No. ARB/15/29, Procedural Order No 3: the Organization of the Hearing (12 August 2020).

73 *Gabriel Resources Limited and Gabriel Resources (Jersey) Limited v. Romania*, ICSID Case No. ARB/15/31, Procedural Order No 33 (18 September 2020) para 9.

74 ibid.

75 *HSH Nordbank AG v. Spain*, ICSID Case No ARB/15/45, Decision on the Second Proposal to Disqualify All Members of the Tribunal (15 December 2020) para 33.

76 ibid.

77 ibid para 135.

to a videoconference constituted 'unequal treatment'.[78] The Chair concluded that a mere disagreement of the party with the tribunal's assessment of the risk that COVID-19 posed and a decision to switch the modality of the hearing did not violate the requirements on independence and impartiality set by the ICSID Convention.[79] The Chair observed that '[n]either the ICSID Convention, nor the ICSID Arbitration Rules contemplate a disqualification proceeding as a mechanism to overturn procedural decisions that dissatisfy one of the Parties'.[80]

In this context, the states and the arbitral institutions participating in the ISDS reform may wish to consider the possibility of providing general guidance on the applicable procedures in the circumstances of force majeure, such as the pandemic. Arguably, the departure from the ad hoc nature of the pandemic-related response can increase the efficiency of the ISDS proceedings and ensure that the parties do not advance unnecessary challenges to delay the proceedings.

The second issue relates to staying the enforcement of awards in the context of the pandemic. For instance, in *Tethyan Copper v. Pakistan*, Pakistan argued that the immediate enforcement of the award could impede its 'capacity to meet public needs, including the loss of life and the impact on programs designed to face the crisis of the COVID-19 pandemic'.[81] Furthermore, the respondent state argued that due to this hardship, it would not be able to fulfil its international obligations under the *International Covenant on Civil and Political Rights* (ICCPR), specifically the right to life.[82] Pakistan also referenced the International Regulations adopted by the WHO, which stipulated as follows: '[s]tate must develop, strengthen and maintain [...] the capacity to respond promptly and effectively to public health risks and public health emergencies of international concern'.[83] According to the Government, if the tribunal were to lift the stay, it would impact Pakistan's ability to 'effectively' protect public health since the public funds would be directed to paying the investor.[84] Notably, Pakistan made references to the ICCPR and the WHO

78 ibid para 141.

79 ibid paras 140–143.

80 ibid para 143.

81 *Tethyan Copper Company Pty Limited v. Islamic Republic of Pakistan*, ICSID Case No. ARB/12/1, Decisions on Stay of Enforcement of the Award (17 September 2020) para 64.

82 ibid para 43.

83 ibid.

84 ibid.

Regulations in light of article 52(5) of the ICSID Convention. For clarity, article 52(5) of the Convention provides that

> [t]he Committee may *if it considers that the circumstances so require*, stay enforcement of the award pending its decision. Accordingly, if the applicant requests a stay of enforcement of the award in his application, enforcement shall be stayed provisionally until the Committee rules on such request.[85]

The Committee, thus, has the discretion to stay in enforcement of the award.

The Committee did not deem these concerns valid for lacking the immediacy of the impact to stay the enforcement of the award.[86] Specifically, it observed that 'while the Committee recognises the potential hardship that Pakistan may suffer due to a lifting of the stay, it is not convinced of the likelihood that Pakistan would suffer severe hardship on an immediate basis to the degree it claims'.[87] The Committee further denied the relevance of the WHO Regulations and the ICCPR, in part, on the basis that previous committees never 'considered them, or anything comparable'.[88] The Committee noted, however, that even if it applied the ICCPR and the WHO Regulations, '[t]he chain of events that exists between lifting a stay of enforcement and the triggering of the right to life, public health rights, or public health emergencies of international concern appears too long and tenuous'.[89] Regardless of whether one agrees or disagrees with the Committee's reasoning, Pakistan's arguments and the Committee's assessment signal a need to further examine the relevance of other treaties, such as the international human rights treaties, to the interpretation of article 52(5) of the ICSID Convention. The provisions of the VCLT, specifically article 31(3)(c) permits for a holistic approach to interpreting the ICSID Convention.[90] In light of these developments, the states and arbitration institutions that engage in the reform efforts could analyse the issue of

---

85 *Convention on the Settlement of Investment Disputes between States and Nationals of Other States* (opened for signature 18 March 1965, entered into force 14 October 1966) (ICSID Convention) art 52(5) (emphasis added).

86 *Tethyan Copper* (n 81) paras 154–56.

87 ibid para 157.

88 ibid para 133.

89 ibid.

90 Daniel Rosentreter, *Article 31(3)(c) of the Vienna Convention on the Law of Treaties and the Principle of Systemic Integration in International Investment Law and Arbitration* (Nomos Verlag 2015) 261.

balancing states' obligations in the context of article 52(5) of the Convention, particularly so in the context of the pandemic and other emergencies.

In *ConocoPhillips Petrozuata BV v. Venezuela*, the Venezuelan Government has argued in favour of maintaining the stay because 'it will suffer irreparable harm if the stay is not maintained'.[91] According to the government, 'an immediate payment of the Award, should it be subsequently annulled, would put it at risk of not being able to recover the amount paid'.[92] To justify its request, the Government referenced '[t]he COVID-19 crisis' that contributed to its precarious economic position 'on top of the crisis', which resulted from the economic sanctions imposed by the USA.[93] The Committee disregarded the COVID-related concerns. Specifically, it noted that '[a]bsent a demonstration that the worldwide sanitary crisis has worsened the perspectives of payment of the Award, we consider the argument as moot'.[94] The Committee made the following observation:

> [i]f we follow this line of argumentation on Venezuela's financial condition, the issue would be more about Venezuela's impossibility to pay the amounts of the award than about a limited deferral of payment pending these proceedings. Venezuela has not proven that enforcement before a decision on annulment will cause more catastrophic consequences which did not already exist.[95]

The *ConocoPhillips* decision raises an important question on the circumstances that can justify the stay of enforcement in the context of the pandemic or similar events. The states participating in the reform process can scrutinize this issue in greater detail to guide other ISDS participants in the future.

Third, many governments worldwide introduced various pandemic-related measures to curb the infection. In this context, the *United Nations Conference on Trade and Development* (UNCTAD) warned that specific provisions in the IIAs 'could come into friction with state measures adopted to address the pandemic'.[96] For example, the French investors threatened to bring a claim against

---

91 *ConocoPhillips Petrozuata BV v. Venezuela*, ICSID Case No. ARB/07/30, Decision on the Applicant's Request to Continue the Stay of Enforcement of the Award (2 November 2020) para 26.

92 ibid.

93 ibid para 27.

94 ibid para 52.

95 ibid para 54.

96 UNCTAD (n 8) 11. Seattle to Brussels Network, 'Open Letter to Governments on ISDS and COVID-19' <http://s2bnetwork.org/sign-the-pen-letter-to-governments-on-isds-and-covid-19/> accessed 13 December 2022.

Peru for cancelling the tolls to ease the financial strain of the pandemic upon the population.[97] Silvia Steininger explains that '[t]he suspension of toll fees was limited to a state of emergency, which Peru declared in March. Peru has been one of the hardest-hit countries by COVID-19 with more than 52,000 deaths and around 1.5 million infections in the first year'.[98] It will likely take some time before we can see more claims resurfacing.[99]

In the circumstances surrounding the pandemic, the core issue before the tribunals will be to evaluate whether the government appropriately balanced the investment and non-investment concerns. Notably, some investment treaties reaffirm the right to regulate in the public interest.[100] The most recent joint statement by G20 provides that '[g]overnments reaffirm the right to regulate investment for legitimate public policy purposes'.[101] Arguably, such language can be an invitation for the tribunals to exercise balancing between investment and non-investment interests.[102] The treaties with such provisions typically do not prescribe a particular test for the tribunals to balance the objectives of regulating in the interests of the public and protecting investments. In his partial dissenting opinion for the *Eco Oro Minerals Corp v. Colombia* arbitration, Philippe Sands calls for 'sensitivity to the difficulties of governmental decision-making' in evaluating the arbitrariness of the governmental measures.[103] According to Sands,

> [i]n the search for balance, and in the face of competing pressures, different arms of the same government may inevitably give expression to

---

97 IAReporter, 'Three Are in Place to Hear Contract-Based Highway Concession Dispute with Peru' (5 January 2022) IAReporter <www.iareporter.com/articles/three-are-in-place-to-hear-contract-based-highway-concession-dispute-with-peru/> accessed 13 December 2022.

98 Silvia Steininger, 'Investment and Human Rights in the Shadow of the Pandemic: Recent Developments in 2020' in Lisa Sachs, Lise Johnson, and Jesse Coleman (eds), *Yearbook on International Investment Law & Policy* (OUP 2020) para 12.26.

99 ibid para 12.27. UNCTAD, 'Investor-State Dispute Settlement Cases Pass the 1000 Mark: Cases and Outcomes in 2019' (July 2020) <https://unctad.org/system/files/official-document/diaepcbinf2020d6.pdf> accessed 13 December 2022.

100 Catharine Titi, *The Right to Regulate in International Investment Law* (Bloomsbury 2014).

101 G20, 'Guiding Principles for Global Investment Policymaking' para VI <www.oecd.org/daf/inv/investment-policy/G20-Guiding-Principles-for-Global-Investment-Policymaking.pdf> accessed 13 December 2022.

102 Vera Korzun, 'The Right to Regulate in Investor-State Arbitration: Slicing and Dicing Regulatory Carve-outs' (2017) 50 Vand J Transnatl L 355, 363; Titi (n 100).

103 *Eco Oro Minerals Corp v. Colombia*, ICSID Case No. ARB/16/41, Partial Dissent of Professor Philippe Sands (9 September 2021) para 28.

> different and potentially conflicting priorities. As noted above, this is particularly the case when the protection of the environment or human health is at stake (one need only think of the current challenges faced by so many governments around the world as they confront the emerging reality of global warming/climate change and biodiversity losses and their consequences, or the reality of COVID-19, as governments struggle to find a way through the difficulties of protecting human health whilst also securing economic wellbeing).[104]

Given the previous criticisms levied against the ISDS tribunals in their inconsistent and uncertain application of the law, it is unlikely that Sands' appeal will be universally adopted by the tribunals. Even if some states update their IIAs to account for COVID-like emergencies, it is difficult to predict whether the tribunals will be receptive to this change in their approach to balancing investment and non-investment interests. In his most recent book, Wolfgang Alschner has persuasively shown that '[w]riting new treaties to produce new outcomes is tough because the meaning of investment treaty provisions is only partially crafted at the drafting stage. Much of it only emerges through practice'.[105] For example, in practice, the investors use the Most-Favoured Nation (MFN) provisions to import more expansive investment protection standards. Even when the states update the MFN language in the treaties, it is not a guarantee that the existing trends in arbitral practice will be reversed. According to Alschner, 'MFN today threatens to undermine more complete IIAs and to reverse treaty design innovation'.[106] The reason is that arbitral practice constitutes a 'default gap filler' as the tribunals look at previous decisions when giving reasons in the arbitral awards.[107]

Accordingly, states cannot rely on the arbitral practice to shift the balance in favour of public interest regulation including in the circumstances of global emergencies. As such, the participants of the ISDS reform should consider developing guidance on the approaches to be taken by the tribunals on balancing investment and non-investment interests in the circumstances of global challenges, such as pandemics, climate emergency, etc.

104 ibid.

105 Wolfgang Alschner, *Investment Arbitration and State-Driven Reform: New Treaties, Old Outcomes* (OUP 2022) 123.

106 ibid.

107 ibid 219–20.

4 Concluding Remarks

The ISDS reform efforts even continued during the pandemic. The Working Group III and its participants, as well as the arbitral tribunals and the arbitration institutions, adjusted to the pandemic measures. However, they displayed a reactive approach to address the challenges posed by the pandemic. My proposition is that the reform participants need to develop some *ex-ante* guidance on how to manage global challenges based on the lessons learned during the COVID response. Such guidance should focus on two issues.

First, the reform participants should develop principles on virtual engagement during the arbitral proceedings. These principles should follow the values identified by UNCITRAL, namely 'transparency, inclusiveness, flexibility, effectiveness and equality'. Second, given that the pandemic left us with much uncertainty about balancing the interests of investors and the regulatory objectives of states, the reform participants may wish to consider providing more guidance on how the tribunals should balance investment and non-investment interests. For example, the provisions on investment standards could include specific criteria for evaluating the state conduct during emergencies to complement the necessity defence. Such approach is needed because tribunals rely on previous arbitral practice to justify their choices and may be reluctant to shift towards a more balanced approach, even if states introduce new provisions on the right to regulate.

CHAPTER 4

Foreign Direct Investment and Geoeconomic Risk: Sketching the Contours of an Emerging Concept

Jens Hillebrand Pohl and Mikael Wigell

1 Introduction*

Geoeconomic rivalry has been accelerating in recent years, with states increasingly applying economic instruments to advance strategic agendas. As this competition is ramped up, economic interdependence is cast in a new light.[1] The recent COVID-19 pandemic had a catalysing effect on already existing tendencies towards a more adversarial international economic environment, hastening a trend toward geoeconomic rivalry that became very evident during the Trump US presidency.[2] The pandemic prompted states and companies to recognize how vulnerable their economies were (and still are), not only to external shocks like the pandemic, but also to self-seeking behaviour by other states and companies.[3]

Moreover, the pandemic witnessed the weaponization of critical health technology. Labelled 'vaccine war' and 'vaccine diplomacy', states with access to such technologies – chiefly Russia and China, and countered by the United States and Europe – began leveraging access to COVID-19 vaccines for power-political purposes.[4]

---

* Research for this chapter is part of the Finnish Institute of International Affairs research project 'Power Politics by Economic Means: The Geoeconomics Research Initiative' (Project-ID: 355820), funded by the Research Council of Finland.

1 See, e.g., Mark Leonard, *The Age of Unpeace: How Connectivity Causes Conflict* (Penguin Books London 2021); Henry Farrell and Abraham L Newman, 'Weaponized Interdependence: How Global Economic Networks Shape State Coercion' (2019) 44 Intl Secur 42.

2 Henry Farrell and Abram Newman, 'Will the Coronavirus end Globalization as We Know it' (*Foreign Affairs*, 16 March 2020) <www.foreignaffairs.com/world/will-coronavirus-end-globalization-we-know-it> accessed 21 September 2023.

3 ibid.

4 Ville Sinkkonen and Anu Ruokamo, 'Vaccines as Contentious Connectivity in the Indo-Pacific: The Case of US-China Competition during the COVID-19 Pandemic' (2022) Finnish Institute of International Affairs Working Paper 129 <www.fiia.fi/en/publication/vaccines-as-contentious-connectivity-in-the-indo-pacific> accessed 21 September 2023; Sinikukka Saari,

© KONINKLIJKE BRILL BV, LEIDEN, 2025 | DOI:10.1163/9789004711204_006

Economic interdependencies, once heralded as a barrier to conflict, has now turned into a currency of power. Leveraged for strategic ends, they feed a geoeconomic chain reaction with states applying broader economic controls out of concern for their economic autonomy.[5] Foreign direct investment (FDI) is a case in point, and instrumentalized for geoeconomic purposes, it can take many forms.

First, the making of investments abroad can be projected as a means of gaining influence.[6] State-owned enterprises (SOEs) can make investments in foreign countries to gain access to technologies, products, or data that are valuable to the home state. Sovereign wealth funds (SWFs) can make infrastructure investments that significantly support the economic performance of a host state and expect some negotiation leverage in return. A state can subsidize domestic private firms' mergers and acquisitions activities abroad and expect those firms to comply with its instructions on matters of strategic importance when needed, e.g., to cease production or supply of a critical input or resource at a time of crisis, such as vaccines, financial services, or news reporting. This was amply illustrated during the recent COVID-19 pandemic. Access to vaccines became a lever of geoeconomic power, whereby the threat of denial of vaccine deliveries, or the imposition of conditions to such deliveries, provided vaccine manufacturers, and their host states, with unprecedented bargaining leverage.[7]

Second, it is not only the *making* of investments that can be 'weaponized' in the manner illustrated above. One state's *denial* of a target state's investment opportunities abroad can also be a source of geoeconomic leverage – or to be precise the investment opportunities of a target state's nationals (which could be understood as individuals and firms that are the subjects of the target state under international law). Relatedly, states can apply economic sanctions as a kind of 'investment embargo' to starve a non-compliant state of needed *inward* FDI. Following Russia's full-scale invasion of Ukraine that began in

'Russia's Corona Diplomacy and Geoeconomic Competition: A Sputnik Moment?' (2021) Finnish Institute of International Affairs Briefing Paper 315 <www.fiia.fi/en/publication/russias-corona-diplomacy-and-geoeconomic-competition> accessed 21 September 2023.

5 Henrique Choer Moraes and Mikael Wigell, 'Balancing Dependence: The Quest for Autonomy and the Rise of Corporate Geoeconomics' in Milan Babić, Adam D Dixon, and Imogen T Liu (eds), *The Political Economy of Geoeconomics: Europe in a Changing World* (Springer 2022) 29.

6 See, e.g., Carlos Esplugues, *Foreign Investment, Strategic Assets and National Security* (Intersentia 2018).

7 Another illustrative example of the importance of control (through investment) of a critical resource is the speculated acquisition of German vaccine manufacturer CureVac by US interests. Aitor Hernández-Morales, 'Germany Confirms that Trump Tried to Buy Firm Working on Coronavirus Vaccine' (*POLITICO*, 15 March 2020) <www.politico.eu/article/germany-confirms-that-donald-trump-tried-to-buy-firm-working-on-coronavirus-vaccine/> accessed 21 September 2023.

2022, Western powers have turned to economic sanctions with an unprecedented intensity and scope.[8] To a significant extent, these restrictive measures serve to deny Russia investment opportunities in other countries. Screening inbound FDI can also have the effect of restricting a target state's ability to invest abroad, albeit in a more focused way. In recent years, ever more Western allies have introduced investment screening mechanisms, and across the West, the use of existing and new investment screening mechanisms has expanded significantly.[9]

Third, yet another example of how FDI can be employed as an instrument of economic statecraft is when a state seeks to restrict international investments by individuals and firms that are the subjects of the state under international law *into* a target country. States can ban investments into a target state or use *outbound* investment screening to ensure that domestic investors stay clear of making investments in certain states under certain circumstances.[10] These examples illustrate that FDI is not merely an economic transaction involving private enterprises. FDI also has multifarious geoeconomic uses.

In this chapter, we argue that the geoeconomic leveraging of policy instruments, such as FDI, which was amplified by the COVID pandemic, is giving rise to a new sort of risk – what we shall refer to as *geoeconomic risk*.[11] In contrast to

---

8 Jeffrey J Schott, 'Economic Sanctions Against Russia: How Effective? How Durable?' (2023) Peterson Institute for International Economics Policy Brief 23–3 <www.piie.com/publications/policy-briefs/economic-sanctions-against-russia-how-effective-how-durable> accessed 22 September 2023; Kristi Raik and others, 'Tackling the Constraints on EU Foreign Policy Towards Ukraine: From Strategic Denial to Geopolitical Awakening' (2023) JOINT Research Papers No.20 <www.jointproject.eu/2023/04/06/tackling-the-constraints-on-eu-foreign-policy-towards-ukraine-from-strategic-denial-to-geopolitical-awakening/> accessed 22 September 2023.

9 OECD, 'Framework for Screening Foreign Direct Investment into the EU. Assessing Effectiveness and Efficiency' (2022) <www.oecd.org/investment/investment-policy/oecd-eu-fdi-screening-assessment.pdf> accessed 22 September 2023; Sarah Bauerle Danzman and Sophie Meunier, 'The Big Screen: Mapping the Diffusion of Foreign Investment Screening Mechanisms' (2021) <https://papers.ssrn.com/sol3/papers.cfm?abstract_id=3913248> accessed 22 September 2023.

10 Thilo Hanemann and others, 'An Outbound Investment Screening Regime for the United States?' (2022) Rhodium Group US-China Investment Project Report <https://rhg.com/research/tws-outbound/> accessed 22 September 2023; Louis Brennan and Alessandra Vecchi, 'The European Response to Chinese Outbound Foreign Direct Investment: Introducing a Dynamic Analytical Framework' (2021) 52 Dev Change 1066.

11 OECD, 'Investment Screening in Times of COVID-19 and Beyond' (2020) <www.oecd.org/coronavirus/policy-responses/investment-screening-in-times-of-covid-19-and-beyond-aa60af47/> accessed 22 September 2023. See also Mikael Wigell and others, 'Navigating Geoeconomic Risks. Towards an International Business Risk and Resilience Monitor' (2022) Finnish Institute of International Affairs Report 71

traditional geopolitical risk, which is usually circumscribed to particular countries or regions and is highly conjunctural, geoeconomic risk is transnational and systemic. Geoeconomic risk stems from changes in the international economic system and is therefore less conjunctural than geopolitical risk, which is usually coupled with a specific war or sudden regime change in some limited part of the international system, although it may sometimes reverberate broadly throughout the system, such as in the case of Russia's war of aggression in Ukraine.

Geoeconomic risk ultimately arises from the unprecedented economic interdependence and interconnectivity characterizing the contemporary international system, which – particularly in the post-pandemic era – is increasingly viewed as a vulnerability and potential threat to economic security.[12] States therefore feel the need to balance against risky dependence on foreign actors by adopting a host of economic policy instruments that for a long time were considered exceptional. Often, these instruments defy the market-oriented logic underpinning economic policy and global economic relations in recent decades. As such, they not only put pressure on the rules and norms that have governed the international economy in recent decades but also introduce a major new source of risk for economic actors around the world.

This essay takes the COVID-19 pandemic as context for asking (a) how governments' concerns about geoeconomic risk shape the way states treat inbound FDI in today's age of re-emerging great power rivalry and (b) how international legal frameworks for FDI, principally bilateral investment treaties (BITs), cope with geoeconomic state behaviour and how they may change. Inspired by the phenomenon-based research method,[13] we outline a set of answers to these questions, drawing out implications for the law and policy of international investments.

In section 2, we proceed by capturing, describing, and documenting the phenomenon of economic interdependencies as a potential source of vulnerability. For purposes of describing geoeconomic risk, we compare approaches to conceptualizing the degree of uncertainty as to whether such vulnerability

---

<www.fiia.fi/en/publication/navigating-geoeconomic-risks> accessed 22 September 2023; Jens Hillebrand Pohl, 'Emergency, Security and Strategic Autonomy in EU Economic Regulation' (2020) 21 ERA Forum 143.

12 Commission, 'Joint Communication to the European Parliament, the European Council and the Council. On "European Economic Security Strategy"' JOIN (2023) 20 final; Choer Moraes and Wigell (n 5).

13 Georg von Krogh, Cristina Rossi-Lamastra, and Stefan Haefliger, 'Phenomenon-Based Research in Management and Organisation Science: When Is It Rigorous and Does It Matter?' (2012) 45 Long Range Planning 277.

will result in negative outcomes. We then explore how such risk can be recognized, assessed, and measured. Section 3 examines the implications of geoeconomic risk awareness in the context of inbound FDI screening and examines how governments' recognition of such risk is conditioning state behaviour. Mapping geoeconomic strategies across a range of investment-related policy instruments, we assess the explanatory power of geoeconomic risk as a concept in the context under investigation. Section 4 addresses the extent to which geoeconomic risk analysis can and cannot help explaining the host state's behaviour towards FDI. We look at legal mechanisms tempering the use of geoeconomic strategies, including non-discrimination and relative treatment standards in BITs, as well as factors that limit the effectiveness of such mechanisms. Section 5 concludes with a summary of observations and suggestions for further research.

2 Conceptualizing Geoeconomic Risk

2.1 *FDI and Economic Interdependence*

In essence, FDI establishes a relation between two states: the *home* state of the investor and the *host* state where the investment is made. While this relation may not need to involve the governments of the relevant states, it will still create economic interdependence through market forces. A single FDI transaction will contribute only marginally to the increase of this interdependence, but in aggregate FDI has the potential to establish deep interdependence at the national level.

This *inter*dependent character of FDI transactions may not be obvious at first glance. On the one hand, an FDI transaction creates an economic dependency of the investor on the host state to whose jurisdiction and treatment the investor subjects itself.[14] The host state has the factual power to harm the investor economically through expropriation or restrictions on the repatriation of profits regardless of whether it has the legal power to do so. On the other hand, FDI also creates an economic dependency of the host state on foreign investors in aggregate, even if not necessarily towards an individual investor.[15] If

14 Matthias Busse and Carsten Hefeker, 'Political Risk, Institutions and Foreign Direct Investment' (2007) 23 Europ J Pol Econ 397.

15 Susan M McMillan, *Foreign Direct Investment in Three Regions of the South at 20th Century* (Palgrave Macmillan 1999) ch 1, 1–22; Robert JS Ross and Bruce London, 'The Political Sociology of Foreign Direct Investment, Global Capitalism and Capital Mobility, 1965–1980' (1995) 36 Intl J Comp Sociol 198.

the host state acts illegally, arbitrarily, or offensively in any other way towards foreign investors, the host state will suffer harmful economic consequences.[16] It is likely that it will find it more difficult or expensive to raise capital in international financial markets, suffer retaliatory restrictions on its outbound trade or investments, and face international legal claims.

Two types of FDI-related asymmetric interdependencies stand out. First, foreign investors provide much-needed capital at a lower cost than any domestic funding sources available in the host state.[17] If that were not the case, the foreign investor would not be competitive in the host state's capital market. This cheap funding indirectly benefits the host state by contributing to lower funding costs available in general in the host state's capital market, even if it does not directly benefit the government itself. The secondary effects of a lower cost of capital are felt throughout the economy, including notably the labour market. In other words, ready access to FDI supports the labour market and, with that, socio-economic stability. The (sudden) withdrawal of foreign capital and the resulting higher funding costs would be a significant blow to the economic wherewithal of the host state as well as to the host state's political stability.

Second, the technology and transfer of data and knowhow from the foreign investor is another important source of dependency of a host state on foreign investors.[18] As with foreign capital, the host state exposes the foreign investor to the risk of technology theft, to which foreign investors can retaliate. Foreign investors may become wary of locating data – or knowledge-intensive business processes under the jurisdiction of the host state. They may even be able to raise legal claims, such as for forced technology transfer, e.g., on the basis of investment protections of a BIT.[19] As such, the host state will be at risk of being denied access to the benefits of future technological advancements.

16 Claire Cutler, 'Globalization, Law and Transnational Corporations: A Deepening of Market Discipline' in Theodore H Cohn, Stephen McBride, and John Wiseman (eds), *Power in the Global Era: Grounding Globalization* (Palgrave Macmillan 2000).

17 Patrick Kaczmarczyk, 'Foreign Direct Investment in Neoclassical Theory of International Trade: A Conceptual Weak Spot' (2023) 52 Intl J Pol Econ 70; Stephen H Hymer, 'The International Operations of National Firms, a Study of Direct Foreign Investment' (DPhil thesis, Massachusetts Institute of Technology 1960).

18 Zhiqiang Liu, 'Foreign Direct Investment and Technology Spillovers: Theory and Evidence' (2008) 85 J Dev Econ 176; Magnus Blomstrom and Ari Kokko, 'How Foreign Investment Affects Host Countries' (1997) World Bank Policy Research Working Paper 1745 <https://documents1.worldbank.org/curated/en/992201468765633696/pdf/multi-page.pdf> accessed 25 September 2023.

19 Jonathan Bonnitcha, 'Investment Wars: Contestation and Confusion in Debate About Investment Liberalization' (2019) 22 J Intl Econ L 629. See further, Chapter 2.

These economic interdependencies are inherently asymmetrical. The dependencies that constitute the *inter*dependencies are diverse and differ in their importance between the host state and the home state(s) of the foreign investors. Moreover, these economic interdependencies are not static. This is well illustrated in the case of global value chains (GVCs), in which staying connected in a GVC provides many economic benefits to a host state and where the prospect of being excluded becomes a source of vulnerability.[20] However, the host state may also attain a level of bargaining power within a GVC by being positioned to disrupt the GVC. Such chains require significant resources to build up and maintain, which creates leeway for negotiation through the threat of disruption. Such a potential power play between host states and foreign investors is nothing new and goes back to the very nature of FDI.[21] How it plays out depends in large measure on the level of global policy coordination and cooperation.[22]

During the heyday of international economic multilateralism, the prospect of a swift and coordinated retaliatory response by the international community put contours around host states' adventurism.[23] International institutions, governments, and the international business community act in solidarity against a host state's violation of the rule of law. The proliferation of investor-friendly BITs, which increased rapidly from the 1980s onwards, and the opening up of national banking and capital markets to international competition contributed to imposing 'market discipline' across the globe.[24] The consequences for

20 Toby Carroll, 'Constrained, Competing and Eking – the Limits of Economic Statecraft in East Asia after National Development' (2023) 36 Pacific Rev 949; Phoebe W Moon, 'When the Target Fights Back: Economic Coercion and Interstate Conflict in the Era of Global Value Chains' (DPhil thesis, UC Irvine 2022).

21 Asha Kaushal, 'Revisiting History: How the Past Matters for the Present Backlash Against the Foreign Investment Regime' (2009) 50 Harv Intl L J 491; Sanjaya Lall and Paul Streeten (eds), *Foreign Investment, Transnationals and Developing Countries* (Palgrave Macmillan 1977).

22 Mika Aaltola and others, 'Solidarity During COVID-19 at National, Regional and Global Levels: An Enabler for Improved Global Pandemic Security and Governance' (2021) Finnish Institute of International Affairs Briefing Paper 309 <www.fiia.fi/en/publication/solidarity-during-covid-19-at-national-regional-and-global-levels> accessed 25 September 2023.

23 Karen J Alter, 'Contracting v. Multilateralism in Global Economic Governance: Before, During and After the WTO' in Manfred Elsig, Peter van den Bossche, and Rodrigo Polanco (eds), *International Economic Dispute Settlement: Demise or Transformation?* (CUP 2021).

24 Pierre-Olivier Gourinchas and Olivier Jeanne, 'On the Benefits of Capital Account Liberalization for Emerging Economies' (2002) IMF Preliminary Working Paper <https://citeseerx.ist.psu.edu/viewdoc/download;jsessionid=E468FF18DD8DFB6AE53A9C6BA7C6548A?doi=10.1.1.6.7363&rep=rep1&type=pdf> accessed 25 September 2023.

a host state that stepped out of line are richly illustrated by the case of the Argentinian sovereign debt crisis of 2002 and the ensuing saga[25] and by the Greek sovereign debt crisis a decade later.[26]

However, with ever more imperfect policy coordination and eroding policy cooperation, that type of global solidarity weakens. Foreign investors then lose the safety mechanism that a globally coordinated institutional action ensured. As a result, the economic power balance between host states and foreign investors shifts in favour of host states. In these instances, where foreign investors cannot rely on the protection of a global 'community response', they must discover new protection infrastructures, such as falling back on the protection of their home states.[27]

When the protection of foreign investors' economic interests falls mainly on the investors' home states, such interests are easily commingled with the policy interests and concerns of the home states' governments.[28] The home state government may sacrifice investors' interests for some other policy advantage or exploit investors' claims as a diplomatic bargaining chip in exchange for host state concessions on a different policy issue. In this way, FDI becomes enmeshed in the home state's economic and non-economic interests, particularly its vital or critical interests, chiefly security interests.

2.2 *Economic Interdependencies as Geoeconomic Vulnerabilities and Geoeconomic Risks*

In the absence of strong global policy coordination and cooperation, FDI becomes available as an instrument of geoeconomic contestation and diplomacy. The preceding subsection illustrated ways in which the interdependencies created by FDI can result in economic harm, both to the home and host states. Such potential sources of harm may be referred to as *geoeconomic vulnerabilities*, where the subject of vulnerabilities are threats directed by one state (the coercer) against the economic security of another state (the target).[29]

---

25 Alejandro Grimson and Gabriel Kessler, *On Argentina and the Southern Cone: Neoliberalism and National Imaginations* (Routledge 2005); Theodore H Moran (ed), *International Political Risk Management: The Brave New World* (World Bank 2004).

26 Ian Bruff, 'The Rise of Authoritarian Neoliberalism' (2014) 26 Rethinking Marxism 113.

27 Rodrigo Polanco, *The Return of the Home State to Investor-State Disputes: Bringing Back Diplomatic Protection?* (CUP 2019).

28 Christopher A Casey, *Nationals Abroad: Globalization, Individual Rights, and the Making of Modern International Law* (CUP 2020).

29 This terminology is inspired by Kelly M Greenhill, Peter Krause, and Robert Art, 'Coercion: An Analytical Overview' in Kelly M Greenhill and Peter Krause (eds), *Coercion: the power to hurt in international politics* (OUP 2018).

The nature of a vulnerability is that of a potentiality: the potential for successful economic coercion.[30] Vulnerabilities are not themselves economic security threats but open up the *possibility* of such threats by exposing a weakness or a mechanism through which harm can be inflicted or leveraged. Exploiting a target state's vulnerability requires, in addition, capabilities, intent, and resolve on the part of the coercer. In this context, one can talk of *geoeconomic risk*, i.e., the degree of uncertainty as to whether negative outcomes will emerge from such vulnerabilities.

The term 'geoeconomics' has become increasingly popular to describe the transformation in the logic underpinning global economic relations. Governments are turning to policies that integrate economic and security rationales at the national or regional level at the expense of global economic policy coordination.[31] This change is exemplified by the EU's policy of 'open strategic autonomy'. The EU is adapting to geopolitical competition in the economic arena through a panoply of new policy measures. These range from new trade defence and anti-coercion tools, sanctions, and export controls to screening of security threats and state-sponsored subsidies in foreign investments, carbon border adjustment, supply chain due diligence, and a new industrial strategy.[32]

---

30 The present analysis focuses on coercion as the principal strategy of geoeconomics. Coercion is used here to describe one actor's behaviour (the coercer's) influencing another actor's (the target's) behaviour by manipulating the latter's intentions and resolve using negative incentives. When positive incentives are used, one could think of this as 'negative coercion' or more appropriately as 'inducement'. The arguments made in this essay largely applies to both coercion and inducement, but for the sake of simplicity the focus lies on the former.

31 Mikael Wigell, Sören Scholvin, and Mika Aaltola, *Geo-Economics and Power Politics in the 21st Century: The Revival of Economic Statecraft* (Routledge 2018); Anthea Roberts, Henrique Choer Moraes, and Victor Ferguson, 'Toward a Geoeconomic Order in International Trade and Investment' (2019) 22 J Intl Econ L 655; Geoffrey Gertz and Miles M Evers, 'Geoeconomic Competition: Will State Capitalism Win?' (2020) 43 Wash Q 117; Daniel W Drezner, Henry Farrell, and Abraham L Newman (eds), *The Uses and Abuses of Weaponized Interdependence* (Brookings Institution Press 2021); Milan Babić, Adam D Dixon, and Imogen T Liu (eds), *The Political Economy of Geoeconomics: Europe in a Changing World* (Springer 2022).

32 Tobias Gehrke, 'Threading the Trade Needle on Open Strategic Autonomy in Niklas Helwig (ed), *Strategic Autonomy and the Transformation of the EU: New Agendas for Security, Diplomacy, Trade and Technology* (2020) Finnish Institute for International Affairs Report 67 <www.fiia.fi/en/publication/strategic-autonomy-and-the-transformation-of-the-eu> accessed 27 September 2023; Scott Lavery, Sean McDaniel, and Davide Schmid, 'European Strategic Autonomy: New Agenda, Old Constraints' in Milan Babić, Adam D Dixon, and Imogen T Liu (n 31); Niklas Helwig and Mikael Wigell, 'The EU's Quest for Geoeconomic Power' (2022) Finnish institute of International Affairs Briefing Paper 33

In this effort, the EU is reacting to similar moves by other major powers, notably the United States and China. In the past decade, the United States strengthened its national security review (screening) of inbound investments and enhanced its application of existing trade laws to respond to new geoeconomic risks; this includes the novel use of Section 232 investigations into steel and aluminium exports to determine their effect on national security. The United States is considering new instruments, as demonstrated by the 2022 CHIPS and Science Act and the Casey-Cornyn legislative proposal for screening outbound US investment destined for other countries.[33] China's geoeconomic strategy is evident in efforts in the *14th Five-Year Plan* of 2021 to secure critical technologies and data through national security oversight and control.[34] China has embraced 'geo-regulation' by using technical standards as instruments to advance strategic goals, such as the *Made in China 2025* strategy.[35] The COVID-19 pandemic demonstrated the breadth of sectors that are critical to the survival of the state, notably pharmaceutical expertise and technology.[36]

Emerging from the practice of geoeconomic strategies, economic interdependencies are thus reappraised as geoeconomic vulnerabilities that give rise to geoeconomic risks. In the context of FDI, vulnerabilities arise from economic interdependencies. A host state may be vulnerable to the extent of its economic dependency on international capital flows or access to foreign critical resources, mainly technology, knowhow, and data. Conversely, foreign investors or their home states are vulnerable to the extent of their invested capital in

---

<www.fiia.fi/en/publication/the-eus-quest-for-geoeconomic-power> accessed 27 September 2023; Jens Hillebrand Pohl, 'Open Strategic Autonomy and the New Geoeconomics: Consequences for EU Trade Policy' (2023) University of Adelaide Institute of international Trade Policy Brief 18 <https://iit.adelaide.edu.au/news/list/2023/01/09/open-strategic-autonomy-and-the-new-geoeconomics-consequences-for-eu-trade> accessed 27 September 2023.

33 Naoise McDonagh and Jens Hillebrand Pohl, 'Reconceptualizing the Legal-Economic Nexus in the Era of Great Power Rivalry: The Case of Foreign Direct Investment Screening' (The Politics and Regulation of Investment Screening Mechanisms Workshop, Princeton University, 7 October 2022).

34 Nis Grünberg and Vincent Brussee, 'China's 14th Five-Year Plan – Strengthening the Domestic Base to Become a Superpower' (*MERICS*, 9 April 2021) <https://merics.org/en/comment/chinas-14th-five-year-plan-strengthening-domestic-base-become-superpower> accessed 28 September 2023.

35 Mikael Wigell and others, *Europe Facing Geoeconomics: Assessing Finland's and the EU's Risks and Options in the Technological Rivalry* (Prime Minister's Office, Helsinki 2022) <https://julkaisut.valtioneuvosto.fi/handle/10024/163804> accessed 29 September 2023.

36 OECD (n 9); Bauerle Danzman and Meunier (n 9).

the host state and to their access to host-state controlled critical resources that are capable of being 'weaponized', i.e., exploited for coercive ends.

2.3 *Approaches to Conceptualizing and Measuring Geoeconomic Risk*

In general, geoeconomic risk describes the uncertain prospect of economic harm suffered by a state or non-state actor (target) due to a coercive measure adopted by another state or non-state actor (coercer). The contemporary notion of risk originates in the work of American economist Frank H. Wright, who in 1921 conceptualized the role of uncertainty in economic activity, distinguishing 'risk' as 'measurable uncertainty'. This preliminary, proto-theoretical definition serves as a point of departure that can accommodate several conceptual approaches.

First, from the perspective of a target being a foreign investor in the context of FDI, the concept of geoeconomic risk can be understood to capture several unwelcome potential consequences of the host state's inherently uncertain future treatment of the foreign investor. These consequences result not only from the exercise of legal powers of the host state government, which in many jurisdictions include the suspension of an investment transaction during an investment screening process, thus causing delay; placing conditions upon the consummation of the transaction, thus altering the terms anticipated by the parties; and even blocking a transaction altogether or ordering its unwinding. Of even greater practical importance are the factual powers wielded by the host state: public knowledge of pending or ongoing review of an investment transaction can lead to an investor's withdrawal from a transaction altogether, while the target company may face significant loss of market value as a consequence of such review or denied screening approval.

Second, a foreign investor may be mobilized as a geoeconomic agent of its home state, being used as pawns in the home state's power competition, combining geostrategic interests with economic dynamics. From such a perspective, geoeconomic risk is associated with economics being used by states for power political objectives. Target states shore up their resilience against this geoeconomic power politics by increasing their control over businesses in strategic sectors of the economy. This manifests itself in the panoply of new means of trade and export controls, investment screening mechanisms, data localization measures, sanctions, and subsidies.

Third, geoeconomic risk can be conceptualized as a particular form of political risk. There have been many efforts to define political risk. In the context of FDI and from the perspective of a foreign investor and its home state, political risk can be thought of as comprising (i) the risk of nationalization, expropriation and confiscation of property, (ii) the risk of host state exchange restrictions,

(iii) the risk of political violence, and (iv) the risk of sovereign breach of contract. However, it is widely acknowledged that political risk is often used as an omnibus term for a more fundamental and far-reaching concept, which covers the uncertain possibility of losses attributable to any political event, including but not limited to, instances where state powers are exercised.

As of today, there is no unified model of geoeconomic risk that incorporates the various prisms outlined above. Such a model should accommodate various constellations of targets and coercers – home states, host states, foreign investors, and indeed domestic enterprises – while also being agnostic as to both the direction of influence and the balance of capabilities and vulnerabilities among these.

2.4 *Balancing Dependence as Geoeconomic Risk Management*

To understand the logic underpinning geoeconomic competition and the uncertainty it engenders, it is appropriate to begin by analysing the elements of coercion: vulnerability, capabilities, intent, and resolve. While the latter two factors are inherently subjective and difficult to ascertain, the former two are more readily susceptible to objective assessment and measurement. In a sense, they are also related. Where vulnerability expresses the weaknesses of the target, capability expresses the strength of the coercion. Both express the potential for successful coercion.

Geoeconomic risk takes the target's perspective, focusing on potential negative outcomes arising out of uncertainty as a result of vulnerability to economic coercion. That vulnerability is in turn a function of the degree of economic interdependence. A solution therefore presents itself, whereby a target can manage (minimize or optimize) its geoeconomic risk situation by adapting its level of economic interdependence, thus reducing its vulnerability, or expressed equivalently, increase its economic resilience. This management of the level of economic interdependence is captured by the notion of *balancing dependence.*

Inspired by balance of power theory, balancing dependence is a model of geoeconomic competitive behaviour that recognizes that geoeconomic actors integrate into the global flows of capital, data, goods, and resources while simultaneously protecting their economic autonomy.[37] In this model, the ways in which actors weigh integration versus autonomy are contingent on the nature of interdependent relations. In practical terms, economic interdependence is seen as being increasingly instrumentalised for power political

37 Choer Moraes and Wigell (n 5).

ends as the geoeconomic competition between the West, China, and Russia has intensified.[38] As such, it is assumed to precipitate geoeconomic balancing as states seek to reduce their vulnerabilities to offensive geoeconomic statecraft (coercion, binding, and wedging) by reducing economic dependencies on public and private foreign actors (hedging). Such balancing can be assumed to put pressure on the interdependent fabric of the global economy. Similar to 'balancing power', 'balancing dependence' may create an economic security dilemma, as states seek to adjust their level of dependence in relation to similar efforts by others.[39]

Understanding how balance of dependence shapes economic security and sets the direction for reducing vulnerabilities and increasing capabilities in a concrete case requires an analysis of states' economic power relations from a network perspective. From the perspective of a foreign investor as a target, balancing dependence serves to explain host state treatment that seeks to reduce economic vulnerabilities, such as inbound investment screening.[40]

3 Implications of Geoeconomic Risk in the Context of Inbound FDI Screening

Screening inbound FDI serves as a case in point for illustrating the geoeconomic risk faced by a foreign investor. Typical features of investment screening mechanisms are that they apply to FDI (broadly defined) that the host state determines to have an adverse effect on its security or other important public interests. Investors are obliged to notify the host state's screening authority about a contemplated investment and to submit to the subsequent screening procedure. The screening authority will then conduct an investigation of the FDI transaction, the investor, the investor's ultimate beneficial owners, among other factors, and collect data to make an assessment of how the FDI would affect the host state's security or other relevant interests.

With respect to investment screening on security grounds, security threat analysis will almost necessarily be confidential. This is because the mere disclosure of the relevant security concerns would undermine the security of the host state. This confidentiality necessarily makes it difficult for the foreign investor to obtain full transparency of the procedure. As a result, the investor's

38 Drezner, Farrell and Newman (n 31); Leonard (n 1).

39 Choer Moraes and Wigell (n 5).

40 Ashley T Lenihan, *Balancing Power without Weapons: State Intervention into Cross-Border Mergers and Acquisitions* (CUP 2018).

ability to question, challenge, or seek legal remedies against a screening decision is severely hampered. The further consequence of this is that foreign investors are left without meaningful legal guarantees against host-state abuse of its screening legislation. Any allegation of abuse would be very difficult to substantiate; without scrutiny of the investment screening process, the investor would find itself without evidence. The investor may take some comfort in the hypothesis that it would be contrary to the host state's interests to maintain a reputation for a sound investment climate. However, with neoliberal ideals on the wane and with increased geoeconomic competition, that comfort may more appropriately be labelled as unfounded hope.

How exactly host states go about assessing the security risk that an FDI transaction poses is naturally not well understood. Each state's threat assessment methodology is itself a closely guarded state secret, which, if commonly known, would constitute a security vulnerability. Nevertheless, some contours have been envisioned in the literature. Theodore H. Moran, writing in 2009, identified three categories of threats that investment screening served to address.[41]

First, the screening investigates the threat that a foreign-controlled owner of a domestic enterprise in a critical situation would cease operations or otherwise deny, delay, or place conditions on the supply of critical goods or services in the host state (Threat I). In other words, the threat is one of potential coercion or 'binding', i.e., a strategy of making the host state dependent on the investor or ultimately its home state. Such dependency then serves as the basis for economic coercion.

Second, the host state screens FDI transactions to assess the threat that important technologies or expertise would be leaked or otherwise appropriated by a foreign government that owns or controls (directly or indirectly) the foreign investor (Threat II). In a narrow sense, this threat concerns the transfer of military or dual use technologies or expertise. However, in a broader sense, it is about transferring technologies and expertise that would increase the home state's technological capabilities and expertise at the expense of the host state. The ultimate end use of such technologies or expertise need not be military. Even purely civilian uses, including personal data or trade secrets, could be used to shift economic capabilities from the host state to the home state.

Third, host state screening examines the likelihood that FDI would serve as a channel for infiltration, surveillance, or sabotage (Threat III). The idea here

41 Theodore H Moran, *Three Threats: An Analytical Framework for the CFIUS Process* (Peterson Institute for International Economics 2009).

is that FDI could be a 'Trojan Horse' through which a foreign government may facilitate espionage operations, gain crucial insights into the operation of the host state's critical infrastructure or supply lines, and use such intelligence to hamper the host state's mobilization of capabilities in a conflict.

Moran further developed this three-tiered threat analysis to construct a threat-assessment decision tree based on two tests.[42]

First, screening authorities are faced with evaluating the impact of each threat (the criticality test). With respect to Threat I, the authority examines the goods or services supplied by the enterprise in which the foreign investor is investing. The goal is to quantify the impact in terms of costs in the event that the supply of those goods or services was denied, delayed, or subjected to certain conditions. With respect to Threat II, the authority would assess the national security-related advantage that the foreign investor or its home state would gain through FDI. Finally, with respect to Threat III, the authority would investigate the extent of the damage that could be foreseen to result from surveillance or disruption through foreign ownership.

Second, in the event that the overall analysis of Threats I, II and III yields a conclusion of 'high criticality' – i.e., a high cost impact of denied, delayed, or conditioned access to goods or services, a high national-security advantage gained by the foreign investor or home state, and/or a high expected damage from surveillance or disruption – the next test seeks to assess plausible mitigating factors (the plausibility test). Specifically, the screening authority explores whether there are substitute goods or services for those that would be controlled by the foreign investor and how widely available those substitutes are on global markets, how competitive alternative suppliers are, and what the cost would be of switching to new suppliers.

In the event that there are good substitute goods or services, competitive suppliers of such substitutes, and acceptable switching costs, the plausibility test would yield a negative result, implying that the contemplated FDI would not pose an economic security threat and could go ahead. If, on the other hand, there is a plausible threat – because of a lack of substitutes, poor competitiveness in substitute markets, or high switching costs. the authority needs to decide how to deal with FDI transactions. It should block the transaction, according to Moran, only if the blocking would leave the target enterprise capable of being internationally competitive. In other words, blocking should not be used if it would harm the enterprise's international competitiveness.

42 Theodore H Moran and Lindsay Oldenski, *Foreign Direct Investment Benefits, Suspicions, and Risks with Special Attention to FDI from China* (Peterson Institute for International Economics 2010).

Conversely, FDI transactions should be allowed if they are the only way for domestic enterprises to remain internationally competitive.

The position advocated by Moran that international competitiveness should ultimately prevail in national security concerns can readily be disputed, but the preceding analytical steps – the criticality test and the plausibility test – remain useful as a simplified structure of national security threat assessment in the context of FDI. Although the literature on investment screening has proliferated in recent years, Moran's investment-security risk blueprint remains relevant.

What scholarship has yet to undertake, is a systematic treatment of geoeconomic strategy in the area of FDI, including a typology of geoeconomic instruments applied to FDI. Such an attempt would examine the full spectrum of instruments and coercer-target roles. As sketched at the outset of this essay, FDI could be an instrument of the home state against the host state. This includes various kinds of sovereign-driven investments, such as investments by state-controlled or state-affiliated investors (notably SOEs and SWFs), as well as state-financed, state-subsidised, state-contracted, or otherwise (directly or indirectly) state-incentivized privately owned investors. The latter categories are very difficult to detect. Even the most thorough analysis of ultimate beneficial ownership will prove useless, as there is no foreign state ownership involved. Indirect liens of loyalty, including clientelism, are typically clandestine in nature and unlikely to be properly documented or easily discoverable.

Such a typology should also consider FDI used as an instrument of the host state against the home state. This includes a kind 'reverse influence' whereby the host state, using lawful or perhaps unlawful means (such as strategic corruption), gains access to the investor's upstream ownership structure. The host state could thereby deny or manipulate access to goods or services in the *home* state. Alternatively, the host state could gain a national-security advantage vis-à-vis the home state, e.g., by being able to seize control of the investor's assets and operations. Alternatively, the host state may gain access to technology and expertise higher up in the corporate structure of the foreign investor. Recent policy debate and scholarly discussions about *outward* FDI screening have partly considered these types of scenarios.

4 Promises and Limitations of Geoeconomic Risk as a Conceptual Approach

Applying the prism of risk indicates an aspiration to rein in the uncertainty generated by geoeconomic competition and strategies. By forging a common understanding of the mechanisms animating such competition and the aims and means of such strategies, a risk approach can reduce the complexity of geoeconomic power plays and render, at least some aspects, susceptible to analysis and remedies. Nevertheless, there are important conceptual limitations.

First, geoeconomic risk focuses on economic vulnerabilities and capabilities, both of which have, in theory, observable or tangible manifestations, such as infrastructure, technologies, supplies of economic inputs, or otherwise intersubjectively (objectively) ascertainable manifestations, such as data or knowledge. Geoeconomic risk does not capture *subjective* elements, notably the geoeconomic competitors' interests (intent) or their willingness to sacrifice other interests in pursuit thereof (resolve). The same limitation often applies to risks. The risk perspective does not promise certainty but rather an analytical approach to deal with a particular kind of *un*certainty.

Second, meaningful geoeconomic risk requires accurate data, which can be particularly difficult to come by when the subject matter of the risk relates to state secrets or otherwise confidential matters. Considering the data required to carry out the three-step threat assessment analysis discussed in the previous subsection, it should be obvious just how difficult the data gathering may be. The criticality test regarding Threat I and the plausibility test both require extensive market data, whereas the other aspects of the criticality test require foreign policy and intelligence data. Data on ultimate beneficial owners are essential but insufficient, as discussed above. It is therefore safe to presume that meaningful geoeconomic risk analysis requires privileged access to the required information as well as superior data processing capabilities.

Third, geoeconomic risk does not address the effect of risk mitigants. Tools that may contribute to mitigating geoeconomic risk posed by a foreign investor and its home state are (third-party) political risk insurance and (bilateral) investment guarantees contained in investment treaties (e.g., BITs), the host-state's national legislation, or contracts specifically concluded between the host state and the foreign investor (investor-state contracts).

The highly standardized terms of BITs are illustrative of how such mitigants operate. When applied to a host state's screening of inward FDI, BITs offer principally two kinds of protection. The first kind is guarantees against discriminatory treatment of a foreign investor or its investment. These are of two types: discrimination compared to the treatment of national (non-foreign) investors or investments (national treatment standard) and discrimination compared to the treatment afforded to other, more favourably treated foreign investors or investments (most favoured treatment or MFN standard). In theory, both of these standards could be invoked to support a case against the host state for compensation. In practice, however, these discrimination standards have been interpreted to incorporate general, public interest exceptions.[43]

According to the second kind of guarantee, the host state must live up to certain absolute standards of treatment. The most typical kind of standard is the 'fair and equitable treatment' (FET) standard. Expropriation can also be considered an absolute standard of treatment. However, these standards leave some room for arbitral deference to executive decisions, with the emphasis being on procedural justice.[44] While it is arguable that procedural justice is in jeopardy in the event of limitations on transparency, one should perhaps caution one's optimism in that regard. As the well-known Ralls case demonstrated, judicial transparency, notably rights to due process, may be interpreted to apply only to publicly available information, not secret intelligence, and other confidential evidence, which may determine the outcome of screening decisions.[45]

Moreover, it is by no means certain that the relevant treatment standards would even apply to an investment subject to screening. This may be because the BIT in question only applies to investments that have been completed, and the screening only applies to investments that have not been completed.[46] Indeed, some treaties expressly state that the standards of treatment do not apply to the pre-establishment phase or to matters of market access.[47] It is also possible that the investor could not invoke rights derived under the BIT because of its links to a foreign government.[48] Moreover, the BIT may include exceptions for conduct that the host-state deems necessary for its national security.[49] Finally, even if none of the above restrictions apply, an investment tribunal may simply defer to the host state's investment screening authority on matters concerning the host state's national security concerns.[50]

43 Jens Hillebrand Pohl, 'The Impact of Investment Treaty Commitments on the Design and Operation of EU Investment Screening Mechanisms' in Steffen Hindelang and Andreas Moberg (eds), *YSEC Yearbook of Socio-Economic Constitutions 2020: A Common European Law on Investment Screening* (*CELIS*) (Springer 2021) 725.

44 ibid.

45 *Ralls Corp. v. Committee on Foreign Investment in the US*, 758 F.3d 296 (D.C. Cir. 2014); see further Kristen E Eichensehr and Cathy Hwang, 'National Security Creep in Corporate Transactions' (2023) 123 Colum L Rev 549, 592–594.

46 Pohl (n 43).

47 ibid.

48 ibid.

49 ibid.

50 ibid.; see also Thomas Verellen, 'When Integration by Stealth Meets Public Security: The EU Foreign Direct Investment Screening Regulation' (2021) Leg Issues Econ Integ 19; see generally, Esmé Shirlow, *Judging at the Interface: Deference to State Decision-Making Authority in International Adjudication* (CUP 2021).

5 Concluding Remarks

The present essay surveyed the emerging concept of geoeconomic risk in light of the experiences of the recent COVID-19 pandemic. Increasing rivalry between states has turned economic interdependence into a source of vulnerability. FDI creates multifarious economic interdependencies that states have not been slow to exploit. Awareness of the possibility of using FDI as a means of exercising influence has resulted in defensive measures, such as inward FDI screening, which allows a host state to block or condition foreign investors' investments on security grounds. However, as of yet, there is no commonly accepted theory of how and with what aims states 'weaponize' FDI. This essay has illustrated how host states' concerns about geoeconomic risk determine their treatment of inbound FDI, notably in the case of inbound FDI screening. As the examples show, geoeconomic risk holds great promise as a step towards delimiting the uncertainty involved in geoeconomic strategies but also has significant limitations. Most notably, geoeconomic risk analysis requires significant resources, including access to intelligence and data processing capabilities. It also does not obviate the need for hard choices. Rivalling powers intentions and resolve remain non-modellable variables, which cannot meaningfully be reduced to an algorithm.

This essay encourages scholars of geoeconomics and risk theory to engage across disciplinary boundaries and actively work on an agenda to lay out a theoretical framework for conceptualizing and measuring geoeconomic risk. This work will have to involve compiling a typology of geoeconomic strategies applied to FDI. Another task for future research concerns measuring geoeconomic vulnerabilities and capabilities, i.e., the measurable aspects of geoeconomic power. This would involve devising a syncretic model of power involving relational, structural, and resource aspects. A formidable amount of conceptual and theoretical work remains. However, there can be little doubt about the need to foster a deeper understanding of the processes shaping geoeconomic competition and the uncertainty they generate.

CHAPTER 5

Controlling Foreign Direct Investment in the Wake of the COVID Pandemic: Enhanced and Supplementary Screening Procedures among EU Member States

Antonino Alì

1 Government Responses to the Economic Crisis Caused by the Pandemic: Changing and Strengthening FDI Screening Policies

The pandemic-induced economic crisis has manifested itself in a number of significant ways. It has led to a significant reduction in economic output, triggering recessions and severe economic downturns in many countries. The negative effects were compounded by business closures, reduced consumer spending, disrupted supply chains, and reduced investment, all of which contributed to a temporary general economic downturn. Financial markets experienced unprecedented volatility during this period, prompting governments around the world to implement fiscal stimulus packages. These measures aimed to mitigate the economic fallout and support recovery, particularly in the face of reduced international trade, which suffered from travel restrictions and lower global demand.

The impact of the crisis varied across sectors. Some, such as aviation, tourism and traditional retail, experienced significant setbacks, while others showed resilience and adaptability. The period also saw an increase in government spending against a background of lower tax revenues, contributing to higher public debt and budget deficits. These factors are likely to have contributed to the recent wave of inflation.

In response to these economic challenges and the vulnerabilities exposed by the pandemic, many governments reassessed their strategies for national security and economic stability. This led to the rapid development and expansion of foreign direct investment (FDI) screening mechanisms. These mechanisms focused on two main areas: public health and national security. Governments increased scrutiny of foreign investment in key health-related sectors and

© KONINKLIJKE BRILL BV, LEIDEN, 2025 DOI:10.1163/9789004711204_007

strategic industries to prevent over-dependence on foreign investors and to protect critical national assets.[1]

The impact of the pandemic on investment patterns was profound, creating a climate of caution among investors who had to adapt to evolving regulatory landscapes and increased due diligence requirements. These changes are indicative of a broader shift in FDI screening processes worldwide, reflecting an increased focus on protecting public health, national security, and domestic industries.[2]

In addition, the pandemic highlighted the delicate balance between protecting national interests and complying with international investment obligations. Navigating this balance became a major challenge for governments, underscoring the need for a predictable and open investment environment.[3]

As the pandemic recedes, the evolution of FDI screening mechanisms continues to shape the international investment landscape. In addition, the growing economic and political rivalry between major powers such as China and the United States has led to a phenomenon known as 'fragmentation'.[4] This refers to the disintegration of previously harmonised global systems such as

---

1 Emily Xueref-Poviacas and others, 'The Evolving Concept of National Security' in Veronica Roberts (ed), *Foreign Direct Investment Regulation Guide* (Law Business Research Ltd 2022) 23; 'The Evolving Global Foreign Direct Investment and National Security Review Landscape' (*Dechert LLP*, 2022) <https://docs.dechert.com/view/322665140/> accessed 25 November 2023; UNCTAD, *Investment Policy Monitor. National Security-Related Screening Mechanisms for Foreign Investment: An Analysis of Recent Policy Developments. Special Issue* (United Nations, 2019).

2 OECD, 'Transparency, Predictability and Accountability for investment screening mechanisms' (*OECD*, 2021) <www.oecd.org/daf/inv/investment-policy/2009-Guidelines-webinar-May-2021-background-note.pdf> accessed 25 November 2023.

3 Philipp Eckhardt and Anne-Carine Pierrat, 'Foreign Investment Screening: Protectionism in Corona-Times?' (2020) cepAdhoc <www.cep.eu/fileadmin/user_upload/cep.eu/Studien/cepAdhoc_Foreign_investment_screening/cepAdhoc_Foreign_Investment_Screening_Protectionism_in_Corona-Times.pdf> accessed 25 November 2023; UNCTAD, 'Investment policy responses to the COVID-19 Pandemic' (*Investment Policy Monitor*, 2020) <https://unctad.org/system/files/official-document/diaepcbinf2020d3_en.pdf> accessed 23 November 2023; Sara Pugliese, 'Toward a New EU Strategic Dimension: Common Purchase and Investment Screening Mechanisms as a Means of Crisis Preparedness and Management' (2022) Il diritto dell'Unione Europea 391; Cheng Bian, 'Investment Screening Put to the Test of the COVID-19 Pandemic: Typology, Legality and Externality' (2023) Asia Pacific Law Review 380.

4 See Shekhar Aiyar, Andrea F Presbitero, and Michele Ruta (eds), *Geoeconomic Fragmentation: The Economic Risks from a Fractured World Economy* (CEPR 2023) 11. This Report arises from a conference on the economic impact of geoeconomic fragmentation, organised by the International Monetary Fund in May 2023.

trade and finance, which can lead to significant welfare losses for countries that are heavily dependent on global trade and capital flows.

2 The Evolution of FDI Screening Policies over the Last Decades

In order to understand the changes that have taken place in the field of FDI screening in recent years, it is useful to summarise some of the critical stages of this development. FDI screening has changed considerably since its inception. Initially, FDI screening policies were more limited in scope, targeting mainly acquisitions in military and defense-related sectors. Investments were mainly between allied countries and the primary objective was to protect national security interests.[5] In the privatisation era of the late 20th century, the focus was primarily on selling off state-owned infrastructure (so-called privatisations). These privatisations opened up new opportunities for international investment and led to a surge in FDI flows.

Nevertheless, with the acceleration of infrastructure denationalization, governments began to recognize the need to protect critical assets from potential threats posed by specific entities. In the early 2000s, countries began to update their policies on foreign investment in response to a changing global market. This period coincided with some important economic events such as the rise in oil prices, which led to increased acquisitions by oil-exporting economies and less transparent sovereign wealth funds (SWFs).[6] These investments raised concerns about the control and influence of foreign companies over strategic assets and sensitive industries. To address these fears, there was growing recognition of the need for internationally agreed standards of behavior for SWFs. Efforts were made to establish guidelines and principles that would promote transparency, accountability, and responsible investment practices. The International Monetary Fund (IMF) and the Organisation for Economic Cooperation and Development (OECD) played an important role in progressing these standards, contributing to greater confidence and acceptance of SWF investments.

5 For a general overview see Jens Velten, *Screening Foreign Direct Investment in the EU Political Rationale, Legal Limitations, Legislative Options* (Springer 2022).

6 See Fabio Bassan, *The Law of Sovereign Wealth Funds* (Edward Elgar 2011); Maria Rosaria Mauro, 'The Emergence of Sovereign Wealth Funds as New "Foreign Investors"': Problems and Perspectives' in Maria Rosaria Mauro and Federico Pernazza (eds), *State and Enterprise. Legal Issues in the Global Market* (Giappichelli Editore 2023) 215.

The introduction of universally accepted standards for SWFs, albeit soft law as exemplified by the Santiago Principles, has helped to allay some of the fears and ambiguities associated with foreign investment in key sectors.[7] These standards have provided a blueprint to ensure that SWFs operate with an ethos of transparency and accountability, thereby fostering trust and reducing the perceived dangers associated with their investment activities.

3 The Role of OECD and UNCTAD in the Field of FDI Screening Mechanisms

Since its launch in 2006, the OECD's Comprehensive Dialogue on Global Investment Policy has consciously recognised the need to reconcile the importance of maintaining an open attitude towards foreign investment with the duty of governments to protect their national security interests. The OECD's Freedom of Investment (FOI) Roundtables, launched in 2006, have made a significant contribution to monitoring and sharing data on the evolution of investment policies. These roundtables provide a forum for governments, business, and other stakeholders to discuss and share best practices, challenges and lessons learned on investment policies.

On a parallel track, UNCTAD's work focused on the escalating utilisation of investment screening frameworks driven by national security concerns and emphasized various policy practices that are instrumental in bolstering the predictability, transparency, and administrative effectiveness of these screening mechanisms.[8] This plays a pivotal role in shaping and guiding these investment policies. These objectives aim to be achieved by establishing explicit procedural guidelines for investors and providing comprehensive decision-making guidance for the authorities tasked with implementation.

An important milestone was reached in 2009 at OECD level with the adoption at unanimity on the Guidelines for Recipient Country Investment Policies Relating to National Security.[9] They provide guidance for governments

---

7 International Working Group of Sovereign Wealth Funds (IWG), 'Sovereign Wealth Funds, Generally Accepted Principles and Practices "Santiago Principles"' (October 2008) <www.ifswf.org/sites/default/files/santiagoprinciples_0_0.pdf> accessed 23 November 2023.

8 UNCTAD, 'The Evolution of FDI Screening Mechanisms' (*UNCTAD*, February 2023) <unctad.org/system/files/official-document/diaepcbinf2023d2_en.pdf> accessed 23 November 2023.

9 OECD, 'Guidelines for Recipient Country Investment Policies Relation to National Security' (*OECD*, 25 May 2009) <www.oecd.org/daf/inv/investment-policy/43384486.pdf> accessed

considering or updating national security investment policies. They aim to provide clarity and transparency in the implementation of such policies, while promoting non-discrimination, proportionality, predictability, and accountability. These documents stress the critical importance of maintaining an open investment climate and urge governments to consider alternative methods, such as risk assessment, mitigation measures, and stakeholder engagement, before resorting to investment restrictions. Since their adoption, the Guidelines served as a benchmark for governments, providing a structure for reviewing and assessing national security investment policies. These endeavors aim to cultivate a setting that supports responsible investment beneficial to all, while also addressing legitimate national security interests.[10]

However, in 2018, the OECD noted that despite more than a decade of extensive discussion and transparency requirements on FDI screening, States have largely followed divergent paths with only modest progress towards uniformity. This continued diversity in national policies suggests that the expected convergence in FDI screening practices has been minimal.[11]

On a parallel track, UNCTAD's work focused on the escalating utilization of investment screening frameworks driven by national security concerns and emphasized various policy practices that are instrumental in bolstering the predictability, transparency, and administrative effectiveness of the screening mechanisms. These objectives can be achieved by establishing explicit procedural guidelines for investors and providing comprehensive decision-making guidance for the authorities tasked with implementation.

---

23 November 2023; OECD, 'Recommendation of the Council on OECD Legal Instruments Guidelines for Recipient Country Investment Policies relating to National Security' (*OECD*, 2024) <legalinstruments.oecd.org/public/doc/227/227.en.pdf> accessed 26 August 2024; Frédéric Wehrlé and Joachim Pohl, 'Investment Policies Related to National Security: A Survey of Country Practices' (2016) 3 OECD Working Papers on International Investment <https://doi.org/10.1787/5jlwrrf038nx-en> accessed 23 November 2023.

10 In March 2018, the OECD organised a workshop entitled 'Investment Policies Related to National Security: New Policies to Address New Threats?', with the aim of exploring the evolving landscape of policymaking in this area and gaining a better understanding of emerging trends in investment policies related to national security. See OECD, 'Investment Policies Related to National Security: New Policies to Address New Threats?' (*OECD*, 13 March 2018) <www.oecd.org/investment/investment-policy/National-security-investment-policies-workshop-agenda-2018.pdf> accessed 23 November 2023.

11 OECD, 'Current Trends in Investment Policies Related to National Security and Public Order' (*OECD*, November 2018) 4, <www.oecd.org/investment/Current-trends-in-OECD-NatSec-policies.pdf> accessed 23 November 2023, where it underlines that '[o]ver a decade of policy dialogue on the subject and transparency obligations would typically lead to some convergence in many areas, but this effect is felt only moderately in this area'.

4 Foreign Direct Investment in Innovation and Technology: The Imperative for Reciprocity

The Treaty of Lisbon, which entered into force in December 2009, has significantly reshaped the investment landscape within the European Union (EU). This pivotal treaty shifted responsibility for FDI to the EU level, bringing it within the scope of Article 207 of the Treaty on the Functioning of the European Union (TFEU), which governs the EU's common commercial policy. At the same time, this Treaty introduced Article 4(2) into the Treaty on European Union (TEU), which requires the EU to respect the essential functions of its Member States, such as maintaining law and order, safeguarding territorial integrity, and protecting national security. It is explicitly recognised that the responsibility for national security remains firmly with each Member State.

The scope of this shift in competence, particularly the challenges involved in developing an EU-wide investment screening mechanism similar to the US's Committee on Foreign Investment (CFIUS), becomes clear when considering the need to balance the individual interests of Member States with the EU's exclusive competences.

In addition, the expansion of sensitive assets – potentially impacting on national security – has been amplified by technological advances (specifically in areas such as artificial intelligence, quantum computing, and robotics) and global economic shifts, leading to concerns about supplier diversity, access to advanced technologies with defence applications, and the complex value chains behind various products.[12] As the FDI screening environment develops, there is a growing focus on developing rules and regulations that tackle the shifting complexities of the global investment scene. This shift involved moving away from limited restrictions targeted at specific assets or sectors to broader, more inclusive, cross-sectoral screening and review processes.

Investment screening mechanisms have existed since the 1960s, but many countries lacked such mechanisms until recently. There has been a considerable surge in policymaking activity in this area since 2016.

The increased international political and economic competition, along with the surge in Chinese investment that peaked in 2016, has intensified concerns among EU member states and prompted a reassessment of their FDI screening mechanisms. Specific acquisitions, such as the takeover of Kuka, a German

12 See Zenobia T Chan and Sophie Meunier, 'Behind the Screen: Understanding National Support for a Foreign Investment Screening Mechanism in the European Union' (2022) Rev Int Organ 513.

robotics manufacturer, by China's Midea Group, as well as other advanced technology companies in Europe, have been particularly noteworthy.[13]

5 The EU's Strategy for Mitigating National Security and Public Order Risks in Foreign Investment

In response to these developments, a joint letter was sent from the ministers of France, Germany, and Italy to the EU Trade Commissioner in February 2017.[14] This letter and the document attached underlined the urgent need to recalibrate the EU's approach to FDI, particularly in the technology sectors. It focused on the increasingly striking pattern of acquisitions by non-EU investors of European companies with key technological competencies. Acquisitions that, according to governments, were not driven by market forces but by strategic imperatives. It's not just about foreign investment per se, which can bring much-needed capital and innovation, it's more about the asymmetry of the relationship and the potential siphoning off of technological and intellectual resources to external entities. Such a dynamic creates vulnerabilities, especially when European investors don't enjoy similar access or rights in the investing countries.

In essence, governments highlighted the incongruity ('lack of reciprocity'): the EU maintains a relatively open attitude towards foreign investors, while European companies often face significant obstacles when they venture to invest in the same foreign markets. They also called for 'effective instruments', underlining the inadequacy of the EU's response to the potential loss of control over its technological and intellectual assets. This letter can be described as a defining moment in the EU's economic policy, from which point investment openness should have been judiciously weighed against long-term strategic interests. By jointly authoring a paper, these governments are clearly indicating their aspiration to unify their strategies at the level of the EU. This

13 A prominent example involved the failed acquisition of Aixtron, a German semiconductor firm, by Fujian Grand Chip, a Chinese enterprise. The transaction was halted by United States regulators through the Committee on Foreign Investment in the United States (CFIUS) due to Aixtron's business operations within the US. This case underscored the broader security considerations of foreign acquisitions that extend beyond a single EU Member State, such as Germany, and have implications for allied nations, including the US.

14 See 'Letter from Brigitte Zypries, Michel Sapin and Carlo Calenda to Cecilia Malmström' (10 February 2017) <www.bmwi.de/Redaktion/DE/Downloads/S-T/schreiben-de-fr-it-anmalmstroem.pdf?__blob=publicationFile&v=5> accessed 23 November 2023.

collaborative effort underlines the shared understanding among these pivotal member states that the challenge at hand calls for a coordinated, collective solution. In a related development, the Commission issued a White Paper in May 2017 titled 'Harnessing globalisation'. For the first time, this document hinted at the possibility of establishing a Europe-wide framework for the control of foreign investments, which, incidentally, was dismissed by several Member States.

6 Pre-pandemic Enactment of European Union Regulation 452/2019

In response to the concerns raised by governments, in the first part of 2017, the European Commission presented a proposal for regulation aimed at coordinating the mechanisms for controlling FDIs among Member States. Thus, the intention was not to establish a European control mechanism, but rather to create a system that would align and coordinate the efforts of the Member States.[15]

In short, the legislation on the control of foreign direct investment in the EU was adopted on 20 November 2018, with the final text approved by the European Parliament in February 2019. This legislation aimed to protect the essential interests of Member States, taking into account concerns about non-EU investments that could threaten security or public order. In March 2019, the EU Regulation (2019/452), was finally adopted and became fully operational from 11 October 2020.[16]

The objective of the Regulation was twofold: on the one hand, it aimed to create a legal framework for Member States to screen foreign direct investments entering the Union because of security or public order considerations. On the other, it wanted to establish a mechanism for cooperation between Member States and between Member States and the Commission, specifically for those foreign investments that could have an impact on security and public order. The framework also includes the possibility for the Commission to issue formal opinions on such investments.

---

15 For a general overview on screening mechanism see Steffen Hindelang and Andreas Moberg (eds), YSEC *Yearbook of Socio-Economic Constitutions 2020* (Springer 2021); Veronica Roberts (n 1). On the process that led the adoption of Regulation 452, see Joanna Warchol, 'The Birth of the EU Screening Regulation' in Hindelang and Moberg (n 14) 53.

16 Regulation (EU) 2019/452 of the European Parliament and of the Council of 19 March 2019 establishing a framework for the screening of foreign direct investments into the Union [2019] OJ L079I/1.

The new legislation didn't introduce a comprehensive mechanism at Union level for the screening of FDI. Under the Regulation, Member States retain the power to maintain, amend or introduce screening procedures for FDI within their borders on the basis of security and public order criteria.

Indeed, the FDI Screening Regulation at EU level does not prescribe in detail the specific form and content that Member States' FDI screening mechanisms should take. It does, however, outline certain essential elements that should be included in national FDI screening mechanisms and establishes a framework for cooperation and exchange of information between EU Member States and the European Commission.[17] In particular, art. 3 of the FDI Screening Regulation imposes obligations on EU Member States with FDI screening mechanisms to ensure that their mechanisms adhere to specific requirements. These key elements serve as guidelines to ensure a certain level of consistency and coherence among FDI screening mechanisms across the EU while allowing flexibility for Member States to tailor their mechanisms to their specific needs and circumstances.

7 COVID-19 Measures and the Triggering Effect of Regulation EU 452/2019

As has been highlighted, the advent of COVID-19 came at a particularly crucial moment for FDI screening mechanisms.

The pandemic not only intensified the scrutiny of FDI, but also potentially recalibrated the parameters of what constitutes a 'strategic' or 'critical' sector. Indeed, the health crisis added a layer of complexity to an already complex regulatory landscape, forcing countries to reassess their stance on foreign investment in sectors such as healthcare, supply chains and technology. In this context, even investments that had previously been considered benign came under scrutiny. Before 2017, around half of the EU member states had legislation regulating FDI, with a limited degree of harmonisation. However, it must be emphasised that all the larger states had some control mechanisms with limited convergence in the criteria and procedural designs of national security-related investment policies.

---

17 ibid art 3 imposes some general obligations on EU Member States with FDI screening mechanisms to ensure that such mechanisms comply with certain requirements: coverage; notification; timeframes; grounds for screening; confidentiality; prevention of circumvention.

Between 16 September 2019 and 15 March 2021, just before and during the early stages of the COVID pandemic, a significant number of countries (39 out of 62 invited to the Freedom of Investment process hosted by the OECD Investment Committee)[18] made changes to their investment policies. It is worth noting that none of these recent policy changes were explicitly justified by pandemic-related imperatives.[19] States continued to focus on the need to mitigate security risks associated with foreign investment.

The analysis of policies reveals an important evolution: many countries that now have or plan to have complex policies in this area had no such policies in the recent past. The assessment also identifies a trend towards more precise and thorough regulation of new mechanisms, accompanied by a renewed emphasis on managing investment in advanced technologies.

This data confirms the accelerated policy change observed in 2020, which was independent of the COVID-19 concerns and their economic consequences. It is worth noting that after July 2020, governments no longer cited circumstances related to the pandemic as a justification for these policy changes. It seems that the COVID-19 crisis did not significantly alter the trajectory of national security investment policy development. In addition, contrary to the expectations of convergence, the pandemic had little impact in terms of common criteria and procedural designs. Instead, countries have had diverse approaches, each focusing on its specific circumstances, priorities and national security considerations.

By contrast, the COVID-19 pandemic has had a significant impact on the concept of national security and related policy approaches. The pandemic accelerated an ongoing process of change, further highlighting the interdependencies and vulnerabilities of global supply chains. It has highlighted the

18 See 'Freedom of Investment Roundtables: Summary of Discussions' (OECD) <www.oecd.org/daf/inv/investment-policy/oecdroundtablesonfreedomofinvestment.htm> accessed 23 November 2023.

19 See OECD, 'Freedom of Investment Roundtables: Summary of Discussions, 33th Roundtable (*OECD*, 30 March 2021) 8 <https://one.oecd.org/document/DAF/INV/WD(2021)13/FINAL/en/pdf> accessed 23 November 2023. The following economies were invited to participate in the Roundtables: Argentina, Australia, Austria, Belgium, Brazil, Bulgaria, Canada, Chile, China, Colombia, Costa Rica, Croatia, Czech Republic, Denmark, Egypt, Estonia, Finland, France, Germany, Greece, Hungary, Iceland, India, Indonesia, Ireland, Israel, Italy, Japan, Jordan, Kazakhstan, Korea, Latvia, Lithuania, Luxembourg, Malaysia, Mexico, Morocco, Netherlands, New Zealand, Norway, Paraguay, Peru, Poland, Portugal, Romania, Russian Federation, Saudi Arabia, Singapore, Slovakia, Slovenia, South Africa, Spain, Sweden, Switzerland, Thailand, Tunisia, Turkey, Ukraine, United Kingdom, United States, Uruguay, and the EU.

need for countries to safeguard essential industries, as well as protecting critical resources and technologies.

The European Commission has also played a supportive role through the Communication it published in March 2020, in which points related to the COVID-19 impact on screening control were raised.[20]

The COVID-19 pandemic has increased the potential risk to strategic industries in the EU, particularly those related to health, including health infrastructure and the supply of critical inputs. Recognising this, the Commission emphasised the importance of ensuring the resilience of these sectors to meet the needs of EU citizens. It called on Member States to protect key economic and industrial players, including SMEs, from foreign takeovers that could pose security or public order risks. To this end, the Commission urged Member States to make effective use of their existing FDI screening mechanisms and to establish comprehensive mechanisms where they do not exist. This would ensure that foreign acquisitions or control in sensitive sectors, in particular health-related infrastructure, and critical input supply chains, were thoroughly assessed.

The Communication underlined that Regulation 2019/452 on the FDI national screening, which applies to all sectors of the economy and to FDI from third countries without thresholds, is a key tool in this context. The transaction assessment should not be the sole determinant of screening, underlining the broader objective of preserving the EU's strategic autonomy, particularly in health-related capacities.

The EU's strategy not only includes the robust implementation of Regulation 452, but also the promotion of cooperation and regular updating of frameworks among Member States to address evolving threats and protect critical sectors. Where a full screening mechanism is not in place, Member States were encouraged to use alternative measures, such as existing regulatory frameworks and in-depth assessments or cooperation with other Member States, to mitigate potential risks. These steps were considered essential for the EU to effectively manage and mitigate risks and to ensure that its openness to foreign investment is consistent with the overarching objective of safeguarding key sectors, particularly in the context of health infrastructure and critical supply chains.

20 Communication from the Commission, Guidance to the Member States concerning foreign direct investment and free movement of capital from third countries, and the protection of Europe's strategic assets, ahead of the application of Regulation (EU) 2019/452 (FDI Screening Regulation) (2020/C 99 I/01) (2020) OJ C99I/1.

In 2021, the European Commission in its Communication on the Trade Policy Review urged all Member States to establish national screening mechanisms, stating that:

> [i]n the security field, under the FDI Screening Regulation, the Commission restates its call to all Member States to set up and enforce a fully-fledged FDI screening mechanism to address cases where the acquisition or control of a particular business, infrastructure or technology would create a risk to security or public order in the EU. The Commission will continue implementing the cooperation mechanism with Member States' authorities to protect security and public order from risky foreign direct investments and consider enhancing the cooperation mechanism established by the FDI Screening Regulation.[21]

It is worth noting that, in April 2022 with the Communication on Russia's military actions in Ukraine, the Commission highlighted the increased risks associated with investments from Russia and Belarus, which could potentially jeopardise security and public order. Following on from the previous 2020 Communication, the Communication advocates the systematic application of screening procedures by Member States to identify and mitigate these risks. It also underlined the need for a concerted effort between the authorities responsible for sanctions and those responsible for investment screening, and emphasised the need for thorough due diligence and comprehensive risk assessments on Russian and Belarusian investors.

As a result of the changing geopolitical situation, and in particular the increased competition between the US and China, COVID-19, and the Russia-Ukraine conflict, there has been a significant increase in the number of review mechanisms and broader government intervention in various sectors of the economy.[22] This has been achieved by introducing new mechanisms, strengthening existing ones, expanding the sectors and assets subject to review, introducing more detailed rules and lowering trigger thresholds.[23]

---

21 Communication from the Commission to the European Parliament, the Council, the European Economic and Social Committee and the Committee of the Regions, Trade Policy Review – An Open, Sustainable and Assertive Trade Policy (2021) COM(2021) 66.

22 As to the review mechanisms triggered by the pandemic, see Chapter 6.

23 See Regulation (EU) 2019/452 (n 15). Jens Hillebrand Pohl and others (eds), *Weaponising investment*, vol 1 (Springer 2023).

8 The Annual Reports of the Commission on the Enforcement of Regulation 452/2019: The Status of FDI in Europe and of the National Screening Mechanisms

According to Art. 5 of Regulation 452, EU Member States are required to submit a consolidated report of FDI data from within their borders in the previous calendar year, to the Commission by the 31st March each year.

The report includes a summary of requests for information received from other Member States, a process described in other articles of the Regulation. If a Member State has an FDI screening mechanism in place, it must provide additional aggregated data on the application of this mechanism during the reporting period. The Commission is required to compile these national reports into a comprehensive annual report on the implementation of the Regulation. This comprehensive report is then submitted to both the European Parliament and the Council of the European Union and made available to the public.

The reports in question, of which three have been published to date, serve to assess the landscape of FDI screening in the European Union. To this end, Art. 5 establishes a structured process for monitoring and discussing the effectiveness and application of these rules. The reports evaluate the current level of cooperation both among EU Member States and between each Member State and the European Commission. Each report provides a comprehensive review of the screening mechanisms in place in individual EU Member States offering a snapshot of how each country approaches the scrutiny of foreign investments, including the criteria they use, the sectors they focus on, and the processes they follow. Furthermore, it describes the state of investments in EU.

For our purposes, these documents are particularly interesting to understand the trend towards strengthening existing screening mechanisms and the establishment of new ones. By documenting the evolution of these mechanisms, the reports highlight the growing emphasis on safeguarding critical industries and technologies from potentially harmful foreign investments. This trend reflects a broader global movement towards more stringent controls on FDI for reasons of national security and public order to understand the changing dynamics of investment screening (a barometer for the state of FDI screening within the EU).

The first report, adopted after the start of the COVID-19 pandemic and in the 'new era' of Regulation 452, shows that the landscape of investment transactions in the European Union has changed significantly due to the impact of the pandemic. All EU Member States experienced a decline in M&A activity (France and Sweden were particularly hard hit while Germany experienced a relatively moderate decline). In Germany, there was a general drop in investment from China and the United States. Chinese investment in Europe, while representing a smaller share of total M&A activity, experienced the sharpest decline from November 2019 (two months before the Wuhan lockdown), and this decline continued despite the relatively early resumption of economic activity in China around mid-2020. The impact of the pandemic was not uniform across economic sectors in Europe. Medical supplies, pharmaceutical manufacturing and e-commerce sectors experienced a surge in activity, riding the wave of increased demand. In contrast, sectors related to tourism, leisure, aviation and shipping were negatively affected. The manufacturing sector, which accounts for a quarter of all outbound M&A transactions, also saw a significant drop in the number of deals in 2020, down 40% year-on-year. However, the Information and Communication Technologies (ICT) sector stood out for its resilience in the face of the pandemic and other global challenges, suffering only a modest decline and going on to lead the recovery in the first quarter of 2021, bringing activity in the sector back to pre-pandemic levels.[24]

When the European Commission proposed the regulation in 2017, only 11 EU Member States had established a national FDI screening mechanism, either covering specific sectors or a wider range. As of 1 July 2021, this number increased to 18. What is more interesting is that the scope of the existing mechanisms has been significantly enhanced and broadened, with many Member States amending their mechanisms to reflect (sometimes in exact wording) or make explicit reference to key provisions of the Regulation.[25]

As previously underlined in the March 2020 ('COVID') and April 2022 ('Russia') Communications, the European Commission, in its first report, urged all 27 EU Member States to implement national FDI screening mechanisms in order to create a legislative/institutional network to protect individual Member States against risky investments from non-EU countries and to maintain the collective security of the Member States and the Union and to support the integrity of the internal market. In response to the economic impact of COVID-19, five Member States – France, Italy, Hungary, Poland, and Slovenia – introduced temporary measures to address vulnerabilities related to the pandemic and the resulting decline in EU asset values. During the reporting period, 24 of the 27 EU Member States have either introduced a new FDI screening mechanism, amended an existing one, or initiated a process that is

24 Report from the Commission to the European Parliament and the Council, First Annual Report on the screening of foreign direct investments into the Union (2021) COM(2021)714 final 1–6.

25 ibid 6–10 and n 13.

expected to lead to new or revised mechanisms. Monitoring of national screening systems is facilitated by Article 3 of the Regulation, which requires Member States to notify the European Commission of their screening mechanisms and any changes to them (paragraph 7), and for the Commission to maintain an updated and publicly available list of these mechanisms (paragraph 8).

The second report, somewhat in line with the first, shows that while there are striking similarities between national screening mechanisms, there are significant differences in the formalities of investment screening, review timeframes, coverage, notification protocols, and various other procedural aspects. In the second annual report, global FDI rebounded significantly from the previous year's COVID-19-induced slump. Global inflows rose to EUR 1.5 trillion, an increase of 52% compared to 2020 and 11% higher than pre-pandemic levels in 2019. The European Union's contribution to this recovery was notable, although its share of global FDI inflows fell from 27% in 2019 to 8%, representing a 31% decline compared to 2020 and a sharp 68% decline compared to 2019. There was a general upward trend in the EU's outward flows, highlighting the region's openness to foreign investment despite the challenges of the pandemic. In 2021, the US was the leading source of FDI in the EU, followed by the UK. However, Chinese and Japanese investment didn't reach their 2020 levels, with China suffering a significant decline.[26] The hopeful outlook for a robust economic recovery in 2022 was overshadowed by rising financial uncertainty, fueled by the ongoing conflict in Ukraine, rising energy prices and ongoing supply chain disruptions. In terms of foreign investment, Germany emerged as the top destination for acquisitions in 2021, with Spain, France and the Netherlands also seeing a surge in such transactions. Spain took the lead for greenfield investments within the EU, with France and Germany close behind. Most industrial sectors have returned to pre-pandemic levels of activity, with ICT and manufacturing at the forefront of the EU FDI recovery. In particular, ICT dominated acquisitions and played a significant role in greenfield investments, with significant growth compared to the previous year.

On the regulatory front, the European Commission has noted that the pandemic and subsequent supply chain issues have highlighted the need for strong industry oversight, forcing EU countries to improve their investment screening protocols. In 2021, three member states introduced new FDI screening mechanisms, while six revised their existing frameworks. In addition, seven member states initiated processes to either establish or improve their

26 Report from the Commission to the European Parliament and the Council, Second Annual Report on the screening of foreign direct investments into the Union, (2022) COM(2022)433 final.

screening systems. By the end of 2021, a substantial two-thirds of EU Member States had enacted legislation on FDI: a decisive step towards safeguarding key industries and ensuring that FDI is in line with the EU's strategic interests and economic security.

The landscape of FDI screening in the European Union has undergone a dynamic transformation, with Member States collectively moving towards more nuanced and comprehensive screening systems. These changes represent an effort to tighten controls on investment from outside the EU and to protect strategic sectors. As signaled in the Report,[27] France significantly lowered the threshold at which non-EU investments are subject to review, while requiring a more detailed submission process. Germany recalibrated its procedural framework and extended its scrutiny to new sectors deemed sensitive, particularly in new technologies. This recalibration also includes adjusted benchmarks for acquisitions of capital and voting rights requiring formal notification. Italy broadened the scope of its investment review process, ensuring that a wider range of transactions fall within the scope of national security considerations. Some States, such as Latvia, have empowered their regulators to require more detailed information from investors, ensuring a deeper insight into investments. Others, such as Lithuania, have updated the list of vital companies and infrastructure, reflecting a proactive approach to protecting critical assets. Hungary has widened the scope of business activities that trigger mandatory reporting of proposed transactions, thereby strengthening its screening process. The second report illustrates a clear trend towards a strengthened regulatory environment, several other EU Member States are actively considering improvements to their current FDI screening frameworks.

In its last annual report released in October 2023,' the 2022 landscape of global FDI increased to EUR 1.2 trillion, rising sharply from 2020 thanks to post-pandemic growth. The evolution of FDI signaled a decline in the EU (mainly due to the collapse of Luxembourg's FDI), the US, and China. In the medium term, the EU 27's cumulative outward transactions from 2015 to 2022 showed a positive trend, with the economic slowdown and higher financing costs caused by inflation being one of the main reasons for the slowdown. Investor confidence in the global market has been hit by escalating inflation due to Russia's aggression in Ukraine, rising energy and commodity prices, and extensive supply chain challenges, leading investors to adopt a cautious stance and wait for more favorable circumstances. In terms of destinations in the EU 27, and despite the overall decline, Germany remained the main destination for FDI in

27 ibid 9.

2022, with Spain in second place, followed by Italy, France, and the Netherlands also recording falls in outward transactions, with only Sweden and Portugal bucking the trend with increases in the number of acquisitions. The ICT sector will continue to attract the most investment in 2022. Conversely, manufacturing, the second most acquisitive sector, saw a decline in both acquisitions and greenfield projects.

In its efforts to promote consistency in national screening, the Commission has offered Member States technical assistance and policy advice, as well as opportunities for meetings and exchange of information, in particular on best practices.

However, despite ongoing cooperation, significant differences remained between Member States' screening mechanisms. These differences were highlighted in a 2022 evaluation study of the FDI Screening Regulation and included differences in what qualifies as formal FDI screening, the timing of these screenings, the sectors involved and the notification requirements.

The ongoing conflict between Russia and Ukraine has highlighted the strategic value of key sectors such as energy, aerospace, defence, and critical technologies. This scenario has prompted many EU Member States to either introduce new frameworks for monitoring FDI or to improve and extend the scope of their existing regulatory frameworks. In 2022, one Member State introduced an additional screening device, while another eight Member States adopted revisions to their existing systems (notably Italy and France). Concurrently, eight Member States embarked upon consultative or legislative procedures to formulate novel screening protocols, with several poised to either ratify these initiatives or implement them in the ensuing year of 2023. By the termination of 2022, two-thirds of EU Member States had legislated formal mechanisms for the screening of foreign direct investments.[28]

Specifically, regarding revisions to current frameworks, France has prolonged the provisional mandate necessitating foreign investors to declare their acquisitions in publicly traded firms upon reaching a threshold of 10% in voting rights. Simultaneously, Italy has enacted expedient provisions to mitigate the economic and humanitarian repercussions emanating from the hostilities involving Russia, with a particular emphasis on domains like cybersecurity and the procurement of raw materials.

28 For an updated list see European Commission, 'Trade' (*European Commission*, 2023) <https://policy.trade.ec.europa.eu/enforcement-and-protection/investment-screening_en> accessed 23 November 2023.

9 Concluding Remarks: Economic Security Policies and the Prospective Landscape of Inbound and Outbound Investment Scrutiny

According to a UNCTAD study, since the mid-1990s, 37 countries around the world have established structures to screen foreign investments for national security risks. Developed European States predominate, accounting for 22 of these frameworks, with the remainder spread across various developed and emerging economies in Asia, North America, Oceania, Latin America, and Africa.[29]

The COVID-19 pandemic has significantly accelerated the pre-existing trend towards improved FDI screening mechanisms. These advances are expected to significantly change investment screening policies and reshape governmental and societal views on the benefits and risks of foreign investment. While FDI is recognised as a driver of growth, innovation and job creation, it also poses security risks to host countries, a concern heightened by the pandemic.

In contrast to the response to the 2008 financial crisis, many countries have tightened controls on foreign investment. This shift reflects changing perceptions of the benefits and risks of international investment, with increased scrutiny of state-owned enterprises (SOEs) linked to foreign governments. Various strategies have been employed to expand FDI screening mechanisms during the pandemic. These include implementing stand-alone policy guidelines, lowering foreign acquisition monetary thresholds, and expanding sector-specific reviews, with a particular focus on public health and related industries. For instance, the EU and Canada developed independent policy guidelines, while Australia and France adjusted monetary thresholds. France and Germany extended sectoral coverage, and India instituted case-by-case screening for investments from specific neighbouring countries.[30]

Europe, with its single market and diverse screening laws, coupled with EU Regulation 452, is an ideal setting for refining screening procedures. The Regulation has emerged as a catalyst for change,[31] particularly since its

---

29 UNCTAD, 'The Evolution of FDI Screening Mechanisms. Key Trends and Features' (2023) 25 Investment Policy Monitor.

30 Cheng Bian (n 3); OECD, 'Investment Screening in Times of COVID-19 and Beyond' (*OECD*, 7 July 2020) <www.oecd.org/coronavirus/policy-responses/investment-screening-in-times-of-covid-19-and-beyond-aa60af47/> accessed 23 November 2023.

31 OECD, 'Framework for the Screening of Foreign Direct Investment in the EU. Assessing Effectiveness and Efficiency' (*OECD*, 2022) <www.oecd.org/investment/investment-policy/oecd-eu-fdi-screening-assessment.pdf> accessed 23 November 2023. This report is the result of an analysis by the OECD's Investment Division, commissioned by the EU

adoption just before the pandemic. It requires disclosure of national mechanisms to the EU Commission, sets minimum procedural and substantive standards, and encourages the assessment of transactions against specific factors (as per Article 4 of the Regulation). Increased transparency and data collection have been key outcomes, influencing legislative changes in Member States. Most adaptations and new mechanisms after 2019 are in line with the Regulation's standards, and ongoing developments reflect its recommendations. Commission's latest report suggests a push for greater harmonisation. It is important to recognise that, while the trend towards the development of control mechanisms continues, there is an increasing focus on outbound investment. This shift is evidenced by the strengthening of dual-use legislation and the establishment of new regimes specifically designed to control outbound investment.[32] This progressive development marks a significant change in the approach to investment regulation, going beyond the traditional control of inbound investment.

According to Article 15(1) of Regulation 452, the Commission should have conducted a comprehensive evaluation of the functioning and effectiveness of the Regulation on the screening of foreign direct investment (FDI) by October 12, 2023. This evaluation, made even more necessary by the changing global economic landscape and emerging security concerns, was to culminate in a comprehensive report to the European Parliament and the Council. The timing of this review period coincided with the unveiling of the European Economic Security Strategy in June 2023,[33] which indicated a strategic alignment of the EU's broader economic security policies with specific investment screening

Commission to assess the efficiency and effectiveness of the EU Regulation's investment screening framework.

32 See US President Joe Biden, 'Executive Order on Addressing United States Investments in Certain National Security Technologies and Products in Countries of Concern' (*The White House*, 9 August 2023) <www.whitehouse.gov/briefing-room/presidential-actions/2023/08/09/executive-order-on-addressing-united-states-investments-in-certain-national-security-technologies-and-products-in-countries-of-concern/> accessed 23 November 2023. The Order aims to regulate certain types of US investment abroad, represents a significant shift in the US national security approach to foreign investment in high-tech sectors such as semiconductors, microelectronics, quantum information technologies and artificial intelligence. See Gisela Grieger, 'US Approach to Outbound Investment Screening' (*Think Tank European Parliamentary*, 2023) <www.europarl.europa.eu/thinktank/en/document/EPRS_ATA(2023)751470> accessed 23 November 2023. The EU is considering a comparable initiative. See also the recent European Commission's White Paper on outbound investments (2024) COM(2024) 24 final.

33 See Joint Communication to the European Parliament and the European Council and the Council on 'European Economic Security Strategy (2023) JOIN(2023) 20 final.

mechanisms. This strategy highlighted potential future directions for the EU, specifically pointing to a significant revision of the current FDI Screening Regulation.

Further advancing this trajectory, as this book neared completion, on January 24, 2024, the European Commission launched its long-awaited Economic Security Package, which introduced five strategic initiatives aimed at enhancing EU competitiveness, protecting against emerging threats, and building key international coalitions.[34] These initiatives covered a variety of focus areas, from inbound and outbound investment to export controls and the security of research and development, particularly in dual-use technologies. A remarkable element of this package is the proposed new FDI Screening Regulation, which sought to refine the existing framework.[35] This refinement included clearer definitions of FDI, the expansion of screening mechanisms, the obligation for Member States to establish such mechanisms based on specific criteria, and the improvement of procedural coherence. These developments signal a pivotal moment in the EU's approach to safeguarding its economic interests in a landscape of global geopolitical tensions and emphasize the dynamic interplay between openness and security in the context of international investment.

---

34 See European Commission, 'Commission proposes new initiatives to strengthen economic security' (*Press release*, 24 January 2024) <ec.europa.eu/commission/presscorner/detail/en/IP_24_363> accessed 25 January 2024.

35 Proposal for a Regulation of the European Parliament and of the Council on the screening of foreign investments in the Union and repealing Regulation (EU) 2019/452 of the European Parliament and of the Council (2024) COM/2024/23 final; see Hannah A Madatali, Lucia Torlai, '*Revision of the EU Foreign Direct Investment Screening Regulation*', (*Think Tank European Parliamentary*, 2024) <www.europarl.europa.eu/RegData/etudes/BRIE/2024/762844/EPRS_BRI(2024)762844_EN.pdf> accessed 22 August 2024.

CHAPTER 6

Preventing Unwanted Acquisitions before and after the COVID Crisis

Francesco Salerno and Marco Grantaliano

1 Introduction

Regulation (EU) 2019/452 (Regulation), approved on 19 March 2019, established a framework for the screening of foreign direct investment.[1] The Regulation does not afford the European Commission (Commission) new powers but sets out common requirements with which national screening mechanisms must comply, establishing a cooperation mechanism between Member States and the Commission.

The deadline for Member States to comply with the Regulation was 11 October 2020.[2] However, on 26 March 2020, right after the start of the COVID-19 pandemic, the Commission issued a Communication (Communication), which urged Member States to enforce their Foreign Direct Investment (FDI) screening regimes and speed up the implementation of the Regulation via the full use of existing screening mechanisms or the setup of new ones.[3] More specifically, the Communication spelled out the link between the COVID-19 pandemic and FDI enforcement in the following terms:

> In the context of the COVID-19 emergency, there could be an increased risk of attempts to acquire healthcare capacities (for example for the productions of medical or protective equipment) or related industries such as research establishments (for instance developing vaccines) via foreign direct investment. Vigilance is required to ensure that any such FDI does

1 Regulation (EU) 2019/452 of the European Parliament and of the Council of 19 March 2019 establishing a framework for the screening of foreign direct investments into the Union [2019] OJ L079I/1.

2 ibid art 17.

3 Commission, 'Communication from the Commission – Guidance to the Member States concerning foreign direct investment and free movement of capital from third countries, and the protection of Europe's strategic assets, ahead of the application of Regulation (EU) 2019/452 (FDI Screening Regulation)' [2020] OJ C099I/1.

© KONINKLIJKE BRILL BV, LEIDEN, 2025 | DOI:10.1163/9789004711204_008

not have a harmful impact on the EU's capacity to cover the health needs of its citizens.

To this end, the European Commission calls upon Member States to:

- *Make full use already now of its FDI screening mechanisms to take fully into account the risks to critical health infrastructures, supply of critical inputs, and other critical sectors as envisaged in the EU legal framework;*
- For those Member States that currently do not have a screening mechanism, or whose screening mechanisms do not cover all relevant transactions, to set up a full-fledged screening mechanism and in the meantime to use all other available options to address cases where the acquisition or control of a particular business, infrastructure or technology would create a risk to security or public order in the EU, including a risk to critical health infrastructures and supply of critical inputs.[4]

The Communication and the Regulation were further complemented by the introduction of a yearly report by the Commission (FDI Screening Report), which, in its 2021 edition, confirms a substantial increase in FDI screening activities.[5] The FDI Screening Report confirms that the vast majority of Member States now has an FDI screening mechanism in place, and that many Member States were in the process of updating their existing ones.

As a matter of fact, enforcement of FDI screening mechanisms in the period 2020–2022, measured by the number of notifications, has increased significantly: the number of yearly notifications under the Italian FDI screening regime increased from 8 in 2014 to 608 in 2022, while in Germany it increased from 78 in 2019 to 306 in 2022, and in France comparable figures amounted respectively to 137 in 2017 and to 325 in 2022.[6]

---

4 ibid (emphasis added).

5 Commission, 'Report from the Commission to the European Parliament and the Council: Second Annual Report on the screening of foreign direct investments into the Union' COM (2022) 433 final (FDI Screening Report).

6 Data sourced respectively: for Italy, from Sottosegretariato di Stato alla Presidenza del Consiglio dei ministri 'Relazione concernente l'attività svolta sulla base dei poteri speciali sugli assetti societari nei settori della difesa e della sicurezza nazionale, nonché per le attività di rilevanza strategica nei settori dell'energia, dei trasporti e delle comunicazioni – anno 2021' (2022) DOC LXV, N 4; for France, from Direction Générale du Trésor 'Contrôle des Investissements Etrangers en France Rapport Annuel 2023' (2023) <www.tresor.economie.gouv.fr/Articles/5ed9606f-f37e-4517-ae5d-445dab7ecad0/files/68cd8466-0b98-44d2-9182-777b8768cee0> accessed 23 September 2023; for Germany, from Federal Ministry of Economic Affairs and Climate Action (*Bundesministerium für Wirtschaft und Klimaschutz*)

However, the data available from 3 key jurisdictions – France, Germany, and Italy – show that other factors were already in place well before the COVID crisis and the enactment of the Communication of March 2020. This chapter tries to disentangle the COVID-related FDI control from FDI controls that were due to other factors, which would have likely taken place even in absence of the pandemic.

The analysis of EU data, shown further on in this chapter, reveals that, while the overall level of screening activity has increased, in most cases the rise in enforcement is not directly attributable to COVID-19 as the explaining factor. Rather, it seems linked to other causal variables which form part of trend towards the evolution of EU FDI control which is independent from COVID-19. Moreover, while the volume of filings concerning FDI screening regimes has increased, the number of vetoed transactions has remained limited.

In conclusion, it will be argued that the impact of the COVID pandemic on FDI screening has been somewhat overstated.

2 The Screening Regimes of Selected EU Member States

The chapter presents a comparative analysis of FDI screening practices in France, Germany, and Italy, from the period before the onset of the COVID pandemic until 2022. All three countries have implemented very extensive FDI screening regimes that are overall very similar, with differences mainly related to procedures.

The first similarity is in terms of scope, in that the FDI screening regimes cover a wide range of sectors, and broadly refer to key national interests, such as 'national security', 'national defence', 'public order', 'critical activities', and 'public health'. The respective definitions, while provided in the legal texts and/or in their implementing acts, are broad and, in most cases, do not allow readers to establish a clear line between exempted investments and those that fall within the scope of the FDI screening regimes. Out of caution, investors tend to notify deals even with tenuous connections to the aforementioned areas. Still, governments seem to have increased their level of attention, and tend to investigate more transactions than before. In the words of the 2021 FDI Screening Report:

'Investment Screening in Germany: Facts & Figures' (2023) <www.bmwk.de/Redaktion/EN/Publikationen/Aussenwirtschaft/investment-screening-in-germany-facts-figures.pdf?__blob=publicationFile&v=6> accessed 23 September 2023 (BMWK Report).

> There is an apparent trend towards screening more cases formally. Indeed, out of the 1 563 authorisation requests and ex-officio cases, roughly 29% of the cases were formally screened. This seems to mark an increase in the proportion of formally screened cases from 2020. It could be explained by a greater attention of what national authorities consider as potentially 'critical', as well as a change in overall investment trends. About 71% of all applications were deemed ineligible or did not require formal screening because of an evident lack of impact on security and public order.
>
> [...]
>
> In comparison to 2020, Member States have considered the requests received as more sensitive in 2021, as the proportion of formally screened cases has increased. [7]

The sectors concerned by FDI scrutiny increased between 2020 and 2022 and are essentially the same; they all include core areas like defence, telecommunications, essential infrastructure (among which, energy and transportation), semi-conductors, health, research and development in key areas, and advanced life sciences. The widening in the scope of FDI screening regimes is in line with the general EU-wide trend, and it has led to an increase in FDI notifications in all three countries.

Another shared characteristic is the absence of general turnover thresholds for State intervention. By contrast, there are shareholding thresholds related to the stake object of the acquisition, which vary according to the sectors concerned. For example, under the Italian FDI screening regime an acquisition of a stake as low as 3% triggers a filing obligation in the sector of defence, while the generally applicable threshold is set at 10%. Moreover, in Germany, specific thresholds are applied depending on the characteristics of the asset that is the object of the scrutinised transaction.[8]

The absence of general turnover thresholds must be read in conjunction with the fact that all regimes at hand have some kind of 'catch-all' provision, which enable competent authorities to intervene *ex officio*. This is most likely

7 FDI Screening Report (n 5) 11–12.

8 For example, a comparison of Italy's and Germany's FDI screening regimes to airports is very telling of the differences in threshold use by the two governments. Whereas the Italian regime is limited to 'airports of national interest' – whose definition is not completely clear and requires an in-depth analysis of national law – the German regime clearly states that it only applies to a passenger handling system with a minimum of 20 million passengers per year.

due to the will to avoid any enforcement gaps, by being able to review even apparently small transactions if they are deemed relevant to national interests.

As one could expect in matters of national security, the level of publicly available information regarding FDI screening is scant compared to other areas of national law, which leads most scholars to define screening regimes as 'opaque'[9] or even 'obscure'.[10] For example, in France a public report on the application of the FDI regime has only been available since 2021 – whereas, for previous years, there is minimal data.[11]

The opacity is further exacerbated by the fact that FDI decisions are not public, in that, in all three countries, they are not published in Official Journals, and their text is not otherwise made available to interested parties that are not directly concerned by the decisions. In any event, experience shows that the decisions themselves tend to state reasons very succinctly.

Finally, as regards procedure, all the three screening regimes hinge on prior notification, have a suspensory effect on notified transactions or investments (notably, also on actions completed in breach of notification obligations), and afford the Governments, besides the noted *ex officio* powers, broad investigative powers.

Sanctions for failure to notify are significant and are both criminal and monetary.

3 Germany

The German FDI screening regime is based on the Foreign Trade and Payments Act (AWG)[12] and the Foreign Trade and Payments Ordinance (AWV),[13] which regulates the implementation of the provisions of the AWG. The AWG was

---

9 Falk Schöning and Stefan Kirwitzke, 'The Rise of Foreign Investment Control in Europe and Beyond Under the Impact of COVID-19' (2020) 16 Competition L Intl 31.

10 Keyan Lai, 'National Security and FDI Policy Ambiguity: A Commentary' (2021) 4 J Int Bus Policy 496.

11 According to publicly disclosed data on the French Ministry of Treasury: <www.tresor.economie.gouv.fr/services-aux-entreprises/investissements-etrangers-en-france> accessed 23 September 2023.

12 Foreign Trade and Payments Act (*Außenwirtschaftsgesetz – AWG*) of 6 June 2013 (Federal Law Gazette I p 1482), as last amended by Article 1 of the Act of 23 May 2022 (Federal Law Gazette I p 754).

13 Foreign Trade and Payments Ordinance (*Außenwirtschaftsverordnung – AWV*) of 2 August 2013 (Federal Law Gazette [BGBl] Part I p 2865), as last amended by the Ordinance of 25 April 2022 (BAnz AT 02.05.2022 V1).

first published in 2013, and, together with the AWV, has been amended several times in recent years.

Under AWG and the AWV, the Ministry of Economic Affairs and Climate Action (BMWK) can review foreign direct investments and has the power to either prohibit the investment project or impose approval conditions whenever the review procedure should highlight that the project may affect public order and/or national security. The approval conditions, named 'restrictive measures' in BMWK documents in their official translations, include, inter alia, commitments to carry out positive actions or the exclusion of a division or component of the targeted company or asset deemed critical.

Compared to the French and Italian FDI screening regimes, Germany appears to have a stricter focus on the sector involved with investment, with specific rules that vary significantly depending on the sector concerned. By contrast, while the Italian FDI screening regime also provides for sectoral rules, a more substantial distinction is made between defence-related assets and other sensitive assets. Moreover, the German regime also provides parameters to assess the 'critical' nature of sensitive assets.

Data provided by the BMWK show that, while the number of notifications increased dramatically with COVID-19 (from 78 in 2018 to 306 in 2022), the number of scrutinised transactions by the BMWK stayed constant in absolute terms.[14] This is due to the fact that, under relevant German law provisions, notified investments can be subject to a less stringent procedure leading to expedited clearance (i.e., Phase I proceedings), or to an in-depth investigation. Only cases subject to an in-depth investigation can result in restrictive measures being imposed.

As regards the data analysis, summarised in Chart 1 below, in-depth review was reserved to 38 cases in 2018, to 49 cases in 2020 and to 40 cases in 2021.[15] The same is true for decisions imposing restrictive measures: in 2018; 10 cases resulted in such measures being adopted (13% of cases), while in 2020 12 cases did (7.5%) and in 2021 14 cases (4.5%).

The data above clearly show the impact of COVID-19-related amendments on the volumes of *notifications*, which increased fourfold. While in 2018 the total number of cases was 78, in 2020 the same figure reached 160 (+105%) and, in 2021 and 2022, it amounted to 306 (+292% compared to 2018).

However, the number of cases which required restrictive measures (as defined above) has remained stable.

14 BMWK Report (n 6).

15 Provisional figures for 2022 are available, but 39 cases remained pending at the time of publication. Therefore, they were not included in the present study.

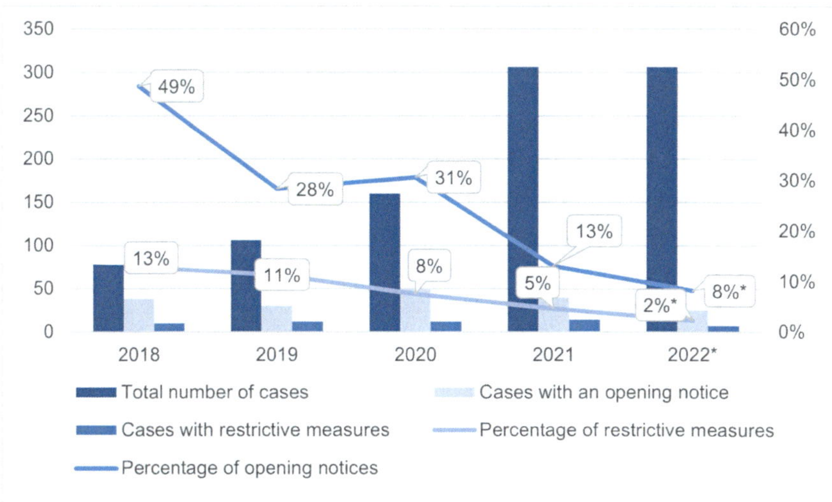

FIGURE 1 FDI screening activity in Germany
* Data for 2022 is provisional and may be subject to changes

It appears, thus, that while COVID-19 was an occasion to expand the *possibility* of scrutiny, the actual level of State intervention regarding FDI has not changed. In particular, the data show that the widening of the scope of the FDI screening regime led to a much higher number of notifications. However, the number of Phase-II cases and restrictive measures has remained unchanged in absolute numbers and even decreased in terms of percentage of the total number notifications.

Therefore, the real priorities of the German government remain unchanged, and they seem to hinge on strategic national security and geopolitical evaluations rather than on the pandemic.

3.1 *Pre-COVID Period*

Before the COVID pandemic, the scope of the German FDI screening regime was substantially narrower than it is today and left wide gaps. Traditionally, Germany had a more liberal stance regarding government intervention in the economy compared with France and Italy, and actively supported free trade.

In the German system, public control was mainly exercised via direct and indirect shareholding in key enterprises and via public banks, through which the German State guarantees easy credit access to private enterprises. The expansive public banks network finds its expression in the Bundesverband Öffentlicher Banken Deutschlands (VÖB), among which one of the leading members is the federal development bank – Kreditanstalt für Wiederaufbau (KFW).

In 2018, a Chinese investor expressed the intention of purchasing a 20% stake in major power grid operator 50Hertz. Power grids are usually considered a key piece of infrastructure, as they enable the transmission of electricity. However, the German FDI rules applicable at the time did not warrant the German government the power to intervene. Thus, German authorities were left scrambling for a creative solution that could warrant the protection of a key national interest even in lack of a clear legal basis for action. The solution was found thanks to State-owned KFW, which, instructed by public authorities, offered to buy – and eventually bought – the contentious stake in 50Hertz instead of the Chinese investor. The German government confirmed that the involvement of KFW had the objective of protecting the power grid, deemed a critical infrastructure.

Although this acquisition did not fall within FDI jurisdiction under the screening regime applicable at the time, national interests were eventually protected via the cooperation of State-owned actors.

The case of 50Hertz shows that the widening of the scope of FDI regimes does not necessarily imply a higher level of vetoes and/or enforcement, as governments may manage to prevent unwelcome takeovers even in the absence of a specific legal instrument. Conversely, the legal possibility of using a protective legal framework does not mean that it will be used, in practice, to its fullest extent.

Another relevant intervention of the government in 2018 involved the takeover of the engineering company Leifeld, a machine tool maker, by the Chinese firm Yantai: due to the government willingness to intervene, on the basis of protection of national security, the investor withdrew its bid.

In 2020 – before the pandemic – two transactions were vetoed. Both cases involved Chinese firms investing in German companies that employed technologies with potential military applications.

3.2 *COVID Period*

After the start of the COVID pandemic, the German government enacted a series of new regulations that widened the scope of FDI control. However, rather than pandemic-related issues, the key interests protected by the new provisions were matters of national interest because of their impact on the economy, while the defence sector was already among those subjected to stricter scrutiny.

In Q1 2020, Chinese medical supply company Aenomed acquired the operations of German breathing ventilators manufacturer Heyer Medical AG.

Aenomed filed the transaction for clearance after closing under German law, which allows a 'non-objection certificate'. After a prolonged review process, the transaction was prohibited due to security concerns in late April 2022.

In January 2022, the BMWK failed to clear the public takeover of Munich-based company Siltronic AG by the Chinese competitor Global Wafers within 13 months after filing, and thus before the 'long stop date' of the public take-over offer. Consequently, the acquisition failed.

Later in 2022 China's State-owned shipping company COSCO Shipping Port Ltd. targeted the acquisition of 35% of one of Hamburg Port's container terminals.

However, in Q4 2022, the German government authorised the acquisition of only 24.9% of the said terminal, prohibiting the acquisition of any right beyond those related to the 24.9% minority shareholding.

Additionally, in Q4 2022, German authorities blocked the acquisition of German semi-conductor manufacturer Elmos Semiconductor SE by a subsidiary of Chinese electronics company Sai Microelectronics.

Overall, among the blocked acquisitions, the only veto directly connected with the pandemic regarded Heyer Medical AG. In contrast, the other blocked acquisitions had, as their chief national security object concerns, the risk of IP flight in the sensitive areas of defence and semiconductors, i.e., a long-standing objective of FDI scrutiny unrelated to COVID-19.

4 France

The French Government's approach aligns with the traditional dirigiste doctrine, with control on FDI dating back to 1966. However, the enforcement style is quite different from Germany in so far as authorities make an extensive use of 'soft' powers, discouraging unwelcome bids by menacing vetoes and openly exhibiting some degree of hostility. This system can indeed be characterized as a 'dissuasion doctrine', wherein the French government sends a clear message to foreign investors that any attempt to seize the 'crown jewels' of French entrepreneurship is unwelcome and will be blocked. The government emphasizes that it will respond with the full force of the law, even before any concrete steps have taken place, implementing a political pre-emptive deterrent.[16]

16 See the Couche Tard / Carrefour case explained above.

Prior to the COVID-19 pandemic, France's FDI screening system had already been amended and expanded. Notably in 2014,[17] the amendments followed the takeover of Alstom's energy business by US-based giant General Electric, which was met with some consternation by the *hautes spheres*.[18] Further modifications to the screening system were introduced in 2019.[19] The pandemic provided an opportunity to further strengthen the government's scrutiny capabilities, as a temporary regime was introduced to lower the threshold for intervention.[20] The temporary regime is set to expire on 31 December 2023.[21]

In addition to the scarcity of formal vetoes, it is worth noting that the French Government is far more active when it comes to imposing conditions: out of

17 See Décret n° 2014–479 du 14 mai 2014 relatif aux investissements étrangers soumis à autorisation préalable which included energy, water supply, transportation, telecoms, and public health among scrutinised sectors.

18 Alstom, widely regarded as a French key enterprise, has long been the interest of the French government. Notably, it had been previously rescued thanks to public capitals in 2004 by the intervention of the French Ministry of the Finances, then led by Nicolas Sarkozy. It then returned a fully private company in 2006 with the intervention of Bouygues in its capital. The fact that its energy business was sold to GE Electric spurred a heated debate regarding the protection of national strategic companies in 2014, which echoed until recent years. In 2014, French Ministry of the Economy Arnaud Montebourg had prohibited the sale of Alstom's energy business by way of an administrative decree based on Article L151–3 of the French Monetary and Financial Code. However, the decree was overturned later in 2014 by the new Ministry of Economy, Emmanuel Macron, who validated the sale on 4 November 2014. The political conflict on the sale is viewed a clear sign of the fact that it was a contentious issue.

19 Loi n° 2019–486 du 22 mai 2019 relative à la croissance et la transformation des entreprises, the so-called PACTE Law. The PACTE Law reinforced the Ministry of Economy's powers in the case of breach of prior authorisation requirements and was further implemented by Décret n° 2019–1590 du 31 décembre 2019 relatif aux investissements étrangers en France, and the Arrêté du 31 décembre 2019 relatif aux investissements étrangers en France, relating to foreign investments, which, together considered, reformed the French foreign investment control regime. The reform notably aligned the French FDI screening regime the coordination mechanism introduced by the Regulation.

20 The measure has the effect of lowering the threshold for government screening of FDI in companies listed on regulated markets. Specifically, the ordinary threshold is 25% of voting rights, while the emergency threshold is 10% of voting rights. The threshold only refers to non-EU investors. The measure was first adopted in 2020 amid the COVID-19 pandemic and was subsequently extended.

21 The lowered threshold referred to voting rights in French companies referred to in n 20 above were set to expire on 31 December 2022. However, by Décret n° 2022–1622 du 23 décembre 2022 relatif à l'abaissement temporaire du seuil de contrôle des investissements étrangers dans les sociétés françaises dont les actions sont admises aux négociations sur un marché réglementé, the French government further extended the measure until 31 December 2023.

328 transactions notified in 2021, 124 have received formal authorization and 67 have been authorized with conditions. The figure related to notified transactions represents a growth of over 30% with respect to 2020.[22] As another proxy for the French Government's activity, 108 transactions were reported to the European Commission's coordination mechanism between 11 October 2020 and 11 October 2021. These data points underscore the active role of the French government in the EU coordination mechanism under the Regulation.

4.1 *Pre-COVID Period*

An illustrative example of a pre-COVID transaction, French electro-optics manufacturer Photonis was eyed by several US-based companies in late 2019. Photonis was owned by French investment fund Ardian and was considered an essential defence company by the government. Following news of the offers received by Ardian, the government suggested that French defence companies Safran and Thales should buy Photonis instead – but the suggestion was declined. Thus, US engineering and electronics group Teledyne formally entered into negotiations with Ardian for the acquisition of Photonis, which led the Ministry of Economic Affairs to call upon French enterprises to 'roll up their sleeves'.[23] However, the call was not heeded.

Facing the inability to find a French buyer, the government authorised the sale imposing heavy conditions, which were refused by Teledyne. It appeared the deal was off, but, some weeks later, Teledyne came back with a lower offer for Photonis, and agreed to comply with all previously imposed conditions. Still, on 18 December 2020, the French government formally vetoed the transaction, as the conditions were still considered inadequate to ensure the long-term protection of strategic assets.

---

22 As stated in Direction Générale du Trésor 'Le Contrôle des Investissements Étrangers en France en 2021' (2022) 3 <www.tresor.economie.gouv.fr/Articles/5ed9606f-f37e-4517-ae5d-445dab7ecad0/files/68cd8466-0b98-44d2-9182-777b8768cee0> accessed 23 September 2023.

23 Declaration on BFM Business of 4 March 2020 by Minister of Economic Affairs Bruno Le Maire: 'Je sais que c'est difficile, on m'explique toujours que c'est difficile, mais je souhaite que, pas seulement l'Etat, mais que toutes les entreprises industrielles se relèvent les manches pour trouver une solution industrielle française pour reprendre Photonis qui produit du matériel qui équipe l'armée française'. Pascal Samama, 'Photonis: Bruno Le Maire veut Convaincre Thales de Faire une Offre de Reprise' *BFM Business* (4 March 2020) <www.bfmtv.com/economie/entreprises/industries/photonis-bruno-le-maire-veut-convaincre-thales-de-faire-une-offre-de-reprise_AV-202003040286.html> accessed 23 September 2023.

4.2 COVID *Period*

During the COVID period, only one case emerged as worthy of notice. In early 2021, the Canadian supermarket chains operator Couche-Tard made a non-binding offer to buy French supermarket chain Carrefour. However, the French Minister of Economy swiftly expressed disapproval of the offer, reminding Couche-Tard of their power to ban FDI in 'strategic sectors' – which notably include the food supply chain. Couche-Tard took the hint and never followed through with the offer.

Indeed, provisional conclusions can be drawn in the French case. On the one hand, it is likely that the renovated attention to supply chains brought by the pandemic did have an influence in the Government's stance in the Couche-Tard / Carrefour debacle. However, it is important to note that the general trends observed in France regarding FDI scrutiny and government intervention have deeper roots that precede the COVID-19 pandemic.

5 Italy

Italy's FDI screening traces back its origins to the so-called 'Golden Share' power, which granted the Government special powers and influence over a select number of formerly public enterprises through a share in the equity, carrying special powers. However, the Golden Share regime was found not compatible with EU law by the Court of Justice.[24] The decision emphasized the need to uphold the principles of free movement of capital and non-discrimination among EU member states.

As a result, Golden Share mechanisms were abolished by the Italian legislator via Law-Decree No. 21 of 15 March 2012, which introduced a general FDI screening regime known as 'Golden Power'. Its scope was subsequently expanded multiple times with the insurgence of the pandemic and to meet the obligations under the Regulation.[25] Moreover, several other implementing

24 The 'Golden Share' was not a unified FDI screening regime, but rather a multitude of single provisions in laws and corporate bylaws, which generated several court cases both domestically and at EU level. Among the latter, the most significant rulings by the Court of Justice are the Judgment of the Court of 23 May 2000, in Case C-58/99 *Commission v. Italy* [2000] ECR I-03811, and Judgment of the Court of 26 March 2009, in Case C-326/07 *Commission v. Italy* [2009] ECR I-02291.

25 Among the most relevant modifications: Decreto legge 16 ottobre 2017, n 148, converted into Legge 4 dicembre 2017, n 172, extended FDI rules to the high-tech sector; Decreto legge 25 marzo 2019, n 22, converted into Legge 20 maggio 2019, n 41, extended FDI screening to certain transactions in the 5G sector; Decreto legge 16 ottobre 2019, n 105, converted

regulations were also published, in the form of either a Decree of the President of the Republic or a Decree of the President of the Council of Ministers, to discipline procedural aspects and, among others, to clarify scrutinised sectors and the notion of strategic assets.[26]

A distinct feature of the amendments carried out during the pandemic was a 'temporary regime' (which expired on 31 December 2022), under which acquisitions in sensitive sectors were subject to scrutiny, even in case the purchaser was EU-based.[27] Not surprisingly, the number of notifications went

---

into Legge 18 novembre 2019, n 133, extended FDI screening to all sectors mentioned by article 4, paragraph 1, of EU Regulation 2019/452 (by the insertion of new article 2, paragraph 1-*ter* in Decreto legge 15 marzo 2012, n 21), subject to the adoption of implementing decrees (pending the adoption of these implementing decrees, the pre-existing implementing decrees continued to apply); Decreto legge 8 aprile 2020, n 23 (known as the Liquidity Decree), converted into Legge 5 giugno 2020, n 40, introduced a temporary regime in the context of the COVID-19 outbreak; article 10-ter of Decreto legge 28 ottobre 2020, n 137, converted into Legge 18 dicembre 2020, n 176, which extended the application of the temporary regime until 30 June 2021; article 11-quinquies of Decreto legge 22 aprile 2021, n 52, converted into Legge 17 giugno 2021, n 87, which extended the application of the temporary regime until 31 December 2021; article 17 of Decreto legge 30 dicembre 2021, n 228, converted into Legge 25 febbraio 2022, n 15, which extended the application of the temporary regime until 31 December 2022; and Decreto legge 21 marzo 2022, n 21, converted into Legge 20 maggio 2022 n 51, which introduced the obligation to jointly notify transactions, amended government powers in 5G and broadband, and expanded the scope of the FDI control, which now permanently captures: purely national and intra-EU transactions in specified sectors, and; greenfield investments and the setup of new companies in specified sectors.

26 Among which, Decreto del Presidente della Repubblica 19 febbraio 2014, n 35, on the procedural rules in the military and defence sectors; Decreto del Presidente della Repubblica 25 marzo 2014, n 86, on the procedural rules in the energy, transportation, and communication sectors; Decreto del Presidente del Consiglio dei ministri 6 giugno 2014, n 108, setting out the relevant strategic assets in the military and defence sectors; Decreto del Presidente del Consiglio dei ministri 6 agosto 2014, n, on the organisation of the activities related to the exercise of the special powers; Decreto del Presidente del Consiglio dei ministri 18 dicembre 2020, n 179, setting out the relevant strategic assets in the sectors listed in article 4 of EU Regulation 2019/452; Decreto del Presidente del Consiglio dei ministri 23 dicembre 2020, n 180, setting out the relevant strategic assets in the energy, transportation and communication sectors; and Decreto del Presidente del Consiglio dei ministri 1 agosto 2022, n 133, introducing the prenotification procedure and setting out the organisation of the administrative activities related to the exercise of special powers.

27 Decreto legge 8 aprile 2020, n 23 (n 25) introduced a temporary regime in the context of the COVID-19 outbreak by amending Decreto legge 16 ottobre 2019, n 105 (n 25) with the introduction of article 2-*ter*, paragraphs 3-*bis* and 3-*quater*. The temporary regime expired on 31 December 2022 and was not renewed. Pursuant to the described law provisions, *inter alia*, all foreign purchases in companies operating in specified sectors (i.e., those described in Article 2, paragraphs 1, 2 and 5, of Decreto legge 15 marzo 2012, n 21, and those

from an average of less than 40 per year between 2014 and 2019 to over 500 in 2022 alone, reflecting the increased scrutiny and monitoring of FDI during the temporary regime period.

5.1 *Pre-COVID Period*

As noted, the pre-COVID period had already seen a gradual expansion of FDI screening in Italy, with the insertion of new scrutinised sectors and the setting of screening procedures. However, the number of Golden Power notifications was quite low overall, starting with only 8 notifications in 2014 and averaging around 40 notifications per year between 2014 and 2019.

In addition, before COVID, only one transaction was vetoed by the Italian Government – namely, the acquisition of defence engineering system provider Next AST S.r.l. by Altran Italia S.p.A., the Italian subsidiary of France-based Altran group (now named Capgemini Engineering) in 2017. By contrast, several transactions had seen the imposition of conditions, notably in the sectors of telecommunications (the TIM-Vivendi transaction and transactions connected with 5G equipment) and defence (especially as regards aerospace, avionics, and robotics).

5.2 *COVID Period*

The COVID-related emergency, together with the Communication's push to enforce FDI and a heightened awareness of geopolitical factors, especially in relation to the deployment of 5G infrastructure on the national territory, spurred the Italian legislator to take immediate action to close enforcement gaps.

Most notably, the Italian government drafted a long-awaited list of scrutinised sectors in December 2020,[28] which, among others, aligned national law with the Regulation. In line with other regimes, while the sectors are listed and the relevant concepts are defined, the definitions are generic and leave ample room for interpretation, which leads to the exercise of caution in the assessment of transactions. As a result, FDI filings increased manifold.

The legislative reforms enacted in the COVID period did entail the vetoing and the imposition of conditions in more transactions, compared to the

recalled in the implementing decrees published pursuant to Article 2, paragraph 1-*ter*, of Decreto legge 15 marzo 2012, n 21) were subject to prior notification, regardless of the nationality of the purchaser.

28 Pursuant to Decreto del Presidente del Consiglio dei ministri 18 dicembre 2020, n 179, and Decreto del Presidente del Consiglio dei ministri 23 dicembre 2020, n 180.

pre-COVID era. Still, as argued infra, the higher level of enforcement activity is not strictly related to COVID but is rather an evolution of pre-existing trends.

In October 2020 the Italian government exercised its veto to block the purchase of 5G components from Huawei Technologies by telecommunication provider Fastweb S.p.A. This decision highlighted concerns over security and potential risks associated with the use of Huawei's equipment in critical infrastructure.

Throughout 2021, three major transactions were vetoed, namely the acquisition of global seed production company Verisem by seed giant Syngenta, and the acquisition of Italian solar cell manufacturer Applied Materials Italia S.r.l. by China-based entities Zhejiang Kesheng Intelligent Equipment Company Limited and Zhejiang Jingsheng Mechanical & Electrical.

The veto on the acquisition of drone manufacturer Alpi Aviation S.r.l. by Chinese entity Mars (HK) Information Technology Co. Limited is also relevant as it concerns a transaction from July 2018 that was only notified in late 2021, after the proceedings for the imposition of the sanction were started.

The year 2022 saw a sustained level of activity, mainly concerning the semiconductor sector and robotics.

Three transactions were blocked in said sectors, all concerning the acquisition of Italian companies by Chinese actors. Furthermore, Russian investments became a matter of concern, and, consequently, the Italian government blocked the attempt by Rosatom to acquire Italian company Faber Industrie, which has hydrogen as its core business.

In 2023, the Italian government vetoed the acquisition of Italian company Tecnologia Intelligente S.r.l. by the Netherlands-based Nebius, due to concerns of proximity between Nebius and Russia, as Nebius was founded by Russian technology giant Yandex.

Based on the information provided, it can be observed that while the Syngenta/Verisem transaction may have COVID-related implications for reasons of security of the food supply chain, the other vetoes do not appear to be directly COVID-related. Instead, they focus on areas such as semi-conductors, 5G, and traditional areas of defence and energy. This suggests that the Italian government's scrutiny and vetoes in these cases were driven by broader strategic and security concerns rather than solely influenced by the COVID-19 pandemic.

6 Concluding Remarks

An increase in FDI screening took place at the same time as the COVID pandemic. However, data from three key jurisdictions show that the trend towards a more proactive approach by EU Governments was already in place before the pandemic.

In fact, the key factor for the increase in scrutiny can be traced back to heightened geopolitical tensions and a deeper awareness of the impossibility to replace essential assets.

While the pandemic surely helped to prove the importance of national control over supply chains and was arguably a triggering factor for a temporary tightening of control, previous FDI screening practice and the Regulation signal that EU Member States have long had the desire to inspect FDI. Furthermore, it is also arguable that FDI screening is only part of the mechanisms devised to limit foreign influence on the internal market, as proven by the Foreign Subsidies Regulation, which is conceptually not linked to the pandemic.

Thus, the increase in FDI screening is somewhat independent from the COVID pandemic, its impact having been somewhat exaggerated.

This finding implies that, once the pandemic has gone, one should expect significant FDI enforcement to continue. In other words, it indicates that an increased level of scrutiny by national authorities in monitoring and regulating foreign investments has become the new normal.

CHAPTER 7

Full Protection and Security and the COVID-19 Pandemic

Sebastián Mantilla Blanco

1 Introduction

The COVID-19 pandemic has been the single most disruptive event in the world for generations, affecting the life of virtually all inhabitants of the planet and every sector of the economy.[1] Legal issues around the pandemic transcend domestic law and reach into most areas of international law, including international investment law.[2] In 2021, French airport concessionaries announced their intention to file an investment arbitration claim against Chile regarding the decline in the number of passengers during the pandemic.[3] In Peru, the suspension of highway tolls during the pandemic without compensation for concessionaries triggered fears of arbitration claims.[4] The COVID-19 years have shown that pandemics are scenarios of potential legal conflict between investors and host states.

1 See generally Doron Teichman, 'Law, Economics, and Compliance in the Times of COVID-19: A Behavioural Perspective' in Klaus Mathis and Avishalom Tor (eds), *Law and Economics of the Coronavirus Crisis* (Springer 2022) 3; Christopher Buttigieg and Gerd Sapiano, 'The COVID-19 Pandemic: A Regulatory Perspective' in Gavin Barrett and others (eds), *The Future of Legal Europe: Will We Trust in It?* (Springer 2021) 81.

2 See generally Charles Jalloh, 'Pandemics and International Law' (2021) 36(5) Am U Intl L Rev 979.

3 Lisa Bohmer, 'Chile is Put on Notice of Treaty-Based Airport Concession Dispute' (20 January 2021) IAReporter <www.iareporter.com/articles/chile-is-put-on-notice-of-treaty-based-airport-concession-dispute/> accessed 14 January 2023.

4 Cf. Lisa Bohmer, 'Updated: Highway Concessionaire Initiates Contract-Based ICSID Arbitration Against Peru' (11 June 2021) IAReporter <www.iareporter.com/articles/highway-concessionaire-initiates-contract-based-icsid-arbitration-against-peru/> accessed 14 January 2023; IAReporter, 'Second Highway Concessionaire Lodges Contract-Based ICSID Arbitration Against Peru' (24 September 2021) IAReporter <www.iareporter.com/articles/second-highway-concessionaire-lodges-contract-based-icsid-arbitration-against-peru/> accessed 14 January 2023. The suspension was introduced by an act of Congress: Ley No. 31018 (09.05.2020). This law was eventually found to be unconstitutional: *Sentencia 359/2020*, 25 August 2021, Exp. No. 0006-2020-PI (Constitutional Tribunal of Peru). There is, however, no clarity on the specifics of pending claims and their actual relation to the pandemic.

© KONINKLIJKE BRILL BV, LEIDEN, 2025 | DOI:10.1163/9789004711204_009

International investment law provides standards of conduct for state authorities in their relation to individuals and corporations.[5] In this sense, it has been described as a form of 'global administrative law'.[6] Just as measures adopted in response to the pandemic gave rise to administrative law and constitutional law disputes at the domestic level, they could also prompt claims concerning alleged breaches of international standards of investment protection. Future cases will showcase the tension and interplay between public health and investors' private interests.[7] These claims will likely include alleged breaches of the guarantee of 'full protection and security' (FPS) under investment treaties and customary law, which embodies an obligation to exercise due diligence in the protection of investments.[8] This chapter considers the potential application of the FPS standard in connection with COVID-related measures.[9]

The argument has been divided in four parts. Following this introduction (section 1), section 2 discusses the extent to which the COVID-19 pandemic fits into the categories of risk covered by the FPS standard. Section 3 considers the scrutiny of the state's reaction to the pandemic through the prism of due diligence. Finally, section 4 draws a general conclusion.

2 Pandemic Risks and the Scope of Application of the Standard of 'Full Protection and Security'

Prospective FPS claims about measures adopted in response to the COVID-19 pandemic raise the preliminary question, whether the FPS standard covers the risks involved. This question is intertwined with the definition of the scope of the FPS obligation, a most contentious subject dominated by inconsistent

5 Gus Van Harten and Martin Loughlin, 'Investment Treaty Arbitration as a Species of Global Administrative Law' (2006) 17(1) EJIL 121, 127.

6 ibid.

7 See generally Freya Baetens, 'Protecting Foreign Investment and Public Health Through Arbitral Balancing and Treaty Design' (2022) 71(1) ICLQ 139.

8 On due diligence see section 3 below.

9 The author has already addressed the 'full protection and security' standard elsewhere: Sebastián Mantilla Blanco, *Full Protection and Security in International Investment Law* (Springer 2019); Sebastián Mantilla Blanco, 'Full Protection and Security and the Rule of Law' in August Reinisch and Stephan Schill (eds), *Investment Protection Standards and the Rule of Law* (OUP 2023) 81ff. This chapter mirrors the arguments of these previous works, to the extent they are useful for the application of the FPS standard in pandemic-related investment claims.

arbitral practice.[10] Relevant arbitral decisions can be classified in three groups.[11]

In a first group of cases, tribunals have interpreted the FPS standard as a general guarantee of security, without defining the specific risks covered by the standard.[12] The broadness of this approach facilitates the application of the FPS standard to measures involving changes in the regulatory framework of foreign investments introduced in response to the Coronavirus pandemic. However, it also creates significant overlaps with other treaty-based standards, such as fair and equitable treatment (FET), at the risk of reducing substantive treaty provisions to redundancy.[13] This outcome runs against the *effet utile* principle of treaty interpretation.[14] For this reason, in the absence of express wording giving a wider meaning to the security obligation,[15] adjudicators should – and normally will – avoid the broad approach.

The second group of decisions define the FPS standard in terms of 'protection from physical harm'.[16] This approach comes at odds with the definitions of 'investment' in most investment agreements, which typically include non-physical assets.[17] Notwithstanding this objection, the physical security criterion is widespread and has found expression in recent treaties defining the FPS obligation in terms of 'physical protection'.[18] Under this approach, successful FPS claims related to the pandemic will require proof of physical damage.[19] There might be scenarios where the pandemic unleashed events that posed physical risks to the investment (e.g. protests and riots against COVID-related

10 See generally Mantilla Blanco, *Full Protection and Security* (n 9) 9ff, 145ff.

11 For a critical analysis of these approaches see ibid 206ff., 269ff. See also Mantilla Blanco, 'Full Protection and Security and the Rule of Law' (n 9) 84ff.

12 For example, *Global Telecom v. Canada*, ICSID Case No. ARB/16/16, Award (27 March 2020) para 664.

13 *Infinito Gold Ltd. v. Costa Rica*, ICSID Case No. ARB/14/5, Award (03 June 2021) para 623.

14 *Crystallex International Corp. v. Venezuela*, ICSID Case No. ARB(AF)/11/2, Award (04 April 2016) para 634.

15 For example, *Convial Callao et al. v. Peru*, ICSID Case No. ARB/10/2, Award (21 May 2013) para 642 (noting that article 4.1 of the Argentina-Peru BIT referred to 'legal security').

16 *Gold Reserve v. Venezuela*, ICSID Case No. ARB(AF)/09/1, Award (22 September 2014) paras 622ff. See also *Eurus Energy v. Spain*, ICSID Case No. ARB/16/4, Decision on Jurisdiction and Liability (17 March 2021) paras 385–386.

17 For example, Canada-Venezuela BIT (adopted 01 July 1996, entered into force 28 January 1998) art 1(f) (definition of "investment"). For a classic example of this argument see *National Grid P.L.C. v. Argentina*, UNCITRAL, Award (3 November 2008) para 187.

18 Hong Kong-United Arab Emirates BIT (adopted 16 June 2019, entered into force 06 March 2020) art 3(4)(b).

19 Cf. for example, *BayWa r.e. et al. v. Spain*, ICSID Case No. ARB/15/16, Decision on Jurisdiction, Liability and Directions on Quantum (02 December 2019) para 531 (without specific reference to pandemics).

measures), giving rise to claims that squarely fit into the notion of physical security.[20]

Potential allegations of insufficient protection against the pandemic as such are more intricate. Numerous investment treaties guarantee FPS to the *investment*.[21] The COVID-19 pandemic certainly had an economic effect over investments, but rarely posed a direct threat of physical harm to the invested assets as such. By contrast, some FPS clauses extend security and protection to both *investments* and *investors*.[22] This language arguably opens the door for the application of the FPS standard in factual settings where the COVID-19 pandemic posed risks to the life and integrity of natural persons who qualify as investors under the treaty.

The third approach defines the standard as an obligation to prevent and redress injuries that originate in a source of risk other than conduct of the host state.[23] It departs from the observation that FPS claims are archetypically about the reaction of the host state against some external risk (e.g. insurgent acts or ordinary private offences).[24] While this approach remains a minority view in academic literature, it has gained increasing acceptance in arbitral practice.[25] The third-party approach is the one that best crystallizes the customary core of the FPS standard.[26] References to the exercise of due diligence in the protection of aliens have traditionally appeared in cases where the immediate cause

---

20 On the raise of protests and riots as a corollary of the pandemic see Koen van der Zwet, 'Emergence of Protests During the COVID-19 Pandemic' (2022) 9(68) Humanit Soc Sci Commun. 1ff.

21 See, for example, Agreement between the United States of America, the United Mexican States, and Canada (USMCA) (signed 30 November 2018, entered into force 01 July 2020) art 14.6(1).

22 EU-Canada Comprehensive Economic and Trade Agreement (adopted 30 October 2016, provisionally in force 21 September 2017) (CETA) art 8.10(5). See also EU-Chile Advanced Framework Agreement (signed 13 December 2023) arts 17.17(1), 17.17(4).

23 For example, *Mobil Exploration et al. v. Argentina*, ICSID Case No. ARB/04/16, Decision on Jurisdiction and Liability (10 April 2013) para 999; *Oxus Gold v. Uzbekistan*, UNCITRAL, Award (17 December 2015) para 354. See also (n 25) below.

24 *Ampal-American Israel Corp. et al. v. Egypt*, ICSID Case No. ARB/12/11, Decision on Liability and Heads of Loss (21 February 2017) paras 245–246, 254, 288.

25 For example, *El Paso Energy v. Argentina*, ICSID Case No. ARB/03/15, Award (31 October 2011) para 522; *Mercer International v. Canada*, ICSID Case No. ARB(AF)/12/3, Award (06 March 2018) para 7.80. See also the analysis of the tribunal in *Hydro Energy 1 et al. v. Spain*, ICSID Case No. ARB/15/42, Decision on Jurisdiction, Liability and Directions on Quantum (09 March 2020) paras 560ff, 566. Some tribunals have limited FPS to *physical* security against *third-party* offences. See *Infinito Gold Ltd. v. Costa Rica*, ICSID Case No. ARB/14/5, Award (03 June 2021) para 623.

26 Mantilla Blanco, 'Full Protection and Security and the Rule of Law' (n 9) 88ff.

of the injury to a foreign citizen was not an act of the host state, but of a third party, so that state responsibility was established on account of an *omission* in the prevention and redress of such injury.[27] In the context of COVID-related claims, the third-party approach leads to a twofold distinction.

On the one hand, claims related to the pandemic might coincide with traditional areas of application of the FPS standard. Wants of diligence in the protection of the investment from pandemic-related riot violence provide a textbook example of this scenario. Private violence falls within the scope of the FPS standard, regardless of the role of the pandemic in the chain of events. On the other hand, tribunals following the third-party approach will likely face the question, whether the pandemic itself triggered the FPS obligation. Pandemics are different from risks conventionally falling within the FPS standard in that they originate in nature rather than human conduct, albeit human behaviour arguably influences their spread and damaging effects.[28] International law already recognises the existence of prevention obligations for the protection of persons from natural hazards.[29] In a 2014 report, the International Law Association placed 'natural disasters' within the FPS obligation.[30] Arbitral practice in this area remains however scarce. The investor in *Allard v. Barbados* submitted an FPS claim related to the deterioration of assets due to pollution,[31] but the Tribunal missed the opportunity to address the issue.[32]

Analogical deduction provides a suitable vehicle to overcome this paucity of sources.[33] Hazards caused by nature resemble mob injuries, revolutionary damages, and other traditional areas of application of the FPS standard, in that the source of the injury is different from the host state's conduct.[34] The FPS

27 See the discussion and examples in Mantilla Blanco, *Full Protection and Security* (n 9) 207ff.

28 The author has already addressed the application of the FPS standard in respect of natural hazards elsewhere: ibid 263ff. (advancing a similar argument and discussing the sources below).

29 ILC, 'Draft Articles on the Protection of Persons in the Event of Disasters' (2016) UN Doc A/71/10, art 10(1).

30 ILA Study Group on Due Diligence in International Law, 'First Report' (07 March 2014) 9. See also Jeswald Salacuse, *The Law of Investment Treaties* (3rd edn, OUP 2021) 444.

31 *Peter A. Allard v. Barbados*, UNCITRAL, Award (27 June 2016) para 231.

32 ibid para 252. On the *Allard* case see also Gian Maria Farnelli, 'Investors as Environmental Guardians? On Climate Change Policy Objectives and Compliance with Investment Agreements' (2022) 23 JWIT 887, 907–908.

33 On resort to analogical deduction for identifying customary international law see Stefan Talmon, 'Determining Customary International Law' (2015) 26(2) EJIL 417, 426ff.

34 See Mantilla Blanco, *Full Protection and Security* (n 9) 267, 612.

standard refers to the host state's reaction against external sources of risk.[35] Pandemic-related hazards are such external risks. Responsibility can therefore be established on account of a state's omission in the prevention or redress of a pandemic-related injury that did not directly originate in acts attributable to host authorities.

3 Due Diligence and the Application of the FPS Standard to Pandemic-Related Claims

Sources generally coincide in defining the content of the FPS standard in terms of due diligence.[36] This notion falls within the formal category of 'standards', i.e., 'legally defined measures of conduct, to be applied by or under the discretion of the tribunal'.[37] Due diligence is not an abstract rule susceptible of syllogistic application but a flexible yardstick for evaluating relevant state conduct.[38] Two key features of due diligence will gain prominence in pandemic-related FPS claims: the objective character of due diligence (3.1) and the need to consider scientific evidence in the assessment of the host state's diligence (3.2).

3.1 *The Objective Character of Due Diligence and Non-discrimination*

States all around the globe adopted unprecedented measures to respond to the Coronavirus pandemic. Lockdowns, limits or bans on public gatherings, constraints on the use of workplace facilities, among others, were at the order of the day.[39] Measures did not typically include distinctions based on nationality, with some important exceptions, such as travel bans.[40] Host states could hence reasonably argue that their response to the pandemic imposed similar burdens on foreigners and nationals, and granted similar protection to both groups. Non-discrimination will, however, have only a very limited effect in the assessment of alleged breaches of the FPS obligation.

---

35 ibid.

36 ibid 327ff.

37 Roscoe Pound, 'The Administrative Application of Legal Standards' (1919) 42 Annu Rep ABA 445, 456.

38 See generally Mantilla Blanco, *Full Protection and Security* (n 9) 456–457.

39 For an overview see Alessandra Asteriti, 'State Measures in Response to the COVID-19 Pandemic', in Yulia Levashova and Pascale Accaoui Lorfing (eds), *Balancing the Protection of Foreign Investors and States Responses in the Post- Pandemic World* (Kluwer 2022) 7, 13ff.

40 See ibid. See also OECD, *International Migration Outlook* (OECD 2022) 69.

The reason is that the FPS standard is one of the key components of the customary international minimum standard of treatment.[41] In turn, the minimum standard is quintessentially a universal bottom line for the treatment of aliens, which is independent from the treatment that the host state accords to its own citizens.[42] In the *Roberts v. Mexico* case of 1926, the US-Mexico General Claims Commission held that 'equality [between citizens and aliens] is not the ultimate test of the propriety of the acts of authorities in the light of international law'.[43] In 1945, Hersch Lauterpacht observed that the 'paradoxical' implication of the minimum standard is that the host state could owe a greater degree of protection to foreigners than to its own nationals.[44] This feature of the minimum standard suggests that the diligence required of a state under the FPS standard cannot be reduced to a subjective standard similar to the private law notion of *diligentia quam in suis rebus* (the diligence displayed in one's own affairs), which in this case would be equivalent to the diligence displayed in the protection of the host state's own domestic investors.[45]

The diligence required under the FPS standard, as an element of said minimum standard, must necessarily be an objective yardstick.[46] This gauge is not blind to the specific circumstances faced by the host state.[47] Arbitral tribunals have understood due diligence as a 'modified objective standard' which is sensitive to the resources available to the host state.[48] This standard of diligence specifically allows taking into consideration the level of development of the host state.[49] The modified standard remains objective, as it measures the acts of domestic authorities against the reaction that could be expected from a diligent average state with similar resources and in similar circumstances as those of the host state.[50] In deciding on the occurrence of an FPS breach, arbitral tribunals must consider the extraordinary challenges states faced during the

41 See, for example, the formulation of FPS in the USMCA (n 21) art 14.6.

42 Elihu Root, 'The Basis of Protection of Citizens Residing Abroad' (1910) 4(3) AJIL 517, 522; *Al Tamini v. Oman*, ICSID Case No. ARB/11/33, Award (03 November 2015) paras 382ff.

43 *Harry Roberts v. Mexico* (02 November 1926) IV RIAA 77, 80 para 8.

44 Hersch Lauterpacht, *An International Bill of the Rights of Man* (Columbia University Press 1945) 48.

45 Mantilla Blanco, *Full Protection and Security* (n 9) 435f.

46 For example, *Naturgy Energy et al. v. Colombia*, ICSID Case No. UNCT/18/1, Award (12 March 2021) para 563.

47 See generally Mantilla Blanco, *Full Protection and Security* (n 9) 449ff.

48 *Pantechniki v. Albania*, ICSID Case No. ARB/07/21, Award (30 July 2009) paras 81–82.

49 See, for example, the analysis in *(DS)2, S.A., Peter de Sutter et al. v. Madagascar II*, ICSID Case No. ARB/17/18, Award (17 April 2020) para 310.

50 See *Strabag SE v. Libya*, ICSID Case No ARB(AF)/15/1, Award (29 June 2020) para 234 (referring to the circumstances of Libya during the Arab spring).

pandemic. This holds true for cases about both prevention and redress of injuries to aliens.[51] Thus, alleged delays or deficiencies in the administration of justice could be justified on the extraordinary circumstances created by the pandemic, such as the need to implement virtual proceedings.[52]

Specific FPS clauses may however deviate from the customary core of the standard and create a subjective guarantee of protection. For example, Article 8(2) of the Colombia-Spain BIT of 2021 provides that '[t]he physical full protection and security encompasses, in any case, no greater police efforts than those granted to the inhabitants of the Contracting Party hosting the Investment or to the Investors and Investments of third countries in similar circumstances'.[53] In the absence of clear and unambiguous language reducing the FPS standard to non-discrimination, absence of discriminatory treatment of domestic and foreign investors will not suffice to exclude a breach of the FPS standard.[54] Still, unjustified differential treatment could be considered as a *factual* circumstance in the analysis of due diligence.[55] Discrimination reveals risk awareness, the ability to react against a threat, and unwillingness to provide foreign investors the protection that was readily extended to domestic investors.[56] In *De Sutter v. Madagscar II* (2020), the Tribunal recognised that the differences in the protection of nationals and foreigners is an 'indicator' of unreasonable state conduct.[57]

3.2 *Scientific Evidence in the Context of FPS Claims*

The FPS standard embodies an obligation to exercise due diligence.[58] The yardstick of diligence involves the evaluation of questions of fact,[59] including the foreseeability of risks or actual knowledge about the risk,[60] the investors' own

51 On the redress aspect see *Electrabel S.A. v. Hungary*, ICSID Case No. ARB/07/19, Decision on Jurisdiction, Applicable Law and Liability (30 November 2012) para 7.146.

52 See the analysis in *Vannessa Ventures v. Venezuela*, ICSID Case No. ARB(AF)04/6, Award (16 January 2013) para 227 (addressing delays in justice administration, without specific reference to pandemics).

53 Original in Spanish. Colombia-Spain BIT (signed 16 September 2021, not in force) art 8(2). Other Colombian treaties reduce the scope of the FPS standard to national treatment and inconsistently characterize it as an element of the minimum standard. See e.g. Colombia-Turkey BIT (signed 28 July 2014, not in force) arts 4(1), 4(6); Colombia-UAE BIT (signed 12 November 2017, not in force) arts 5(1), 5(4).

54 See, for example, the analysis in *(DS)2, S.A., Peter de Sutter et al.* (n 49) paras 306ff.

55 Mantilla Blanco, *Full Protection and Security* (n 9) 477–478.

56 ibid.

57 *(DS)2, S.A., Peter de Sutter et al.* (n 49) para 308.

58 For example, *Mobil Exploration et al. v. Argentina*, ICSID Case No. ARB/04/16, Decision on Jurisdiction and Liability (10 April 2013) para 999.

59 Mantilla Blanco, *Full Protection and Security* (n 9) 456ff. (discussing the relevant factors).

60 *MNSS et al. v. Montenegro*, ICSID Case No. ARB (AF)/12/8, Award (04 May 2016) paras 354ff.

conduct and decisions,[61] compliance with applicable provisions of domestic law,[62] and the host state's need to pursue 'reasonable public policy goals'.[63] In the specific context of COVID-related claims, many of these factors will be intrinsically intertwined with science. State behaviour in the context of the global pandemic cannot be dissociated from the initial absence of reliable information about the nature of the virus and the manner how it spreads, the evolution of scientific knowledge about the virus, and the invention of the first COVID-19 vaccines. FPS claims about the pandemic will likely revolve around the objectiveness of risk assessment, the actual use of available scientific evidence, and consistency of policies on sanitary precaution.

This interplay between scientific evidence, rationality of state action, and due diligence, is not new in investment arbitration. In *Allard v. Barbados*, the Tribunal considered an FPS claim related to the alleged failure of Barbadian authorities to take certain measures, including the enforcement of their own laws, for the prevention of entry of contaminants into a bird sanctuary owned by the investor.[64] The Tribunal acknowledged that 'consideration of a host state's international obligations may well be relevant in the application of the [FPS] standard to particular circumstances'.[65] The arbitrators considered the specific steps taken by local authorities to prevent environmental hazards, considering hydrogeological studies and scientific data.[66] The Tribunal found that '[i]t was therefore no easy issue to establish the hydrology of the whole area and to administer it in the interests of all the stakeholders'.[67] The Tribunal concluded that, under the FPS standard, 'a host [s]tate is not required to take any specific steps that an investor asks of it' because '[t]he obligation is limited to reasonable action'.[68] The acts of local authorities were part of Barbados' 'governance of the entire area' as well as 'appropriate and sufficient for purposes of the duty of due diligence'.[69]

---

61 *PACC v. Mexico*, ICSID Case No. UNCT/18/5, Decision on Claimant Application for Additional Award (09 May 2022) para 50.

62 *Marion Unglaube et al. v. Costa Rica*, ICSID Cases No. ARB/01/1, ARB/09/20, Award (16 May 2012) para 286.

63 *AES Summit Generation et al. v. Hungary*, ICSID Case No. ARB/07/22, Award (23 September 2010) para 13.3.2.

64 *Peter Allard v. Barbados* (UNCITRAL), Award (27 June 2016) paras 244ff.

65 ibid para 244.

66 ibid paras 245ff.

67 ibid para 248.

68 ibid para 244.

69 ibid para 249.

Arbitral practice about the use of scientific evidence in the assessment of FPS claims remains, however, rather scant. Still, these questions are not unchartered territory in international economic law. They resemble the evaluation of sanitary and phytosanitary measures (SPS) under the law of the World Trade Organization (WTO) and, specifically, the Agreement on the Application of Sanitary and Phytosanitary Measures (SPS Agreement).

The SPS Agreement covers, among others, measures applied 'to protect human life or health [...] from the entry, establishment or spread of pests'[70] and 'to prevent or limit other damage within the territory of the Member from the entry, establishment or spread of pests'.[71] It requires that any SPS measure 'is based on scientific principles and is not maintained without sufficient scientific evidence'.[72] SPS measures may be either based on international standards, conform to international standards, or entail a higher degree of sanitary protection, in which case there is an obligation to conduct an objective risk assessment.[73]

In their interpretation and application of these rules, WTO panels and the Appellate Body have delivered a large body of adjudicatory practice regarding health measures.[74] While this practice refers to the carefully negotiated terms of the SPS Agreement, it could provide guidance to investment tribunals tasked with the evaluation of governmental responses to the COVID-19 pandemic. Investment tribunals have resorted to WTO law, for example, in the assessment of the national treatment obligation under investment agreements.[75] Particular cases may call for a specific 'mix of specializations' and hence open the door for a holistic analysis across different sub-disciplines of international economic law.[76] The argument has been made that '[t]he quality of the WTO Appellate Body's jurisprudence in cases involving competing public values (health and the environment vs. free trade, for instance) may in part

70 Agreement on the Application of Sanitary and Phytosanitary Measures (adopted 15 April 1994, entered into force 1 January 1995) 1867 UNTS 493 (SPS Agreement) Annex A, 1(c).

71 ibid Annex A, 1(d).

72 ibid art 2.2.

73 ibid arts 3.1, 3.2, 3.3, 5.1, 5.2. On the general structure of the SPS Agreement and these alternatives see Peter van den Bossche and Denise Prévost, *Essentials of WTO Law* (2nd edn, CUP 2021) 182ff., particularly at 187.

74 For an overview see Lucasz Gruszczynski, *Regulating Health and Environmental Risks under WTO Law* (OUP 2011) 107ff; Mitsuo Matsushita and others, *The World Trade Organization* (3rd edn, OUP 2015) 464ff.

75 See the critical discussion of this practice in Jürgen Kurtz, 'The Use and Abuse of WTO Law in Investor–State Arbitration' (2009) 20(3) EJIL 749.

76 Robert Howse and Efraim Chalamish, 'The Use and Abuse of WTO Law in Investor-State Arbitration: A Reply to Jürgen Kurtz' (2009) 20(4) EJIL 1087, 1094.

be attributable to a broader public international law outlook of a number of its members'.[77] There are two key avenues for an integrative analysis.[78]

At least in cases where both the home and the host state are Members of the WTO, investment tribunals could arguably consider the SPS Agreement as providing 'relevant rules of international law applicable in the relations between the parties' within the meaning of Article 31(3)(c) VCLT.[79] It has been observed, however, that rules pertaining to horizontal inter-state relations cannot always be easily transferred into the vertical framework of investor-state relations.[80] Moreover, the SPS Agreement is only applicable to measures that fit into the definition of 'SPS Measure' under Annex A of the SPS Agreement and 'affect international trade', either directly or indirectly.[81] Measures challenged in investor-state arbitration will not always fit into this definition. This could raise doubts as to whether the SPS Agreement contains rules 'relevant' and 'applicable' for the purposes of Article 31(3)(c) VCLT.[82]

The second possible approach is to use the rules of the SPS Agreement through 'intradisciplinary analogies',[83] a notion coined to describe 'analogies [that] are drawn with other areas of international law'.[84] Reference to external legal rules does not necessarily operate through the vehicle of Article 31(3)(c) VCLT and 'as a matter of law'.[85] Adjudicators may merely recognise that 'textual or functional similarities between these fields [e.g. trade and investment] make it instructive to draw comparisons when resolving difficult issues'.[86]

Either through the principle of systemic integration or through an intradisciplinary analogy, as may appear proper for the case, WTO reports about

77 ibid.

78 See generally Anthea Roberts, 'Clash of Paradigms: Actors and Analogies Shaping the Investment Treaty System' (2013) 107 AJIL 45, 51–52.

79 Vienna Convention on the Law of Treaties (signed 23 May 1969, entered into force 27 January 1980) 1155 UNTS 331 (VCLT), art 31(3)(c). On the use of the principle of systemic integration in international investment law see generally Daniel Rosentreter, *Article 31(3)(c) of the Vienna Convention on the Law of Treaties and the Principle of Systemic Integration in International Investment Law and Arbitration* (Nomos 2015) 283ff. See particularly the discussion of trade law at 341ff.

80 Roberts (n 78) 51.

81 SPS Agreement (n 70) art 1(1), Annex A.

82 On the requirements for the application of Article 31(3)(c) VCLT see Mark Villiger, *Commentary on the 1969 Vienna Convention on the Law of Treaties* (Martinus Nijhoff 2009) 433ff; Oliver Dörr, 'Article 31' in Oliver Dörr and Kirsten Schmalenbach (eds), *Vienna Convention on the Law of Treaties: A Commentary* (2nd edn, Springer 2018) 559, 604ff.

83 Roberts (n 78) 52.

84 ibid.

85 ibid 51.

86 ibid.

the SPS Agreement could offer valuable orientation to investment arbitrators. In reference to the 'fair and equitable treatment' standard, it has been argued that WTO law offers a 'process-driven methodology' to consider science in the assessment of 'regulatory rationality'.[87] Similarly, the state's use or disregard of scientific evidence is a relevant factor in the assessment of its conduct against the prism of due diligence. Reference to the SPS Agreement facilitates the determination of knowledge or foreseeability of risk calling for state action, while leaving a broad margin of discretion for domestic decision-makers. Guidance may operate on at least three fronts.

First. WTO practice may guide the evaluation of risk assessments conducted by state agencies during the pandemic. The SPS Agreement requires SPS measures to be science-based.[88] WTO Members must conduct their own objective risk assessment when adopting levels of sanitary protection that exceed international standards.[89] This risk assessment 'shall take into account available scientific evidence; relevant processes and production methods; relevant inspection, sampling and testing methods'.[90] The standard of review is limited, as panels are not called upon to step into the shoes of domestic decision-makers and conduct an entirely new assessment, but rather to examine whether authorities reasonably relied on scientific facts.[91]

Second. Beyond risk assessment, investment tribunals could also find orientation in WTO adjudicatory practice regarding risk management. This comprises two elements, namely, the determination of the level of precaution or sanitary protection and the design of measures to attain it.[92] As regards the first element, the SPS Agreement allows WTO Members to determine their own 'appropriate level of sanitary or phytosanitary protection' but requires them to consider the goal of reducing negative impacts on international trade,[93] ensuring that the measures adopted 'are not more trade-restrictive than required

87 Jürgen Kurtz, *The WTO and International Investment Law: Converging Systems* (CUP 2016) 167.

88 SPS Agreement (n 70) art. 2.2. On this requirement see *Costa Rica – Measures Concerning the Importation of Fresh Avocado from Mexico*, Panel Report (13 April 2022) WT/DS524/R, paras 7.1728ff. See also Matthias Herdegen, *The International Law of Biotechnology* (2nd edn, Elgar 2023) 148–150.

89 SPS Agreement (n 70) arts 3.3, 5.1. van den Bossche and Prévost (n 73) 187.

90 SPS Agreement (n 70) art 5.2.

91 *Costa Rica–Measures Concerning the Importation of Fresh Avocados* (n 88) paras 7.318-7.319.

92 On the notions of 'risk assessment' and 'risk management' see van den Bossche and Prévost (n 73) 187ff.

93 SPS Agreement (n 70) arts 3.3, 5.4. See also *European Communities – Measures Concerning Meat and Meat Products (Hormones)*, Appellate Body Report (16 January 1998) WT/DS26/AB/R and WT/DS48/AB/R, paras 172, 177.

to achieve their appropriate level of sanitary or phytosanitary protection'.[94] If the level of protection pursued by a Member is higher than that resulting from international standards, 'scientific justification' is required.[95] The second element of risk management requires identifying 'a rational or objective relationship' between the risk assessment and the implemented measures.[96] The SPS Agreement also proscribes arbitrary distinctions in the management of sanitary risks, where such differential treatment results in disguised restrictions on international trade or discrimination.[97]

Third. WTO law and practice may guide the analysis of states' reaction to the pandemic through time. Scientific information about the pandemic evolved from an initial absence of scientific information to a fairly accurate knowledge about the virus. States can justify shortcomings in measures of protection in the fact that the state of scientific knowledge at any specific time did not allow for a fully-fletched risk assessment and the identification of effective measures of sanitary protection.

Article 5.7 of the SPS Agreement contains specific rules for 'cases where relevant scientific evidence is insufficient'.[98] As recognised in *EC-Hormones*, 'responsible, representative governments commonly act from perspectives of prudence and precaution where risks of irreversible, e.g. life terminating, damage to human health are concerned'.[99] The situations covered are those where 'the body of available scientific evidence does not allow, in quantitative or qualitative terms, the performance of a risk assessment'.[100] Insufficiency is determined at the moment of adoption of the challenged measure.[101] A divergence in scientific opinions does not necessarily create an insufficiency unless it sheds doubt on previous assessments of risk.[102] If scientific information

94 SPS Agreement (n 70) art 5.6.

95 ibid art 3.3.

96 *India – Measures Concerning the Importation of Certain Agricultural Products*, Appellate Body Report (04 June 2015) WT/DS430/AB/R, para 5.16; *United States–Measures Affecting the Importation of Animals, Meat and Other Animal Products from Argentina*, Panel Report (24 July 2015) WT/DS447/R, para 7.325.

97 SPS Agreement (n 70) arts 2.3, 5.5. See generally *Russian Federation – Measures on the Importation of Pig Products from the European Union*, Panel Report (19 August 2016) WT/DS475/R, paras 7.1402ff.

98 SPS Agreement (n 70) art 5.7.

99 *EC-Measures Concerning Meat and Meat Products* (n 93) para 124.

100 *European Communities – Measures Affecting the Approval and Marketing of Biotech Products*, Panel Report (29 September 2006) WT/DS291/R, WT/DS292/R, WT/DS293/R, para 7.3237.

101 Ibid para 7.3253.

102 *US/Canada – Continued Suspension of Obligations in the EC-Hormones Dispute*, Appellate Body Report (16 October 2008) WT/DS321/AB/R, paras 677, 725. For an overview of the

is insufficient, the SPS Agreement allows members to impose SPS Measures on a provisional basis, relying on 'available pertinent information'.[103] This information may stem both from WTO members or from 'relevant international organizations'.[104] This last condition indicates that insufficiency of scientific evidence is not a *carte blanche* for arbitrariness, as some form of risk assessment supporting these temporary SPS measures is still required.[105] Provisional authorization is coupled with the obligation to 'seek to obtain the additional information necessary for a more objective assessment of risk and review the sanitary or phytosanitary measure accordingly within a reasonable period of time'.[106] These rules are a consequence of the temporary character of measures adopted under Article 5.7 of the SPS Agreement.[107]

Reference to the framework of the SPS Agreement might help ensure that the scrutiny of pandemic-related measures remains deferent to domestic margins of discretion, without turning a blind eye on blatant disregards of scientific evidence and objective facts. In cases about regulatory conduct, analysis of due diligence will involve an assessment of the 'rationale and urgency of a particular regulatory change'.[108] Diligent states facing a global pandemic can be expected to attend to facts and science. The evaluation of the 'rationale' and 'urgency' of COVID-related measures would certainly profit from the body of WTO law about sanitary measures.

Intradisciplinary reference to the framework of the SPS Agreement may serve both to investors and to states in investor-state arbitrations. On the side of the investor, proof of the existence of scientific evidence about the presence or nature of a risk, coupled by the state's decision not to act on that evidence, could provide a solid basis for an FPS claim. On the side of the state, evidence that measures were science-based and would stand scrutiny under the standards of the SPS Agreement may serve as an indication of due diligence. The FPS standard is an element of the minimum standard, which sets a bottom line for

---

interpretation of the SPS Agreement see WTO, Analytical Index: Guide to WTO Law and Practice <www.wto.org/english/res_e/publications_e/ai17_e/sps_e.htm> accessed 14 January 2023.

103 SPS Agreement (n 70) art 5.7.

104 ibid art 5.7.

105 See *European Communities – Measures Affecting the Approval and Marketing of Biotech Products* (n 100) para 7.2992.

106 SPS Agreement (n 70) art 5.7.

107 *US/Canada – Continued Suspension of Obligations in the EC-Hormones Dispute* (n 102) paras 678, 679.

108 *Eskosol S.p.A. v. Italy*, ICSID Case No. ARB/15/50, Award (4 September 2020) para 481 (discussing extensive approaches to the FPS standard).

state conduct.[109] Reasonable state conduct in line with the more stringent standards set by the SPS Agreement will, in principle, comply with – and likely exceed – the minimum degree of diligence required under the FPS obligation.[110]

4 Conclusion

The coronavirus pandemic unleashed fears about the constrains that the investment protection system could impose on domestic decision-makers, affecting their ability to properly respond to the pandemic.[111] There were calls for an accelerated reform of the system, suspension of investment treaties, and withdrawal by host states of consent to investment treaty arbitration.[112] Discussion largely centered on legal vehicles to shield regulatory action from investment claims, such as treaty-based exceptions and circumstances precluding wrongfulness.[113] Except for some works on fair and equitable treatment[114] and expropriation,[115] the peculiarities of the application of substantive standards of investment protection to pandemic-related claims has received far less attention. This has been particularly the case of the FPS standard.

This chapter has explored existent approaches regarding the scope of the FPS standard and their effect on the applicability of the FPS standard to

109 See section 3.1.

110 See Mantilla Blanco, *Full Protection and Security* (n 9) 487ff. (compliance with other international obligations as an indicator of due diligence).

111 See e.g. Nathalie Bernasconi-Osterwalder and others, 'Protecting Against Investor–State Claims Amidst COVID-19: A call to Action for Governments' (IISD 2020) <www.iisd.org/system/files/publications/investor-state-claims-covid-19.pdf> accessed 14 January 2023.

112 See ibid 7–8. See also Kabir Duggal and others, 'Consequences of Crisis and the Great Re-Think' (2021) 14 J World Energy Law Bus 133, 145.

113 See e.g. Federica Cristani, 'How Pandemics (May) Affect State Defences', in Yulia Levashova and Pascale Accaoui Lorfing (eds), *Balancing the Protection of Foreign Investors and States Responses in the Post-Pandemic World* (Kluwer 2022) 61ff; Charles-Emmanuel Côté and others, 'Pandemics and the Use of Exceptions in International Economic Law' in Philippe Bourbeau and others (eds), *A Multidisciplinary Approach to Pandemics* (OUP 2022) 155, 163ff.

114 Yulia Levashova, 'The Legitimate Expectations of Investors under the Fair and Equitable Treatment in Times of Pandemic and Aftermath' in Yulia Levashova and Pascale Accaoui Lorfing (eds), *Balancing the Protection of Foreign Investors and States Responses in the Post-Pandemic World* (Kluwer 2022) 109ff.

115 Roland Ziadé and Bo Ra Hoebeke, 'Perspectives on Expropriation Claims in a Post-Pandemic World' in Yulia Levashova and Pascale Accaoui Lorfing (eds), *Balancing the Protection of Foreign Investors and States Responses in the Post-Pandemic World* (Kluwer 2022) 131ff.

pandemic-related claims. The study revealed a high likelihood that prospective pandemic claims will be assessed under the FPS standard.[116] Acknowledging that the FPS standard imposes an obligation to exercise due diligence, the argument focused on the application of the flexible yardstick of due diligence in the context of pandemic-related claims.[117] While the standard of due diligence remains objective, it is sensitive to the specific circumstances and resources available to the host state.[118] The evaluation of the diligence displayed by states facing global pandemics must consider the consistency and rationality of their policies. This will likely entail some scrutiny of the underlying risk assessment and risk management policies. WTO adjudicatory practice on the SPS Agreement provides useful guidance for the evaluation of diligence in this new context.[119]

116 See section 2.
117 See section 3.
118 See section 3.1.
119 See section 3.2.

CHAPTER 8

Revisiting the FET Standard and the Right to Regulate in Times of Crisis: The Notion of Stability in an Assessment of Legitimate Expectations

Yulia Levashova

1 Introduction

The outbreak of the COVID-19 pandemic brought the subject of potential investment claims, arising as a result of government measures under the fair and equitable treatment (FET) standard, to the forefront of investment law discussions. So far, we have not witnessed an explosion of investor-state dispute settlement (ISDS) cases as feared by some commentators at the beginning of the pandemic. However, the indirect consequences of the pandemic may cause a serious financial recession especially in developing and least developed countries that are currently experiencing a significant rise in debt levels. The COVID-19 pandemic has significantly increased the external debt burden on many developing countries undermining their recovery and prompting a financial and economic crisis.

In the years to come, many countries may enter a period of recession resulting from a multitude of factors, including the impact of the pandemic, the effect of the war in Ukraine, and the food and fuel crises around the world. The latter economic adverse impacts may have serious financial repercussions for foreign investors, prompting new ISDS claims. Furthermore, the pandemic is anticipated to impact an increasing number of changes in investment law that were already underway before the pandemic, such as the rising importance of FDI screening mechanisms and procedural arbitration reforms, e.g., the introduction of measures to increase transparency in arbitration proceedings.[1] The pandemic has also questioned the ability of the current investment law system to respond to unpredictable events. The latter feature of the pandemic

1 See book introduction.

© KONINKLIJKE BRILL BV, LEIDEN, 2025 | DOI:10.1163/9789004711204_010

has implications for interpreting the right to regulate in the context of a FET standard addressed in Section 2 of this Chapter.

In this context, the FET standard under international investment agreements (IIAs) is likely to play an important role. The wide scope of possible breaches under the FET standard has led to an extensive use of this provision by investors to challenge the host state's measures in ISDS proceedings. Indeed, one of the most debated issues in investment law is the scope of permitted regulatory changes under the obligation of stability emerging from the FET standard. The latter issue is especially pertinent with respect to possible direct and indirect COVID-19-related claims, or any claims prompted by the state's measures to address an emergency or crisis. The tension between safeguarding an investor's legitimate expectations and upholding a state's prerogative to implement regulations stands at the centre of this discussion.

The state's right to regulate has a key role in determining the limits of the protection of the investor's legitimate expectations. Regardless of whether the investor makes a claim for the protection of its legitimate expectations on the grounds of a reversal of a specific representation made to it by the host state, or based on a substantial change to the general regulatory framework, a state will likely justify its regulatory measures by the public interest involved in both scenarios. The question of how tribunals evaluate the state's right to regulate and the protection of an investor's legitimate expectations in cases involving a strong public interest, such as the protection of public health or the stabilisation of an economic system, remains a highly debated one. Arbitral tribunals are constantly shaping the content of the FET standard as the body of investment decisions grows.

This chapter seeks to capture recent developments in the context of the FET standard and the right to regulate, as well as to identify and analyse the emerging factors addressed by tribunals in balancing an investor's financial interests and the interests of a state in times of crisis or emergency.

2 The Right to Regulate and the FET Standard

State sovereignty, as a fundamental concept of international law, forms the legal basis of the state's right to regulate.[2] Together with the principle of sovereign equality, it constitutes one of the basic concepts of international law

2 Samantha Besson, 'Sovereignty, International Law and Democracy' (2011) 22(2) EJIL 376.

reflected in Article 2 of the UN Charter.[3] Under international law, a state has the right to freely choose and develop its economic, political, social, and cultural systems. This right is expressed in the Friendly Relations Declaration and other authoritative legal instruments.[4]

A state may freely exercise its right to regulate, subject to limitations placed on its state sovereignty, by entering international treaties, including IIA.[5] The limitations that may occur upon conclusion of an IIA are, in essence, a manifestation of the state's right to regulate, as a state chooses how to organise its foreign economic relations. As stated by the Permanent Court of International Justice (PCIJ) in the *Wimbledon* case, the state's prerogative to enter international agreements is 'an attribute of state sovereignty'.[6] Upon entering an IIA, a state continues to exercise its right to regulate, while complying with its international obligations under the IIA.

The existence of an intricate balance between a state's right to regulate and other state commitments was addressed in various international court judgments. In the *Lotus* case, the PCIJ had to decide whether Turkey had regulatory freedom to exercise its jurisdiction over a French citizen in a legal dispute resulting from the collision of a Turkish and a French steamer. The PCIJ found that the Turkish regulatory actions were permissible provided that they did not violate an explicit prohibition imposed by international law.[7] The Court asserted that the state has the right to regulate within its territory by exercising

---

3 The UN Charter stipulates in Article 2 (1): 'The Organization is based on the principle of the sovereign equality of all its members.' Charter of the United Nations (adopted 26 June 1945, entered into force 24 October 1945) XV UNCIO 355. 'The 'sovereign equality' should be understood according to the following principles: (1) that states are judicially equal; (2) that they enjoy the right inherent in their full sovereignty; (3) that the personality of the state is respected, as well as its territorial integrity and political independence; (4) that the state should, under international order, comply faithfully with its international duties and obligations.' 'United Nations Conference on International Organisation, Commission 1, General Provisions' (1 June 1945) Un Doc 739/I/1/A/19 (a).

4 Declaration on Principles of International Law concerning Friendly Relations and Cooperation among States in accordance with the Charter of the United Nations, UNGA Res 2625 (XXV) (24 October 1970) 4; Charter of Economic Rights and Duties of States, UNGA Res 3281 (XXIX) (12 December 1974) art 1; International Covenant on Civil and Political Rights, UNGA Res 2200A (XXI) (16 December 1966).

5 Joachim Karl, 'International Investment Arbitration: A Threat to State Sovereignty' in Wenhua Shan and others (eds) *Redefining Sovereignty in International Economic Law* (Hart Publishing 2008) 230.

6 *United Kingdom and others v. Germany*, Judgment, PCIJ Rep Series A No 1, 15.

7 *The Case of the S.S. Lotus* (*France v. Turkey*), Judgment, PCIJ Rep Series A No 10, 19.

discretionary powers in interpreting international legal obligations. This right can only be limited by explicit prohibitive rules to which the state has agreed.[8]

In the last decade, investment disputes concerning public health and environmental issues have sparked discussion on the extent to which IIAs can limit a state's internal sovereignty. From one perspective, there is consensus among tribunals that the state's right to regulate constitutes an element of state sovereignty.[9] Thus, in the absence of a specific treaty provision or customary international law defences, most tribunals, in assessing the FET standard under a relevant IIA, affirm the state's right to regulate as an element of state sovereignty. However, the right to regulate has been subject to diverse interpretations by tribunals.[10] As of 2006, tribunals have begun recognising the state's right to regulate in the public interest, when assessing the investor's rights under the FET standard.[11] To this end, tribunals have acknowledged the state's ability to modify its laws as part of the right to regulate. Moreover, in an increasing number of decisions, tribunals have stressed the relevance of measures adopted in the state's legitimate public interest, for example, the protection of public welfare with a view to remedying the negative consequences of a financial and/or economic crisis. Tribunals have indicated that such arguments need to be taken into consideration when judging the fairness of a host state's conduct towards an investor.[12]

8 An Hertogen, 'Letting Lotus Bloom' (2015) 26(4) EJIL 901.

9 *ADC v. Hungary*, ICSID Case No. ARB/03/16, Award (2 October 2006) para 423; *Cavalum SGPS, S.A. v. Spain*, ICSID Case No. ARB/15/34, Decision on Jurisdiction, Liability and Directions on Quantum (31 August 2020) para 424, with the reference to *Saluka Investments B.V. v. The Czech Republic*, UNCITRAL, Partial Award (17 March 2006) para 305 and *Total S.A. v. The Argentine Republic*, ICSID Case No. ARB/04/01, Decision on Liability (27 December 2010) para 115; also see: *Hydro Energy 1 S.à r.l. and Hydroxana Sweden AB v. Kingdom of Spain*, ICSID Case No. ARB/15/42, Decision on Jurisdiction, Liability and Direction on Quantum (9 March 2020) para 582. Also see concluding remarks in Yulia Levashova, *The Right of States to Regulate in International Investment Law: The Search for Balance Between Public Interest and Fair and Equitable Treatment* (Kluwer Arbitration 2019).

10 David Gaukrodger, 'The Balance Between Investor Protection and the Right to Regulate in Investment Treaties: A Scoping Paper' (2017) 2 OECD Working Papers on International Investment <www.oecd-ilibrary.org/finance-and-investment/the-balance-between-investor-protection-and-the-right-to-regulate-in-investment-treaties_82786801-en> accessed 26 June 2023.

11 Levashova (n 9) 269.

12 E.g., *Total* (n 9) para 123; *National Grid plc v. The Argentine Republic*, UNCITRAL, Award (3 November 2008) para 180; *MamidoilJetoil Greek Petroleum Products Société S.A. v. Republic of Albania*, ICSID Case No. ARB/11/24, Award (30 March 2015) para 626; *Charanne Construction v. Spain*, SCC Case No. 062/2012, Award (21 January 2016) para 514.

In recent decisions on the application of a FET standard, tribunals stressed that (i) the balancing of the state's right to regulate with the interests and rights of an investor is a component of the right to regulate; (ii) states' ability to modify their laws is an inherent component of the right to regulate; (iii) in some recent cases concerning the environment and climate change issues, the notion of a 'strong' public interest must be recognised. These three emerging factors will be analysed further in this chapter.

2.1 *The Balancing of the State's Right to Regulate with the Investor's Rights*

The starting point emphasised by numerous investment tribunals is that the right to regulate is articulated by international law, and that this right is limited by, *inter alia*, investment treaty obligations. This point was summarised in *ADC v. Hungary* where the tribunal underlined that:

> while a sovereign State possesses the inherent right to regulate its domestic affairs, the exercise of such right is not unlimited and must have its boundaries. As rightly pointed out by the Claimants, the rule of law, which includes treaty obligations, provides such boundaries. Therefore, when a State enters into a bilateral investment treaty like the one in this case, it becomes bound by it and the investment protection obligations it undertook therein must be honoured rather than be ignored by a later argument of the State's right to regulate.[13]

A more nuanced specification emerges from several recent Energy Charter Treaty (ECT) tribunals' decisions, which state that the FET clause implies an inherent balancing of the state's right to regulate and the rights of an investor. In the case *Cavalum v. Spain,* the tribunal emphasised that the 'FET standard may legitimately involve a balancing or weighing exercise by the host state'.[14] To this end, the *Cavalum v. Spain* and *Hydro Energy v. Spain* tribunals offer seven identical criteria according to which the state's right to regulate and the legitimate expectations of an investor should be balanced.[15] In both

13 *ADC* (n 9) para 423.

14 *Cavalum SGPS* (n 9) para 424.

15 ibid paras 424–430. These criteria are: "*First,* the State's sovereign right to regulate has been affirmed in many awards, and the State is entitled to a 'high measure of deference.'" *Second,* the idea that legitimate expectations, and therefore FET, imply the stability of the legal and business framework does not mean the virtual freezing of the legal regulation of economic activities. There has to be a weighing of an investor's expectations and the state's regulatory interests. *Third,* in the absence of specific promises or representations

decisions, the first criterion asserts that 'the State's sovereign right to regulate has been affirmed in many awards, and the State is entitled to a "high measure of deference."'[16]

In *Renergy v. Spain*, the tribunal refers to the host state's *undisputed right to regulate*. The tribunal emphasises that in cases 'where the propriety of legislative change lies at the heart of the dispute, the Tribunal must balance the host State's undisputed right to regulate with the legitimate interests of an investor who committed resources on the basis of the earlier legal regime'.[17] According to the tribunal, this balancing exercise departs from the 'very concepts of fairness and equity themselves' and 'from the object and purpose of the ECT'.[18]

In *Silver Ridge Power BV v. Italy*, the tribunal elaborated on the purpose of the ECT in the context of the FET standard: 'The ordinary meaning of the term "fair and equitable treatment" contains a clear indication that the host State is not free to act vis-à-vis investors protected under the ECT ad libitum', however 'the protection of the investors' position is not absolute and unqualified, but rather a matter of degree and balancing'.[19]

In *Sevilla Beheer B.V. and others v. Italy* and *PV Investors v. Spain*, the tribunals emphasised that the objective of maintaining stability is not absolute and does 'not prevent sovereign States from exercising their regulatory powers

---

by the State to the investor, the investor may not rely on an investment treaty as a kind of insurance policy against the risk of any changes in the host state's legal and economic framework. *Fourth*, it has been said that it is inconceivable a state would make a general commitment never to change its legislation whatever the circumstances, and it would be unreasonable for an investor to rely on such a freeze, in particular where times and needs change, or where crisis arises. *Fifth*, economic, social, environmental and legal circumstances and problems are by their nature evolutionary, dynamic and bound to constant change, and it is indispensable for successful public infrastructure and public services to be adaptable to change in evolving circumstances. *Sixth*, consequently, the FET standard preserves the regulatory authority of the host state to make and change its laws and regulations to adapt to changing needs, including fiscal needs, subject to respect for specific commitments made. *Seventh*, the expression "margin of appreciation," can be used to convey the point that the State's right to regulate is subject to a wide latitude, subject to its compliance with its duties under the ECT and customary international law' (emphasis added).

16 ibid para 424, with the reference to *Saluka* (n 9) para 305 and *Total* (n 9) para 115; also see: *Hydro Energy* (n 9), para 582.

17 *Renergy S.à r.l. v. Kingdom of Spain*, ICSID Case No. ARB/14/18, Award (6 May 2022) para 608.

18 ibid.

19 *Silver Ridge Power BV v. Italian Republic*, ICSID Case No. ARB/15/37, Award (26 February 2021) para 396.

in a manner consistent with international law'.[20] The *PV Investors* tribunal explained:

> the Parties to the ECT aimed at realizing a balance between the sovereign rights of the State over energy resources and the creation of a climate favorable to the flow of investments on the basis of market principles. In other words, while the purpose of "promot[ing] long-term cooperation in the energy field" which is stipulated in Article 2 of the Treaty may be facilitated by stability of the investment framework, the requirement of stability is not absolute; it must be balanced with other principles, including those that are directly derived from "[s]tate sovereignty", for instance the [s]tate's right to regulate and to adapt the regulatory framework to changed circumstances. More generally, the protection of investments and the right to regulate operate in a balanced way under the ECT as in all other investment treaties.[21]

In *Urbaser v. Argentina,* the tribunal went one step further in interpreting the FET standard under the Argentine – Spain BIT by explicitly affirming that the state has the right to regulate and that the '[FET] standard encompasses the entire legal, social and economic framework'.[22] In assessing the FET standard, the tribunal noted that in privatising water resources the important objective of the government was 'to ensure the population's health and access to water' according to its Constitution.[23] The tribunal noted that a host state is 'bound by obligations under international and constitutional laws', i.e., the right to water.

The *Urbaser* tribunal emphasised:

> When measures had been taken that have as their purpose and effect to implement such fundamental rights protected under the Constitution, they cannot hurt the fair and equitable treatment standard because their occurrence must have been deemed to be accepted by the investor when entering into the investment and the Concession Contract. In short, they were expected to be part of the investment's legal framework.[24]

---

20 *Sevilla Beheer B.V. and others v. Kingdom of Spain,* ICSID Case No. ARB/16/27, Decision on Jurisdiction, Liability and the Principles of Quantum (11 February 2022) para 714.

21 *ES Solar and others (PV Investors) v. Spain,* PCA Case No. 2012–14, Final Award (28 February 2020) para 565. Also see: *Sevilla Beheer* (n 20) para 714.

22 *Urbaser S.A. and Consorcio de Aguas Bilbao Bizkaia, Bilbao Biskaia Ur Partzuergoa v. The Argentine Republic,* ICSID Case No. ARB/07/26 Award (8 December 2016) paras 618–625.

23 ibid para 622.

24 ibid.

In assessing the state's objective to provide water to its population, the tribunal underscored that the state's conduct should be compatible with the FET standard.[25] At the same time, the investor cannot invoke 'the protection of its own interests as a prevailing objective, because these interests were part of a legal environment also covering core interests of the host state, as protected by sources of law prevailing over the Contract based on international or on constitutional law'.[26] Therefore, the state's objective to provide water to its citizens forms part of Argentina's regulatory framework in which the investor made their investment.[27]

Also, the tribunal in *Mamidoil v. Albania*, in determining the meaning of the FET under Article 10 (1) ECT, underlined that 'the fair and equitable standard brings foreign investors into the normative sphere of rational policy in the general interest. It is not meant to favor the investors' interests over other economic and social interests'.[28] In this case, the tribunal stated that the disputed measures had been taken in the general interest as they involved the 'responsibility [of the state] to provide long-term physical and social infrastructure such as public transport, including sustainable port facilities […]'.[29] By taking into account the inevitable changes in the social, economic and legal environment that affect regulations in the field of public infrastructure,[30] and the specific socio-political circumstances in Albania,[31] the tribunal determined that the state's measures had 'a legitimate objective of public policy, [and] were carried out in a transparent way, were proportionate and not arbitrary, and did not lead to unreasonable instability'.[32]

In these examples, tribunals emphasised that a FET standard departs from the 'very concepts of fairness and equity themselves' and implies an inherent balancing of the state's right to regulate and the rights of an investor.[33] Since the first assessments of a FET standard, tribunals in most decisions attempted to balance these conflicting interests.

However, in more recent FET decisions, a conceptual understanding among tribunals that a FET standard, independently of its formulation in an IIA,

25 ibid.
26 ibid.
27 ibid para 624.
28 *Mamidoil* (n 12) para 614.
29 ibid para 612.
30 ibid para 617.
31 ibid paras 625, 658.
32 ibid para 657.
33 *Renergy* (n 17) para 608.

inherently encompasses the necessity of balancing the rights and obligations of investors and host states, has emerged.

The effect of such theoretical underpinning adopted by some tribunals requires consideration of the state's policy objectives against the economic implications of a state's measure on the investor by a way of structural analysis such as the proportionality review. So far, however, tribunals have been inconsistent in their position on the use of proportionality,[34] such as in the example of *ESPF v. Italy* where the tribunal considered the proportionality of the measure to be an irrelevant criterion for an assessment of legitimate expectations.[35]

2.2 *The Recognition of a State's Ability to Modify Its Laws as a Part of the Right to Regulate*

The key component of the state's right to regulate, shaped by arbitral tribunals in the context of an assessment of an investor's legitimate expectations, is the state's right to modify its laws. This right has been emphasised by tribunals as a result of multiple claims in which investors challenged regulatory amendments made by host states. The reasoning employed by investors in such claims was that such alterations negatively affected their investment and had, therefore, frustrated their legitimate expectations.

As of 2006, tribunals have acknowledged a state's ability to modify its laws as part of the right to regulate.[36] Consequently, the *leitmotif* in every decision on legitimate investor expectations is the affirmation that a state may alter its regulatory framework and that an investor cannot expect laws and regulations to be frozen in time.[37]

In *Saluka v. Czech Republic*, the tribunal stated that 'no investor may reasonably expect that the circumstances prevailing at the time the investment is

---

34 Eric de Brabandere and Paula B M da Cruz, 'The Role of Proportionality in International Investment Law and Arbitration: A System-Specific Perspective' (2020) 89(3–4) Nord J Intl L 471.

35 *ESPF Beteiligungs GmbH, ESPF Nr. 2 Austria Beteiligungs GmbH, and InfraClass Energie 5 GmbH & Co. KG v. Italian Republic*, ICSID Case No. ARB/16/5, Award (14 September 2020) para 584.

36 See *Saluka* (n 9) para 305. In this award the tribunal for the first time explicitly referred to the 'host state's legitimate right subsequently to regulate domestic matters in [the] public interest'.

37 *Hydro Energy* (n 9) para 585; *Watkins Holdings S.à r.l. and others v. Kingdom of Spain*, ICSID Case No. ARB/15/44, Decision on Jurisdiction, Liability and Directions on Quantum (7 March 2020) para 543; *Glencore International A.G. and C.I. Prodeco S.A. v. Republic of Colombia*, ICSID Case No. ARB/16/6, Award (27 August 2019) para 1311; *Mobil Investments v. Canada*, ICSID Case No. ARB(AF)/07/4, Decision on Liability and Principles of Quantum (22 May 2012) para 153; *Renergy* (n 17) para 639.

made remain totally unchanged'.[38] In a similar vein, the *Parkerings v. Lithuania* tribunal emphasised that 'it is each state's undeniable right and privilege to exercise its sovereign legislative power. A state has the right to enact, modify or cancel a law at its own discretion'.[39] In *El Paso v. Argentina*, the tribunal in assessing the FET standard stated that 'the state has to be able to make the reasonable changes called for by the circumstances and cannot be considered to have accepted a freeze on the evolution of its legal system'.[40]

In *InfraRed v. Spain,* the tribunal stated that the freezing of a regulatory framework cannot arise in the absence of 'a specific commitment tendered directly to the investor or industry sector at issue'.[41] The *InfraRed* tribunal provided that the later finding is in accordance:

> with the principle of state sovereignty – enshrined in the ECT and considered by tribunals as part of the balancing exercise carried out when assessing an investor's bilateral relation with the state. The Tribunal is mindful of the significant limitation that a "stability" obligation would impose on the host state's sovereign legislative powers. The Tribunal cannot give effect to such a significant limitation of state sovereignty in the absence of a specific expression of consent by the host state.[42]

In the same vein, the *PV Investors v. Spain* tribunal further clarified the state's right to alter its laws and policies:

> the requirement of stability is not absolute; it must be balanced with other principles, including those that are directly derived from 'State sovereignty', for example, the State's right to regulate and to adapt the regulatory framework to changed circumstances. More generally, the protection of investments and the right to regulate operate in a balanced way under the ECT as in all other investment treaties.[43]

38 *Saluka* (n 9) para 305.

39 *Parkerings-Compagniet AS v. Republic of Lithuania,* ICSID Case No. ARB/05/8 Award (11 September 2007) para 332.

40 *El Paso Energy International Company v. The Argentine Republic,* ICSID Case No. ARB/03/15 Award (31 October 2011) para 365.

41 *InfraRed Environmental Infrastructure GP Limited and others v. Kingdom of Spain,* ICSID Case No. ARB/14/12, Award (2 August 2019) para 366.

42 ibid.

43 *ES Solar* (n 21) para 570.

In the above mentioned *Cavalum v. Spain case,* which contains one of the most explicit elaborations on the state's right to regulate under a FET standard, the tribunal emphasised that it would be 'inconceivable that a state would make a general commitment never to change its legislation whatever the circumstances, and it would be unreasonable for an investor to rely on such a freeze, especially upon changing needs, or in a time of a crisis'.[44]

In another case, *Renergy v Spain*, the tribunal spoke of 'Relative Stability'. The *Renergy* tribunal clarified that investors will receive protection if 'legislative changes [have] exceeded a (wide) acceptable margin, i.e., general legislation creates the legitimate expectation that it will not be subjected to any such changes'.[45] In assessing whether the legislative changes exceeded an (wide) acceptable margin according to Article 10(1) ECT, the *Renergy* tribunal identified the specific criteria that play a role when balancing legitimate expectations of an investor based on stability with the state's right to regulate. These criteria are as follows: the magnitude of the change; the economic impact; the abruptness of the change; the change in external circumstances: public interests involved; prior legislative practice; stability assurances.[46]

The criteria specified by the *Renergy* tribunal attempt to clarify the factors for an assessment of the scope of permitted regulatory changes under an applicable treaty. For the first time, the tribunal clearly stressed the 'public interest involved' was/is among the factors in an assessment of legitimate expectations based on stability. The *Renergy* tribunal, in particular, explained that '[t]he more important the public interests involved are, which often coincides with a high level of regulation, the more a diligent investor could have expected change'.[47]

To summarise, the tribunals affirm that the state's right to change its laws is a part of the right to regulate. While they generally agree that the regulatory framework cannot be frozen for the lifetime of an investment, the extent of permitted changes, however, is subject to different interpretations.[48] A prevalent number of tribunals underlined that a state has an obligation to ensure a stable economic and legal regime and that the FET only protects against

44 *Cavalum SGPS* (n 9) para 427.

45 *Renergy v. Spain* (n 17) para 642.

46 ibid para 681.

47 ibid.

48 Federico Ortino, 'The Obligation of Regulatory Stability in the Fair and Equitable Treatment Standard: How Far Have We Come?' (2018) 21(4) J Intl Econ L 845.

drastic changes and changes in the 'essential characteristics of the regulatory regime relied upon by investors'.[49]

In recent decisions, attempts were made to clarify the scope of permitted regulatory changes and to introduce the balancing test. In this context, some decisions refer to a proportionality review, the technique that more frequently appears in an assessment of legitimate expectations based on stability. In some other cases, like *Renergy v Spain,* the balancing test comprises of a number of criteria against which the disputed change to a regulatory framework is assessed.

2.3 *Public Interest as a Part of an Assessment under a FET Standard*

When balancing the state's right to regulate and the rights of an investor under the FET standard, tribunals assess whether a disputed state measure pursued a legitimate objective. The legitimacy of a state's objective is typically one of the criteria for judging the lawfulness of a state's conduct under the principles of reasonableness, proportionality, and the prohibition of arbitrariness. The evaluation of whether the objective of a state measure was to serve the public interest is central in cases addressing a crisis or emergency, like the pandemic. As case law demonstrates, it is likely that the more importance tribunals attach to the decision of a state, the greater is the deference (margin of appreciation) that tribunals will give to the legitimate objectives underlying countries' regulatory changes.

In determining a breach of legitimate investor expectations, tribunals tend to consider – to various degrees – the involved public interest and legitimate policy objectives. The express acknowledgement of public interest as a factor in the assessment of the existence of legitimate expectations based on stability was recognised in the aforementioned *Renergy v. Spain*. The tribunal stated:

> The more important the public interests involved are, which often coincide[s] with a high level of regulation, the more a diligent investor could have expected change. This is because, as rightly noted by the Respondent: [t]he host State is not required to elevate the interests of the investor above all other considerations, and the application of the

---

49 *Opera Fund v. Kingdom of Spain,* ICSID Case No. ARB/15/36, Award, (6 September 2019) para 508; *Antin Infrastructure Services Luxembourg S.à.r.l. and Antin Energia Termosolar B.V. v. Kingdom of Spain,* ICSID Case No. ARB/13/31 Award (15 June 2018) para 556; *Novenergia v. Spain,* SCC Case No. 2015/063, Final Award (15 February 2018); *Infracapital F1 S.à r.l. and Infracapital Solar B.V. v. Kingdom of Spain,* ICSID Case No. ARB/16/18, Decision on Jurisdiction, Liability and Directions on Quantum, (13 September 2021) para 527.

> FET standard allows for a balancing or weighing exercise by the State and the determination of a breach of the FET standard must be made in the light of the high measure of deference which international law generally extends to the right of national authorities to regulate matters within their own borders.[50]

In *Antaris v. Czech Republic*, the tribunal also specified that the 'exercise of the host State's normal regulatory power in the pursuance of a public interest' that does not alter the regulatory framework beyond the acceptable margin of change, will not frustrate the investor's expectations based on stability.[51]

In some cases, tribunals tend to afford a higher degree of deference to state decisions focusing on strong public interest and motivated by compliance with international legal obligations. In *Blusun v. Italy*, the tribunal concluded that the alteration of the conditions for receiving feed-in tariffs was a measure that was proportionate to the state's public interest objective, i.e. a 'response to a genuine fiscal need, given the large take-up under the earlier Energy Accounts'.[52] The tribunal found that the national legislation served a public interest because they were adopted to implement the EU Directive on the promotion and use of renewable energy. Hence, Italy had to comply with the specific obligations under this directive.[53] In *Renergy v. Spain*, even though the tribunal found in favour of the violation of legitimate expectations of an investor, it nevertheless stressed the importance of the commitment of states to protect the environment in accordance with EU legal instruments. To this end, the tribunal observed:

> increasing the use of green energy is likewise of vital public interest, given in particular the positive impact on the environment. Indeed, the Respondent itself committed to pursuing this interest many times, not least in the Preamble of Law 54/1997,1152 and is also under an obligation to do so under EU law, in particular pursuant to EU Directive 2009/28/EC. As it seems difficult to deny that, at least in the short term, the Disputed Measures make investments in green energy projects in Spain

50 *Renergia* (n 17) para 681.

51 *Antaris Solar GmbH and Dr. Michael Göde v. Czech Republic,* PCA Case No. 2014–01, Award (2 May 2018) para 360(7).

52 *Blusun v. Italy,* ICSID Case No. ARB/14/3 Award (27 December 2016) para 342.

53 Directive (EU) 2009/28, of the European Parliament and of the Council on the Promotion of the Use of Energy from Renewable Sources and Amending and Subsequently Repealing Directives 2001/77/EC an 2003/30/EC, [2009] OJ L140.

> less attractive to investors, the disputed measures could be seen to run counter to the public interest in saving the environment.[54]

In the case *Plama Consortium Ltd v. Republic of Bulgaria*, the tribunal had to determine whether the alteration of Bulgarian environmental laws constituted a breach of Article 10 (1) of the ECT. The tribunal found that the claim was inadmissible due to the fact that investors' investments were in breach of Bulgarian law. Although the FET claim was inadmissible, the tribunal still commented on it, noting that:

> the ECT does not protect investors against any and all changes in the host country's laws. Under the fair and equitable treatment standard the investor is only protected if (at least) reasonable and justifiable expectations were created in that regard. It does not appear that Bulgaria made any promises or other representations to freeze its legislation on environmental law to the Claimant or at all.[55]

The focus on the state's right to regulate to protect the environment has been emphasised by *Al Tamimi v. Oman* tribunal. In this case, the investor failed to obtain necessary permits, including environmental permits, which eventually led to the termination of the investor's lease agreements. In deciding on the breach of the minimum standard of treatment obligation under the US-Oman FTA, the tribunal noted that the treaty placed 'a high premium on environmental protection'.[56] The tribunal rejected the claim of an investor, stressing the importance of investor's compliance with the environmental laws and pointing out that for the violation of the minimum standard of treatment, a 'gross or flagrant disregard for the principles of fairness consistency, even-handedness, due process, or natural justice expected by and of all States under customary international law', is required.[57]

Compliance with obligations under international treaties, other than the applicable IIA, has, in some cases, served as a factor for justifying state measures. For example, in *Chemtura v. Canada*, *David Aren v. Costa Rica*, *Philip Morris v. Uruguay*, and *Urbaser v. Argentina*, the obligations of the state under

54 *Renergy v. Spain* (n 17) para 900.

55 *Plama Consortium Limited v. Republic of Bulgaria*, ICSID Case No. ARB/03/24, Award (27 August 2008) para 219.

56 *Adel A Hamadi Al Tamimi v. Sultanate of Oman*, ICSID Case No. ARB/11/33, Award (3 November 2015) para 387.

57 ibid para 390.

international treaties and European treaties regulating public health, the protection of environment, and the right to water were taken into account.

In *Chemtura v. Canada*, decided under the NAFTA, the tribunal took the Aarhus Protocol, and the obligation of Canada to reassess the use of lindane (a pesticide), as required by the Protocol, into account. The dispute arose as a result of Canada's delay in reviewing lindane produced by a US based chemical company and its subsequent refusal to register it.[58] In alleging the violation of Article 1105 (minimum standard of treatment), the investor argued that the Canadian Pest Management Regulatory Agency had undertaken a Special Review 'as a result of a trade irritant and not of health and environmental considerations'.[59] The claimant also contended that the review process was flawed and unfair. Canada asserted that reviewing the lindane-based pesticides was part of the mandate of its national pest management regulatory agency. During this review, it was established that the registration of these types of products should be terminated or suspended because of the threat to workers' health and certain adverse environmental effects. Furthermore, the state argued that it had acted in accordance with its international obligations under the Aarhus Protocol concerning the Convention on Long-Range Transboundary Air Pollution and its Protocol on Persistent Organic Pollutants (LRTAP).

In evaluating Canada's objectives motivated by health and environmental concerns, the tribunal afforded a high level of deference towards the state's measures. As a starting point, the tribunal underlined that it was not appropriate for the tribunal to second guess decisions of the state's scientific agencies. Also, the tribunal emphasised the fact that lindane had been raising serious concerns in other countries and at an international level since the 1970s, and that Canada had international obligations under the Protocol on Persistent Organic Pollutants. The tribunal herewith found the objective to be legitimate and properly substantiated. The investor argued that its legitimate expectations had been breached due to the violation of a commitment in the withdrawal agreement which provided that lindane products could be used to treat canola seed until 1 July 2001, with no limitations on when seed so treated could be sold or planted.[60] The tribunal arrived at the conclusion that 'the disingenuous position taken by the Claimant with respect to the content of the withdrawal agreement cannot justify a "reasonable" or "legitimate" expectation to be treated in disregard of the 1 July deadline in the meaning just established'.[61]

58 *Chemtura v. Canada*, NAFTA-UNCITRAL Arbitration, Award (2 August 2010) para 93.
59 ibid para 133.
60 ibid para 164.
61 ibid para 179.

In light of the state's legitimate objectives, justified by environmental and health concerns, it was considered unreasonable for an investor to expect that lindane treated seed could be sold or planted after the established deadline.

In *David Aren v. Costa Rica*, brought under the Dominican Republic-Central America Free Trade Agreement, the tribunal affirmed the state's right to enforce its environmental laws as part of international law. The tribunal established that Costa Rica was party to numerous international environmental conventions that, according to the tribunal, constituted 'the environmental legal framework in Costa Rica that applied[d] to this dispute'.[62]

To this end, the tribunal emphasised that the 'Respondent ha[d] both adopted international conventions and ha[d] enacted internal legislation in environmental matters that are not only consistent with most international conventions but are at the forefront of most jurisdictions'.[63] In interpreting the provisions of the treaty, the tribunal, relying primarily on Article 10.11 (environmental exception clause),[64] concluded that the rights of investors are subordinate to environmental concerns. However, this rule was considered to be subject to limitations. Namely, that environmental laws should be adopted in a fair and non-discriminatory manner through due process of law.[65]

A notable observation of the *David Aren* tribunal concerns the interpretation of treaty provisions for the purpose of determining 'whether there has been a breach to the standards of "fair and equitable treatment" and "full protection and security" under the Treaty, and under customary "international law" as well'.[66] In addition to paragraph 1 of Article 31 of the Vienna Convention on the Law of Treaties (VCLT), the tribunal also referred to sub-paragraph (3)(c) stipulating that 'any relevant rules of international law applicable in the relations between the Parties' must be taken into account, together with the context, in interpreting treaty texts. This led to the tribunal's conclusion that not only other provisions of the DR-CAFTA and general principles of law should be taken into account, but also 'custom, in construing in context the proper meaning of DR-CAFTA provisions, such as Articles 10.5 [minimum standard of treatment] and 10.7 [Expropriation and Compensation]'.[67]

62 *David R. Aven and Others v. Republic of Costa Rica*, ICSID Case No. UNCT/15/3, Award (18 September 2018) para 423.

63 ibid para 439.

64 The tribunal also applied Article 17(1)-(2) (enforcement of environmental laws).

65 *David R. Aven* (n 62) paras 412–413.

66 ibid para 410.

67 ibid para 411.

In *Philip Morris v. Uruguay*, in assessing the state's objectives in the context of the alleged violation of the FET standard, the tribunal stressed the deference to states' regulation of public health.[68] The tribunal accepted the argument of Uruguay that the challenged measures had been adopted in order to comply with the provisions of the Framework Convention on Tobacco Control (FCTC).[69] In the assessment of the legitimate expectations based on changes to the regulatory framework, the tribunal underlined that the investor's expectations can be frustrated if the state's measures exceed the exercise of the host state's normal regulatory power, and if the regulatory change lies 'outside of the acceptable margin of change'.[70] In the view of the tribunal, Uruguay had exercised normal regulatory power and there could therefore not be:

> any legitimate expectation of the Claimants vis-à-vis Uruguayan tobacco control regulations. Manufacturers and distributors of harmful products such as cigarettes can have no expectation that new and more onerous regulations will not be imposed, and certainly no commitments of any kind were given by Uruguay to the Claimants or (as far as the record shows) to anyone else.[71]

By stressing the legitimacy of the state's objective to safeguard public health, the tribunal concluded that the investor should have anticipated stricter anti-tobacco measures in light of growing awareness of the negative effects of smoking. The tribunal also concluded that the state's measures were not 'outside of the acceptable margin of change'. Without elaborating on the latter threshold, the tribunal simply ruled that the impact of the state's measures on the investor was limited.[72]

As has been seen, in *Cavalum v. Spain,* the tribunal also referred to the 'margin of appreciation' and a 'high level of deference.' In the context of an assessment of legitimate expectations, the tribunal ruled that a state is free to amend its legislation and that this falls within the state's margin of appreciation.[73] The

68 See a discussion on the implications of this case in Freya Baetens, 'Protecting Foreign Investment and Public Health through Arbitral Balancing and Treaty Design' (2022) 71(1) ICLQ 139.

69 *Philip Morris v. Uruguay*, ICSID Case No. ARB/10/7 Award (8 July 2016) para 401: 'The first point to be made is that both measures were adopted in an effort to give effect to general obligations under the FCTC'.

70 ibid para 423.

71 ibid para 429.

72 ibid para 433.

73 ibid para 419.

latter principle confirms that 'the State's right to regulate is subject to a wide latitude, subject to its compliance with its duties under the ECT and customary international law'.[74] According to the tribunal's analysis the Spanish measures, which amounted to a replacement of an incentive system, were taken in the public interest and fell within the state's margin of appreciation.[75] The explicit reference to both the margin of appreciation and a high measure of deference demonstrates the importance placed by the tribunal upon the state's right to regulate when weighing the commercial interests of an investor under the ECT.

Concluding this section, the observation can be made that the role of a public interest in an assessment of legitimate expectations has been reflected more prominently in some of the latest decisions. Traditionally, the spectrum of public interests recognised by tribunals has been broad and included the protection of public welfare, the safeguarding of ecological and environmental values, the maintenance of basic labour standards, the protection of cultural rights and vulnerable groups of citizens, the banking sector reform, the fight against corruption, the protection of consumers, and the elimination of excessive costs for various groups of consumers and companies. An extensive list of public interests recognised by tribunals is also codified in the new generation of IIAs, for example, in the provision on the state's right to regulate. In cases discussed above where the legitimate public interest was clearly involved, the turning point for a tribunal in judging the state's conduct is primarily dependent on the methodology and the standard of review applied. Tribunals tend to afford more deference to state decisions focusing on a strong public interest, such as health and environmental protection and motivated by compliance with international legal obligations. Furthermore, tribunals using the proportionality review in conjunction with the margin of appreciation. In *Philip Morris v. Uruguay* tribunals were more inclined to attach greater importance to a state's decision in an overall balancing of the investor's and the state's interests.

In assessing the FET standard, however, tribunals are unclear on the hierarchy and allocation of weight among various factors involved in the case.[76] Specifically, a state's legitimate objective in serving the public interest, such as public health, is only one among other intermediary factors in tribunals' assessments. In cases involving the protection of public health as a primary response to the pandemic, tribunals should be able to establish a hierarchical relationship among diverse factors relevant to the case, with the public interest

74 ibid para 430.

75 *Cavalum SGPG* (n 9) paras 615, 620.

76 See, e.g., *ESPF* (n 35) para. 581.

taking precedence. Certainly, tribunals ought to remain flexible in evaluating the state's objective of implementing a measure taken in the public interest. However, if a tribunal determines that a state's measure serves a legitimate goal, the first prong of proportionality, namely the review of suitability, can guide tribunals in making a final decision. In this way, the pursued policy aim is prioritised and must be assessed against the interests of investors in a systematic manner. To ensure that investors' economic rights are properly addressed, authorities must use a non-discriminatory and non-arbitrary approach with a view to achieving their public policy objectives.

3 Concluding Remarks

The crises affecting international investment law, such as the pandemic, armed conflicts, and climate change, highlight the need to further clarify and resolve the tension between the state's right to regulate and the protection provided by a FET standard. In the growing body of FET decisions, tribunals deal with complex issues involving sensitive public concerns that require a systematic approach to balancing the state's right to regulate with the economic interests of an investor. The notion of the right to regulate in the context of a FET assessment has evolved from an abstract legal concept to a practical mechanism containing a set of elements, developed by tribunals. In addition to the recognition that states have an 'undisputed' right to regulate under general international law, some tribunals have recently emphasized that a FET standard implies an inherent balancing of the state's right to regulate and an investor's rights. Also, the definition of the right to regulate is extended to the recognition of the state's ability to modify its laws. Tribunals have consistently held that the state's right to modify its laws is inherent to its sovereign powers. The requirement of 'stability is not absolute' and must be balanced with the state's right to regulate and changed circumstances.[77]

The evolutionary clarifications on the FET standard and the right to regulate by recent tribunals have, however, not solved the systematic problem of inconsistent analysis. Tribunals have created a 'list of requirements' for the assessment of legitimate expectations of an investor. Its starting point is an evaluation of the type of commitments on which the investor relies. Supplementary factors that may be considered include the severity of the economic impact; the extent of change and the procedure followed by a state; the public interest

77 ES *Solar* (n 21) para 570.

involved; external circumstances; and an investor's due diligence. The issue with this approach, though, is a persistent lack of clarity regarding the hierarchy and weight allocation of these factors in a tribunal's final determination of a breach of legitimate expectations. More importantly, in many cases, a state's legitimate goal of serving the public interest is only one of several intermediary factors considered by tribunals.

The lack of prioritisation of public interest in sensitive cases concerning the measures adopted to respond to the pandemic might further undermine the legitimacy of ISDS, as voiced by critics of the system. When making decisions affecting both private parties and the general public, tribunals must strike a careful balance. In circumstances where it has been decided that the state's measure was implemented in a non-discriminatory and non-arbitrary manner and was motivated by a significant public interest, tribunals may employ a different methodological approach to assessing a FET standard. The incorporation of structured reasoning through the application of the first prong of proportionality combined with the duty to defer to the margin of appreciation of state authorities, as done by some tribunals, may serve as a pillar for a coherent methodological approach in FET cases.[78]

78 Yulia Levashova, 'The Way Forward in Reforming the Legitimate Expectations Test' (2022) Columbia FDI Perspectives <https://ccsi.columbia.edu/sites/default/files/content/docs/fdi%20perspectives/No%20346%20-%20Levashova%20-%20FINAL.pdf> accessed 23 June 2023.

CHAPTER 9

Indirect Expropriation in the Context of the Pandemic: Confronting Investment Treaty Provisions with COVID-Related Regulatory Measures

Niccolò Zugliani

1 Introduction

The multitude of emergency measures adopted by states to face the COVID-19 pandemic has reignited, if ever needed, the long-standing debate as to the potential of the international investment regime to unduly fetter the state's ability to regulate. Over the past decades, states have dedicated much effort to negotiating international investment agreements (IIAs) that would recalibrate the protection offered to foreign direct investment (FDI), perceived as unbalanced in favour of foreign investors, with the continuous exercise of the host state's sovereign powers. Despite these changes, whether new-generation IIAs have effectively reached a balanced protection of FDI is still to be tested. At the same time, the regime still registers the widespread presence of old-generation treaties, as well as the continuous operation of IIAs already terminated but whose effects linger on, due to the presence of sunset clauses.

The current architecture of the international investment regime calls into question the capacity of the state to enact emergency legislations to safeguard the health of its citizens during crises without incurring any international responsibility. The issue was presented in all its urgency after the outbreak of COVID-19 in 2020. In the wake of the emergency, states swiftly adopted a wide range of across-the-board health-related policies, with sweeping effects on domestic and international business endeavours. States confiscated numerous types of medical products, mandated manufacturers to switch their production to medical equipment, forced producers to sell at reduced prices, issued compulsory licences to avoid the monopolization of health supplies, or disseminated intellectual property, to mention but a few of these measures.[1]

1 UNCTAD, 'Investment Policy Responses to the COVID-19 Pandemic' (2020) Investment Policy Monitor 4/2020, 9 <https://investmentpolicy.unctad.org/publications/1225/investment-policy-monitor-special-issue---investment-policy-responses-to-the-covid-19-pandemic>

© KONINKLIJKE BRILL BV, LEIDEN, 2025 | DOI:10.1163/9789004711204_011

States then strongly intervened in internal markets to aid domestic producers and to fight the economic disruption connected to the COVID-19 emergency.[2]

Even though the dreaded wave of expected investment arbitral proceedings has not materialised so far, state reactions to the pandemic have the potential to run afoul of the favourable treatment to FDI provided by IIAs. Among the substantive grounds of protection whose breach might be raised in connection with the exercise of health-related measures is the protection from indirect expropriation, usually granted in IIAs.[3] This chapter will investigate the legal issues that emerge in connection with the presence of indirect expropriation provisions in IIAs, focusing on the most likely scenario in which a claim might be raised, namely that of regulatory expropriation. The chapter will proceed as follows: Section 2 will summarize the main tenets of the protection from indirect expropriation, especially with regard to the adoption of general regulatory measures. Section 3 will address how new-generation provisions on indirect expropriation safeguard the state's regulatory space. Section 4 will elaborate on the application of the police powers doctrine in the context of COVID-related regulatory measures.

2 Protecting FDI from General Regulatory Measures

The protection from unlawful expropriation is a long-standing feature of the international regulation of FDI, rooted in customary international law and widely present in IIAs.[4] As a general rule, international law does not prohibit states from expropriating alien property in their territory, but it places certain conditions upon states for expropriation to be legal. These are the fulfilment of

---

accessed 9 February 2023; Cecilia Olivet and Bettina Müller, 'Juggling Crises: Latin America's Battle with COVID-19 Hampered by Investment Arbitration Cases' (*Longreads*, 1 September 2020) <https://https://longreads.tni.org/jugglingcrises> accessed 9 February 2023.

2 'COVID-19 EMEA Life Sciences Survey' (Baker McKenzie 8 April 2020) <www.bakermckenzie.com/-/media/files/insight/publications/2020/04/emea_survey_presentation_20200409.pdf?la=en> accessed 9 February 2023.

3 States have often resorted to expropriation to face crises. For an overview of expropriation as a means to face emergencies, see Roland Ziad and Bo Ra Hoebeke, 'Perspectives on Expropriation Claims in a Post-Pandemic World' in Yulia Levashova and Pascale Accaoui Lorfing (eds), *Balancing the Protection of Foreign Investors and States Responses in the Post-Pandemic World* (Wolters Kluwer 2022) 155–59.

4 On the legality of expropriation under general international law, see August Reinisch and Christoph Schreuer, *International Protection of Investments: The Substantive Standards* (CUP 2020) 5–11.

a public purpose, the absence of discriminatory and arbitrary actions, and the provision of compensation to the investor.[5]

Expropriation can take place in two distinct ways. *Direct* expropriation, as is known, consists in the formal deprivation of the investor's title in favour of the host state.[6] Starting from the second half of the 20th century, however, direct expropriation has become rare and much more prominence has been gained by *indirect* expropriation.[7] The latter takes place whenever a state's interference with property rights does not affect the title of the investment, but 'still result[s] in the effective loss of management, use or control of, or a significant depreciation of the value of, the assets of a foreign investor'.[8] Protection from indirect expropriation is frequently provided in IIAs, which usually expand the scope of expropriation provisions to measures 'having effect equivalent to nationalization or expropriation',[9] 'tantamount to expropriation',[10] or achieving substantially similar effects.[11]

While scholars have attempted, with little success, to define indirect expropriation, some indications have been drawn from the mounting case law of investment arbitral tribunals on the matter.[12] Tribunals do not always employ consistent criteria and their analysis ultimately remains case-specific, although some main lines of reasoning have emerged.[13] First, consensus can

---

5 Consensus on the customary features on the legality of expropriation is, however, less monolithic than it is usually portrayed. See August Reinisch, 'Legality of Expropriations' in August Reinisch (ed), *Standards of Investment Protection* (OUP 2008) 173–76.

6 Reinisch and Schreuer (n 4) 39.

7 Barnali Choudhury, 'Recapturing Public Power: Is Investment Arbitration's Engagement of the Public Interest Contributing to the Democratic Deficit' (2008) Vand J Transnatl L 775, 130.

8 UNCTAD, 'Taking of Property' (2000) UNCTAD Series on issues in international investment agreements UNCTAD/ITE/IIT/15, 2 <https://unctad.org/publication/taking-property> accessed 9 February 2023.

9 The Energy Charter Treaty (signed 17 December 1994, entered into force 16 April 1998) 2080 UNTS 95 (ECT) art 13(1).

10 See, among the many, North American Free Trade Agreement (signed 17 December 1992, entered into force 1 January 1994) (NAFTA) art 1110(1).

11 An overview of the numerous examples of indirect expropriation provisions can be found in Rudolf Dolzer and others, *Principles of International Investment Law* (3rd edn, OUP 2022) 154ff.

12 See, e.g., the non-overlapping definitions offered by Muthucumaraswamy Sornarajah, *The International Law on Foreign Investment* (4th edn, CUP 2017) 437; Rudolf Dolzer, 'Indirect Expropriations: New Developments?' (2002–03) 11 NYU Envtl LJ 64. Authors generally agree that it is difficult to define the situations which are covered by the notion of expropriation. See Campbell McLachlan and others, *International Investment Arbitration: Substantive Principles* (2nd edn, OUP 2017) 389.

13 See the analysis of case law carried out in Reinisch and Schreuer (n 4) 250; Anne K Hoffmann, 'Indirect Expropriation' in August Reinisch (ed), *Standards of investment*

be registered as to the intensity of the interference with property rights. The state action must impact the investment in a way that causes substantial or severe deprivation of its economic value and for a significant period of time.[14] The interference shall substantiate in the investor's loss of use, enjoyment of, or control of the investment,[15] so that a mere depreciation of the investment is not considered sufficient for a finding of indirect expropriation.[16] Accordingly, state measures that merely diminish the profit of the investment without preventing the investor from carrying out their day-to-day operation, or maintaining managerial control, have not been considered expropriatory.[17] The second pivotal requirement of indirect expropriation concerns the assessment of whether the state has breached the investor's legitimate expectations not to be substantially deprived of the value of the investment, especially when specific assurances were given to the investor.[18] Investment tribunals have then further expanded on other elements of indirect expropriation, admitting the existence of partial expropriation when only specific rights are expropriated,[19] or of 'creeping expropriation' whenever the cumulative effect of a series of measures, non-expropriatory if analysed in isolation, would lead to a deprivation of the value of the investment as described above.[20]

protection (OUP 2008); Sondra Faccio, *Indirect Expropriation in International Investment Law. Between State Regulatory Powers and Investor Protection* (Editoriale Scientifica 2020) 129–64; Aniruddha Rajput, *Regulatory Freedom and Indirect Expropriation in Investment Arbitration* (Wolters Kluwer 2019) 32–45.

14 Reinisch and Schreuer (n 4) 112ff. As a matter of example, in the health-related ban of a pesticide in the *Chemtura v. Canada* case, this requirement led the tribunal to conclude that 'the sales from [the pesticide] were a relatively small part of the overall sales of Chemtura Canada at all relevant times [and that, consequently] the interference of the Respondent with the Claimant's investment [could] not be deemed 'substantial'. *Chemtura Corporation v. Government of Canada*, UNCITRAL Award (2 August 2010) para 249.

15 See the sources quoted at footnote 13.

16 *El Paso Energy International Company v. The Argentine Republic*, ICSID Case No. ARB/03/15, Award (31 October 2011) para 245.

17 See, e.g., *LG&E Energy Corp, LG&E Capital Corp, and LG&E International, Inc. v. Argentine Republic*, ICSID Case No. ARB/02/1, Decision on Liability (3 October 2006); *Azurix Corp v. The Argentine Republic*, ICSID Case No. ARB/01/12, Award (14 July 2006).

18 *Metalclad Corporation v. The United Mexican States*, ICSID Case No. ARB(AF)/97/1, Award (30 August 2000) para 107; *Técnicas Medioambientales Tecmed SA v. United Mexican States*, ICSID Case No. ARB (AF)/00/2, Award (29 May 2003) para 149.

19 *Middle East Cement Shipping and Handling Co SA v. Arab Republic of Egypt*, ICSID Case No. ARB/99/6, Award (12 April 2002) para 107.

20 *Siemens AG v. The Argentine Republic*, ICSID Case No. ARB/02/8, Award (17 January 2007) para 263.

In the last few decades, many of the cases regarding indirect expropriation concerned the adoption of general regulatory measures.[21] It is generally accepted that legitimate regulatory measures in the public interest do not constitute indirect expropriation and that they should not entail international responsibility on the state even when they are detrimental to the economic value of the investment.[22] Although arbitral tribunals have often admitted that the state enjoys a certain degree of regulatory freedom, they have however found that indirect expropriation might take place when the expropriatory effect was the result of general regulations.[23] This is commonly referred to as a case of *regulatory* expropriation. Identifying when general regulations are a lawful exercise of sovereign powers and when they are expropriatory instead has emerged as one of the most relevant issues concerning FDI protection.[24] In the silence of most treaty texts,[25] tribunals have developed different approaches to identify regulatory expropriation.

Under the so-called 'sole effect' doctrine, regulatory expropriation takes place whenever the impact of the measure(s) is equivalent to that of formal expropriation.[26] The effect of the state's action on the investment is considered the determinant criterion for a finding of regulatory expropriation, regardless of the presence of expropriatory intent on the part of the state.[27]

In contrast to the sole effect doctrine, another stream of case law considers general regulatory measures adopted in the public interest as an expression of the state's police powers and denies the existence of regulatory expropriation

21 See, e.g., Jesuald W Salacuse, *The Law of Investment Treaties* (OUP 2010) 327, according to whom '[t]he precise differentiation between [regulatory expropriation] and the category of indirect expropriation is ephemeral at best'. An interchangeable usage among scholars is recorded, with some criticism, in Kenneth J Vandevelde, *Bilateral Investment Treaties. History, Policy, and Interpretation* (OUP 2010) 278.

22 Although there have been some contrary voices that deny the relevance of the state's right to regulate. See, e.g., *Compañía del Desarrollo de Santa Elena, SA v. The Republic of Costa Rica*, ICSID Case No. ARB/96/1, Award (17 February 2000) para 72; Rajput (n 13) 34.

23 *El Paso Energy* (n 16) para 234.

24 See the publication of books dedicated to this specific aspect, such as Faccio (n 13); Rajput (n 13).

25 For an overview of the few treaties that, until 2004, exceptionally dealt with the issue of regulatory expropriation, see Katia Yannaca-Small, '"Indirect Expropriation" and the "Right to Regulate" in International Investment Law' (2004) OECD Working Papers on International Investment 2004/04, 6 <www.oecd.org/daf/inv/investment-policy/WP-2004_4.pdf> accessed 25 April 2023.

26 *Metalclad* (n 18) para 111, in which the tribunal found a violation of NAFTA Article 1110 and stated that in order to decide on an indirect expropriation, it "need not decide or consider the motivation, nor intent of the adoption" of the piece of legislation under scrutiny.

27 Dolzer (n 12) 79ff.

whenever an overriding public interest emerges. The recognition of the state's police powers by arbitral tribunals has proven difficult to implement, as emerged in several awards.[28] Some tribunals have focused on the nature of the regulation and have concluded that non-discriminatory measures, enacted in accordance with due process and to fulfil the public interest, were not expropriatory, regardless of the destruction of the value of the affected investment. This approach, labelled by some commentators as 'radical police powers',[29] first emerged in *Methanex v. United States* and *Saluka v. Czech Republic*. In the Methanex award, the tribunal found that:

> a non-discriminatory regulation for a public purpose, which is enacted in accordance with due process and, which affects, inter alios, a foreign investor or investment is not deemed expropriatory and compensable unless specific commitments had been given by the regulating government to the then putative foreign investor contemplating investment that the government would refrain from such regulation.[30]

While these awards have been criticized for virtually eliminating FDI protection in the case of regulatory expropriation,[31] they have influenced the subsequent reasoning of arbitral tribunals, which in some cases have interpreted the state's police powers accordingly.[32] However, contemporary arbitral case law often steers from placing exclusive emphasis on the existence of a non-discriminatory public purpose and moderates the approach followed in *Methanex* and *Saluka* by introducing additional criteria, such as the

---

28 See, e.g., *Continental Casualty Company v. The Argentine Republic*, ICSID Case No. ARB/03/9, Award (5 September 2008) para 277.

29 Ursula Kriebaum, 'Regulatory Takings: Balancing the Interests of the Investor and the State' (2007) 8 J World Investment & Trade 717, 727.

30 *Methanex Corporation v. United States of America*, UNCITRAL Final Award of the Tribunal on Jurisdiction and Merits (3 August 2005) Part iv, Chapter D, 4, para 7. Similarly, the tribunal in *Saluka Investment BV (The Netherland) v. The Czech Republic*, UNCITRAL Partial Award (17 March 2006) para 225, recalled the *Methanex* award when stating that '[i]t is now established in international law that [s]tates are not liable to pay compensation to a foreign investor when, in the normal exercise of their regulatory powers, they adopt in a non-discriminatory manner bona fide regulations that are aimed at the general welfare'.

31 See, e.g., Sornarajah (n 12) 445; Kriebaum (n 29) 727, labelling this approach to the police powers doctrine as 'radical police powers'.

32 See, e.g., *Bayindir Insaat Turizm Ticaret Ve Sanayi AS v. Islamic Republic of Pakistan*, ICSID Case No. ARB/03/29, Award (27 August 2009).

proportionality or the reasonableness of the measure,[33] to determine the legality of the interference with the investment.[34]

Overall, certain types of regulatory actions such as those aimed at safeguarding, among other things, workers' rights, human health, or the environment, are increasingly seen as legitimate regulatory efforts.[35] Though case law on the specific issue is scarce, health-related measures have so far been at the core of two high-profile investor-state dispute settlement (ISDS) proceedings in the field of tobacco regulation.[36] In the only case that reached the merits stage, namely *Philip Morris v. Uruguay*, the tribunal clearly endorsed the moderated version of the *Saluka/Methanex* jurisprudence when it required that 'the action [...] be taken bona fide for the purpose of protecting the public welfare, [...] be non-discriminatory and proportionate'.[37]

3 Safeguarding the State's Regulatory Powers: Expropriation Provisions in New-Generation IIAs

Although most traditional IIAs do not regulate the treatment of non-compensable regulatory measures,[38] the last two decades have witnessed increasing attention in treaty drafting to accommodate the state's regulatory needs. As regards expropriation provisions, this has materialized in two main trends that point to a clarification of the elements of indirect expropriation and to the exclusion of certain regulatory measures from the scope of indirect expropriation respectively.[39]

33 The reasonableness of the regulation has been addressed in *El Paso Energy* (n 16) para 233. Linking reasonableness to the burden on the investment, see *Continental* (n 28) para 276.

34 The inclusion of additional requirements to the 'radical police powers' doctrine has been defined by some as 'mitigated police powers' doctrine. See Gebhard Bücheler, *Proportionality in Investor-State Arbitration* (OUP 2015) 129–32; Reinisch and Schreuer (n 4) 104–05.

35 Allen S Weiner, 'Indirect Expropriations: The Need for a Taxonomy of "Legitimate" Regulatory Purposes Recurring Themes: Indirect Expropriation in International Law' (2003) 5 Intl LF D Intl 166, 174.

36 *Philip Morris Brands Sàrl, Philip Morris Products SA and Abal Hermanos SA v. Oriental Republic of Uruguay*, ICSID Case No. ARB/10/7, Award (8 July 2016); *Philip Morris Asia Limited v. The Commonwealth of Australia*, UNCITRAL, PCA Case No. 2012–12, Award on Jurisdiction Admissibility (17 December 2015).

37 *Philip Morris* (n 36) para 283.

38 Yannaca-Small (n 25) 6.

39 For a classification of new treaty developments from a different angle, see chapter 2.

As to the first trend, provisions on indirect expropriation have started listing the criteria for distinguishing indirect expropriation from legitimate regulation. This approach was originally adopted by the United States (US) and Canada in their model investment treaties and in their subsequent IIAs,[40] but it has also informed numerous IIAs by other countries, which specify the factors on which the determination of indirect expropriation must be based, either in their text or in annexes to the text.[41] These are usually 'the economic impact of the government action [...]; the extent to which the government action interferes with distinct, reasonable investment-backed expectations; and the character of the government action'.[42] While initially following a different approach, recent practice of the European Union (EU), as well as of the majority of states, is slowly converging towards the north-American model.[43] Some treaties, such as the 2016 Canada-EU CETA, expand these requirements, adding 'the duration of the measure or series of measures'[44] and 'the character of the measure or series of measures, notably their object, context and intent.'[45] However, despite an attempt to clarify indirect expropriation provisions, these developments have been deemed incapable of solving the uncertainties connected to the identification of expropriation as they run the risk of simply re-drafting uncertain terms in equally vague language.[46]

40 UNCTAD, 'Expropriation: A Sequel' (2012) UNCTAD Series on Issues in International Investment Agreements II, 60 <https://unctad.org/system/files/official-document/unctaddiaeia2011d7_en.pdf> accessed 20 May 2023. See, e.g., Australia-US FTA (signed 18 May 2004, entered into force 1 January 2005); Canada-Peru BIT (signed 29 May 2008, entered into force 20 June 2007).

41 Salacuse (n 21) 347–48.

42 US Model BIT (2012) Annex B, art 4(a) <https://ustr.gov/sites/default/files/BIT%20text%20for%20ACIEP%20Meeting.pdf> accessed 30 May 2023; an equivalent formulation can be found, as a matter of example, in Colombia-United Kingdom BIT (signed 17 March 2010, entered into force 10 October 2014) art 6(2).

43 Eric De Brabandere, 'States' Reassertion of Control over International Investment Law – (Re)Defining "Fair and Equitabe Treatment" and "Indirect Expropriation"' in Andreas Kulick (ed), *Reassertion of control over the investment treaty regime* (CUP 2017) 304.

44 EU-Canada Comprehensive Economic and Trade Agreement (signed 30 October 2016, provisionally in force 21 September 2017) (CETA) Annex 8-A, Expropriation, 2(b).

45 ibid Annex 8-A, Expropriation, 2(d).

46 Ying Zhu, 'Do Clarified Indirect Expropriation Clauses in International Investment Treaties Preserve Environmental Regulatory Space' (2019) 60 Harv Intl LJ 377, 406–11. This is not, however, entirely supported by the case law of arbitral tribunals. In some cases, the tribunal has resorted to the elements listed in the relevant IIA to clarify indirect expropriation. See, e.g., *Bear Creek Mining Corporation v. Republic of Peru*, ICSID Case No. ARB/14/21, Award (30 November 2017) para 374ff.

A more effective trend might be that of excluding some types of regulatory measures from the scope of indirect expropriation. Once again, this is in line with the broader shift of the international investment regime towards a recalibration of FDI protection, that witnesses the inclusion of state's defences by means of specific exceptions in IIAs.[47] Focusing on expropriation provisions, these have long excluded general regulations in specific sectors, such as taxation measures or intellectual property rights.[48] More recently, an increasing number of IIAs have excluded health measures from the scope of indirect expropriation. Even in this case, the yardstick is set by the US Model BIT, which already in 2004 provided that

> [*e*]*xcept in rare circumstances*, non-discriminatory regulatory actions by a Party that are designed and applied to protect legitimate public welfare objectives, such as public health, safety, and the environment, do not constitute indirect expropriations.[49]

This exact wording appeared not only in US treaties, but also in treaties concluded by the EU and in a number of IIAs by other states.[50] Despite its success, the exception is not without problems, mainly related to the unclear scope of the *caveat* 'except in rare circumstances'. For this reason, IIAs that replicate the provision of the US Model BIT tend to modify this part. In some cases, the formulation 'except in rare circumstances' does not appear, arguably expanding the scope of the regulatory exception.[51] In other cases, the *caveat* is limited

---

47 The emergence of state's defences under international investment agreements is dealt with in chapter 11.

48 See, e.g., Canadian Model FIPA (2021) art 9(6) <www.international.gc.ca/trade-commerce/trade-agreements-accords-commerciaux/agr-acc/fipa-apie/2021_model_fipa-2021_modele_apie.aspx?lang=eng> accessed 30 May 2023, carving out the scope of indirect expropriation with regard to measures consistent with the TRIPS Agreement. As to taxation measures, see e.g., US-Uruguay BIT (signed 4 November 2005, entered into force 31 October 2006) art 21(3).

49 US Model BIT (2004) Annex B, art 4(b) <https://ustr.gov/sites/default/files/U.S.%20model%20BIT.pdf> accessed 30 May 2023; an identical provision is contained in the 2012 US Model BIT (n 42) (emphasis added).

50 US-Uruguay BIT (n 48) Annex B, art 4(b); EU-Singapore Investment Protection Agreement (signed 15 October 2018, not in force) Annex 1(2); an equal result is reached, through a slightly different approach, by the Colombia-United Kingdom BIT (n 42) art 6(2)(c).

51 See, e.g., Pakistan-Turkey BIT (signed 22 May 2012, not in force) art 7(2): '[n]on-discriminatory legal measures designed and applied to protect legitimate public welfare objectives, such as health, safety and environment, do not constitute indirect expropriation'. The same wording can be found, e.g., in Nigeria-Turkey BIT (signed 2 February 2011,

in its scope and reads 'except in the rare circumstance when the impact of a measure or series of measures is so severe in light of its purpose that it appears manifestly excessive'[52] or 'except in rare circumstances, such as when a measure, or series of measures, are so severe in the light of their purpose that they cannot be reasonably viewed as having been adopted and applied in good faith'.[53] A third set of cases builds a bridge with the GATT-style general exceptions increasingly present in IIAs. The 2008 Japan-Peru BIT, for instance, states that '[n]on-discriminatory measures [...] that are designed and applied to protect legitimate public welfare objectives stated in [the provision on General Exceptions] do not constitute indirect expropriation'.[54] The provision links the carve-out to the treaty's Article 19, which in turn replicates Article XX GATT and excludes measures 'necessary to protect human, animal or plant life or health'.[55]

Yet, new-generation provisions do not automatically entail that tribunals will shield regulatory measures from a finding of indirect expropriation. Legal scholars have criticized the indeterminacy of the *caveat* 'in rare circumstances', suggesting the need for including lists of determinative elements that give meaning to the clause.[56] Indicative, in this sense, is the recent case *Bear Creek Mining v. Peru*, based on the 2008 Canada–Peru Free Trade Agreement, which contained an expropriation provision that excluded legitimate public measures by replicating, at Annex 812.1 (c), the exception of the US Model BIT.[57] When deciding upon the state's exercise of its police powers, the tribunal not only disregarded this specific exception, but further excluded the applicability of the police powers doctrine given the detailed list of GATT-style general

not in force) art 7(2); India Model BIT (2015) art 5(5) <https://jusmundi.com/en/document/treaty/en-bilateral-investment-treaty-between-the-government-of-the-republic-of-india-and-india-model-bit-2016-friday-1st-january-2016> accessed 30 May 2023.

52 CETA (n 44) Annex 8-A(3); Italy Model BIT (2022) Annex 2(3) <https://edit.wti.org/document/show/7bf07a89-63c7-44b8-9d38-6e4bc70034be> accessed 12 June 2023.

53 Canada-Mali BIT (signed 28 November 2014, entered into force 6 August 2016) Annex B.10; Canada-Jordan BIT (signed 28 June 2009, entered into force 6 July 2016) Annex B.13.1(c).

54 Japan-Peru BIT (signed 21 November 2008, entered into force 12 October 2009) Annex IV(c).

55 ibid art 19.

56 Maryam Malakotipour, 'The Chilling Effect of Indirect Expropriation Clauses on Host States' Public Policies: A Call for a Legislative Response' (2020) 22 Int CL Rev 235, 257, 267–68.

57 'Canada-Peru BIT (n 40) Annex 812.1(c): 'Except in rare circumstances, such as when a measure or series of measures is so severe in the light of its purpose that it cannot be reasonably viewed as having been adopted and applied in good faith, non-discriminatory measures of a Party that are designed and applied to protect legitimate public welfare objectives, such as health, safety and the environment, do not constitute indirect expropriation'.

exceptions contained in the treaty.[58] The tribunal went on to say that even if the police powers doctrine did apply, it would not insulate Peru from liability for unlawful expropriations.[59] It did however suggest that its conclusion would differ if the measure under scrutiny had been adopted for the protection of human life or health.[60]

4 Regulatory Expropriation in the Context of the COVID-19 Pandemic

The difficulty in reconciling the state's regulatory needs with the protection of FDI from indirect expropriation has fuelled speculations as to the possibility that investment claims be filed for the alleged breach of investment protection from indirect expropriation stemming from the adoption of COVID-related regulatory measures. Unsurprisingly, direct expropriation seems to play little relevance when addressing state responses to the COVID-19 pandemic. States have occasionally put forward nationalisations as means to react to the economic collapse determined by the sudden disruption of commercial activities, although such policies were never implemented.[61]

Swiftly after the outbreak of the pandemic, states enacted a wide range of emergency responses with the aim of safeguarding the health of their citizens, with potentially sweeping effects on FDI.[62] Among the most relevant sets of policies, numerous measures were enacted to face the shortage of medical equipment that national healthcare systems were in dire need of. States seized medical equipment and healthcare materials or prevented private operators from trading such products in the international markets through temporary limitations of goods.[63] Numerous countries imposed companies to redirect

58 *Bear Creek Mining* (n 46) paras 473–474.

59 ibid paras 477–78.

60 ibid para 475.

61 Nationalization was implemented in the case of Italy's Alitalia, the largest domestic airline operator. The company, however, was heavily subsidized by the State after it had defaulted numerous times and had long been placed under receivership of the state. See UNCTAD (n 1) 6.

62 A list of measures can be found at International Social Security Association, 'Coronavirus Country Measures' <https://ww1.issa.int/coronavirus/country-measures> accessed 10 March 2023; 'Policy Responses to COVID 19' (*IMF*, 2022) <www.imf.org/en/Topics/imf-and-covid19/Policy-Responses-to-COVID-19> accessed 10 March 2023.

63 UNCTAD (n 1) 9; Sophia Ankel, 'At Least 5 Countries – Including a Small Caribbean Island – Are Accusing the US of Blocking or Taking Medical Equipment They Need to

their production lines toward medical supplies.[64] Spain temporarily put the private healthcare system at the disposal of the autonomous local communities, allowing them to take control over private hospitals.[65] Another set of policies was aimed at managing social distancing and preventing circulation of people in promiscuous ways. An example of this were the flights that were brought to a halt almost everywhere, with severe consequences on transport operators,[66] while in some cases states suspended the collection of toll fees on roads to foster individual mobility.[67] A third set of policies dealt with the mitigation of the economic effects of the pandemic, following the disruption of domestic economies. Among other things, states suspended the payments of utility bills by private operators, including energy or water supplies, telephone and internet bills, mortgages, and the like.[68]

Depending on the effects that the specific state measure had on FDIs, COVID-related policies might well be at risk of constituting regulatory expropriation. Although most of the emergency actions were temporary, it is possible that they ultimately led to a substantial interference with the value of the investment, or with some of its assets.[69] The analysis of COVID-related regulatory measures will most likely lead arbitral tribunals to address whether they constitute a lawful exercise of the state's police powers. Police powers have

---

Fight the Coronavirus' (*Business Insider*, 7 April 2020) <www.businessinsider.com/coronavirus-us-accused-of-diverting-medical-equipment-from-countries-2020-4> accessed 10 March 2023.

64 David Waldstein, 'With Games Paused, Sports Companies Shift to Making Medical Supplies (Published 2020)', (*The New York Times*, 7 April 2020) <www.nytimes.com/2020/04/07/sports/formula-one-bauer-coronavirus-ppe.html> accessed 10 March 2023.

65 Adam Payne, 'Spain Has Nationalized All of Its Private Hospitals as the Country Goes into Coronavirus Lockdown' (*Business Insider*, 16 March 2020) <www.businessinsider.com/coronavirus-spain-nationalises-private-hospitals-emergency-covid-19-lockdown-2020-3> accessed 10 March 2023.

66 Jack Ballantyne, 'Chile Threatened over Airport Pandemic Disruption' (20 January 2021) <https://globalarbitrationreview.com/chile-threatened-over-airport-pandemic-disruption> accessed 10 March 2023.

67 Cosmo Sanders, 'Peru Warned of Potential ICSID Claims over COVID-19 Measures' (*Global Arbitration Review*, 9 April 2020) <https://globalarbitrationreview.com/article/peru-warned-of-potential-icsid-claims-over-covid-19-measures> accessed 10 March 2023.

68 Paolo Mastropietro and others, 'Emergency Measures to Protect Energy Consumers during the COVID-19 Pandemic: A Global Review and Critical Analysis' (2020) 68 Energy Res Soc Sci 101678.

69 *Olin Holdings Ltd v. Libya*, ICC Case No. 20355/MCP, Final Award (25 May 2018) para 165; Oliver Hailes, 'Epidemic Sovereignty? Contesting Investment Treaty Claims Arising from Coronavirus Measures' (*EJIL: Talk!*, 27 March 2020) <www.ejiltalk.org/epidemic-sovereignty-contesting-investment-treaty-claims-arising-from-coronavirus-measures/> accessed 7 February 2023.

historically been rooted in public health regulation,[70] and have informed the analysis of investment arbitral tribunals in the few cases in which they have been confronted with the protection of public health.[71]

In line with the moderated version of the *Saluka/Methanex* approach to police powers emerging in investment tribunals' case law, state measures will most likely be analysed against the requirements of public interest, due process, non-discrimination, legitimate expectations, and proportionality or reasonableness. The requirement that the measure be taken for a public interest seems easily fulfilled.[72] States are traditionally accorded wide margins of discretion in defining their own public interest.[73] The protection of public health then generates a 'strong presumption of legality' of the regulatory measure.[74] In this regard, COVID-related measures can be linked to the protection of public health, as also highlighted by the WHO in its recommendations.[75]

The remaining requirements will be highly case-specific. Non-discrimination might not be met when measures selectively target foreign operators,[76] although tribunals often require evidence that the actions have been taken with discriminatory intent for a finding of indirect expropriation.[77] As to legitimate expectations, case law on indirect expropriation has generally shown a more-cautious approach than that applied for the fair and equitable treatment standard, where some tribunals have found investor's expectations to stem from the general legal framework. Legitimate expectations are usually

70 Catharine Titi, 'Police Powers Doctrine and International Investment Law' in Andrea Gattini and others (eds), *General Principles of Law and International Investment Arbitration* (Brill Nijhoff 2018) 324–25.

71 Reinisch and Schreuer (n 4) 102; *Philip Morris* (n 36) para 291: '[p]rotecting public health has since long been recognized as an essential manifestation of the [s]tate's police power'.

72 Thomas Lehmann, 'Police Powers Doctrine: A Reliable State Defense in Times of COVID-19?' (2021) 18 Braz J Intl L 73, 80; See *Chemtura* (n 14) para 266.

73 Nico Schrijver, *Sovereignty over Natural Resources: Balancing Rights and Duties* (CUP 1997) 344–46. The requirement of public purpose has been deemed as imposing 'relatively modest' limitations on the right to expropriate already by the jurisprudence of the Iran-US Claims Tribunal. See Ben Mostafa, 'The Sole Effects Doctrine, Police Powers and Indirect Expropriation under International Law' (2008) 15 Austl Intl LJ 267, 275.

74 *Señor Tza Yap Shum v. The Republic of Peru*, ICSID Case No. ARB/07/6 (7 July 2011) para 95.

75 By way of example, see already World Health Organization, 'Statement on the First Meeting of the International Health Regulations (2005) Emergency Committee on the COVID-19 Pandemic' (23 January 2020). See also chapter 12.

76 *Philip Morris* (n 36) para 402.

77 See, e.g., *Methanex* (n 30) para 7; *Eureko BV v. Republic of Poland*, Partial Award (19 August 2005) para 242.

identified whenever the investor has received *specific* assurances as to the stability of the existing conditions.[78]

Although the proportionality or reasonableness tests are, to a greater extent, inherently vague, some indications can be drawn from case law that has dealt with health measures. First, in the *Philip Morris v. Uruguay* case, the analysis was informed by the presence of international obligations. The WHO Framework Convention on Tobacco Control (FCTC) was defined as a point of reference on the basis of which to determine the reasonableness of the contested piece of legislation and used accordingly by the tribunal.[79] As discussed further in chapter 12, despite the absence of specific international health obligations, COVID-related measures were often based on the findings and recommendations regularly released by the WHO to halt the spreading of the virus.[80] WHO guidelines lacked any binding force but they were the only international benchmark in times of profound scientific uncertainty and might thus be considered relevant when deciding upon the reasonableness of COVID-related measures.[81] Second, the *Philip Morris* tribunal noted that 'the responsibility for public health measures rests with the government and investment tribunals should pay great deference to governmental judgments of national needs in matters such as the protection of public health.'[82] The tribunal followed suit and applied a high degree of deference when deciding upon the proportionality of the state's decisions. Its analysis was limited to whether the measures 'bann[ed] the production and sale of tobacco altogether',[83] without enquiring any further into the interference with the use of a trademark and ultimately finding them proportional.[84] Third, state policies adopted on the basis of specialised national regulatory agencies should be granted a high degree of deference. The limited expertise of the international tribunal as opposed to the scientific decision-maker is one of the reasons for courts to be deferential to

---

78 See, e.g., *MTD Equity Sdn Bhd and MTD Chile SA v. Republic of Chile*, ICSID Case No. ARB/01/7, Award (25 May 2004) para 214.

79 *Philip Morris* (n 36) para 401.

80 See chapter 12. See also Sondra Faccio, 'The World Health Organization's Response to the Health Emergency and its Impact on Investment Arbitration and Human Rights Case Law' (2023) 25 Int CL Rev 476.

81 Concerning the WHO's role in providing scientific knowledge in investment arbitration, see further chapter 12. See, e.g., WHO, 'COVID 19 – How to Select, Implement and Adjust Public Health and Social Measures' (11 December 2020) <www.who.int/publications/m/item/update-44-how-to-select-implement-and-adjust-public-health-and-social-measures> accessed 10 March 2023.

82 *Philip Morris* (n 36) para 399.

83 ibid para 306, footnote 405.

84 ibid para 409.

the decisions of the reviewed body.[85] In line with this, in *Chemtura v. Canada*, the tribunal noted how its role was 'not to second-guess the correctness of the science-based decision-making of highly specialized national regulatory agencies.'[86]

Ultimately, the few cases brought so far before investment arbitral tribunals over the adoption of health-related measures in the public interest have recognized the state's right to use their regulatory powers vis-à-vis foreign nationals, usually by displaying a high degree of deference towards the state's action, provided that the latter respected the other criteria of the police powers test. This is in line with the long-standing approach of domestic courts on the matter.[87]

5 Conclusion

Among the many legal questions triggered by the pandemic, the compatibility of general regulatory measures to safeguard public health with FDI protection from indirect expropriation is far from being settled. In the silence of old-generation IIAs, investment arbitral tribunals have not uniformly recognized a margin of manoeuvre in state action in the public interest, leaving the door open to speculation as to possible findings of international responsibility, should ISDS proceedings be initiated.

While these concerns are inescapable due to the inherent traits of the international protection of FDI, some trends must be accounted for. Even when confronted with old-generation expropriation provisions, arbitral tribunals have generally recognized the existence of a regulatory capacity of the state through a moderated police powers doctrine, especially when proceedings were triggered by health-related measures. The exceptionality of the pandemic, the existence of guidelines by the WHO, and the fact that virtually all states enacted such measures, might all come into play in the determination of whether a measure constitutes a lawful exercise of regulatory powers. This approach might be further reinforced if the proceedings are based on new-generation IIAs, which clarify the scope of regulatory expropriation or

85 Joshua Paine, 'Standard of Review: Investment Arbitration' (*Max Planck Encyclopedia of Public International Law*, January 2018) <https://opil.ouplaw.com/view/10.1093/law-mpeipro/e3664.013.3664/law-mpeipro-e3664> accessed 30 October 2019.

86 *Chemtura* (n 14) para 134.

87 Tim Hagemann, 'Corporate Wealth over Public Health? Assessing the Resilience of Developing Countries' COVID-19 Responses against Investment Claims and the Implications for Future Public Health Crises' (2021) 34 Pace Intl L Rev 25, 51–52.

specifically carve out health measures,[88] although the *Bear Creek* case warns about the effectiveness of these developments.[89] Specific regulatory exceptions contained in expropriation provision must then not be read in isolation, as they will be brought forward along with state defences under customary law or under IIAs, dealt with in other parts of this book.[90]

Still, case law has amply proven how international investment proceedings remain highly unpredictable. Despite the attempts by states – through their IIAs – and certain arbitral tribunals to set some tools to balance the regulatory needs of states and the protection of FDI from unlawful expropriation, there are no guarantees as to how arbitral tribunals will interpret and apply IIAs provisions in the future, nor that they will adhere to the trends or main approaches identified above. Ultimately, a finding of regulatory expropriation will depend on how the state action is carried out and will be highly dependent on the specific circumstances of each case.

---

88 Although scholars have highlighted the existence of reasons that might run counter the application of police powers by arbitral tribunals. See, e.g., Nicholas J Diamond, 'Pandemics, Emergency Measures, and ISDS' (*Kluwer Arbitration Blog*, 13 April 2020) <https://arbitrationblog.kluwerarbitration.com/2020/04/13/pandemics-emergency-measures-and-isds/> accessed 7 February 2023.

89 On the need that arbitral tribunals address the specific regulatory exceptions contained in expropriation provisions, see Guangyi Qu and Wei Shen, 'Public Health and Investment Protection in the Context of the COVID -19 Pandemic; From the Sustainable Perspective of Exception Clauses' (2022) 14 Sustainability 11, 1, 15.

90 See chapter 10 and chapter 11.

CHAPTER 10

Responses to the COVID-19 Pandemic and Customary Law Defences: Force Majeure and the State of Necessity

David Collins

1 Introduction

Many countries around the world instigated measures to combat the transmission and adverse health effects of the COVID-19 pandemic to varying degrees, shutting down innumerable businesses and destroying livelihoods in the process. Some of these businesses were foreign in origin, raising the prospect of claims of excessive interference or regulatory over-reach, necessitating compensation. These strict measures were thought by many to be the only way to deal effectively with the pandemic, at least at the beginning. Other chapters of this book have examined the types of measures that were applied,[1] such as cancelled contracts, restrictions on capital flows and the general anti-business consequences of 'lockdowns,' investigating the potential claims which may generated under investment treaties.[2]

Since we now know that COVID-19 is a serious health risk to a small minority of the population,[3] it may be argued, with some legitimacy, that the response to the crisis was disproportional. This is arguably compounded by the fact that there is convincing evidence that 'lockdowns' did not even work to supress the virus, nor, according to some, did travel bans[4] or mask mandates.[5] It is arguable

1 See for example chapters 2, 9 and 12.

2 See e.g. Julien Chaisse, 'Both Possible and Improbable: Could COVID-19 Measures Give Rise to Investor-State Disputes?' (2020) 13 Contemporary Asian Arbitration Journal 99, 165.

3 'Coronavirus (COVID-19) Mortality Rate' (*Worldometer*, 14 May 2022) <www.worldometers.info/coronavirus/coronavirus-death-rate/> accessed 20 November 2023. Age and co-morbidities were the major risk factors: 90% of deaths from COVID-19 under the age of 65 involved underlying medical conditions; average age of death from COVID-19 was 80, equal to normal life expectancy.

4 'Do Restrictions on Travel Work Against COVID?' *BBC News* (4 January 2023) <www.bbc.com/news/59461861> accessed 20 November 2023.

5 Tom Jefferson and others, 'Physical Interventions to Interrupt or Reduce the Spread of Respiratory Viruses' (2023) 1 Cochrane Database of Systematic Reviews CD006207.

© KONINKLIJKE BRILL BV, LEIDEN, 2025 | DOI:10.1163/9789004711204_012

that governments went beyond the WHO's recommendations in January 2020, which did not recommend any travel or trade restriction based on the current information available.[6] In the UK for example, the government departed from its own influenza pandemic preparedness strategy. This did not advocate actions which subsequently became known as 'lockdowns'[7] yet which became universally accepted policy, often unchallenged, in the UK and elsewhere since first instigated by China and duplicated by Italy in the early weeks of the pandemic. The lack of scientific evidence in support of measures such as lockdowns and restrictions on businesses, such as social distancing and masking, suggests that the response by many countries was not proportional to the actual risk, which again is now known to be much less than was gauged by mathematical modelling of expected deaths, which turned out to be grossly inaccurate.[8] These mis-judgments, now known in hindsight, but perhaps partially justifiable at the time, could, or perhaps should, play a role in states' ability to take advantage of available legal defences.

When assessing the potential of investment claims against states on the basis of COVID-19 response, or, as in the case of this chapter, evaluating the way in which states might defend themselves against such claims through customary international law, it is important not to fall into the trap of 'exceptionalism' in international economic law, a term used to describe a paradigm of justification according to which deviations from primary rules are absolved by way of 'exceptions' (express or implied), and in which claims of exceptionalism can be expected to proliferate. By allowing exceptional, adjudicators accepting responses to the COVID-19 pandemic as negating legal obligations pose significant risks for the legitimacy and stability of international investment law.[9] Conventional, established understandings of international investment law, including customary international law (CIL), must therefore be the basis of

6 'Statement on the Second Meeting of the International Health Regulations (2005) Emergency Committee regarding the outbreak of novel coronavirus (2019-nCoV)' (*World Health Organization*, 30 January 2020) <www.who.int/news/item/30-01-2020-statement-on-the-second-meeting-of-the-international-health-regulations-(2005)-emergency-committee-regarding-the-outbreak-of-novel-coronavirus-(2019-ncov)> accessed 20 November 2023.

7 Department of Health and Social Care, 'UK Influenza Pandemic Preparedness Strategy' (*GOV.UK*, 5 June 2014) <www.gov.uk/government/publications/review-of-the-evidence-base-underpinning-the-uk-influenza-pandemic-preparedness-strategy> accessed 1 August 2022.

8 See e.g. John PA Ioannidis, Sally Cripps, and Martin A Tannerc, 'Forecasting for COVID-19 has Failed' (2022) 38(2) International Journal of Forecasting 423.

9 Julian Arato, Kathleen Claussen, and Benton J Heath, 'The Perils of Pandemic Exceptionalism' (2020) 114(3) AJIL 627.

an appropriate legal assessment of how states might resist challenges to their responses and whether these might (or should) be successful.

CIL is a primary source of international law, along with treaties and general principles of law.[10] CIL is also a body of law arising from established practices that states consider to be binding. As a consequence of its unwritten nature, CIL is difficult to pin down, in contrast to the more specific provisions typically found in treaties. Its precise contents defy definitive identification. Nevertheless, the International Law Commission (ILC)'s Articles on State Responsibility for Internationally Wrongful Acts, 2001 (ARSIWA) are often regarded as a 'codification' of CIL, capturing many of CIL's essential principles.[11] Chapter V of the ARSIWA contains six defences that states may invoke to avoid responsibility: referred to as 'circumstances precluding wrongfulness.' These exist in addition to defences which may be specified in treaties, including investment treaties, which will be explored in chapter 11.

Three of the defences listed in ARSIWA may be appropriate CIL defences for COVID-19 response measures which harmed foreign investors: force majeure, distress, and necessity.[12] Several commentators have argued that these are the most likely defences that states will seek to rely on in defending themselves against COVID-19 response claims.[13] The police powers doctrine, which may be part of CIL,[14] may also be relevant. Each of these defences will now be explored in turn. Conclusions will be presented in the final section, generally illustrating the conflicted position of states being seen to have done either too much or too

10 Statute of the International Court of Justice (adopted 26 June 1945, entered into force 24 October 1945) USTS 993, art 38(1).

11 James Crawford, 'The ILC's Articles on Responsibility of States for Internationally Wrongful Acts: A Retrospect' (2002) 96(4) AJIL 874.

12 The other three defences under UNGA 'Articles on State Responsibility' UN Doc A/56/10 (2001) (ARSIWA), consent, self-defence and countermeasures do not easily fit the circumstances. Consent concerns acts committed to other states, not private parties. Self-defence normally relates to armed attacks. Countermeasures involve responses by states to acts of other states which is not the focus of this chapter.

13 Chaisse (n 2) 99; Federica Paddeu and Freya Jephcott, 'COVID-19 and Defences in the Law of State Responsibility: Part I' (17 March 2020) EJIL Talk <www.ejiltalk.org/covid-19-and-defences-in-the-law-of-state-responsibility-part-i/> accessed 1 August 2022; Federica Paddeu and Freya Jephcott, 'COVID-19 and Defences in the Law of State Responsibility: Part ii' (17 March 2020) EJIL Talk <www.ejiltalk.org/covid-19-and-defences-in-the-law-of-state-responsibility-part-ii/> accessed 1 August 2022.

14 The police powers doctrine is found in state practice and in judicial practice of international courts and tribunals, as well as in the writings of learned societies and eminent publicists.

little to deal with the pandemic to make much use of CIL in protecting themselves against legal action by foreign investors.

2 Customary International Law Defences

2.1 *Force Majeure*

Force majeure enables a state to claim that it is materially impossible to fulfil an international obligation, such as those featured in investment treaties. It is indirectly relevant that China's Supreme Court, for example, declared *force majeure* in relation to some contracts signed by Chinese companies, as a way to shield them from claims for non-delivery or non-purchase of products and product inputs contracted before the pandemic.[15] According to the ARSIWA, *force majeure* as an exception precluding wrongfulness will apply only if several conditions are satisfied:

(i) the act in question must be brought about by an irresistible force or an unforeseen event;
(ii) which is beyond the state's control; and
(iii) which makes it materially impossible in the circumstances to perform the obligation.[16]

Furthermore, the state applying the measure must not have contributed to the situation and not have assumed the risk of the situation occurring.[17]

Force majeure often applies to acts of war.[18] The assertion of *force majeure* is rarely successful outside these circumstances. For example, in a claim brought by a foreign investor for breach of contract, Venezuela failed to justify its failure to increase highway toll fees due to civil unrest on the basis of *force majeure*.[19]

---

15 The Supreme People's Court of the Pople's Republic of China, 'Guiding Opinions of the Supreme People's Court on Several Issues Concerning Properly Handling Civil Cases Related to COVID-19 Epidemic in Accordance with the Law (III)' (20 April 2020) <https://english.court.gov.cn/2021-10/23/c_761746.htm> accessed 1 August 2023.

16 International Law Commission (ILC), 'Draft articles on Responsibility of States for Internationally Wrongful Acts, with commentaries' (2001) 2 Yearbook of the International Law Commission 76.

17 ARSIWA (n 12) arts 23(a), 23(b).

18 Crawford (n 5) 564; Ian Brownlie, *Principles of Public International Law* (3rd edn, Clarendon Press 1979) 465.

19 *Autopista Concesionada de Venezuela, C.A. v. Bolivarian Republic of Venezuela*, ICSID Case No. ARB/00/5, Award (23 September 2003) paras 111–129. See also *Strabag SE v. Libya*, ICSID Case No. ARB(AF)/15/1, Award (29 June 2020) paras 784, 813.

Commentators agree that host states will encounter difficulties in proving material impossibility in the performance of their COVID-19 related actions.[20] States will bear a high burden in establishing that the pandemic rendered the performance of their obligations impossible.[21]

It would seem as though most countries 'lost control' to varying degrees intermittently throughout the pandemic. On the other hand, there was no breakdown of government or society – order prevailed, subject to severe constraints. COVID-19's status as an irresistible force is uncertain, as clearly the vaccines have been able to 'resist' it to a degree. It also has a very low infection fatality rate for all but the most vulnerable.[22] Regarding foreseeability, it is not certain that the spread of COVID-19 could have been both anticipated and mitigated against in light of previous outbreaks of diseases such as Severe Acute Respiratory Syndrome (SARS) and Middle East Respiratory Syndrome (MERS) seen in the last decades. Many countries had pandemic preparedness protocols in place, suggesting that they were aware that one was a distinct possibility.[23] Finally, it is arguable that states contributed to the worsening of the pandemic, for example by not shutting borders or locking down sooner (although the efficacy of both of these strategies in dealing with COVID-19 is now highly questionable).[24]

2.2 *Distress*

A state may rely on distress to justify its actions if resulting measures aimed to prevent loss of life. Distress refers to a factual situation of extreme peril, where there is no other reasonable way, of saving the lives of other persons entrusted to the state's care. Such a defence can be used where a state that acted wrongfully and did not conform to an international commitment, yet it can be shown

20 Paddeu and Parlett (n 6), Chaisse (n 2).

21 *CMS Gas Transmission Company v. The Republic of Argentina*, ICSID Case No. ARB/01/8, Award (12 May 2005) para 356; *Autopista Concesionada de Venezuela, C.A. v. Bolivarian Republic of Venezuela*, ICSID Case No. ARB/00/5, Award (23 September 2003).

22 'Coronavirus (COVID-19) Mortality Rate' (n 3).

23 E.g. the UK Influenza Preparedness Strategy (n 7) 15.

24 The UK government acknowledged that morbidity from restrictions would be worse than from COVID-19 itself: Department of Health and Social Care, Office for National Statistics, Government Actuary's Department and Home Office, 'Direct and Indirect Impacts of COVID-19 on Excess Deaths and Morbidity: Executive Summary' (*GOV.UK*, 15 July 2020) 2 <https://assets.publishing.service.gov.uk/media/5f6342438fa8f51063ce4ecf/S0650_Direct_and_Indirect_Impacts_of_COVID-19_on_Excess_Deaths_and_Morbidity.pdf > accessed 1 August 2023: 'when morbidity is taken into account, the estimates for the health impacts from a lockdown and lockdown induced recession are greater in terms of Quality Adjusted Life Years (QALYS) than the direct COVID-19 deaths'.

that the state had no other rational means in an emergency situation and that the act was taken for the purpose of saving lives. Distress has been infrequently asserted in international investment arbitration, often unsuccessfully. The *von Pezold v Zimbabwe* tribunal noted that the respondent's claim of distress was not properly pleaded, coming too late in the proceedings and without sufficient evidence. The tribunal appeared to suggest that the respondent had used the word 'distress' in its common, dictionary sense rather than to signify the defence of distress as captured by customary international law.[25]

Under the ARSIWA, to use distress, the state will have to prove:

(i) a special relationship between the state organ and the persons in question whose life were in danger;
(ii) the impossibility to deal with the threat differently;
(iv) that it did not contribute to the situation; and
(v) that the measures were proportionate.[26]

The criterion of reasonableness is designed to provide a level of 'flexibility regarding the choice of action'.[27] In such situations, the government must take strong, rapid action to minimise the loss of life.[28] Some commentators believe that host states could cite the defence of distress in response to claims by investors, in certain circumstances.[29] A successful defence on this basis would require a state to prove that there was a particular connection between that nation and those whose lives were endangered.[30]

Since public health and the life of the citizens were at stake during the COVID-19 pandemic, the threat to life conditions would appear to have been met. The 'special relationship' condition must be established between the state organs adopting the measure and the people concerned. The control between

---

25 *Bernhard von Pezold and Others v. Republic of Zimbabwe*, ICSID Case No. ARB/10/15, Procedural Order No. 9 (15 October 2013) para 36.

26 See ARSIWA (n 12) arts 24, 79, 80.

27 ibid.

28 Michael Ostrove and others, 'State Defences to Investment Claims Arising from COVID-19' (*DLA Piper*, 29 April 2020) <www.dlapiper.com/fr/france/insights/publications/2020/04/state-defences-to-investment-claims-arising-from-covid-19/> accessed 1 August 2022.

29 'COVID-19: Public Health Emergency Measures and State Defenses in International Investment Law' (*Cleary Gottlieb*, 28 April 2020) <www.lexology.com/firms/dla-piper-llp/michaCOVID-19:%20COVID-19: Public Health Emergency Measures and State Defenses in International Investment LawPublic%20Health%20Emergency%20Measures%20and%20State%20Defenses%20in%20International%20Investment%20Lawl_ostrove> accessed 1 August 2022.

30 Ostrove and others (n 14).

the state entity and the individuals whose lives are under threat is essential.[31] It could be argued that, as states are required to safeguard the health and safety or their citizens (indeed this is arguably the primary function of a government), the state had to protect those who were vulnerable to COVID-19 and took measures such as social distancing, confinement or business closures to meet this objective. Moreover, since the central government has the authority to instigate lockdowns, some contend that it is plausible that the special relationship criterion is met because there is such a relationship when 'the fate of the population is within the control of the central authorities'.[32] However, others have argued that this condition may be difficult to meet as COVID-19 measures were only implemented to protect the entire population.[33] Indeed, targeted protection of the vulnerable appeared to have been completely disregarded as a strategy across most of the world.

As mentioned, the requirement for reasonableness aims at providing a 'certain degree of flexibility in the assessment of the conditions of distress'.[34] The concept of proportionality requires that the measures go no further than required to address the harm, striking a balance between the means used and the intended aim. Some measures taken to cope with COVID-19, such as social distancing, were arguably reasonable since they were believed, at the time, to have reduced the transmission rate of the disease, ultimately saving lives by reducing the burden on healthcare systems.[35] On the other hand, the arbitrary nature of some of the social distancing rules (varying distances, changing distances over time, different distances for different sizes of room etc.) makes this assertion more dubious.

The issue is more problematic in relation to country-wide lockdowns and travel bans.[36] The success of Sweden, as well as US states such as Florida, which did not implement severe restrictions and with substantially lower death rates than many other countries, suggests that many of the measures, such as social distancing in its various forms, were not necessary.

---

31 Onur Inan, 'Can States Successfully Resort to the Customary International Defences against the Possible Claims Arising out of COVID-19 Measures?' (2020) 14 Romanian Arbitration Journal 131.

32 Paddeu and Jephcott (n 6).

33 Ostrove and others (n 14).

34 ILC (n 16) 80 para 6.

35 Felix Richter, 'Coronavirus: This Chart Shows Why Social Distancing is so Important' (*World Economic Forum*, 19 March 2020) <www.weforum.org/agenda/2020/03/social-distancing-measures-coronavirus-covid19/> accessed 1 August 2023.

36 Paddeu and Jephcott (n 6).

Distress can only preclude wrongfulness where the interests sought to be protected (e.g. the lives of passengers or crew) clearly outweigh the other interests at stake in the circumstances. If the conduct sought to be excused endangers more lives than it may save or is otherwise likely to create a greater peril it will not be covered by the plea of distress.[37] In that regard, we do not know how many lives were lost because of the lockdown. In the UK this is believed to potentially be in the millions (cancelled medical treatment, psychological harm etc).[38]

The defence of distress will not apply if: (a) the situation of distress is due, either alone or in combination with other factors, to the conduct of the state invoking it; or (b) the act in question is likely to create a comparable or greater peril.[39] The interest protected must 'clearly outweigh the other interests at stake in the circumstances'.[40] A potential difficulty here is that that the measures were not implemented with regards to a specific section of the population (the shielding strategy), but rather to the entire population.

2.3 *Necessity*

The defence of distress does not extend to more general cases of emergencies.[41] Instead, the doctrine of necessity is invoked by respondent states facing international legal claims to cover more general situations of crisis. It then can function as an excuse for the breach of an international law obligation, such as the obligations contained in an IIA as determined by an arbitration tribunal. The defence of necessity, as circumstance precluding wrongfulness under customary international law, thereby empowers host states to breach their commitments to investors during times of crisis.

A state can only invoke the defence of necessity if the following conditions are met:

(i) the act in question must be the only way for the state to safeguard an essential interest against a grave and imminent peril;

---

37 ILC (n 16) 80 para 10.

38 See e.g. Larry Elliott 'A Year of COVID Lockdowns has Cost the UK Economy £251 Billion' *The Guardian UK* (London, 22 March 2021) <www.theguardian.com/business/2021/mar/22/a-year-of-covid-lockdowns-has-cost-the-uk-economy-251bn-study-says#:~:text=2%20years%20old-,A%20year%20of%20Covid%20lockdowns%20has%20cost,economy%20%C2%A3251bn%2C%20study%20says&text=A%20year%20of%20Covid%2D19,a%20report%20published%20on%20Monday> accessed 1 August 2023.

39 ARSIWA (n 12) arts 24(2)(a), 24(2)(b).

40 ILC (n 16) 80 para 10.

41 ibid para 7.

(ii) the state's act must not seriously impair an essential interest of another State or of the international community as a whole; and
(iii) the state cannot invoke this defence if it has contributed to the situation.[42]

States have to be careful to ensure the measures they enact under this defence are necessary and in proportion to the stated objective and achieve a legitimate policy outcome. Some believe that host states had a responsibility to prevent the spread of the pandemic through the imposition of strict measures, such as shutting down businesses, since this was thought to be the only way to deal effectively with the pandemic.[43] Qualifying for a defence of necessity is based on identifying a need to uphold public's safety by preventing harm to the community, and secondly, whether any delay in taking action might lead to imminent or future harm to the community.[44] Tribunals constituted under the Argentina-US BIT examined the necessity defence outlined in that treaty, in some cases conflating it with that found in customary international law.[45] Scholars note that there are some superficial similarities between treaty exceptions referring to measures 'necessary for the maintenance of public order' and the prerequisites for the invocation of the customary plea. Both forms require the identification of a legitimate objective and an analysis of whether the challenged measure is necessary to achieve that objective. The key difference is that in the context of exception clauses found in IIAs, the necessity functions as a primary rule: successful invocation of the clause means that there is no treaty breach and therefore no state liability. The customary plea of necessity, on the other hand, may be used only where a breach of an international obligation has been established according to the rules of the particular regime.

42 ARSIWA (n 12) arts 25, 80.

43 Riddhi Joshi, 'Force Majeure under the ILC Draft Articles on State Responsibility: Assessing its Viability against COVID-19 Claims' (2020) 24(24) ASIL <www.asil.org/insights/volume/24/issue/24/force-majeure-under-ilc-draft-articles-state-responsibility-assessing> accessed 1 August 2022.

44 Paddeu and Jephcott (n 6).

45 *CMS* (n 21) Decision of the ad hoc Committee on the Application for Annulment of the Argentine Republic (15 Sept 2007) para 146; *Sempra Energy International v. The Argentine Republic*, ICSID Case No. ARB/02/16, Award (18 Sept 2007) para 376; *Enron Corporation and Ponderosa Assets, L.P. v. Argentine Republic*, ICSID Case No. ARB/01/3, Award (22 May 2007) para 334.

Here it operates as a secondary rule to determine whether wrongfulness is precluded.[46]

Finally, it is important to note that an essential interest may be valid if it might affect the international community, even when it does not threaten the host state.[47] From this perspective, it can be argued that it was essential for governments to shut down businesses during the global pandemic, since again these types of measures, along with travel bans were seen (rightly or wrongly) as only way for the state to manage the spread of the virus and limit associated fatalities.[48]

There have been several investment arbitration cases dealing with necessity, making it one of the more well-developed defences available under CIL in international investment law.[49] In the aftermath of the Argentinean economic crisis in the early 2000s, the state of Argentina invoked the defence of necessity with varying degrees of success. The similar factual background has led to the Argentina cases becoming somewhat of a test-case for the applicability of the defence of necessity to international investments as it applies to various adaptations across several across sectors.

While the *CMS* and *Enron* tribunals recognised the severity of the economic crisis which had gripped Argentina,[50] they felt that Argentina had contributed to the crisis in both cases, defeating a claim of necessity. The *CMS* Annulment Committee[51] upheld the tribunal's rejection of the defence although in that case the arbitrators erroneously considered whether Argentina qualified for the defence of necessity at all.[52] The Annulment Committee in *Enron*[53] also annulled parts of the award because the tribunal had concluded too promptly that the defence of necessity would only apply if the challenged measures were the 'only' means available to the state to protect its essential interests. The

46 Caroline Henckels, *Proportionality and Deference in Investor-State Arbitration* (CUP 2015) 7–88; August Reinisch, 'Necessity in Investment Arbitration' (2010) 41 Netherlands Yearbook of International Law 137.

47 ibid.

48 Ostrove and others (n 14).

49 Especially the Argentina cases, noted above: *CMS* (n 21), *Sempra* (n 45) and *Enron* (n 45).

50 *CMS* (n 21) para 324.

51 Contained in Convention on the Settlement of Investment Disputes between States and Nationals of Other States (opened for signature 18 March 1965, entered into force 14 October 1966) (ICSID Convention) art 52(1), an annulment procedure is a form of review for a narrow range of procedural errors – it is not a substantive appeal.

52 Fiona Marshall, '*CMS Gas Transmission Co. v. Republic of Argentina,* ICSID Case No. ARB/01/8' (*IISD*, 18 October 2018) <www.iisd.org/itn/en/2018/10/18/cms-v-argentina/> accessed 30 June 2023.

53 *Enron* (n 45) paras 306, 312.

tribunal also ruled that Argentina could not benefit from the defence because it had contributed to the state of necessity.[54] The tribunal reasoned that the Argentine economic crisis did compromise the very existence of the state and its independence, qualifying as involving an essential interest of the state.

Argentina did succeed in using the defence of necessity as it had restricted transfers out of its territory. The tribunal in *Continental Casualty* held that necessity precluded Argentina's liability for breaching its obligations.[55] It also observed, somewhat expansively, that international law was not 'blind to states' needs to exercise their sovereignty in the interest of their populations, free from internal as well as external threats to security'.[56]

These exercises of sovereignty could well include protecting citizens' health.[57] This purpose must be assessed objectively, according to the *Continental Casualty* tribunal, and it must contain 'a significant margin of appreciation for the state applying the particular measure: a time of grave crisis is not a time for nice judgments, particularly when examined by others with the [advantage] of hindsight'.[58] It would seem as though states should be accorded a wide degree of discretion in assessing the nature of the risks and appropriate responses.

In another case, the *LG&E* tribunal found that Argentina's actions were taken during a state of necessity between December 2001 and April 2003 (during the worst period of its economic crisis). It should be absolved from its responsibility for losses that occurred during this period.[59] Argentina was able to demonstrate that the provision of water and sewage services were vital to its population and were an essential interest of the state.[60] By analogy, states

54 Lise Johnson, 'Second Argentine Award Annulled in One Month Enron Creditors Recovery Corporation and Ponderosa Assets, L.P. v. Argentine Republic (ICSID Case No. ARB/01/3) – Annulment Proceeding' (*IISD*, 23 September 2010) <www.iisd.org/itn/en/2010/09/23/awards-and-decisions/> accessed 1 August 2022.

55 *Continental Casualty Company v. The Argentine Republic*, ICSID Case No. ARB/03/9, Award (5 September 2008) para 193.

56 ibid para 175.

57 ibid para 177.

58 ibid para 181.

59 *LG&E Energy Corp., LG&E Capital Corp., and LG&E International, Inc. v. Argentine Republic*, ICSID Case No. ARB/02/1, Decision on Liability (3 October 2006) para 229.

60 *Suez, Sociedad General de Aguas de Barcelona S.A., and Inter Aguas Servicios Integrales del Agua S.A. v. The Argentine Republic*, ICSID Case No. ARB/03/17, Decision on Liability (30 July 2010) para 238; *Suez, Sociedad General de Aguas de Barcelona, S.A. and Vivendi Universal, S.A. v. Argentine Republic*, ICSID Case No. ARB/03/19, Decision on Liability (30 July 2010) para 260; *Impregilo S.p.A. v. Argentine Republic*, ICSID Case No. ARB/07/17, Award (21 June 2011) para 346.

will probably be able to successfully argue that public health qualifies as an essential interest.

Investment tribunals will most likely consider that the COVID-19 pandemic was a 'grave and imminent peril', having led to the deaths of almost 6 million people by mid-2022.[61] This is despite the fact that we now know that the disease posed a serious threat only to the most vulnerable members of society. A state may have more difficulty proving that the measures that it implemented in response to the pandemic were 'the only way' to safeguard against the peril.[62] This is all the more so now that data is available to show that many of the measures such as lockdowns had a dubious effect on suppression of the disease. Targeted isolation for the *vulnerable*, along the lines of the strategy advocated in the much-maligned Great Barrington Declaration,[63] may have achieved the same reduction in mortality with far less adverse consequences on society and the economy.

A state also has an obligation to ensure that its actions do not seriously impair an essential interest of another state or of the whole community. States may accordingly struggle to justify their ban on exports of personal protection equipment or vaccines as these measures arguably shifted harms to countries that were less able to bear them.[64] It is worth noting, however, that there does not appear to be a clear correlation between GDP per capita and COVID-19 fatalities.[65]

Also, problematically, the state cannot invoke the defence of necessity if it contributed to the situation of necessity, meaning that the causal contribution of the state was 'sufficiently substantial or merely incidental or peripheral'.[66] The proportionality and reasonableness of the state's conduct in this regard will be examined on a case-by-case basis. It will also be evaluated in light of the conduct of other states 'in comparable circumstances.'[67] While there were outliers which imposed limited suppression measures, such as Sweden, most

61 See World Health Organization, 'WHO Coronavirus (COVID-19) Dashboard' <https://covid19.who.int/> accessed 1 August 2022.

62 *Enron* (n 45) para 308; *CMS* (n 21) para 323.

63 'Great Barrington Declaration' <https://gbdeclaration.org/> accessed 1 August 2022. See further Mark Woolhouse, *The Year the World Went Mad* (Sandstone Press, 2022).

64 Ostrove and others (n 14).

65 Rich Countries May Have Suffered a Slightly Larger Loss of Life Years Than Poor Countries: Francisco HG Ferreira, 'Inequality in the Time of COVID' (*International Monetary Fund*, September 2021) <www.imf.org/external/pubs/ft/fandd/2021/06/inequality-and-covid-19-ferreira.htm> accessed 1 August 2023.

66 *CMS* (n 21) para 328.

67 *Continental* (n 55) para 227.

countries in the world readily embraced lockdowns and other strict measures at various points throughout the pandemic, suggesting that there was a policy consensus regarding appropriate responses.

2.4 *Police Powers*

Some have argued that the 'police powers' doctrine could provide a way for states to avoid liability for the actions they took to combat COVID-19 which adversely affected foreign investors.[68] The police powers doctrine, often associated with defences to claims of indirect expropriation, states that non-discriminatory measures that aim to achieve a public purpose will not give rise to a duty to compensate investors for losses incurred. It is widely believed that there does not need to be an express police powers clause in a treaty. But if police powers are expressly excluded, this could be sufficient for a tribunal to deny this defence.[69]

Although some investment tribunals have treated the police powers doctrine as a customary rule of international law,[70] this is far from settled.[71] ICSID tribunals have refused to apply the police powers doctrine when addressing defences to expropriation, instead turning to the 'solo effects doctrine'.[72] Under this doctrine, the test to determine whether a regulation constitutes an expropriation entitling the investor to compensation depends entirely on the effect of the measure on the investment with no regard for its objective. In *Vivendi v. Argentina*, for example, the tribunal ruled that 'the effect of the measure on the investor, not the state's intent, is the critical factor'.[73] It is clear that states

---

68 Nathalie Potin, 'Lines of Attack and Defences for Foreign Investors and States in Future Investment Disputes Post-Pandemic' (2022) 28(2) International Trade Law and Regulation 90.

69 Noam Zamir, 'The Police Powers Doctrine in International Investment Law' (2017) 14 Manchester J Int'l Econ L 318; Chaisse (n 2).

70 E.g. *Chemtura Corporation v. The Government of Canada*, UNCITRAL, Award (2 August 2010). See further Ursula Kriebaum, 'Regulatory Takings: Balancing the Interests of the Investor and the State' (2007) 8(5) JWIT 717; Erlend M Leonhardsen, 'Looking for Legitimacy: Exploring Proportionality Analysis in Investment Treaty Arbitration' (2011) 3(1) J Int Dispute Settl 95; Sondra Faccio, *Indirect Expropriation in International Investment Law. Between State Regulatory Powers and Investor Protection* (Editoriale Scientifica 2020) 93ff.

71 Catherine Titi, 'Police Powers Doctrine and International Investment Law' in Andrea Gattini, Attila ME Tanzi, and Filippo Fontanelli (eds), *General Principles of Law and International Investment Arbitration* (Brill 2018).

72 Rudolf Dolzer, 'Indirect Expropriations: New Developments?' (2002) 11 NYU Environmental Law Journal 79.

73 *Compañía de Aguas del Aconquija S.A. and Vivendi Universal S.A. v. Argentina*, ICSID Case No. ARB/97/3, Award (20 August 2007) para 7.5.20.

may rely on the police powers doctrine to respond to claims from international investors.[74] Police powers was denied in several cases,[75] but was successfully pleaded in several situations where claims were rejected which challenged regulatory measures designed to protect public health.[76]

States bear the obligation of protecting and preserving life within their boundaries. Police powers accordingly justify that governments act as agents for the protection of society's interests and adopt measures as necessary, even if those measures deprive an investor of benefits or control of their investment. In doing so, though, governments must demonstrate a reasonable balance between the extent of the deprivation and the aim sought. In *Azurix Corp. v Argentina*,[77] the tribunal established that this intent must be demonstrated and cannot simply be asserted.

In enacting lockdown and other disease suppression measures, governments were arguably exercising their police powers. Some may view these as inadequate whereas others might suggest that they were excessive. In the *Philip Morris v Uruguay* dispute, the arbitral tribunal rejected a claim of indirect expropriation against legislation enacted by Uruguay on public health grounds. Instead, the tribunal accepted that Uruguay's measures protected public health and were adopted 'in good faith' in a 'non-discriminatory' fashion, and were 'proportionate to the objective they meant to achieve'.[78] Since the incidence of smoking declined as sought, the Philip Morris tribunal felt that the plain packaging requirement for tobacco products was 'a valid exercise' of Uruguay 'police powers for the protection of public health'.[79] That governments pursued COVID-19 suppression strategies in good faith may hopefully be presumed. Proportionality between costs and benefits will be more difficult to demonstrate.

A case from near the turn of the 20th Century may be illustrative with regards to the specific situation engendered by COVID-19 and the legality of state action. *Bischoff's Case* of 1903 dealt with the taking of a carriage by

---

74 Zamir (n 50); Prabhash Ranjan, 'Police Powers, Indirect Expropriation in International Investment Law, and Article 31(3)(c) of the VCLT: A Critique of Philip Morris v. Uruguay' (2019) 9(1) Asian Journal of International Law 98.

75 *Compañía Del Desarrollo De Santa Elena, S.A. v. The Republic of Costa Rica,* ICSID Case No. ARB/96/1, Award (17 February 2000) para 72; *Pope & Talbot, Inc v. Government of Canada,* UNCITRAL, Interim Award (26 June 2000) para 99.

76 E.g. *Philip Morris Brands Sàrl, Philip Morris Products S.A. and Abal Hermanos S.A. v. Oriental Republic of Uruguay,* ICSID Case No. ARB/10/7, Award (8 July 2016).

77 *Azurix Corp. v. The Argentine Republic,* ICSID Case No. ARB/01/12, Award (14 July 2006).

78 *Philip Morris* (n 76) para 306.

79 ibid para 307.

Venezuela for the purpose of carrying passengers contaminated with smallpox. The court dismissed the claim for damages by the carriage owner, holding that '[c]ertainly during an epidemic of an infectious disease there can be no liability for the reasonable exercise of police powers'.[80] This case indicates that the prevention of the spread of disease entitles governmental authorities to infringe the ownership rights of individuals in a manner that would otherwise be prohibited.

The applicability of police powers as a defence may be a fraught exercise and tribunals will face difficulties in relieving states of claims of indirect expropriation on its basis.[81] Some have cautioned that enabling states to breach their investment obligations through resort to defences premised on the existence of exceptional circumstances, such as a public health crisis, harmfully compels investment arbitrators to adjudicate in relation to health policy, which is outside their disciplinary competence.[82] This is a valid point – indeed, the concept of public health has expanded in recent years, enabling interventions in matters that are arguably extraneous to a government's purview, such as poverty, housing and climate change.

3 Conclusion

The extent to which states were transparent in the application of the COVID-19 response measures as well as their scope and purpose could dictate whether or not any of the above defences are operative. Consulting with potentially affected enterprises and stakeholders when assessing policy options, including the presentation of draft regulations for public scrutiny and comment, could also help.[83] States probably did not pay much regard to the impact of their decisions on foreign investors when deciding emergency interventions or measures such as lockdowns. Indeed, it would seem that the long-term consequences of lockdowns and other measures may have been suppressed by governments eager to be seen to be doing something to assuage the publics' fears.[84]

---

80 'Bischoff Case' (1903) 10 Reports of International Arbitral Awards 420.

81 Zamir (n 50) 333–337.

82 Arato, Claussen, and Heath (n 3).

83 'Perspectives – COVID-19 & International Investment Protection' (*Shearman & Sterling*, 14 April 2020) <www.shearman.com/Perspectives/2020/04/COVID-19-International-Investment-Protection> accessed 1 August 2022.

84 Camilla Turner, 'Mistake to "Empower Scientists" in COVID Pandemic' *The Telegraph* (25 August 2022) quoting the former UK Chancellor of the Exchequer Rishi Sunak.

Some have urged that vagueness of treaty standards will apply to COVID-19 measures, and further the lack of precedent in arbitration may 'incentivize lawyers and third-party funders to speculate by bringing multiple claims challenging similar measures across the globe.'[85] Others controversially proposed that countries should come together 'to suspend the application of treaty-based investor–state arbitration for all COVID-19 related measures or clarify how international law defences apply to this extraordinary situation'.[86] As other chapters of this book have illustrated, claims brought under newer generation IIAs which contain wider rights of states to enact public policy measures (and correspondingly narrower protections for foreign investors) reduce the likelihood that such claims will succeed. Such treaties are more protective of the state's right to regulate and the state's need to safeguard the public interest.[87] Many IIAs contain specialized exceptions for state action in circumstances of 'public emergency,' to protect 'essential security interests,' for 'public order,' or sometimes to 'protect public health,' many of which were probably engaged by the pandemic. The ambiguity of these concepts affords very broad scope for governments to infringe on the activities of investors that might in the past have triggered liability under international law. On the other hand, new generation treaties are fewer compared to old generation ones, that explains the importance of customary law defences. Moreover, it has been argued that tribunals have been unwilling to recognize these powers, preferring instead to import standards from older treaties through MFN clauses, for example.[88]

This chapter has illustrated the CIL defences available to states for claims brought by investors in relation to COVID-19 response measures. *Force majeure* involves an occurrence of an irresistible force or an unforeseen event beyond the control of the state making it materially impossible to perform an obligation. Investment arbitration tribunals have held that *force majeure* can only be used when there is: i) impossibility of performance; ii) unforseeability; and iii) non-attribution to the state, the last of which is probably the hardest to satisfy.

---

85 Nathalie Bernasconi-Osterwalder, Sarah Brewin, and Nyaguthii Maina, 'Protecting Against Investor–State Claims Amidst COVID-19: A Call to Action for Governments' (*IISD*, April 2020), <www.iisd.org/articles/protecting-against-investor-state-claims-amidst-covid-19-call-action-governments> accessed 1 August 2022.

86 Nyaguthii Maina and Suzy H Nikièma, 'The African Union's Declaration on COVID-Related ISDS Risks: Why it matters now' (*IISD*, 2 March 2021) <www.iisd.org/articles/african-union-ministerial-declaration-covid-related-isds-risks-why-it-matters-now> accessed 1 August 2022.

87 Potin (n 49). See chapters 2, 8, 9, 12.

88 Wolfgang Aschner, *Investment Arbitration and State-Driven Reform: New Treaties, Old Outcomes* (OUP 2022).

In the context of COVID-19, it will be difficult for states to prove loss of control and unforseeability given continued functioning of government and experience of previous pandemics. States may have contributed to the worsening of pandemic by not reacting faster, although in hindsight this is unlikely as the many interventions appeared to have a minimal impact on the spread of the disease or its severity.[89]

The defence of distress is available where the state is required to take action to prevent loss of life where there is no other reasonable way. The state must show that there is a special relationship between it and the persons whose lives are in danger. Distress also requires that the state did not contribute to the event and that the measures were proportionate. But distress is narrow in scope – it does not extend to more general cases of emergencies (where defence of necessity is more appropriate). When it comes to the pandemic, the special relationship likely met because of state's responsibility for its citizens' lives, particularly where there is public healthcare. Non-contribution could be problematic because of the perceived slow or inadequate response of some governments. Standards of proportionality and reasonableness are questionable because of uncertain benefits of some measures (e.g. lockdowns, travel bans) possibly even resulting in a worsening of harms. The acceleration of inflation across the industrialized world in 2022 is perhaps the most obvious collateral damage from the COVID-19 responses. Untreated illnesses because of missed doctors' appointments, an explosion of mental illness through isolation and stunted education of children due to closed schools other leading contenders.

The defence of necessity is available when the measure is the only way for state to safeguard an essential interest against a grave an immanent peril. The state's act must not seriously impair the essential interests of another state, or the international community and the state cannot have contributed to the situation. States (notably Argentina) have used necessity as a defence in many investment claims, in some cases successfully. While public health is likely to be viewed as an essential interest, the 'only way' will be difficult to prove because some measures were arguably excessive (e.g. lockdowns, travel bans). States may have contributed to the situation by failing to act faster – but this will be assessed by conduct of other comparable states. It appears that harsh suppression at an early stage, as in the case of China and Italy, did little

89 Phil Kerpen, Stephen Moore, and Casey B Mulligan, 'A Final Report Card on the States' Response to COVID-19' National Bureau of Economic Research (*National Bureau of Economic Research*, April 2022) <www.nber.org/papers/w29928> accessed 1 August 2022.

to alleviate later surges of infections. Additionally, some measures impaired other states' interests (e.g. vaccine & PPE export bans).

Finally, the police powers doctrine, which may be part of CIL, protects the state's right to regulate over important matters such as public health, order or morality. Measures taken under the police powers doctrine will not be subject to claims of expropriation or give rise to compensation to investors. Protecting public health has been viewed as an aspect of police powers by international tribunals, but reasonableness and proportionality must be shown. Again, this could be problematic since many measures may be viewed as excessive.

It would seem that necessity is probably the best avenue for a state to defend itself against a claim from a foreign investor based on responses to the pandemic. Necessity is the most commonly invoked of the discussed defences in investment arbitration and has general application to emergencies such as a serious, widespread public health crisis. The main problems with using necessity, and indeed some of the other defences, seem to be non-contribution, proportionality and reasonableness. Paradoxically these requirements seem to be mutually exclusive: if a state contributed to the worsening of the pandemic because it did not do enough (a claim that is increasingly uncommon) then logically it cannot have acted excessively (a far more prevalent assertion as of mid-2022).

If they are accepted as lawful, there is a danger that some of the pandemic responses may end up remaining in place or being re-tried in similar circumstances. Indeed, some politicians are on record of saying that the pandemic can be used to instigate a new era of state-led interventions in many aspects of society.[90] While CIL defences were designed to respond to once-in-a-generation crises, they are less-well suited to address these kinds of interferences.[91] Consequently tribunals adjudicating international law must ensure that they are not wielded by states lightly. Taking a narrower view of CIL defences to state responsibility could also help forestall overreach in situations when needing to be seen 'doing something' drives decision-making whereas doing nothing, or something markedly less severe, would have been wiser.

---

90 E.g. Canadian Deputy Prime Minister Chrystia Freeland's infamous statement: 'I really believe COVID-19 has created a window of political opportunity', reported in John Tasker, 'Freeland says COVID-19 has created a 'window of opportunity' to launch national child-care program' (*CBC*, 8 April 2021) <www.cbc.ca/news/politics/freeland-child-care-liberal-convention-1.5980851#:~:text=%22A%20lot%20of%20people%20who,for%20the%20women%20of%20today.%22> accessed 1 August 2023.

91 Arato, Claussen, and Heath (n 3).

CHAPTER 11

State Defences under International Investment Agreements

Silvina González Napolitano

1 Introduction

The COVID-19 pandemic led states to rapidly adopt different types of measures in order to prevent the virus from spreading. Some measures impacted the normal compliance with international obligations in relation to foreign investment activities, which prompted some investors to resort to arbitration.[1]

The purpose of this chapter is to identify some of the substantive defences that states could invoke under bilateral investment treaties or investment chapters of bilateral or multilateral free trade agreements (which we will refer to generically as 'investment treaties') to deal with emergency situations, like a pandemic, or to protect essential interests of the state.

To this end, firstly, reference will be made to the evolution of investment treaties, in order to verify at what point states began to be concerned with including rules that safeguard the regulatory power of the state or the ability to manoeuvre in states of emergency. Secondly, the chapter will show what the relevant provisions contained in the new generation of investment agreements are. It will also mention some of the international disputes that were brought before arbitral tribunals, in which various defences related to the right to health, the environment or safety were invoked, and the response given by these tribunals. Finally, based on the above, some concluding observations will be presented.

1 *Concesionaria Peruana de Vías – COVINCA, S.A. v. Republic of Peru*, ICSID Case No. ARB/21/45; *VINCI Highways SAS and VINCI Concessions SAS v. Republic of Peru*, ICSID Case No. ARB/21/60. These claims are reportedly linked to the suspension of toll collection mandated by a Peruvian law during the COVID-19 pandemic.

© KONINKLIJKE BRILL BV, LEIDEN, 2025 | DOI:10.1163/9789004711204_013

2 Investment Treaty Clauses on Emergency Situations or Essential Interests of the State

Investment treaties emerged in the 20th century, hand in hand with their 'cousins', the Friendship, Commerce, and Navigation Treaties (FCN Treaties). In the 18th century, the latter already contained provisions to protect the property of nationals in a foreign country.[2] From 1946 onwards, the United States decided to strengthen its FCN Treaties, while years later other states began to negotiate investment treaties, mainly as a defensive reaction to the expropriations suffered by their national investors.[3] In these new FCN Treaties negotiated by the United States, such as the China-USA FCN (1946), we can already find a clause on non-precluded measures (NPM) to protect essential security interests.[4]

Since the origin of investment treaties, we have also been able to find agreements that contain provisions protecting some essential interests or that are to be applied in emergency situations. Germany was the first country to do so, signing its first BIT on 5 November 1959 with Pakistan (which can be described as a 'first-generation treaty'), thus beginning a new era of foreign investment protection. This was followed by other countries, including Switzerland, the Netherlands, France, and Italy, which negotiated several such treaties in the 1960s.[5] Others, however, such as the United Kingdom, only began to do so in the mid-1970s, while the United States signed its first BIT with Panama in 1982, which contains an NPM clause.

The Protocol attached to the Germany-Pakistan BIT made it clear that '[m]easures taken for reasons of public security and order, public health or morality shall not be deemed as discrimination within the meaning of Article

2 Kenneth J Vandevelde, 'A Brief History of International Investment Agreements' (2005) 12(1) UCDavis JIntl L& Pol'y 157, 158–159.

3 ibid 162, 171.

4 William Burke-White and Andreas von Staden, 'Investment Protection in Extraordinary Times: The Interpretation and Application of Non-Precluded Measures Provisions in Bilateral Investment Treaties' (2008) 48(2) VaJIntl L 312.

5 For example, Switzerland-Tunisia Bilateral Investment Treaty (BIT) (signed 2 December 1961, entered into force 19 January 1964, not in force), Switzerland-Niger BIT (signed 28 March 1962, entered into force 17 November 1972), Netherlands-Tunisia BIT (signed 23 March 1963, entered into force 19 December 1974), Netherlands-Côte d'Ivoire BIT (signed 26 April 1965, entered into force 8 September 1966), France-Tunisia BIT (signed 9 August 1963, entered into force 9 August 1965), Italy-Guinea BIT (signed 20 February 1964, entered into force 20 February 1964), and Italy-Malta BIT (signed 28 July 1967, entered into force 15 October 1973). The text of these agreements can be consulted at UNCTAD, International Investment Agreements Navigator <https://investmentpolicy.unctad.org/international-investment-agreements> accessed 23 September 2023.

2'.[6] On the other hand, the main text of the Germany-Pakistan BIT provided for specific non-discrimination protection with regard to measures taken in respect of losses suffered by investors in cases of 'war or other armed conflicts, revolution or revolt in the territory of the other Party'.[7] While such provisions were not found in agreements concluded by other states at the time, years later the latter were included in most BITs (usually under the heading of 'Compensation for losses'), albeit with some variations as to their scope. Some treaties include, among the situations covered by this provision, the 'state of national emergency'.[8]

Since the end of the 20th and beginning of the 21st century, some states started to introduce specific clarifications in their treaties, which can be called 'second-generation treaties', and then, mainly from 2010 onwards, states have begun to negotiate more balanced agreements to promote investments based on sustainable development principles, with a more complex and detailed structure, which can be called 'third-generation treaties'.[9] These treaties include elements that produce a balance between the obligations that states assume towards investors or foreign investments, and the obligations that investors must fulfil in return. Today, to deal with an emergency, or a situation that requires the protection of essential interests, states can invoke a variety of those provisions to exempt or mitigate their responsibility for the measures they should have taken.[10] Some of them are described below.

6 Protocol annexed to the Germany-Pakistan BIT (signed 25 November 1959, entered into force 28 April 1962) para 2.

7 Germany-Pakistan BIT (n 6) art 3.3.

8 E.g., Panama-US BIT (signed 27 October 1982, entered into force 30 May 1991) art V.

9 According to UNCTAD, 'first-generation treaties' are those concluded before 2010. See UNCTAD, 'Reform of the International Investment Agreement Regime: Phase 2' (2017) 2 TD/B/C.II/MEM.4/14 <https://unctad.org/system/files/official-document/ciimem4d14_en.pdf> accessed 23 September 2023. However, the author believes that investment treaties or chapters should be classified into three categories: first, second and third generation. 'Second-generation of treaties' are those negotiated prior to 2010, and containing some clarifications (such as NAFTA and CAFTA). 'Third-generation of treaties' are those negotiated after 2010 and containing a more complex and detailed structure.

10 See Federica Cristani, 'How the Coronavirus Crisis Challenges International Investment (Customary) Law Rules: Which Role for the Necessity Defense?' (2021) 53 Case Western Reserve JIntlL 89; Dimitrios Katsikis, '"Necessity" due to COVID-19 as a Defence to International Investment Claims' (2021) 36(1) ICSID Rev 46; Orhan Bayrak, 'Economic Crises and the Fundamental Change of Circumstances in Investment Arbitration' (2020) 35(1–2) ICSID Rev 130; Freya Baetens, 'Protecting Foreign Investment and Public Health through Arbitral Balancing and Treaty Design' (2022) 71 ICLQ 139.

2.1 *More Precise Standards of Treatment*

As opposed to the first-generation BITs that enunciated very lax standards of treatment, the new treaties incorporate elements that allow greater precision when determining the scope of each standard. These elements should prevent investment tribunals from making expansive interpretations that deviate from what the negotiating states wanted to agree in each treaty.[11] Undoubtedly, explicit clarifications in the text facilitate the state's defence in the case of a claim that it has violated the BIT.

For example, like many other treaties, the Comprehensive and Progressive Agreement for Trans-Pacific Partnership (CPTPP) (2018) in Article 9.6 details the content of the fair and equitable treatment standard and clarifies that some measures, even if inconsistent with the legitimate expectations of investors, or causing damage to them, do not constitute a violation of such standard of treatment.[12]

In addition, some investment treaties, especially those that do not have a general 'right to regulate' provision, when referring to some standards of treatment, leave out measures that the host state may adopt to protect legitimate public policy objectives, such as health, environment, and safety, amongst others.[13]

With regard to the national treatment and most favoured nation clauses, the new treaties specify that these standards must be accorded to investors or investments that are 'in like circumstances'. Thus, the context of a crisis or emergency situation will be particularly relevant in the framework of this provision for the purpose of comparing the measures adopted by the state with respect to another investor or investment. Furthermore, some investment treaties clarify the expression in 'like

11 On the debate surrounding the new generations of BITs, and its main features, see John Beechey and Antony Crockett, 'New Generation of Bilateral Investment Treaties: Consensus or Divergence?' (2008) Contemporary Issues in International Arbitration and Mediation: The Fordham Papers 5; David Gaukrodger, 'The Future of Investment Treaties – Possible Directions' (2021) OECD Working Papers on International Investment 2021/03 <https://doi.org/10.1787/946c3970-en> accessed 28 March 2023.

12 According to the Comprehensive and Progressive Agreement for Trans-Pacific Partnership (CPTPP) (signed 4 February 2016, not in force) art 9.6(2) '(a) "fair and equitable treatment" includes the obligation not to deny justice in criminal, civil or administrative adjudicatory proceedings in accordance with the principle of due process embodied in the principal legal systems of the world'; and (b) "full protection and security" requires each Party to provide the level of police protection required under customary international law.'

13 For instance, Canada-Moldova BIT (signed 12 June 2018, entered into force 23 August 2019) art 9 on Performance Requirements.

circumstances'.[14] This distinction is relevant in the context of the measures adopted during the COVID-19 pandemic. Indeed, the restrictions imposed by governments were not the same for all economic sectors and workers. For example, companies producing medical or pharmaceutical supplies or health professionals were not in the same circumstances as other sectors and professionals.

In connection with indirect expropriation, some treaties state that non-discriminatory regulatory actions by a contracting party that are designed and applied to protect legitimate public welfare objectives, such as public health, safety and the environment, do not constitute indirect expropriations, except in rare circumstances.[15] Other treaties establish specific criteria to distinguish between an indirect expropriation and a legitimate regulatory measure, which does not require compensation.[16] Furthermore, some of them clarify that 'the revocation, limitation or creation of intellectual property rights, to the extent that these measures are consistent with the TRIPS Agreement [...]', does not constitute an expropriation, nor does a determination that these measures are inconsistent with the TRIPS Agreement constitute expropriation.[17] Provisions such as these, as well as those that safeguard public health objectives, are particularly relevant during a pandemic, where states have made changes to their intellectual property legislation and granted compulsory licences for health reasons, e.g. to ensure the supply of health technologies or the development of vaccines.[18]

In the *Philips Morris v. Uruguay* case, for instance, claimants challenged the tobacco control measures imposed by the Uruguayan government that affected the treatment of registered cigarette trademarks. They argued that the state's exercise of police powers did not constitute a defence against expropriation, or

14 For example, the Pacific Alliance-Singapore FTA (signed 26 January 2022, not in force) art 8.5, para 4. In a more detailed manner, see Hungary-United Arab Emirates BIT (signed 15 July 2021, entered into force 10 April 2022) art 4, para 2.

15 Argentina-Japan BIT (signed 1 December 2018, not in force) art 11.3(b). Likewise, the Turkey-Uruguay BIT (signed 23 April 2022, not in force), Annex A, item 3(b).

16 For instance, we can mention the EU-Canada Comprehensive Economic and Trade Agreement (signed 30 November 2016, provisionally in force 21 September 2017) (CETA) Annex 8-A 'Expropriation' paras 2–3.

17 For example, ibid art 8.12.

18 Notably, due to the exceptional circumstances of the pandemic, the WTO decided that, despite the existence of patent rights in their national legislation, some member states may limit the rights under Article 28.1 of the TRIPS Agreement by authorising the use of the subject matter of a patent necessary for the production and supply of COVID-19 vaccines without the consent of the right holder to the extent necessary to address the pandemic. See, WTO, Ministerial Decision of 22 June 2022, WT/MIN(22)30WT/L/1141, para 1.

exclude the requirement of compensation, because there was no room under Article 5(1) of the Switzerland-Uruguay BIT, or otherwise in the treaty, for carving out an exemption based on the police powers of the state.[19] The tribunal disagreed with this view affirming that

> [p]rotecting public health has since long been recognised as an essential manifestation of the state's police power, as indicated also by Article 2(1) of the BIT which permits contracting states to refuse to admit investments 'for reasons of public security and order, public health and morality.[20]

After reviewing the evolution of expropriation over the years, the tribunal considered that provisions such as those contained in the new treaties, 'whether or not introduced *ex abundanti cautela*, reflect the position under general international law'.[21] The tribunal ended up rejecting not only the expropriation claim but also the rest of the claims.[22]

2.2 *Right to Regulate*

Although every state possesses the inherent power to regulate in order to fulfil its functions, some investment treaties incorporate a general clause to explicitly reaffirm this power in order to achieve public policy objectives.[23] Several of these treaties, by way of example, state some of the objectives. Some of them mention the right to regulate in the preamble in addition to the reference contained in the text of the treaty, or in place of.[24]

Certain treaties include some restrictions, for example, that the regulation is consistent with the treaty or the investment chapter (the formula usually used is 'unless consistent with the Treaty/Chapter'), or non-discriminatory.[25] But investment tribunals have recognised the power of the state to regulate for

---

19 *Philip Morris Brand Sàrl, Philip Morris Products SA and Abal Hermanos SA v. Oriental Republic of Uruguay*, ICSID Case No. ARB/10/7, Award (8 July 2016) para 289.

20 ibid 291.

21 ibid 301.

22 ibid 590.

23 CETA (n 16) art 8.9; EU-Singapore Investment Protection Agreement (signed 15 October, not in force) art 2.2. See further chapters 2, 8, 9, 12.

24 Like the Turkey-Uruguay BIT (n 15).

25 For instance, the Agreement between the United States of America, the United Mexican States, and Canada (USMCA) (signed 30 November 2018, entered into force 1 July 2020) art 14.16, or the Costa Rica-United Arab Emirates BIT (signed 30 October 2017, entered into force 21 October 2020) art 10.

the purpose of achieving public policy objectives, even in the absence of an explicit treaty provision.[26]

The key question is whether the state is exempt from its obligation to compensate since, if it is not, the invocation of this right would be sterile, without useful effect. On the one hand, some tribunals consider that recognising an absolute right to regulate, i.e., to cover any regulatory measure, would be incompatible with the obligations established in the treaty, for example, that of not expropriating without compensation.[27] It is held that 'if one qualifies all substantively and procedurally legitimate measures as an exercise of the right to regulate, then no legitimate measure would engage the duty of compensation'.[28] But, on the other hand, 'encumbering all regulatory changes with the duty of compensation would be unduly burdensome on a state's sovereignty and might induce a so-called regulatory chill'.[29]

By way of defence, in *Pope & Talbot Inc v. Canada*, Canada argued that because the measures under consideration were cast in the form of regulations, they constituted 'an exercise of 'police powers', which, if non-discriminatory, are supposedly beyond the reach of the NAFTA rules regarding expropriations'.[30] The tribunal rejected the argument because it was beyond the coverage of Article 1110 of the NAFTA and stated: 'much-creeping expropriation could be conducted by regulation, and a blanket exception for regulatory measures would create a gaping loophole in international protections against expropriation'.[31]

On the contrary, in the *Methanex v. USA* case, in which the claimant argued that its rights had been expropriated by actions taken by the Government to

26 *Total S.A. v. Argentine Republic*, ICSID Case No. ARB/04/1, Decision on Liability (27 December 201), para 123. In *Philips Morris* (n 19), Uruguay invoked the sovereign right to regulate of the state as an inherent one (see para 382 of the Award). As we already mentioned, the tribunal affirmed that the challenged measures constituted a valid exercise of the state's police power.

27 *Marvin Roy Feldman Karpa v. United Mexican States*, ICSID Case No. ARB(AF)/99/1, Award (16 December 2002) para 105.

28 ibid 157. See also Julie Kim, 'Balancing Regulatory Interests through an Exceptions Framework under the Right to Regulate Provision in International Investment Agreements' (2018) 50(2) Geo Wash Intl L Rev 289; Janice Lee, 'Note on COVID-19 and the Police Powers Doctrine: Assessing the Allowable Scope of Regulatory Measures during a Pandemic' (2020) 13(1) Contemporary Asia Arbitration J 229.

29 David Khachvani, 'Non-Compensable Regulation versus Regulatory Expropriation: Are Climate Change Regulations Compensable?' (2020) 35(1–2) ICSID Rev 154, 155.

30 *Pope & Talbot Inc v. The Government of Canada*, UNCITRAL, Interim Award (26 June 2000) para 99.

31 ibid.

ban a fuel additive (MTBE) that was harmful to public health, the tribunal affirmed that

> the California ban was made for a public purpose, was non-discriminatory, and was accomplished with due process. Hence, *Methanex*'s central claim under Article 1110(1) of expropriation under one of the three forms of action in that provision fails. From the standpoint of international law, the California ban was a lawful regulation and not an expropriation.[32]

Thus, the existence of a non-compensable exercise of regulatory powers is recognised.[33]

Along the same lines, in the *Chemtura v. Canada* case, in which a manufacturer of a noxious agricultural insecticide (lindane), said to be harmful to health and the environment, claimed against Canada for having prohibited its sale, the tribunal concluded that the measure was 'a valid exercise of the [s]tate's police powers and, as a result, does not constitute an expropriation'.[34]

Another example is the already mentioned *Philips Morris v. Uruguay* case, in which the tribunal dismissed all the claims, concluding that, among other reasons, the challenged measures constituted a valid exercise of the state's police power for the protection of public health.[35]

Undoubtedly, to avoid leaving this issue to the discretion of the tribunals, it is advisable to include an express recognition of the right to regulate in light of the regulatory measures imposed during the COVID-19 pandemic (social isolation, compulsory quarantine, restrictions on the movement of persons, trade, transport, import or export of goods; total or partial closure of borders, among others), which affected the normal functioning of businesses.

32 *Methanex Corporation v. United States of America*, UNCITRAL, Final Award of the Tribunal on Jurisdiction and Merits (3 August 2005) Part iv – Chapter D, para 15.

33 ibid 7 ('as a matter of general law, a non-discriminatory regulation for a public purpose, which is enacted in accordance with due process and, which affects, inter alios, a foreign investor or investment is not deemed expropriatory and compensable unless specific commitments had been given by the regulating government to the then putative foreign investor contemplating investment that the government would refrain from such regulation').

34 *Chemtura Corporation (formerly Crompton Corporation) v. Government of Canada*, UNCITRAL, Award (2 August 2010) para 266.

35 *Philips Morris* (n 19) 307.

2.3 *Domestic Law*

Investment treaties may contain various references to domestic law. On certain occasions, these may be invoked by the respondent states in their right of defence.

While in the first-generation treaties, we could find references to compliance with the laws and regulations of the host state at the time of making the investment, some of the new investment treaties establish the obligation to comply with domestic law throughout the life of the investment.[36] Provisions of this kind elevate domestic law to the level of the treaty, similar to the typical umbrella clause often found in some treaties. So, the obligation to comply with domestic law becomes an obligation under the treaty.[37]

This is not only useful to allow the state to counterclaim against the investor in arbitration proceedings in cases where the investor has not complied with domestic law, but also to endorse emergency measures that the state may take in a given situation. In cases of emergencies, like a pandemic, the state may declare a state of siege and suspend individual rights, in accordance with its constitutional law.

In the absence of such a legal basis, states have invoked the applicable law article as a defence, if it refers to domestic law. In the case of the Argentine Republic, in relation to the 2001–2002 crisis, the state sustained that the economic emergency was one of the grounds expressly contemplated in the National Constitution.[38]

In *Metalclad v. Mexico*, in defending against the claim, the respondent referred to domestic environmental legislation. It argued that the Municipality had the power to grant (or deny) construction permits, which constituted a valid exercise of regulatory powers in environmental matters.[39] It also invoked NAFTA's Article 1114(1) in the context of fair and equitable treatment

---

36 Such is the case of the Brazil-India BIT (signed 25 January 2020, not in force) art 11, paragraph a. See also, Argentina-Qatar BIT (signed 6 November 2016, not in force) art 11; Brazil-Suriname BIT (signed 2 May 2018, not in force) art 14, paragraph a.

37 About references to clauses on compliance with domestic law in investment treaties and their effects, see Rumiana Yotova, 'Compliance with Domestic Law: An Implied Condition in Treaties Conferring Rights and Protections on Foreign Nationals and their Property?' (June 2018) University of Cambridge Legal Studies Research Papers Series No 43/2018 9–15 <https://papers.ssrn.com/sol3/papers.cfm?abstract_id=3199812> accessed 28 March 2023.

38 See, for example, *Continental Casualty Company v. The Argentine Republic*, ICSID Case No. ARB/03/9, Award (5 September 2008) para 59.

39 See Counter-Memorial submitted by Mexico (22 May 1998) para 584 <www.italaw.com/sites/default/files/case-documents/italaw7809.pdf> accessed 28 March 2023.

standards.[40] It should be noted that this provision does not establish an obligation to comply with domestic law, but rather the right of the state to adopt, maintain or enforce any measure it considers appropriate to ensure that investment activity in its territory is conducted in a manner sensitive to environmental concerns. Yet in a way, the state's right to the adoption of environmental law constitutes, as a counterpart, an implicit obligation of compliance for the investor. In the tribunal's analysis, it was mentioned that Mexico's environmental legislation grants the Federation the power to authorise the construction and operation of hazardous waste landfills. However, according to the tribunal, even if Mexico was correct that a municipal construction permit was required, the denial of the permit by the Municipality by reference to environmental impact considerations was improper.[41]

In the *Maffezini v. Spain* case, the tribunal considered that Spanish law required an environmental impact study prior to authorising certain projects that could cause significant impacts and that Spain or the Society for the Industrial Development of Galicia (SODIGA) could not be held liable for the decisions taken by the claimant in relation to the mentioned study.[42] According to the tribunal, 'the Kingdom of Spain's action is fully consistent with Article 2(1) of the Argentine-Spain Bilateral Investment Treaty, which calls for the promotion of investment in compliance with national legislation'.[43] Thus, although the Argentina-Spain BIT (1991) did not contain specific provisions regarding environmental compliance, the paragraph referring to the promotion and admission of foreign investments 'in accordance with its legal provisions' was sufficient for the tribunal to take environmental regulations into account.

Moreover, it should be noted that arbitral tribunals have considered the invocation of domestic law as a defence in investment disputes even in the absence of a provision to that effect in the applicable treaty. For example, in the *Philips Morris v. Uruguay* case, the tribunal considered various domestic provisions that Uruguay had invoked to justify the measures taken to protect public health.[44] This was despite the fact that the applicable treaty in this case

40 ibid 838.

41 *Metalclad Corporation v. The United Mexican States*, ICSID Case No. ARB(AF)/97/1, Award (30 August 2000) para 86.

42 *Emilio Agustín Maffezini v. The Kingdom of Spain*, ICSID Case No. ARB/97/7, Award (13 November 2000) paras 65–71.

43 ibid 71.

44 *Philips Morris* (n 19) para 302.

(Switzerland-Uruguay BIT of 1998) did not contain an explicit obligation to comply with domestic law during the life of the investment.

2.4 *Compensation for Losses*

We have already seen that the first BIT signed in 1959 contained a provision on compensation for losses suffered by the investor in situations of emergency or armed conflict, amongst other similar cases.[45] In the current treaties, a typical clause on compensation for losses can be found in Article 10.11 of the Regional Comprehensive Economic Partnership Agreement (RCEP) (2020).[46]

Regardless of the variations in the wording of this clause that may be found in BITs, the fact remains that this provision stipulates the obligation not to discriminate against the investor or its investment in the event that the state decides to grant compensation for losses suffered in a state of emergency. In other words, the provision on compensation for losses, in the majority of treaties, does not oblige the state to compensate in such situations but transfers the application of the obligations of national treatment and most favoured nation to these cases. Some of the measures adopted by states to address the COVID-19 pandemic consisted of economic subsidies, and tax exemptions or benefits to help vulnerable sectors. This could be the factual basis for the application of a compensation for losses clause, as long as the measures are not themselves excluded from the scope of the treaty,[47] or fall under a sectoral reservation (non-conforming measure), or a treaty exception.

45 Germany-Pakistan BIT (n 6) art 4.3: 'Nationals or companies of either Party who owing to war or other armed conflict, revolution or revolt in the territory of the other Party suffer the loss of investments situate there, shall be accorded treatment no less favourable by such other Party than the treatment that Party accords to persons residing within its territory and to nationals or companies of a third party, as regards restitution, indemnification, compensation or other considerations. With respect to the transfer of such payments each Party shall accord to the requests of nationals or companies of the other Party treatment no less favourable than is accorded to comparable requests made by nationals or companies of a third party'.

46 Regional Comprehensive Economic Partnership (signed 15 November 2020, entered into force 1 January 2022) art 10.11: 'Each Party shall accord to investors of another Party, and their covered investments, with respect to measures it adopts or maintains relating to losses suffered by investments in its territory owing to armed conflict, civil strife, or state of emergency, treatment no less favourable than that it accords, in like circumstances, to: (a) its own investors and their investments; and (b) investors of any other Party or non-Party, and their investments'.

47 There are agreements that exclude subsidies or taxation issues, e.g. Argentina-United Arab Emirates BIT (signed 16 April 2018, not in force) arts 2(a), 10.

There could be different interpretations as to whether this clause only benefits investors or can also be useful to the state as a defence. This depends on defining what this provision entails. Specifically, does it grant extra rights to investors outside of those specified elsewhere in the treaty (such as fair and equitable treatment or full protection)? Or is its function primarily regulatory–placing overriding constraints on host states' general obligations towards investors if certain conditions come into play?

In most of the cases brought against Argentina as a result of the 2001–2002 crisis, the state invoked the clause on compensation for losses as a defence. This clause was found in most of the applicable Argentinian BITS.[48] The argument was that in emergency situations the only obligation of the state was not to discriminate against investors, either against its own investors or those of third states. Since the measures adopted by the Argentine Government to face the crisis ('pesification' of the economy, among others) were general, applicable to all economic sectors without distinction of nationality, Argentina had complied with the provisions of each applicable BIT in which there was an article on compensation for losses.

The first of the awards related to the Argentine crisis was rendered in the *CMS v. Argentina* case, in which the Argentina-USA BIT was applied. The tribunal did not endorse the Argentine position. It understood that the measures adopted by Argentina did not have a discriminatory effect, subsequently it did not apply this provision (Article IV.3 of the BIT).[49]

According to the tribunal

> The plain meaning of the Article is to provide a floor treatment for the investor in the context of the measures adopted in respect of the losses suffered in the emergency, not different from that applied to nationals or other foreign investors. The Article does not derogate from the Treaty rights but rather ensures that any measures directed at offsetting or minimizing losses will be applied in a non-discriminatory manner.[50]

With a somewhat different approach, in the *LG&E v. Argentina* case, the tribunal held that Article IV(3) of the Argentina-USA BIT contemplated the national state of emergency as a separate category of exceptional circumstances and

48 It is not, however, found in the Argentina-Spain BIT (signed 3 October 1991, entered into force 28 September 1992).

49 *CMS Gas Transmission Company v. Argentine Republic*, ICSID Case No. ARB/01/08, Award (12 May 2005) para 375.

50 ibid.

that during the crisis that article had not been violated because the measures taken by Argentina were 'across the board'.[51]

Other tribunals emphasized that the article in question applied only 'to measures a [s]tate adopts in relation to the losses referred to in that article, e.g. the investor's right to compensation owing to war and similar situations, but not to measures that cause such a loss'.[52] In conclusion, for these tribunals, the alleged breaches of the treaty could not be excused by the clause on compensation for losses.

For its part, the tribunal in *Total v. Argentina* case, when considering the state's defence on Article 5(3) (compensation for losses) of the Argentina-France BIT (1991), added that this article did not have an exculpatory clause.[53] Subsequently, the basis of the defence was considered without merit.

On the other hand, the Algeria-Morocco BIT (1990) that was applicable in the *Consortium v. Morocco* case contains a clause on compensation for losses with a different content compared to that adopted in most investment treaties, because it obliges to compensate. Indeed, article 4(1) of that treaty provides that if investments made by investors suffer losses in the territory of the other state as a result of wars, armed conflicts, states of emergency, or other similar events, they shall be compensated in a fair and adequate amount by the Contracting Party on whose territory the investment suffered such loss; and article 4(2) adds that investors shall receive the same treatment as provided for the investors of the host state or from third countries. Clearly, the wording of this article benefits investors.

Thus, in the *Consortium* case, the provision in question was invoked by the claimant. The tribunal had to consider a claim relating to compensation for the additional costs of construction stoppages and acceleration measures caused by the exceptional weather conditions.[54] Morocco defended itself by saying that, under the applicable contract, any interruption of the work due to bad weather could not give rise to compensation from the contractor, nor to an extension of the deadline.[55] The tribunal ended up not applying Article 4(1) of

51 *LG&E Energy Corp., LG&E Capital Corp., LG&E International Inc. v. Argentine Republic*, ICSID Case No. ARB/02/1, Decision on liability (3 October 2006) para 244.

52 *Mobil Exploration and Development Inc. Suc. Argentina and Mobil Argentina S.A. v. Argentine Republic*, ICSID Case No. ARB/04/16, Decision on Jurisdiction and Liability (10 April 2013) para 1021. In the same sense, *El Paso Energy International Company v. The Argentine Republic*, ICSID Case No. ARB/03/15, Award (31 October 2011) para 559.

53 *Total* (n 26) 230.

54 *Consortium RFCC v. Royaume du Maroc, ICSID Case No. ARB/00/6*, Arbitration Award (French) (22 December 2003) para 73.

55 ibid 78.

the BIT, considering that the facts of the case did not fall within the situations enumerated in this provision: the host state had not undertaken to compensate investors for losses caused by the climatic situation.[56]

The *LESI and Astaldi v. Algeria* case is related to claims arising from a series of riots and acts of violence in Algeria, which affected a public tender awarded to the claimant for the construction of a dam to supply drinking water to the city of Algiers.[57] The claimants alleged that Algeria had violated the obligation to grant full and complete protection and security under Article 4(1) of the Algeria-Italy BIT (1991). As a defence, Algeria alleged that the only provision of the treaty applicable to the situation in which it found itself at the time, was Article 4(5), a typical compensation for losses clause.[58] The application of Article 4(5) of the BIT, being a more specific rule, would exclude any application of Article 4(1), a more general rule. The arbitral tribunal observed that the terms of Article 4(1) guaranteed investments a level of protection and security that is 'constant, full and complete', which was superior to and hardly compatible with that resulting from the simple obligation of granting a treatment no less favourable than that accorded by the host state to its own nationals or to those of the most favoured nation referred to in Article 4(5).[59] According to the tribunal, both paragraphs, which provided for different levels of investment protection, could not be applied cumulatively. Then, both the internal structure of Article 4 of the BIT and the language used therein led the tribunal to conclude that the intention of the contracting states at the time of the conclusion of the treaty was to make paragraph 5 of Article 4 a special rule derogating from the general rule of the first paragraph in order to allow the states to be released from their obligation of full protection in the event of war or other armed conflicts, revolution, national state of emergency or revolt. The tribunal acknowledged that its conclusion contrasted with that adopted by the tribunal in the *Asian Agricultural v. Sri Lanka* case (by majority, as one arbitrator dissented) in relation to the Sri Lanka-United Kingdom BIT.[60]

However, being an exception to the general principle of full protection, the situations set forth in Article 4(5) should be strictly interpreted. The tribunal considered that the events that occurred in the territory of Algeria, due to their

56 ibid 80.

57 *L.E.S.I. S.p.A. and Astaldi S.p.A. v. People's Democratic Republic of Algeria*, ICSID Case No. ARB/05/3, Award (French) (12 November 2008).

58 ibid 170.

59 ibid 174.

60 *Asian Agricultural Products Limited v. Sri Lanka*, ICSID case No. ARB/87/3, Award (27 June 1990) and Dissenting Opinion of Samuel K. B. Asante (15 June 1990).

seriousness and persistence, fell within the scope of that provision, which referred to situations of armed conflict, national emergency, and revolt.[61] In conclusion, Algeria had complied with the only protection it was required to provide to the investor, i.e., a protection equivalent to that provided to its own nationals.[62]

2.5 *Exceptions and Non-precluded Measures*

In first-generation treaties, some states (like the United States, India, Canada, and the Belgo-Luxembourg Union) already included particular exceptions or non-precluded measures (NPMs).[63] Today, however, the inclusion of this type of clause has become widespread. Indeed, in the new investment treaties currently being negotiated, it is common to find clauses with general or specific exceptions to the treaty that are clearly useful for the state as a defence. Some of the general exceptions usually incorporate *mutatis mutandis* those contained in Article XX of GATT (1994), to protect public morals, human, animal or plant life or health, etc.[64] Specific exceptions may refer to issues related to public order and security,[65] public health, and environment,[66] amongst others. Treaties may also contain restrictions to protect the balance of payments, which may be located within the article on Payments and Transfers, or as part of the final provisions of the treaty.

As NPM, we can mention Article XI of Argentina-USA BIT that was under analysis in many proceedings, which prescribes:

> This Treaty shall not preclude the application by either Party of measures necessary for the maintenance of public order, the fulfilment of its obligations with respect to the maintenance or restoration of international peace or security, or the protection of its own essential security interests.

---

61 *L.E.S.I. and Astaldi* (n 57) 177.

62 ibid 182.

63 For an analysis of the different defences that may qualify as grounds of justification or excuses in international law, see Federica Paddeu, *Justification an Excuse in International Law. Concept and Theory of General Defences* (CUP 2018).

64 E.g., Canada-Peru BIT (signed 14 November 2006, entered into force 20 June 2007) art 10; Canada-Czech Republic BIT (signed 6 May 2009, entered into force 21 January 2012) art IX.

65 E.g., Japan-Republic of Korea BIT (signed 22 March 2002, entered into force 1 January 2003) art 16, or Japan-Vietnam BIT (signed 14 November 2003, entered into force 19 December 2004) art 15.

66 E.g., Uruguay-US BIT (signed 4 November 2005, entered into force 31 October 2006) art 12 (Investment and Environment).

The Argentine Republic invoked this provision as a defence in all cases brought by U.S. investors for measures adopted in the context of the 2001–2002 crisis. The measures challenged were, *inter alia*, the 'pesification' of the economy, freezing of tariffs, suspension and restructuring of public debt. Argentina's position was that the Emergency Law and related measures were necessary to protect public order and essential security interests in the face of the most serious crisis in the country's history. In fact, it was a crisis with various aspects: economic, financial, institutional, social, sanitary, etc., where essential interests of the state were at risk, such as security, public health, and governmental institutions. Argentina first invoked Article XI of the BIT (in addition to the Compensation for losses article) and, as an alternative defence, the state of necessity under customary international law, discussed in the previous chapter.[67]

In analysing these defences, the arbitral tribunals adopted different approaches. The tribunal in the *CMS*, *Enron* and *Sempra* cases began with the defence of necessity under customary international law,[68] and then analysed the treaty clause (Article XI), to which they applied the same requirements under customary international law for a state of necessity (described in Article 25 of the International Law Commission's Articles on State Responsibility).[69] Regarding the relationship between the two defences, the *CMS* annulment committee took the view that 'Article XI is a threshold requirement: if it applies, the substantive obligations under the Treaty do not apply. By contrast, Article 25 is an excuse which is only relevant once it has been decided that there has otherwise been a breach of those substantive obligations'.[70] So, according to the committee 'the requirements under Article XI are not the same as those under customary international law as codified by Article 25' and '[o]n that point, the Tribunal made a manifest error of law'.[71] The tribunals in *CMS*, *Enron* and *Sempra* found that two of the requirements of necessity – 'only mode'[72] and 'non-contribution'[73]– had not been met. Finally,

67 See chapter 10.

68 *CMS* (n 49) paras 309–331; *Enron Corporation Poderosa Assets, L.P v. Argentine Republic*, ICSID Case No. ARB/01/3, Award (22 May 2007) paras 294–342; *Sempra Energy International v. Argentine Republic*, ICSID Case No. ARB/02/16, Award (28 September 2007) paras 333–391.

69 *CMS* (n 49) 378; *Enron* (n 68) 333, 341; *Sempra* (n 68) 375.

70 *CMS Gas Transmission Company v. Argentine Republic*, ICSID Case No. ARB/01/8, Decision of the ad hoc Committee on the application for annulment of the Argentine Republic (25 September 2007) para 129.

71 ibid 130.

72 *CMS* (n 49) 323; *Enron* (n 68) 309; *Sempra* (n 68) 351.

73 *CMS* (n 49) 328–331; *Enron* (n 68) 312; *Sempra* (n 68) 354.

Enron[74] and *Sempra*[75] awards were annulled in their entirety for defects relating to the application of Article XI of the BIT, or of necessity under customary international law.

The *LG&E* tribunal approached the issue from a different perspective. It first analysed Article XI of the BIT and held that this provision had been triggered by the emergency situation Argentina was going through and that it was sufficient to exempt Argentina from liability for a certain period. It then held that 'state of necessity' as defined in international law and contained in Article 25 of the ILC Articles confirmed the tribunal's earlier conclusion.[76] It stated that a severe economic crisis could constitute an essential security interest because of the havoc it could cause on the lives of an entire population and the ability of the Government to lead.[77] The tribunal accepted that under Article XI the state could have multiple responses to maintain public order or protect its essential security interests, it being sufficient to note that the measure taken by Argentina to suspend the calculation of dollar tariffs had been a legitimate measure to protect its economic and social system.[78]

The tribunal in the *Continental* case began by discussing the difference between the two defences (Article XI and the customary state of necessity) – whose requirements were not the same,[79] and then analysed the former. As this was a general exception involving all of the claimant's claims, the tribunal considered that it had to start there before assessing the alleged individual claims of treaty breaches.[80] This tribunal also held that, in a broad sense, a severe economic crisis may qualify under Article XI as affecting an essential security interest and thus applied this provision for the measures adopted by Argentina in 2001–2002 (but not for the restructuring of the 2004 treasury

74 *Enron Corporation Poderosa Assets, L.P v. Argentine Republic*, ICSID Case No. ARB/01/3, Decision on the Application for Annulment of the Argentine Republic (30 July 2010) (the Committee annulled the finding of the tribunal and associated reasoning that the Argentine Republic is precluded from relying on Article XI of the BIT and on the principle of necessity under customary international law, on the ground of manifest excess of powers).

75 *Sempra Energy International v. Argentine Republic*, ICSID Case No. ARB/02/16, Decision on the Argentine Republic's Application for Annulment of the Award (29 June 2010) (the Committee annulled the Award on the ground of manifest excess of powers owing to the failure the tribunal to apply Article XI of the BIT).

76 *LG&E* (n 51) 245.

77 ibid 238.

78 ibid 239.

79 *Continental* (n 38) 167.

80 ibid 160–161.

bills).[81] Consequently, the measures adopted in 2001–2002 did not constitute a violation of the treaty.

In the framework of all these cases, it was discussed whether the clause had self-judging wording since Article XI of the Argentina-USA BIT did not have explicit wording indicating so ('measures necessary for'), unlike other treaties entered into by the United States ('measures that it considers necessary for').[82] This question is linked to the degree of appreciation that the investment tribunal should give to the measures taken by the state to protect its essential security interests.[83] Argentina considered that Article XI of that BIT was self-judging so that it was for the state to determine when measures were necessary for the maintenance of public order or the protection of its essential security interests.[84] Thus, the tribunal was only required to decide whether or not Argentina had acted in good faith. However, none of the tribunals considered that it had such scope.[85] The temporary nature of the state of necessity and its consequences were also discussed. All the tribunals agreed on the temporary nature (the defence applied for the duration of the crisis),[86] but not on the consequences. The *CMS* tribunal considered that the crisis period

81 ibid 178–179, 266.

82 E.g., US-Mozambique BIT (signed 1 December 1998, entered into force 3 March 2005) art XVI; US-Bahrain BIT (signed 29 September 1999, entered into force 30 May 2001) art XIV. The United States first raised the self-judging nature of an essential security interest clause, art XXI(1)(d) of the Nicaragua-US FCN Treaty (signed 21 January 1956, entered into force 24 May 1958), in the 'Nicaragua' case before the ICJ. But the Court considered that it had jurisdiction to determine whether measures taken by the States fall within such an exception, and noted the text of that Article did not employ the wording which was already to be found in Article XXI of the General Agreement on Tariffs and Trade (GATT) (*Military and Paramilitary Activities in and against Nicaragua* (*Nicaragua v. United States*) [1986] ICJ Rep 16, para 222). Since then, the United States have made the language of this kind of provisions more explicit when negotiating its investment and FTA treaties. In this context, in the Letter of Submittal of the US-Mozambique BIT (1 May 2000), the Department of State of USA clarified that '[m]easures to protect a Party's essential security interests are self-judging in nature, although each Party would expect the provisions to be applied by the other in good faith'. Argentina adopted this same position in cases in which it claimed the application of Article XI of the Argentina-US BIT, even though language of the latter was not explicitly self-judging.

83 See Burke-White and von Staden (n 4) 368–381; Gabriel Bottini, 'Protection of essential interests in the BIT era' in Grierson Weiler TJ (ed), *Investment Treaty Arbitration and International Law* (JurisNet 2008) 145, 153–159.

84 *CMS* (n 49) 367; *LG&E* (n 51) 208.

85 *CMS* (n 49) 373; *LG&E* (n 51) 214; *Enron* (n 68) 332; *Sempra* (n 68) 388; *Continental* (n 38) 188.

86 *CMS* (n 49) 382; *Enron* (n 68) 343; *Sempra* (n 68) 392; *LG&E* (n 51) 261.

ended 'sometime between late 2004 and early 2005'.[87] For its part, the tribunal in *LG&E* fixed a period from December 1, 2001, to April 26, 2003, during which it understood that Argentina had gone through a situation of extreme crisis.[88]

Unlike other tribunals that held that the state was not exempt from paying compensation[89] (although they considered the crisis situation when assessing damages), the tribunal in *LG&E* – as in the *Continental* case – interpreted Article XI as enshrining necessity as a ground for excluding the state's wrongfulness and, therefore, making it exempt from liability.[90]

In a more recent decision, issued in *Eco Oro. v. Colombia* case,[91] another tribunal, which had to apply the Canada-Colombia FTA (2008), analysed the application of a general exception to the treaty referring to the environment (provided for in Article 2201, paragraph 3, of the same treaty),[92] which had been invoked by Colombia as a defence. The majority of the tribunal concluded that there was no indirect expropriation because the environmental preservation measures had been taken in good faith, in a legitimate exercise of Colombia's police powers; they were designed and applied to protect the environment and were non-discriminatory. However, Colombia had failed to comply with the Minimum Standard of Treatment contained in Article 805 of the FTA, for which it should compensate the claimant. The tribunal rejected Colombia's position that the general exception invoked excluded its liability and obligation to pay compensation. In this regard, Canada had also presented a non-disputing party submission.[93] According to the tribunal, if the parties had intended for this provision to exclude liability, they would have drafted it in terms similar to those of Annex 811 on police powers. Any contrary interpretation would also conflict with the provisions of that Annex, 'which expressly

87 *CMS* (n 49) 250.

88 *LG&E* (n 51) 226–230. According to the tribunal these dates, which are not identified with the legislative emergency, coincided with the beginning of the de facto emergency, given by the freezing of withdrawals from bank accounts, and the election of President Kirchner.

89 *CMS* (n 49) 323; *Sempra* (n 68) 397.

90 *LG&E* (n 51) 261.

91 *Eco Oro Minerals Corp. v. Republic of Colombia*, ICSID Case No. ARB/16/41, Decision on Jurisdiction, Liability and Directions on Quantum (9 September 2021).

92 Canada-Colombia FTA (signed 21 November 2008, entered into force 15 August 2011) art 2201, paragraph 3: 'Measures necessary "For the conservation of living or non-living exhaustible natural resources"'.

93 *Eco Oro Minerals* (n 91) 836.

acknowledges that in certain circumstances a measure taken for the protection of the environment may constitute indirect expropriation'.[94]

Exceptions or non-precluded measures are especially important in the context of a pandemic such as COVID-19. In particular, those aimed at the maintenance of public order, and the protection of essential security interests, life, health, the environment, and natural resources.

3 Concluding Remarks

Since the origin of investment treaties, we have been able to find agreements that contain some provisions protecting essential interests or to be applied in emergency situations. But as the treaties were developed, new elements were incorporated, many of which can be invoked by respondent states to exempt or mitigate their responsibility for the measures they should have taken. Some of them are, among others, clarifications of the standards of treatment; clauses recognising the right of the state to regulate; explicit obligations to comply with domestic law; exceptions and NPMs.

However, as has been seen above in section 2.5, even with the existence of these elements, some states were unsuccessful in invoking them as a defence to protect their essential interests in the face of certain circumstances. Paradoxically, even without such explicit elements in the treaties, some respondent states succeeded in having the tribunals recognise their sovereign power to adopt certain legitimate regulatory measures, without having to pay compensation to the investor.

The COVID-19 pandemic and its devastating effects forced states to take urgent measures to safeguard the life and health of the population. These measures included: social isolation, compulsory quarantine, restrictions on the movement of people, trade, transport, import or export of goods, total or partial closure of borders, issuance of compulsory licences, amongst others. Investors who considered themselves affected by the measures quickly threatened to initiate claims under the protection of investment treaties, and some of them actually resorted to international arbitration. In light of this, it is necessary to review the content of investment treaties and determine what leeway states have to act in these contexts, what defences are available to them in case

94 ibid 831 (if the measure in question meets the requirements of art 2201(3) then '[…] there is no violation of the Agreement and no State liability').

they were demanded, and how successful they might be in light of the decisions of the arbitral tribunals.

In view of the cases analysed, and the lessons learned from the pandemic, we believe that it is important that the new treaties contain even more precise guidelines to distinguish the scope, limits, and effect of the regulatory power of the state, both in general and in emergency situations. Especially by avoiding ambiguous or contraditory language in the right to regulate clause, to prevent it being interpreted by some tribunal as meaningless, as discussed in section 2.4. This is particularly important, considering that in general international law it is not clear which regulatory measures are free from compensation and which are not, and that existing treaty provisions are still interpreted differently by investment tribunals,[95] largely because of their diverse composition.

95 See also Ridhi Kabra, 'Return of the Inconsistent Application of the "Essential Security Interest" Clause in Investment Treaty Arbitration: *CC/Devas v. India* and *Deutsche Telekom v. India*' (2019) 34(3) ICSID Rev 723.

CHAPTER 12

Scientific Knowledge and Domestic Regulatory Measures: Perspectives from the COVID Pandemic

Sondra Faccio

1 Introduction

Scientific knowledge usually refers to information that is understood through the application of the scientific process of investigating and analysing phenomena pertaining to the physical and natural world, and is therefore beyond the legal field.[1]

In the context of investment arbitration, scientific knowledge has been used by arbitrators to understand the factual background of the dispute and, in turn, whether the measure adopted is appropriate to the circumstances.[2] Scientific knowledge has also been considered by arbitrators to assess whether the measure is adopted in *good faith* and/or is *reasonable* because it relates to the scientific knowledge regarding risk;[3] or, on the contrary, whether it constitutes a *disguised restriction* to investments that entails the obligation of the state to pay compensation to the affected investor.[4] Sometimes, arbitrators have assessed whether the process by which the scientific knowledge is produced, and subsequently collected and used by states in order to understand whether states' reliance on this information, is justified or justifiable.[5]

1 Philip Kitcher, 'Scientific Knowledge' in Paul K Moser (ed), *The Oxford Handbook of Epistemology* (OUP 2005).

2 *Peter Allard v. Barbados*, PCA Case No. 2012–06, Award (27 June 2016) paras 87–139, 163; *Chemtura Corporation v. Government of Canada*, UNCITRAL, Award (2 August 2010) para 123.

3 *Philip Morris v. Uruguay*, ICSID Case No. ARB/10/7, Award (8 July 2016) paras 306, 307, 401; *Crystallex International Corporation v. Bolivarian Republic of Venezuela*, ICSID Case No. ARB(AF)/11/2, Award (4 April 2016) paras 593, 597.

4 *Methanex Corporation v. United States of America*, UNCITRAL, Final Award (3 August 2005) Part iv, Chapter E, para 19. See also, *Olympic Entertainment Group AS v. Ukraine*, PCA Case No. 2019–18, Award (15 April 2021) para 93–95 where scientific knowledge is used to understand whether Ukrainian Gambling Ban Law was adopted in *good faith* and therefore be part of the police powers of the state.

5 *Methanex* (n 4) para 101; *Chemtura* (n 2) para 154, stating that scientific divergence cannot constitute a basis for a finding of unfair or bad faith treatment under the FET standard.

© KONINKLIJKE BRILL BV, LEIDEN, 2025 | DOI:10.1163/9789004711204_014

So far, the need to refer to scientific knowledge has only emerged significantly in some investment disputes involving public health and environmental issues. However, in the near future, scientific knowledge is expected to play a major role in relation, for example, to controversies arising from measures undertaken in the context of pandemics and the implementation of states' climate policies. In this regard, it is worth mentioning that some new generations of international investment agreements (IIAs) expressly

> recognise the importance [that states take into account] of scientific, technical and other information, and relevant international standards, guidelines and recommendations, if existing, when preparing and implementing measures related to the *environment* and *labour conditions* that affect trade and investment.[6]

Consequently, these provisions will require arbitrators to assess the state's decision process and the weight given to scientific information in undertaking the regulatory measure.

Against this backdrop, this chapter aims to discuss whether, and to what extent, scientific knowledge may play a role in drawing the line between the state's legitimate exercise of regulatory powers and the violation of international standards and norms for the protection of foreign direct investments (FDIs). The chapter will focus on IIAs containing clauses that preserve the states' regulatory space to undertake measures for environmental and health purposes,[7] and it will argue that scientific knowledge may help arbitrators understand whether the state's measures fall within the scope of the application of these clauses.

The chapter will conclude by observing that the use of scientific knowledge for the assessment of the state's regulatory measures may entail differences

6 For example: EFTA-Philippines FTA (signed 28 April 2016, entered into force 1 June 2018) art. 11.3(2) (emphasis added); EFTA-Georgia FTA (signed 27 June 2016, entered into force 1 September 2017) art. 10.3(2); EFTA-Ecuador FTA (signed 25 June 2018, entered into force 1 November 2020) art. 8.3(2); China-Switzerland FTA (signed 6 July 2013, entered into force 1 July 2014) art. 12.2(3).

7 For example: EU-Canada Comprehensive Economic and Trade Agreement (signed 30 November 2016, provisionally in force 21 September 2017) (CETA) Annex 8-A (3) (Expropriation); India-Korea CEPA (signed 7 August 2009, entered into force 1 January 2010) art. 10.18(1) (Exceptions); Slovak Republic-Iran (signed 19 January 2016, entered into force 30 August 2017) art 6(5) (Expropriation); Burkina Faso-Canada BIT (signed 20 April 2015, entered into force 11 October 2017) art 18(1) (General Exceptions) and Annex I(3) (Expropriation).

between countries that have limited economic resources available for scientific research and richer countries.[8] In this regard, general standards and guidelines elaborated by NGOs or by international organizations such as the WHO may become pivotal in granting equal opportunities to all countries.

Accordingly, in addition to the present introduction, the chapter will be structured in four sections: section two and three will analyse some relevant investment arbitration decisions and IIA's provisions respectively, which have made use of scientific knowledge; section four will discuss the application of scientific knowledge to discriminate between legitimate regulation and violation of treaty standards and norms, with special focus on arbitral practice on health matters. Finally, section five will provide some concluding remarks.

2 Investment Arbitration Decisions and the Use of Scientific Knowledge in the Assessment of States' Regulatory Measures

Scientific knowledge has been employed by arbitrators in the context of indirect expropriation and fair and equitable treatment (FET) standard to assess whether the measure adopted by the state is in good faith and for public purpose in the case of indirect expropriation, and whether it is reasonable or arbitrary in the case of the FET standard.

For example, in *Olympic Entertainment Group AS v. Ukraine*,the arbitral tribunal referred to scientific knowledge to understand whether a law adopted by the Ukrainian Parliament to stop gambling and its negative impact on human health and morality was in good faith and therefore amounted to a legitimate exercise of the police powers of the state (rather than a form of indirect expropriation). In this case, arbitrators admitted that a state is not expected 'to critically analyse every aspect of whatever studies might be available';[9] but, it is expected that '[the state] would at least reasonably consider and discuss some of the evidence' before taking actions which would effect radical changes for the investor.[10] The tribunal concluded that the Ukrainian Parliament adopted the measure in good faith,[11] as the 'Gambling Ban Law was passed with wide support from politicians from all over the political spectrum' and 'the issue of gambling and the problems that are related to it were previously debated in

8 Marcos A Orellana, 'The Role of Science in Investment Arbitrations Concerning Public Health and the Environment' (2006) 17(1) YBIntl EnvL 48–72.

9 *Olympic Entertainment* (n 4) para 93.

10 ibid.

11 ibid para 95.

[the] Ukraine', with 'more than 35 draft laws that sought to address the problem of gambling [...] between the years of 1998 and 2009'.[12] Previous debates and proposals within the parliament were considered sufficient discussion of some evidence to deem the measure in good faith.

In the case *Methanex Corp. v. United States,* the tribunal emphasised that science cannot 'merely provide[d] a convenient excuse' to the state to undertake measures to the detriment of investors.[13] The tribunal concluded that the state of California made 'a careful assessment of the problem and thereafter responded reasonably to independent findings';[14] the respondent state acted in good faith and for public purpose 'with a view to protecting the environmental interests of the citizens of California, and not with the intent to harm foreign methanol producers'.[15]

In another case concerning *inter alia* a denial of a permit to exploit gold deposits in Venezuela,[16] an investment tribunal argued that the state 'ha[s] the burden to elucidate the reasons for [undertaking a given measure] with some kind of supporting data to explain why it was reaching the conclusion it reached'.[17] In the case at stake, the tribunal found that – although the state mentioned some environmental concerns – it invoked them 'in vague terms and without any supporting authority', with the consequence that '[the measure] [was] so fundamentally deficient that, to the eyes of a reasonable third person, [it] "surprise[s] a sense of juridical propriety"'.[18] The tribunal therefore concluded that the permit denial frustrated the investor's legitimate expectation and amounted to a violation of the FET standard under the Canada – Venezuela BIT of 1996.[19]

12 ibid para 94.

13 *Methanex* (n 4) Part iv, Chapter E, para 19: 'the question is whether the scientific conclusions which were presented to the Governor were so faulty that the Tribunal may reasonably infer that the science merely provided a convenient excuse for the hidden regulation of methanol producers'.

14 ibid.

15 ibid para 20.

16 *Crystallex* (n 3) para 7, the claimant challenged both 'Venezuela's April 2008 denial of a permit to Crystallex to exploit the gold deposits at Las Cristinas' and 'the rescission by the Corporación Venezolana de Guayana (CVG), a state-run corporation tasked with stimulating economic activity in the Guayana region, of the Mine Operation Contract (MOC) in February 2011'.

17 ibid para 593.

18 ibid paras 593, 597.

19 ibid para 597. In relation to the application of the FET standard, arbitrators considered scientific knowledge also to assess the investor's legitimate expectations. For example, in *Peter A. Allard*, the investor alleged a breach of the Barbados-Canada BIT, as Barbados denied him fair and equitable treatment 'by making representations that it would [...]

In the landmark case *Philip Morris v. Uruguay*, the arbitral tribunal used the WHO Framework Convention on Tobacco Control (FCTC) of 2003 as 'a point of reference' to evaluate the reasonableness of the anti-smoking measures adopted by Uruguay. The tribunal assessed whether they amounted to a violation of the FET standard.[20] The tribunal observed that Uruguay's measures 'were adopted based on the substantial body of evidence that had been made available in the course of its active participation in the FCTC negotiations and in the drafting of implementing guidelines'.[21] In the Tribunal's view, 'there was no requirement for Uruguay to perform additional studies or to gather further evidence in support of the Challenged Measures'.[22] The tribunal concluded that the measures were reasonable, not arbitrary, grossly unfair, unjust, discriminatory or disproportionate, and were potentially an 'effective means to protecting public health'.[23]

According to arbitrators, states are expected to gather and consider scientific or technical knowledge before issuing measures that could significantly impact on foreign investors. Some tribunals valued states' 'careful assessments' of 'independent findings' (*Methanex*) or 'substantial body of evidence' based on specialised international organisations' studies (*Philip Morris*); others argued that it is sufficient for states to 'consider and discuss some of the evidence' (*Olympic Entertainment*) or at least 'some kind of supporting data' (*Crystallex*).

Scholars and tribunals have observed that 'it is beyond [arbitrators'] task to investigate the factual scientific truth behind host states' regulatory decisions', rather arbitrators shall focus on 'the process in which regulatory science has been produced' and 'investigate the credibility of science used in

uphold its environmental policies [...] and then failing to act in accordance with those representations'. The respondent submitted that the investor's legitimate expectations had to be assessed in light of the investor's obligation to exercise due diligence at the time of making the investment. In the view of Barbados, Mr. Allard did not exercise due diligence: he 'bought the Sanctuary "impulsively" [...] without conducting any environmental study' and his environmental management plans 'lacked scientific rigor'. Although the tribunal did not discuss the investor's due diligence in relation to the application of the FET standard, it nonetheless confirmed the respondent's view that the investor made the investment out of 'philanthropic intentions and of enthusiasms', overlooking the environmental issues connected to the investment, and ultimately dismissed the investor's claim on the FET standard. *Peter A. Allard* (n 2) paras 172, 191, 220, 224–228.

20 *Philip Morris* (n 3) para 401.

21 ibid para 394.

22 ibid para 396.

23 ibid paras 306, 307, 410, 420.

the regulatory process'.[24] The reasons being that arbitrators are often not well equipped to assess the validity of scientific information and may not always be able to discriminate between apparently equally 'valid' information produced by party-appointed experts. This problem emerged clearly in the case *Perenco v. Ecuador*:

> The Tribunal has set out the main issues of fact and law which have divided the experts. However, with regard to many of the [...] differences, the Tribunal does not feel able to prefer one above the other. It seems to the Tribunal that each was attempting to achieve the best result for the party by whom they were instructed, and that they crossed the boundary between professional objective analysis and party representation. It is clear to the Tribunal that the experts were effectively shooting at different targets and this has made the work of this Tribunal most difficult.[25]

According to some scholars, these type of problems can be overcome by making reference to the findings of and/or standards set by specialised international organisations, such as the World Health Organisation,[26] or by allowing investment tribunals to appoint their own experts,[27] or by applying the precautionary principle.[28] As it will be illustrated in the subsequent section, some recent IIAs have endorsed the above approaches with the aim of tackling concerns that emerged in the practice of investment tribunals.

24 Katalin Sulyok, *Science and Judicial Reasoning. The Legitimacy of International Environmental Adjudication* (CUP 2022) 225, 234, 239; Jorge E Viñuales, *Foreign Investment and the Environment* (CUP 2012) 378; Orellana (n 8) 64–65; *Chemtura* (n 2) para 134.

25 *Perenco Ecuador Ltd. v. Republic of Ecuador and Empresa Estatal Petróleos del Ecuador (Petroecuador)*, ICSID Case No. ARB/08/6, Interim decision on the environmental counterclaim (11 August 2015) para 581. The statement is made by the tribunal in relation to Ecuador's counterclaim for environmental damages. According to Ecuador, the investor created 'an "environmental catastrophe" in the two oil blocks situated in the country's Amazonian rainforest', where it was operating. The investor responded to the counterclaim arguing that the pollution was caused by previous activities in the area (para 34).

26 Sondra Faccio, 'The World Health Organization's Response to the Health Emergency and its Impact on Investment Arbitration and Human Rights Case Law' (2023) 25(5) Int'l Comm L Rev 476-507, 506.

27 Sulyok (n 24); Orellana (n 8) 64.

28 Orellana (n 8) 65–66.

3 International Investment Agreement Provisions on the Right to Regulate and the Use of Scientific Knowledge

The new generation of free trade agreements (FTAs) and IIAs now incorporate the consideration of scientific knowledge in connection with the states' right to regulate and tribunal-appointed experts.

For example, scientific information is expressly referred to in relation to the right to regulate and the levels of protection to be granted to trade and investments in the most recent EFTA's FTAs. In this regard, the relevant 'Trade and sustainable development' chapters state:

> The Parties recognise the importance of taking account of scientific, technical and other information, and relevant international standards, guidelines and recommendations, if existing, when preparing and implementing measures related to the environment and labour conditions that affect trade and investment between them.[29]

Similarly, article 12.2(3) of the China-Switzerland FTA (2013) on Multilateral environmental agreements and environmental principles establishes that '[t]he Parties recognise the importance, when preparing and implementing measures related to the environment, of taking account of scientific, technical and other information, and relevant international guidelines'.[30] Reference to international standards, guidelines, and recommendations becomes particularly valuable in case of health emergencies, where time constraints may not permit an extensive scientific inquiry.[31] In such circumstances, the findings and recommendations of specialised organisations, such as the WHO's, may provide guidance to all states on how to approach the emergency in a fair and reasonable manner.[32]

It is worth mentioning that FTAs are concerned with the development of trade and investment, but they do not usually provide for standards of treatment of FDIs. Nonetheless, it might be argued that, based on systematic interpretation,[33] their provisions may be considered by arbitrators in disputes

29 EFTA-Philippines FTA (n 6) art 11.3(2); EFTA-Georgia FTA (n 6) art 10.3(2); EFTA-Ecuador FTA (n 6) art 8.3(2).

30 China-Switzerland FTA (signed 6 July 2013, entered into force 1 July 2014) art 12.2(3).

31 Orellana (n 8) 64.

32 Faccio (n 26).

33 ILC, 'Report of the International Law Commission on the Work of its 58th Session' (1 May-9 June and 3 July-11 August 2006) UN Doc A/CN.4/L.702.

concerning the application of investment treaties.[34] Indeed, Article 31(3) of the Vienna Convention on the Law of Treaties (VCLT) identifies some elements that the interpreter shall 'take into account, together with the context' in the interpretation of treaties, including: a) subsequent agreements, b) subsequent practice, and c) international law applicable to the treaty parties. In relation to Article 31 (3) (c), the International Law Commission has observed:

> Article 31 (3) (c) [also] requires the interpreter to consider other treaty-based rules so as to arrive at a consistent meaning. Such other rules are of particular relevance where parties to the treaty under interpretation are also parties to the other treaty, [and these rules …] provide evidence of the common understanding of the parties as to the object and purpose of the treaty under interpretation or as to the meaning of a particular term. […]
> Rules of international law subsequent to the treaty to be interpreted may be taken into account especially where the concepts used in the treaty are open or evolving. This is the case, in particular, where: (a) the concept is one which implies taking into account subsequent technical, economic or legal developments; […] or (c) the concept has a very general nature or is expressed in such general terms that it must take into account changing circumstances.[35]

In light of the points mentioned above, it may be argued that FTAs' provisions that encourage states to consider scientific and technical knowledge, when formulating and implementing regulatory measures, may be viewed as a 'common understanding of the parties' as to the meaning of 'the right to regulate', which is typically expressed in general terms in investment agreements. This could be illustrated with an example. Article 9 of the Switzerland-Georgia BIT of 2014 recognises the contracting states' right to adopt, maintain or enforce measures in the public interest, such as 'measures to meet health, safety, labour or environmental concerns or reasonable measures for prudential purposes'. Section 2 of Article 9 further states that '[t]he adoption, maintenance or enforcement of such measures is subject to the requirement that they are *not applied in an*

34 Concerning the relation to other international agreements, the EFTA-Ecuador FTA (n 6) art 1.4 states: '[t]he Parties confirm their rights and obligations under the WTO Agreement and the other agreements negotiated thereunder to which they are a party, and any other international agreement to which they are a party'.

35 ILC (n 33) 15–17; Tarcisio Gazzini, *Interpretation of International Investment Treaties* (Hart 2016).

arbitrary or unjustifiable manner or do not constitute a disguised restriction on investments of investors of the other Contracting Party'.[36] Article 10.3 (2) of the subsequent EFTA-Georgia FTA of 2016 invites states to take into account scientific and technical information when preparing and implementing measures related to the environment and labour conditions that affect investment.[37] It may be argued that, with Article 10.3 (2) of the FTA, Georgia and Switzerland intended to clarify what could be a 'reasonable measure for prudential purposes' or when a measure could be considered 'not [to be] applied in an arbitrary or unjustifiable manner' under the BIT, i.e. when it is based on scientific and technical information.

With reference to tribunal-appointed experts, a number of IIAs incorporate provisions on 'Expert Reports' or 'Information and Technical Advice' that allow arbitral tribunals to appoint their own experts in a view to get assistance in approaching and understanding cases involving complicated scientific knowledge or where science does not offer conclusive parameters.

For example, according to the Australia-Hong Kong Investment Agreement of 2019

> a tribunal [...] unless the disputing parties disapprove, on its own initiative, may appoint one or more experts to report to it in writing on any factual issue concerning scientific matters raised by a disputing party in a proceeding, subject to such terms and conditions that the disputing parties may agree [to].[38]

The Kyrgyz Republic-India BIT of 2019 expressly refers to 'any factual issue concerning environmental, health, safety, technical or other scientific matters';[39] which usually emerge in relation to the adoption of states' regulatory measures. As in the case of the Australia-Hong Kong Investment Agreement, the arbitral tribunal may not appoint an expert if the disputing parties disagree.[40]

36 Switzerland-Georgia BIT (signed 3 June 2014, entered into force 17 May 2015) art 9 (emphasis added).

37 EFTA-Georgia FTA (n 6).

38 Australia-Hong Kong Investment Agreement (signed 26 March 2019, entered into force 17 January 2020) art 33; See also, Kyrgyz Republic-India BIT (signed 14 June 2019, not in force) art 25; Belarus-India BIT (signed 24 September 2018, entered into force 5 March 2020) art 25; Argentina-United Arab Emirates BIT Argentina-United Arab Emirates BIT (signed 16 April 2018, not in force) art 31; Canada-Mongolia BIT (signed 8 September 2016, entered into force 24 February 2017) art 33.

39 Kyrgyz Republic-India BIT (n 38) art 25. See also, Canada-Mongolia BIT (n 38) art 33.

40 These provisions do not affect the appointment of other kinds of experts where the appointment is authorized by the applicable arbitration rules. The UNCITRAL Arbitration

This provision aims to prevent the uncontrolled increase of costs and length of the arbitral proceedings, but it significantly limits the capacity of arbitrators to autonomously ascertain scientific matters.

In contrast, the EU's IIAs, establish that '[t]he Tribunal, [...] on its own initiative, may appoint one or more experts', having it only the obligation to consult the disputing parties.[41] This wording should be interpreted in the context of the Union's efforts to promote a reformed approach to Investor-State Dispute Settlement (ISDS) mechanisms with a view to ensuring the highest possible standards of legitimacy, transparency, consistency, predictability, and legal correctness.[42] According to the EU's Commission, the adjudicator's 'ability to [freely] call on experts for technical or scientific information', together with his or her legal expertise, may contribute to responding to the legitimacy concerns as regards the current ISDS system.[43]

4 Scientific Knowledge to Discriminate between Legitimate Regulation and the Violation of Treaty Standards in the Context of Pandemics

In the context of health emergencies, scientific knowledge may confirm the existence of a health risk or, in the worst case, of a veritable pandemic, in the first place. Further, scientific knowledge may justify the response of the state

Rules and the IBA Rules on the Taking of Evidence in International Arbitration regulate tribunal-appointed experts, providing that 'the arbitral tribunal may appoint one or more independent experts to report to it, in writing, on specific issues to be determined by the arbitral tribunal'. See, Report of the United Nations Commission on International Trade Law, UNCITRAL Arbitration Rules (with new Article 1, paragraph 4, as adopted in 2013) (28 June–16 July 2021) UN Doc A/76/17, art 29; IBA Council, IBA Rules on the Taking of Evidence in International Arbitration (17 December 2020) art 6; Chapter 14.

41 For example, Proposal for a Council Decision on the conclusion of the Investment Protection Agreement between the European Union and its Member States, of the one part, and the Socialist Republic of Viet Nam of the other part of 2019 (17 October 2018) COM/2018/693 final, Annex, arts 3.20, 3.52; the EU-Singapore Investment Protection Agreement (signed 15 October, not in force) art 3.41.

42 European Commission, Government of Canada, Expert meeting 13 (14 December 2016) Discussion Paper 'Establishment of a Multilateral Investment Dispute Settlement System', 1 <https://circabc.europa.eu/ui/group/7fc51410-46a1-4871-8979-20cce8df0896/library/a3002620-408d-4469-8d27-4131bc3e1bb6/details> accessed 28 June 2023. See also, The European Commission Concept Paper, 'Investment in TTIP and Beyond: The Path for Reform. Enhancing the Right to Regulate and Moving from Current and Hoc Arbitration towards an Investment Court' (2015).

43 European Commission, Government of Canada (n 42) 5.

in relation to the risk, *i.e.* whether the response is an '*effective means* to protecting public health'.[44] The adoption of a methodical and well-structured process that includes a thorough evaluation of the issue based on available scientific data may establish the '*bona fide*' nature of a measure and avoid its qualification as a '*disguised restriction*' to investment.[45]

The consideration of scientific information may also play a role in deciding whether a measure is not only conceived, but also '*applied* in an arbitrary or unjustifiable manner', or not.[46] For example, during the COVID emergency, the WHO issued a number of temporary recommendations concerning the handling of the pandemic, inviting states to continuously re-assess domestic measures in light of 'risk assessments, transmission patterns, cost-benefit analysis, the evolution of the pandemic, and new knowledge of COVID-19'.[47] Thus, arbitrators may state that a measure is reasonable if the state has set up an orderly process to re-assess it in light of evolving scenarios and scientific information. Moreover, a careful analysis of health and economic costs and benefits of the measure over time may contribute to justifying the state's choice on the basis of the principle of proportionality and exempting the state from responsibility of treaty violation.[48]

Specialised international agencies, such as the WHO, along with international organisations or non-governmental organisations, may play a crucial role in providing 'independent findings' (*Methanex*) to states.[49] Arbitrators have already observed that the substantial body of evidence made available by the WHO (with reference to tobacco control) can be effectively used as a point of reference by states without the need 'to perform additional studies or to gather further evidence in support of the Challenged Measures' (*Philip*

---

44 *Philip Morris* (n 3) paras 306, 307, 410, 420 (emphasis added).

45 *Methanex* (n 4) para 19.

46 Switzerland-Georgia BIT (n 36) art 9 (emphasis added).

47 For example, WHO, 'Statement on the First Meeting of the International Health Regulations (2005) Emergency Committee on the COVID-19 Pandemic' (23 January 2020); WHO, 'Statement on the Second Meeting of the IHR Emergency Committee' (30 January 2020) (Statement on the second meeting). As to the use of scientific knowledge produced by the WHO, see *Philip Morris v. Uruguay* (n 3) para 394–396.

48 Faccio (n 26).

49 In the context of the COVID-19 pandemic, a number of states relied on the WHO's guidance. See, Italy, Decree of the President of the Council of Ministers (3 December 2020) (Italian decree) Annex 14; WHO, 'New Zealand takes early and hard action to tackle COVID-19' (15 July 2020) <www.who.int/westernpacific/news-room/feature-stories/item/new-zealand-takes-early-and-hard-action-to-tackle-covid-19#:~:text=New%20Zealand's%20early%20success%20in,weeks%20without%20any%20new%20infections> accessed 23 September 2023.

Morris).[50] Concerns, however, may arise in relation to the credibility of the organisation and/or the available scientific data. The COVID-19 pandemic has shown once more that the development, divulgation, and use of scientific knowledge can be quite heterogeneous and may not always lead to a universal scientific truth. For example, in relation to the definition of 'pandemic', different views have emerged focusing either on the degree of the spread[51] or the number of deaths or illness.[52]

These uncertainties could be particularly problematic when states are called to swiftly react to health emergencies. The same holds true for arbitrators that, in the aftermath of a crisis, may be called to assess the measures adopted by the state in light of treaty standards. However, it is argued that the arbitrators' task is not much to deliberate over the truth of the scientific data, but rather whether such data were derived through the application of scientific principles and proper methods.[53] According to Orellana, 'emphasis on due process reduces the risk that adjudicators will become entangled in questions of scientific validity', moreover in relation to 'the evaluation of appropriate responses to risk [...] [i]n difficult situations of inconclusive science', reference can be made to the precautionary principle.[54]

The precautionary principle, for example, played a central role in the discussions surrounding Canada's ban of the fuel additive Methylcyclopentadienyl Manganese Tricarbonyl (MMT) and its environmental effects in the 1990s.[55] When Canada adopted the ban, it was disputed what the degree of health and environmental risk was created by MMT. In this context, some scholars and experts argued for the application of a precautionary and adaptive approach, which may be useful to '[prevent and ease] environmental [and health] stress

50 *Philip Morris* (n 3) para 396.

51 John M Last (ed), *A dictionary of epidemiology* (OUP 2001). According to the classical epidemiological definition of a pandemic, the latter could be defined as 'an epidemic occurring worldwide, or over a very wide area, crossing international boundaries and usually affecting a large number of people'.

52 Peter Doshi, 'The Elusive Definition of Pandemic Influenza' (2011) 89(7) Bull World Health Org 532; Heath Kelly, 'The Classical Definition of a Pandemic is not Elusive' (2011) Bull World Health Org 540; WHO 'Report of The Review Committee on the Functioning of the International Health Regulations (2005) and on Pandemic Influenza A (H1N1) 2009' (5 May 2011) A64/10, 15.

53 Orellana (n 8) 64–65.

54 ibid. See also, Sulyok (n 24) 220.

55 *Ethyl Corporation v. Canada*, UNCITRAL, Award on Jurisdiction (24 June 1994); Julie Soloway, 'Environmental Trade Barriers under NAFTA: The MMT Fuel Additives Controversy' (1999) 8 Minn J Global Trade 55, 86, 91–94.

well before conclusive evidence concerning damage exists, and [to adapt] policy as new scientific information becomes available'.[56]

5 Concluding Remarks

Science is expected to play an expanding and influential role in investment arbitration, extending beyond pandemics to encompass environmental and energy matters which often 'feature complex questions of policy and science'.[57] As observed, science may be relevant in appraising whether a genuine risk exists, which, in turn, justifies enacting regulatory measures; whether the measures adopted by the state are in good faith and appropriate in light of the risk; whether their application is reasonable.

The use of scientific knowledge, however, may result in disparities between countries that have limited economic resources available for scientific research, and richer countries.[58] In this regard, general standards and guidelines elaborated by NGOs or by international organizations such as the WHO, may become pivotal in granting equal opportunities to all countries. These organisations may also intervene as *amici curiae* in the arbitral proceedings bringing to the attention of the tribunal relevant information and knowledge.[59] In this regard, *amicus curiae* intervention is expected to increase in the future, especially in arbitral cases involving delicate health and environmental matters.

Concerns may arise in relation to the credibility of the organisations involved and their research. Criticism of the WHO's response to the pandemic, accusing the organisation of failing to provide timely and accurate information on COVID-19 and to be 'China oriented', is a paramount example.[60] However, arbitrators shall focus on the production process of scientific knowledge, rather than on its unequivocal truth. In addition, in case of uncertainties or unknown diseases, the precautionary and adaptive approach applies. Precaution may

56 Soloway (n 55) 92; Richard Blackhurst and others, *Trade and Sustainable Development Principles* (IISD 1994) 28.

57 Sulyok (n 24).

58 Orellana (n 8) 48–72.

59 See further Chapter 13; Sondra Faccio, 'Public Participation in Arbitral Proceedings' in Avidan Kent, Eric De Brabandere, and Tarcisio Gazzini (eds), *Public Participation and Foreign Investment Law. From the Creation of Rights and Obligations to the Settlement of Disputes* (Brill Nijhoff 2021) 283, 299.

60 For example, Martin Russel, 'World Health Organization: Is it fit for purpose?' (European Parliament Research Service, May 2020) <www.europarl.europa.eu/RegData/etudes/BRIE/2020/651910/EPRS_BRI(2020)651910_EN.pdf> accessed 23 September 2023.

prevent under-reactions and the risk of an epidemic, especially in the first phase when the potential damage to human health is still uncertain; adaptation may avoid over-reaction and unnecessary limitations to economic and civil rights, especially in the long run.

According to the author's perspective, the precautionary and adaptive approach is evident in the Recommendations issued by the WHO during the COVID pandemic. Indeed, the primary purpose of the Recommendations was to prevent or minimize the international spread of disease, reflecting the precautionary nature of the measures.[61] Moreover, they called for continuous review and adjustment of the measures 'based on regular risk assessments, transmission patterns at origin and destination, cost-benefit analysis, the evolution of the pandemic, and new knowledge of COVID-19'.[62] Arbitrators may well use this approach as a point of reference in the assessment of states' regulatory measures in case of future pandemics.

61 WHO 'Revision of the International Health Regulations' (23 May 2005) WHA58.3, arts 2, 12.

62 Statement on the Second Meeting of the International Health Regulations (2005) Emergency Committee Regarding the Coronavirus Disease (COVID-19) pandemic (30 January 2020) <www.who.int/groups/covid-19-ihr-emergency-committee> accessed 23 September 2023; Statement on the Third Meeting of the IHR Emergency Committee (1 May 2020) <www.who.int/groups/covid-19-ihr-emergency-committee> accessed 23 September 2023; Statement on the Fourth Meeting of the IHR Emergency Committee (1 August 2020) <www.who.int/groups/covid-19-ihr-emergency-committee> accessed 23 September 2023.

CHAPTER 13

Questions of Public Health before Investment Tribunals: Can Amici Curiae Play a Useful Role?

Avidan Kent and Jamie Trinidad

1 Introduction

Amici curiae are 'friends of the court', traditionally defined as independent experts whose role is to assist the court by providing expertise that will inform and improve the judges' decision.[1] While (with a few exceptions[2]) the practice of amicus interventions is now widespread across international courts and tribunals, the rules on this process and the types of interventions vary significantly from forum to forum. The focus of this chapter will be on amicus interventions in the Investor-State Dispute Settlement mechanism (ISDS), an area that has undergone radical transformation over the past 20 years: From the 'secretive', confidentiality-guided, private arbitration model to one of the most amicus-friendly dispute settlement mechanisms in the world of international law.[3]

This volume deals with the pandemic and its impact on, and links with, the international investment regime. The task entrusted to the authors of this chapter was to address the role of amici curiae in providing public health-related knowledge in ISDS proceedings. At the time of writing, the authors are aware of only one COVID-related investment case, which is currently ongoing,

1 See longer discussion of the concept of 'amicus curiae' in our previous work, Avidan Kent and Jamie Trinidad, 'International Law Scholars as *Amici Curiae*: An Emerging Dialogue (of the Deaf)?' (2016) 29(4) LJIL 1081; Avidan Kent and Jamie Trinidad, 'Amicus Curiae Participation in International Proceedings' in Avidan Kent, Nikos Skoutaris, and Jamie Trinidad (eds), *The Future of International Courts* (Routledge 2019); Avidan Kent and Jamie Trinidad, 'The Management of Third Party Amicus Participation Before International Criminal Tribunals: Juggling Effectiveness and Legitimacy' (2017) 17 IntCLR 728. For a comprehensive overview, see Astrid Wiik, *Amicus Curiae Before International Courts and Tribunals* (Hart/Nomos 2018).

2 See for example the very limited practice in tribunals such as the International Court of Justice or the WTO's tribunals, see review in Avidan Kent & Jamie Trinidad, 'Amicus Curiae Participation in International Proceedings' (n 1).

3 Avidan Kent, 'Public Participation as an Evolving Norm: from Rio to Mauritius' in Eric De Brabandere and others (eds), *Public Participation and Foreign Investment Law* (Brill 2021).

© KONINKLIJKE BRILL BV, LEIDEN, 2025 | DOI:10.1163/9789004711204_015

and may or may not end with an award.[4] This analysis, therefore, will be based on the broader practice of amicus interventions in public health-related ISDS proceedings[5] and the lessons that could be learnt from this practice in the context of the COVID (or any other future) pandemic.

2 The Amicus as a Provider of Knowledge

A critical analysis of the role of the amicus as a provider of health-related knowledge in the process of investment arbitration must first consider the *who* and the *how*: which types of entities are intervening as amici, and what are the expectations around their role and input in the process of investment arbitration. After addressing these questions, we will evaluate whether certain types of amicus participation are better suited than others when it comes to supporting tribunals with health-related knowledge.

2.1 *The Practice of Amici Submission in Health-Related ISDS Proceedings*

The traditional notion of the amicus curiae, as a neutral expert supporting the court's work, has for several decades been regarded as overly simplistic. In his seminal Yale Law Journal paper of 1962, Samuel Krislov presented the 'from friendship to advocacy' spectrum:[6] Krislov's main point addressed the amicus' 'neutrality' component. Many amici, he explained, are no longer independent, agenda-less actors whose sole wish is to support the court's operation. Rather, they can be observed openly supporting and promoting a range of external interests, *inter alia* political agendas (e.g. human rights, environmental protection, public health, governance),[7] the interests of states,[8]

4 *ADP International S.A. and Vinci Airports S.A.S. v. Republic on Chile*, ICSID Case No ARB/21/40.

5 We have largely drawn from a list of cases identified by Freya Baetens, from which we excluded cases that did not address health-related matters directly (e.g. the construction of hospitals), see: Freya Baetens, 'Protecting Foreign Investment and Public Health Through Arbitral Balancing and Treaty Design' (2022) 71 ICLQ 139.

6 Samuel Krislov, 'The Amicus Curiae Brief: From Friendship to Advocacy' (1962) 72 Yale LJ 694.

7 See a review of the public interest objectives in amici submissions in ISDS in Sondra Faccio, 'Public participation in arbitral proceedings, in Eric De Brabandere and others (n 3) 283, 294.

8 Krislov (n 6) 700–702, or more recently see a line of submissions by the EU Commission in investment cases (e.g. *European American Investment Bank AG (EURAM) v. Slovak Republic*, UNCITRAL, *Ioan Micula, Viorel Micula, S.C. European Food S.A, S.C. Starmill S.R.L. and S.C. Multipack S.R.L. v. Romania [I]*, ICSID Case No. ARB/05/20, *Electrabel S.A. v. Republic of Hungary*, ICSID Case No. ARB/07/19, and many other cases).

and those of private individuals and entities.[9]

2.1.1 Unsolicited Briefs

The evolving role of the amicus is reflected in the way amici interact with investment tribunals. The vast majority of amicus interventions in ISDS are unsolicited and submitted independently. This type of intervention is widespread in ISDS proceedings and in most cases could be described as a manifestation of the 'amicus-as-advocate' role, motivated by *inter alia* a desire to shape the tribunal's approach to a case or an area of law, as well as the promotion of ideological, political, personal, or professional goals.

Unsolicited amicus interventions are nevertheless rare in health-related investment cases. Out of the 18 public health-related ISDS cases identified by Baetens,[10] only two involved entirely unsolicited submissions: *Philip Morris v. Uruguay*, and *Methanex v. USA*. The *Philip Morris v. Uruguay* arbitration addressed the respondent's right to adopt anti-smoking regulation. This case attracted an amicus submission from the World Health Organization (WHO),[11] which included a wealth of information in the form of a scientific 'literature review' regarding the effectiveness of health warnings, including the size of health warnings, the size of their coverage, their impact on consumers, examples of state practice, and more. Interestingly, in its decision to accept the amicus submission, the Tribunal emphasised the amicus' expertise in the dispute subject matter, but also that accepting this submission 'would *support the transparency of the proceeding and its acceptability by users at large*.'[12]

Following the WHO's intervention, a second intergovernmental organization (IGO) – the Pan American Health Organization (PAHO) – requested to submit an amicus submission containing technical expert information on smoking and its impact on society. Also here, the Tribunal accepted the request, relying on the oft-cited quotation from *Methanex v. USA*:

> the […] arbitral process could *benefit from being perceived as more open or transparent; or conversely be harmed if seen as unduly secretive*. In this

---

9 Krislov, (n 6) 703–704, and see more recent examples e.g. *Angel Samuel Seda and others v. Republic of Colombia*, ICSID Case No. ARB/19/6, or numerous submissions in *Eli Lilly and Company v. The Government of Canada*, UNCITRAL, ICSID Case No. UNCT/14/2.

10 Baetens (n 5).

11 *Philip Morris v. Uruguay*, ICSID Case No. ARB/10/7, Written submission by the World Health Organization and the WHO Framework Convention on Tobacco Control Secretariat (January 28, 2015).

12 *Philip Morris* (n 11) Procedural Order No. 3 (17 February 2015) para 29 (emphasis added).

> regard, the Tribunal's willingness to receive amicus submissions *might support the process in general and this arbitration in particular*, whereas a blanket refusal could do positive harm.[13]

On the face of it, therefore, a primary motivation for engaging with these amici was the Tribunal's own self-interest; to be perceived as legitimate, open and transparent. It is understandable that the Tribunal should be concerned with enhancing the legitimacy of its decision-making process, given the public backlash against the investment regime as a whole and the field's reputational difficulties.[14] In future cases dealing with the pandemic or other public health-related issues – a highly divisive topic that will attract public scrutiny and criticism regardless of a case's outcome – the need to be perceived as legitimate will be particularly acute.

At the same time, it is also clear that the reasons the *Philip Morris* Tribunal accepted the participation of amici were not merely cosmetic. Indeed, as illustrated in chapter 12, the expertise of the amici in matters of public health was relied on to a great extent. The award's 'factual background' is based on data provided by the amici, including citations and quotations from their written briefs. The tribunal also referred to the amicus submissions in its legal analysis, when concluding that: '[c]ontrary to the Claimants' contention, [FN omitted] the Challenged Measures were not "arbitrary and unnecessary" but rather were potentially "effective means to protecting public health," a conclusion endorsed also by the WHO/PAHO submissions'.[15]

A second, more dated, health-related ISDS example is the *Methanex v. USA* case. This was the first ISDS arbitration to admit amicus briefs and is widely regarded as instrumental in changing the ISDS' rules on amicus intervention and transparency more broadly.[16] This case eventually attracted two amicus submissions, the first from the International Institute for Sustainable Development (IISD, a Canadian NGO) and the second from a group of three NGOs – Communities for a Better Environment (CBE), the Bluewater Network of Earth Island Institute (Bluewater) and the Center for International Environmental Law (CIEL). Both of the amicus submissions were legal in

13 *Philip Morris* (n 11) Procedural Order No. 4 (24 March 2015) para 28 (emphasis added).

14 Michael Waibel and others (eds) *The Backlash Against Investment Arbitration: Perceptions and Reality* (Kluwer 2010).

15 *Philip Morris* (n 11) Award (8 July 2016) para 306.

16 For a full review see Kent (n 3).

nature; they were authored by renowned legal experts[17] and addressed investment law and international law more broadly.[18]

The Tribunal proceeded to deliver a decision on whether these entities were entitled to intervene as amici curiae.[19] On the question of whether the amicus could provide any unique and useful expertise, the Tribunal merely stated that while it could not decide at that early stage whether the submissions would be helpful, it 'must also assume that the Petitioners' submissions *could* assist the Tribunal.'[20] The Tribunal did not elaborate on why it must be assumed that international and investment law experts could assist the resolution of the dispute – a notion that, as discussed below, was in fact rejected in later cases. The Tribunal, it seems, responded to these offers of third-party assistance with an open mind, or at least intended to create the appearance of an open mind concerning the potential usefulness of the amicus submissions.

In any event, in its final award there is very little to indicate that the briefs were helpful for the Tribunal (that is beyond their mere acceptance, which was revolutionary at the time) or that the Tribunal relied on the amicus contributions in its analysis in any meaningful way. Of course, the absence of citation is not conclusive evidence that the interventions were not useful; they could have influenced the decision in subtle ways. However, after the Tribunal's initial eagerness to interact with the amici for the purpose of addressing wider legitimacy concerns, the fact that the Tribunal did not refer to the amicus submissions in its decision suggests that it did not, in fact, find them particularly useful.

2.1.2 Solicited Amicus Briefs

It is far less common for international courts and tribunals to solicit amicus briefs. There are however, occasional instances where assistance has been sought from non-partisan third-party experts, whose participation can be understood to fall within the more traditional 'amicus-as-independent expert' role. One notable example is the appointment of Professors Philippe Sands and Diane Orentlicher as amici in the *Charles Taylor* case before the Special Court

17 The IISD amicus brief was authored by Howard Mann and Professor Don McRae for the IISD, and Martin Wagner for CIEL, CBE and Bluewater.

18 *Methanex Corporation v. United States of America*, UNCITRAL, IISD amicus brief (9 March 2004).

19 *Methanex* (*n 18*) Decision of the tribunal on petitions from third persons to intervene as 'amici curiae' (15 January 2001).

20 ibid para 48.

for Sierra Leone in 2004.[21] In the ISDS universe, this form of participation is exceedingly rare, but not non-existent. One public health-related example is the case of *Achmea v. Slovakia*, which addressed *inter alia* a new law requiring health insurance providers to operate as not-for-profit entities. In this case, however, the amici (the European Commission and the Dutch Government) were not invited to contribute public health-related expertise. Rather, they were invited to submit their (non-health-related) observations on the validity of intra-EU investment treaties in light of EU Law.[22]

The amicus briefs in that case were described in the final award at great length, over a number of pages. The points made by the amici were 'considered carefully' and were described by the Tribunal as 'helpful'.[23] After a thorough review and discussion of the submissions, the Tribunal decided that:

> [it] has not found it necessary to rest any part of its decision upon the ostensible attitude of either Party to these arbitration proceedings – still less upon that of the Government of the Netherlands or of the European Commission – to the question of the status of the BIT or the existence, continuation or extent of the jurisdiction of the Tribunal.[24]

In short, the amici in this case presented a legal point; one that was welcomed by the Tribunal, even if eventually rejected.

2.1.3 General Invitations to Intervene as Amici

Finally, there is also a third model: a general invitation to intervene. According to this model, the tribunal does not invite a specific amicus but rather issues an open call for amici with specific expertise to intervene. Such invitations sometimes contain highly targeted requests, with tribunals explaining exactly what kind of information they will welcome.[25] On other occasions (and more commonly in ISDS, mostly based on NAFTA/USMCA rules), the invitation has

---

21 *Prosecutor v. Charles Ghankay Taylor*, Case No. SCSL-2003-01-I, SCSL-03-01-I-059, ICL 25 (SCSL 2004), Decision on Immunity from Jurisdiction, Appeals Chamber (SCSL) (31st May 2004).

22 *Eureko B.V. v. The Slovak Republic*, UNCITRAL, PCA Case No. 2008–13, Award on Jurisdiction (26 October 2010) para 154.

23 ibid para 217.

24 ibid para 219.

25 *Prosecutor v. Tihomir Blaskic* (IT-95-14).

been open-ended with no specification of the type of information the tribunal was hoping to elicit.[26]

The most notable health-related ISDS example in which the open invitation model was relied on is *Eli Lilly v. Canada*.[27] The invitation in this case resulted in no less than nine applications to intervene. Four of the briefs were submitted by groups of experts in Intellectual Property (IP) law, all of whom restricted their comments to their area of expertise. Another four applications were made by representatives of the pharmaceutical industry: these arguments varied from specific points of law to broader public policy arguments (including urging 'the Tribunal to dispose of this arbitration without commenting upon any substantive principles of Canadian patent law', which it argues could 'upset longstanding Canadian jurisprudence' on Canadian patent law).[28] The ninth submission was made by the Canadian Chamber of Commerce.[29] Six of these applications were eventually accepted, and the other three were rejected due to a lack of legal standing (the lack of a relevant nationality, in this case).

Despite accepting a large number of amicus submissions, the Tribunal did not openly engage with the information and arguments presented by amici. The final award did not rely on the amicus submissions, and the very few references made to these submissions were included in the part describing the parties' positions (rather than the Tribunal's own analysis).

While the *Eli Lilly* Tribunal did not engage with the amici, it did engage to a great extent with other external experts. Notably, the *Eli Lilly v. Canada* case folder includes no fewer than 28 expert reports. These reports mainly arrived from experts on different aspects of patent law and regulation. Two of these experts were medical experts, one of whom addressed drug approval

26 See for example ICSID, 'Koch Industries, Inc. and Koch Supply & Trading, LP v. Canada (ICSID Case No. ARB/20/52) – Amici Curiae' (News and Events, 1 February 2022) <https://icsid.worldbank.org/news-and-events/news-releases/koch-industries-inc-and-koch-supply-trading-lp-v-canada-icsid-case-no> accessed 23 September 2023; ICSID, 'Apotex Inc. v. United States of America – NAFTA/UNCITRAL Arbitration Rules Proceeding – Invitation to Amici Curiae' (News and Events, 9 August 2011) <https://icsid.worldbank.org/news-and-events/news-releases/apotex-inc-v-united-states-america-naftauncitral-arbitration-rules> accessed 23 September 2023.

27 ICSID, 'Eli Lilly and Company v. Government of Canada (ICSID Case No. UNCT/14/2) – Amici Curiae' (News and Events, 5 November 2015) <https://icsid.worldbank.org/news-and-events/news-releases/eli-lilly-and-company-v-government-canada-icsid-case-no-unct142-amici> accessed 23 September 2023.

28 The (accepted) amici arguments are summarised at *Eli Lilly* (n 9) Final award, 12–13.

29 See all applications and documents at italaw <www.italaw.com/cases/1625> accessed 23 September 2023.

submission processes in Canada, and the other biostatistics.[30] Unlike the amicus submissions, these expert opinions were heavily relied on by the Tribunal, which cited and quoted from them.[31] Moreover, the Tribunal explicitly acknowledged that these expert opinions were helpful:

> [f]inally, the Tribunal observes that the present case is one in which the facts are the law. Thus, this analysis necessarily touches upon aspects of Canadian patent law previously unfamiliar to the Members of the Tribunal. The Tribunal has been greatly assisted by the Parties' submissions and the testimony of their experts and witnesses, and thereby reaches its conclusions with confidence.[32]

This expression of gratitude for bringing in unique and necessary expertise was not extended to the amici, even though the amici provided similar expertise. Whether the omission of amici from this paragraph was conscious or not, the absence of any reference to the amicus submissions in the award (in contrast with the expert opinions) was surely not accidental.

A similar open-ended invitation to submit amicus briefs was issued in another health-related arbitration: *Apotex v. USA*. The amici in this case asked to contribute legal expertise and knowledge, notably regarding the interpretation of legal terms such as 'investment'[33] and 'Most Favoured Nation'.[34] The Tribunal refused these requests because *inter alia* it did not consider that the investment law expertise of the would-be amici was something the parties did not possess.[35] This position contrasts with the one adopted in *Methanex*, where investment law expertise was regarded as welcome. Nevertheless, in line with the approach in *Methanex*, the Tribunal in *Apotex* stressed the legitimacy-benefits of opening the arbitral process and allowing amicus participation:

> [i]n matters of public interest, the Tribunal considers that the requirement of a different expertise, experience or perspective from that of

30 See expert *Eli Lilly* (n 9) Expert Report of Bruce Levin (7 September 2015); *Eli Lilly* (n 9) Witness Statement of Kimby Barton (26 January 2015).

31 See for example *Eli Lilly*, Final award (n 28) paras 323, 333, 360, 420, 425.

32 ibid para 311.

33 *Apotex Inc. v. The Government of the United States of America*, ICSID Case No. UNCT/10/2, Procedural Order No. 2 on the participation of a non-disputing party (11 October 2011) para 10.

34 *Apotex v. USA* (n 33) Procedural Order on the Participation of the Applicant Barry Appleton as a non-disputing party) para 12.

35 *Apotex v. USA* (n 33) para 21.

> the Disputing Parties ought to be construed broadly, so as to allow the Tribunal access to the widest possible range of views. By ensuring that all angles on, and all interests in, a given dispute are properly canvassed, the arbitral process itself is thereby strengthened.[36]

However, unlike the *Methanex* Tribunal, the *Apotex* Tribunal explained that such legitimacy benefits can only be gained where the expertise being offered is useful for the Tribunal. The amicus' expertise, it was explained, is similar to that of the parties' lawyers, and therefore '[t]here is no reason to conclude that the Disputing Parties will not competently and comprehensively argue all issues regarding jurisdiction, and bring before the Tribunal all relevant perspectives on the meaning and scope of Article 1139 of the NAFTA'.[37] The legitimacy benefits of engaging with amici are thus linked with the nature and quality of expertise being offered, a sensible approach that avoids engagement with amici for the sole purpose of window dressing.

2.2 *The COVID-Context: Who Shall Be Welcomed at the Gates?*

It can be seen that Samuel Krislov's 'friendship to advocacy' spectrum is reflected in the multifarious identities and objectives of amici that emerge from a survey of the ISDS practice, and the varying extent to which tribunals have engaged with amicus submissions. We turn our focus now to investment cases that deal with health-related matters, which raise interesting questions regarding the kind of amici that may (and ought to) contribute to health-related investment cases, and under what conditions.

2.2.1 Assistance with Unique Arguments, Perspectives, and Expertise

First, arbitral decisions[38] and procedural rules[39] emphasise that the amicus role 'is to help the decision maker arrive at its decision by providing the

36 ibid paras 22–23.

37 ibid paras para 25.

38 See for example *Aguas Provinciales de Santa Fe S.A., Suez, Sociedad General de Aguas de Barcelona S.A. and InterAguas Servicios Integrales del Agua S.A. v. Argentina*, ICSID Case No. ARB/03/17, Order in response to a petition for participation as amicus curiae (17 March 2006) para 13; *Bernhard von Pezold and others v. Zimbabwe*, ICSID Case No ARB/1/15, Procedural Order No. 2 (26 June 2012) para 49; *Philip Morris* (n 11) para 21.

39 See for example ICSID, Rules of Procedure for Arbitration Proceedings (2022) Rule 67(2)(b); Agreement between the United States of America, the United Mexican States, and Canada (USMCA) (signed 30 November 2018, entered into force 1 July 2020) art 14.D.7(3); UNCITRAL, Rules on Transparency in Treaty-Based Investor-State Arbitration (January 2014) art 4(3)(b).

decision maker with arguments, perspectives, and expertise that the litigating parties may not provide'.[40] Undoubtedly, certain amici may be in a position to provide unique health-related knowledge in the context of health-related issues, for example by explaining the medical/scientific consensus or by providing a scientific review which may, or may not, justify measures taken by states. Cases such as *Philip Morris, Eli Lilly* and *Achmea* indeed reveal an appetite to interact with experts whose expertise goes beyond that of the Tribunal.[41] On the face of it, tribunals are likely to welcome amicus interventions in the context of COVID and other public health-related cases also, should such cases become common. Such expertise, after all, is well-beyond the expertise that can be expected of an arbitration panel.

The COVID context, however, gives rise to certain complications. The COVID era has been characterised by what could be referred to as the politicization of science. Different groups have harnessed science (or their own definition of 'science'), often for the purpose of achieving a variety of political results. The novelty of the pandemic and the lack of well-established research imply limits to scientific knowledge, a fact that by itself is being used and abused in relevant public debates. Where scientific health-related knowledge is becoming ever more political and divisive, several questions must be asked.[42]

First, as Krislov described, there is an ongoing shift in the amicus' role: from the traditional model of a neutral expert to the nowadays more prevalent model of an advocate. The ISDS universe has in fact harnessed this shift, utilising engagement with 'advocate amici' to improve the system's public perception and legitimacy. But can, and should, investment tribunals rely on (potentially politically-motivated) advocate amici to inform them of the 'science' in COVID-related cases? And do they have the tools to distinguish between 'real' science and its politically perverted version? In the COVID era, it could be that expecting an advocate-amicus to assist a panel by telling it, objectively and dispassionately, what the science is, may be overly optimistic.

40 *Suez* (n 38) para 13.

41 While in other (non-health-related) investment cases tribunals did not always accept help from amici claiming expertise in *non*-investment law areas (e.g. CIEL's claimed expertise in international environmental law was deemed as unrequired by the *Odyssey Marine Exploration v. Mexico* Tribunal), the explanation remains the same – as long as the parties' lawyers can address these matters, the amicus contribution shall not be regarded as unique and necessary. See *Odyssey Marine Exploration, Inc. v. United Mexican States*, ICSID Case No. UNCT/20/1, Procedural Order No. 6 (20 December 2021) para 23 (also other decisions cited by the Tribunal).

42 See further chapters 12 and 14.

Secondly, we explained above that the amicus procedure is important also (some might even say primarily) for democratic/perception/legitimacy reasons. In the context of COVID, one may question the positive contribution of amici to the system's legitimacy. Will amicus interventions by big pharmaceutical companies (e.g. vaccine makers) or, perhaps, anti-vaxxer groups, support the legitimacy of the ISDS? Even if rejected by the tribunal, these actors' mere intervention may be perceived by large segments of the public as problematic.

In short, in the COVID context, it becomes questionable whether the amicus' unique perceptions, knowledge, and expertise, are useful for the tribunal, and what the impact of this process on the legitimacy of ISDS is expected to be. One possible exception to this rule could be solicited amicus interventions, where the Tribunal itself targets the experts that it wishes to hear from. As we have discussed elsewhere,[43] tribunals did find this model useful, especially given its targeted nature and the trusted identity of the amici. This model could also possibly alleviate some of the concerns around legitimacy, although again, it will have to contend with the fact that, in the COVID era, it has become commonplace to question the objectivity of those professing neutral expertise. Even if concerns as to the objectivity of certain experts are misplaced, reliance on such expertise will not necessarily improve the public's perception of a tribunal's legitimacy. Amid the febrile scientific and policy debates that have been a feature of public discourse during the COVID pandemic, tribunals need to be on their guard when evaluating scientific evidence. For instance, they must take care to avoid falling into the 'false balance' fallacy of according weight to questionable as well as reputable sources, for the sake of appearing fair and enhancing their legitimacy in the eyes of the public.

2.2.2 What Kind of Amici Knowledge/Expertise Will Be Welcome?

This chapter concerns the role of the amicus as a provider of *knowledge* in health-related disputes. But what kind of knowledge is truly needed and welcomed by tribunals? As discussed above, tribunals have not always accepted amicus interventions, sometimes because the expertise offered was deemed unnecessary for resolving the dispute. Defining the exact type of knowledge/expertise that tribunals will want to accept seems therefore important, even if it is not always easy to define.

There is no doubt that medical/health-related expertise is remote enough from the typical expertise possessed by tribunals and counsel, and as such it should be regarded as useful in principle. The value of this type of information

---

43 Kent and Trinidad (n 1).

was made clear in the central role that the contributions of amici evidently played in the *Philip Morris* arbitration, and the influence they had on the final decision in that case.

The picture, however, is less clear where the expertise on offer is entirely legal in nature. The practice in this respect has not been consistent. Some tribunals have welcomed legal expertise in different areas of law (e.g. patent law in *Eli Lilly* or EU law in *Achmea*) and, at times, even in the very area of the tribunal's own expertise (e.g. the *Methanex* arbitration, accepting amicus briefs on investment law).[44] On other occasions, tribunals have rejected legal expertise on the basis that the amici's expertise is well-covered by the tribunal and the parties' lawyers,[45] at times even when the offered expertise went *beyond* the realm of investment law. For instance, the *Odyssey Marine Exploration* Tribunal rejected CIEL's amicus application with the following words:

> [i]n relation to CIEL, the Tribunal has no doubt that it has significant experience and expertise on matters of international *environmental* law. However, the Application for Leave has not demonstrated that CIEL can provide assistance on matters not addressed by the parties or that the parties are unable to provide in this arbitration.[46]

Importantly, one of the *Odyssey Marine Exploration* arbitrators – Professor Philippe Sands – dissented, claiming that the CIEL's ability to place the dispute in a wider context (notably that of the investment-environment-human rights interplay) is unique and that it goes beyond the parties' submissions, and as such it should have been accepted.[47]

Turning now to the unique context of COVID-related ISDS disputes, there can be no doubt that expertise in areas such as WHO law, medical law, public protest law, criminal law, etc, might be relevant and useful. It seems sensible that tribunals should accept this type of expertise when it is offered by amici. Equally, according to certain tribunals,[48] where the parties are able to provide this information through their lawyers and expert reports, the amicus

44 See also the practice of other tribunals, notably international criminal law tribunals: ibid.

45 *Apotex* (n 33) para 32; see also a decision on application by the same amicus (this time in collaboration with Professor Robert Howse) in *Resolute Forest Products Inc. v. Government of Canada*, PCA Case No. 2016–13, Procedural Order No. 6 (29 June 2017) para 4.4.

46 *Odyssey Marine Exploration* (n 41) para 23 (emphasis added).

47 See *Odyssey Marine Exploration* (n 41) Dissenting opinion by Philippe Sands (20 December 2021) para 6.

48 *Odyssey Marine Exploration* (n 41) para 23.

contribution will be redundant and deemed unnecessary. There is therefore no certainty that *any type* of expertise will be accepted, or rejected, by tribunals.

The question of what type of expertise will be accepted is also very much linked to a tribunal's objective in a given case. Where some tribunals have truly relied on the information submitted, others appear to have been more interested in promoting the wider legitimacy of the ISDS process. Those who are sceptical of the usefulness of amicus interventions will have their scepticism reinforced by the fact that certain tribunals will openly welcome amicus interventions, and then avoid engaging with the arguments of the amici in their decisions. To put it crudely, where the purpose of accepting amici intervention is mostly legitimacy-driven 'window dressing', it does not matter a great deal what type of expert submissions a tribunal agrees to hear. As long as the amicus is heard, and seen to be heard, the 'legitimacy' objective will be achieved, in a cosmetic sense.

2.2.3 Significant Interest in the Case

The main ISDS rules (e.g. ICSID, USMCA, UNCITRAL) also demand that the amicus demonstrate an 'interest in the case'. On the face of it, if interpreted narrowly, this condition could be problematic for expert amici. The *Apotex* Tribunal summarised the accepted interpretation of this condition in the following manner:

> To meet this requirement, the applicant needs to show that he has more than a 'general' interest in the proceeding. For example, the applicant must demonstrate that the outcome of the arbitration may have a direct or indirect impact on the rights or principles the applicant represents and defends.[49]

The interpretation of this condition could restrict the type of amici that can intervene in health-related matters. 'Advocate amici' may be able to demonstrate a 'significant interest', especially where the amici are NGOs or other organized groups, that are able to demonstrate a link with their organizations' declared goals and principles. Other types of amici – notably 'purely' scientific amici (e.g. university scientists) – will find it much harder to demonstrate a 'significant interest' that is unique to them. Unlike organised groups or NGOs, most scientific experts do not have publicly declared goals and objectives that

---

49 *Apotex* (n 33) para 38. See also *Eco Oro Minerals Corp. v. Republic of Colombia*, ICSID Case No. ARB/16/41, Procedural Order No. 6 (18 February 2019) para 34; *Resolute Forest Products* (n 45) para 4.6.

they are aspiring to promote. One useful example in this respect concerns Mr. Barry Appleton – an investment law expert – whose application to intervene in the *Apotex* dispute was rejected *inter alia* due to the lack of his 'significant interest' in the case.[50] A similar decision was made when Mr. Appleton attempted to intervene together with New York University Professor Robert Howse – a world renowned expert in international economic law – in the *Resolute Forest Products Inc. v. Canada* case.[51] Being an expert, it seems, does not equate with being 'significantly interested'.

In the context of public health (and even more so in the context of COVID), the result of this situation is somewhat perverse. Most will prefer to obtain their medical knowledge from objective sources and not from those with political agendas and specific interests in the case.[52] Accepting submissions from those with a 'general' interest in the case may also be advantageous for broader policy reasons. As noted above, investment tribunals are increasingly leveraging the amicus process to promote the legitimacy of ISDS. In a given COVID-related case, rejecting an amicus submission from a group of university scientists, while accepting one from a pro/anti vaccinations group (whose 'sufficient interest' may be easy to demonstrate) would surely put the legitimacy of the process at risk.

2.2.4 Do I Really Need a Friend?

This leads us to pose a rather provocative, but in our view justifiable, question: is amicus participation in health/COVID-related cases unnecessary or even actively unhelpful? The benefits of the amicus process in the context of ISDS disputes are often described as (1) promoting better decisions by enriching the information available to the panel, and (2) promoting the greater legitimacy of the ISDS process by creating the perception of an open and inclusive legal process.[53] The above discussion casts some levels of doubt on both of these assumptions.

To begin with, do amici really bring new knowledge that tribunals are otherwise unaware of? Perhaps. Others may claim that it is the job of the parties' lawyers to present the tribunal with all the relevant factual and legal background. Where the relevant knowledge is *scientific or legal in nature*, it may be reasonable to assume that this type of knowledge is available to the parties regardless of the amicus interventions, and that the parties' legal teams could

50 *Apotex* (n 33) paras 37–40.

51 *Resolute Forest Products* (n 45) para 4.6.

52 See chapters 12 and 14.

53 Kent (n 3).

present it without the benefit of external input. The health-related information presented by the two IGOs in the *Philip Morris* arbitration was hardly a secret, and indeed the parties were able to present the tribunals with a wealth of smoking-related data. Moreover, given that the IGOs briefs were entirely supportive of one side to the dispute – the state party (as is *very often* the case in ISDS) – there is nothing to stop this party from adding them to their own submissions, should they find it relevant and useful. The difference in these cases between the amici and a party-appointed expert is not entirely clear.

This is not to say that there are no cases where a genuine need for external expert knowledge arises. The expert opinions submitted in *Eli Lilly v. Canada* are a case in point, and the panel's reliance on these documents is indicative of the value that was accorded to them. These opinions, however, were not submitted via an independent third-party amicus route – the *parties* commissioned them and ensured their availability to the panel. Furthermore, where the objective is to obtain expert information beyond that which is available to the panel, there are more obvious – and more easily controllable – ways for a tribunal to do this than opening up the door to amici.[54]

This is not to argue that there are no cases in which the amicus participation could add value to the work of a tribunal. One example that comes to mind is amicus participation on behalf of affected communities who are unable to get their voices heard in the proceedings via a state party. However, in the context of health-related disputes and the pandemic more specifically, it is difficult to think of such cases, perhaps with one exception – groups that oppose state regulatory measures (i.e. lockdowns, vaccinations). Engagement with such groups (which have proliferated in many countries) would bring significant challenges for the integrity of ISDS, and lead us to a second point concerning the ISDS' legitimacy.

The modern preoccupation with the legitimacy of ISDS can be understood as a reaction to a widely propagated image of ISDS as a closed, secretive, corporate-oriented legal field. Indeed, many tribunals have openly stated that accepting amicus interventions will improve the image and legitimacy of ISDS.[55] However, for the reasons we have highlighted above, engagement with

---

54 Lucas Carlos Lima, 'Expert Advisor or Non-Voting Adjudicator? The Potential Function of Assessors in Procedure of the International Court of Justice' (2016) 99 Rivista di Diritto Internazionale 1123; Joost Pauwelyn, 'The Use of Experts in WTO Dispute Settlement (2002) 51(2) ILCQ 325; Giorgio Gaja, 'Assessing Expert Evidence in the ICJ' (2016) 15(3) LPICT 409; Avidan Kent, 'Renewable Energy Disputes Before International Economic Tribunals: A Case for Institutional Greening?' (2015) 12(3) TDM.

55 *Methanex* (n 19) para 48; *Biwater Gauff v. Tanzania* (Procedural Order No. 5) (2007) ICSID Case No ARB/05/22, para 51, and more recently (and with greater detail), Philippe Sands

amici in COVID-related cases is not guaranteed to enhance the legitimacy and public image of ISDS, and it could potentially even bring it into disrepute.

3 Concluding Remarks

We were asked by the editors of this volume to reflect on the potential role of amici in pandemic-related ISDS proceedings. The preceding analysis, which draws lessons from the evolution of amicus participation in international courts and tribunals, and more specific insights from ISDS practice in health-related cases, leave some room for cautious optimism. There is no doubt that expert knowledge and perspectives furnished by amici can contribute (indeed *have* contributed) positively to the resolution of health-related investment disputes. There is equally no doubt that this potential also exists in the more specific context of the pandemic.

It is nevertheless important to question the assumptions that underpin, and serve to justify, amicus participation, as well as the rules that govern it. To the extent that engagement with amici is driven by a desire to enhance the legitimacy of ISDS in the eyes of stakeholders and the broader public, future pandemic-related cases may turn the normal presumption – that engagement with amici is in principle a good thing – on its head. There can be few areas where the public discourse has been more fractious, or where assertions of scientific expertise have been more contested.

It remains to be seen whether the pandemic that has dominated our lives in recent years will also cast a long shadow over the future of ISDS. But if indeed COVID-related cases start to appear in large numbers, tribunals will inevitably have to deal with requests to intervene from a diverse array of amici curiae. They will need to exercise caution when evaluating whether, how and to what extent they should engage with such requests.

---

dissenting opinion in *Odyssey Marine Explorations* (n 41). The idea has also found expression in a recent article on the relevance of the amicus function in post-COVID public health-related ISDS cases: Christian Carbajal Valenzuela and Yolanda Mendoza Neyra, 'La Relevancia de los *Amicus Curiae* en los Arbitrajes Internacionales de Inversion Post-COVID-19 en Materia de Salud Pública' (2021) 39 Agenda Internacional, 201–225.

CHAPTER 14

Remarks on Procedural Issues concerning Scientific and Technical Evidence in Investment Arbitration

Gian Maria Farnelli

1 Introduction

The assessment of scientific and technical facts plays a major role in international adjudication.[1] Suffice to say that in the early *Factory at Chorzów* and *Corfu Channel* cases, respectively before the Permanent Court of International Justice and the International Court of Justice (ICJ), adjudicators already availed themselves of experts to assess points of fact concerning technical issues.[2]

Such relevance of technical expertise is mirrored in investment arbitration. There are many disputes revolving around states' measures based on alleged environmental or health risks which investors claim lack any scientific basis, thus being qualified as arbitrary and violating the fair and equitable treatment (FET).[3] As mentioned in chapters 12 and 13, reliance on scientific and technical facts in investment arbitration is furthermore likely to increase, given the potential of COVID-19 and climate change-issues to prompt investment disputes.[4]

---

1 See John Merrills and Eric De Brabandere, *Merrills' International Dispute Settelment* (7th edn, CUP 2022) 234; Makane M Mbengue, 'Scientific Fact-finding at the International Court of Justice: An Appraisal in the Aftermath of the Whaling Case' (2016) 29 LJIL 529; Jean D'Aspremont and Makane M Mbengue, 'Strategies of Engagement with Scientific Fact-Finding in International Adjudication' (2014) 5 JIDS 240; Laurence Boisson de Chazournes, 'Introduction: Courts and Tribunals and the Treatment of Scientific Issues' (2012) 3 JIDS 479.

2 *Case Concerning the Factory at Chorzów* (*Germany v. Poland*) (Merits) PCIJ Rep Series A No 17, 51; *Corfu Channel* (*United Kingdom of Great Britain and Northern Ireland v. Albania*) (Merits) [1949] ICJ Rep 4, 9.

3 This has occurred particularly in the context of arbitrations concerning obligations stemming from the *North Atlantic Free Trade Agreement* (NAFTA) (signed 17 December 1992, entered into force 1 January 1994, terminated 1 July 2020). See, *inter alia*, the *Methanex Corporation v. United States of America* (UNCITRAL), *Chemtura Corporation v. Government of Canada* (UNCITRAL, PCA Case No. 2008–01), *Campos de Pesé, S.A. v. Republic of Panama* (ICSID Case No. ARB/20/19) and *EcoDevelopment in Europe AB and EcoEnergy Africa AB v. United Republic of Tanzania* (ICSID Case No. ARB/17/33) arbitrations.

4 Merrills and De Brabandere (n 1) 234.

© KONINKLIJKE BRILL BV, LEIDEN, 2025 | DOI:10.1163/9789004711204_016

The knowledge necessary to assess scientific and technical facts is commonly, if not exclusively, acquired through experts, whose task is one of 'help[ing] non-experts [...] to understand the structure and behaviour of the "physical and natural world" through the application of accepted scientific methods such as observation and experiment'.[5] This is demonstrated, *inter alia*, by the widespread use of quantum experts in investment arbitration.[6] In the light of the above statement on the role of experts in introducing scientific and technical knowledge in investment arbitration, any acknowledgement of scientific and technical evidence in investment arbitration must inevitably consider expert-related issues.

However, the relevance of experts has not been met with a corresponding development of the procedural rules governing their use in investment arbitration. Before the 2022 amendments, ICSID Arbitration Rules only established that experts should be examined by the parties, and that the tribunal had the power to admit written expert deposition. Current ICSID Arbitration Rules add little by establishing that rules concerning witnesses also apply to party-appointed experts[7] and by acknowledging the tribunals' power to appoint their own experts unless the parties jointly disagree.[8]

The UNCITRAL Arbitration Rules are similarly vague. They simply refer to the possibility of presenting 'evidence by witnesses, including expert witnesses'[9] and to establish that experts, like witnesses, must testify and be cross-examined during hearings,[10] and regulate tribunal-appointed experts, allowing any party to raise objections regarding qualifications, impartiality, or independence, and to examine the expert.[11]

As is apparent, such bodies of arbitration rules, which *inter alia* equate experts to witnesses, are far from detailed. Tribunals have complemented the scant regulatory framework by invoking their inherent power to conduct

---

5 José E. Alvarez, 'The Search for Objectivity: The Use of Experts in *Philip Morris v. Uruguay*' (2018) 9 JIDS 411, 412.

6 Mélida Hodgson and Melissa Stewart, 'Experts in Investor-State Arbitration: The Tribunal as Gatekeeper' (2018) 9 JIDS 453, 456.

7 ICSID, 'Arbitration Rules' in ICSID, *ICSID Convention, Regulations and Rules* (2022) 88, art 38 <https://icsid.worldbank.org/rules-regulations/convention> accessed 15 December 2022 (ICSID Arbitration Rules).

8 ibid art 39. On the party's power to prevent the tribunal from appointing experts, see ICSID, 'Proposals for Amendment of the ICSID Rules' (2019) 1 Working Paper #3 317 <https://icsid.worldbank.org/resources/rules-amendments> accessed 15 December 2022.

9 UNCITRAL, 'Arbitration Rules' (2021) (UNCITRAL Arbitration Rules) art 17(3) <https://uncitral.un.org/en/texts/arbitration/contractualtexts/arbitration> accessed 15 December 2022.

10 ibid arts 27, 28.

11 ibid art 29.

proceedings in the way they consider necessary for the appropriate administration of justice.[12] They have exercised such power by following soft law rules elaborated by professional associations, with special regard to the International Bar Association Rules on the Taking of Evidence in International Arbitration (IBA Rules),[13] in particular Article 5 on party-appointed experts and Article 6 on tribunal-appointed experts.[14]

This contribution aims at reviewing the current procedural framework concerning the use of experts in investment arbitration in light of the case law. The

12 Such inherent power is commonly linked to art 44 ICSID Convention and art 17 UNCITRAL Arbitration Rules. For an analysis of these provisions see, respectively, Christoph H Schreuer and others, *The ICSID Convention. A Commentary* (2nd edn, CUP 2009) 672 ff; David D Caron and Caplan M Lee, *The UNCITRAL Arbitration Rules: A Commentary* (OUP 2013) 29 ff.

13 International Bar Association, *IBA Rules on the Taking of Evidence in International Arbitration* (2020) <www.ibanet.org/MediaHandler?id=def0807b-9fec-43ef-b624-f2cb2af7cf7b> accessed 15 December 2022. For an overview of the IBA Rules, see Peter Ashford, *The IBA Guidelines on Party Representation in International Arbitration: A Guide* (CUP 2016); Roman Khodykin and Carol Mulcahy, *A Guide to the IBA Rules on the Taking of Evidence in International Arbitration* (OUP 2019); Joseph E Neuhaus, Andrew J Finn, and David S Blackman, 'The 2020 IBA Rules on the Taking of Evidence in International Arbitration: A History and Discussion of the 2020 Revisions' in Amy C Kläsener, Martin Magál, and Joseph E Neuhaus (eds), *The Guide to Evidence in International Arbitration* (Law Business Research 2021) 20. On their relevance in investment arbitration practice, see, among others, *Peteris Pildegovics and SIA North Star v. Kingdom of Norway*, ICSID Case No. ARB/20/11, Procedural Order No 1 (12 October 2020) para 15.1; *Railroad Development Corporation v. Republic of Guatemala*, ICSID Case No. ARB/07/23, Decision on Provisional Measures (15 October 2008) para 32. On the relevance of this kind of 'procedural soft law instrument' in international arbitration, investment and commercial alike, see Felix Dasser, '"Soft Law" in International Commercial Arbitration' (2019) 402 RCADI 392, 492–512; Alexis Mourre, 'About Procedural Soft Law, the IBA Guidelines on Party Representation and the Future of Arbitration' in Patricia Shaughnessy and Sherlin Tung (eds), *The Powers and Duties of an Arbitrator: Liber Amicorum Pierre A. Karrer* (Kluwer 2017) 239.

14 The success of this soft law instrument stems from its being aimed at 'reflect[ing] and amalgamation' of the civil and common law legal tradition, see Hodgson and Stewart (n 6) 457; Siegfried H Elsing and John M Townsend, 'Bridging the Common Law – Civil Law Divide in Arbitration' (2002) 18 Arb Intl 1, 5–6. For the sake of completeness, one has to recall that the IBA is not the only legal association which has produced 'procedural soft law' on experts. Suffice to recall the Chartered Institute of Arbitrators, which has adopted in 2007 a *Protocol for the Use of Party-Appointed Expert Witnesses in International Arbitration* (September 2007) <www.ciarb.org/media/6824/partyappointedexpertsinternationalarbitration.pdf> accessed 15 December 2022.

study will also consider the relevant practice concerning quantum and legal experts[15] who, from a procedural standpoint, are akin to scientific experts.

This contribution will be structured in three parts, in addition to this introduction and the concluding remarks. Firstly, issues concerning the rules governing party-appointed experts, with special regard to requirements for submission of the expert report, will be addressed. Secondly, the above analysis will be mirrored with regard to tribunal-appointed experts, whose use has been limited so far.[16] Thirdly, the study will provide some considerations on the assessment of the probative value of experts' evidence.

2 Party-Appointed Experts

Party-appointed experts must submit an 'expert report' containing the conclusions they have reached.[17] On the basis of the report, experts will be then examined and cross-examined during the hearings.[18] The report will arguably

15 The use of legal experts raises many issues, mostly stemming from their proximity to advocacy. Indeed, while it is generally acknowledged that '[f]rom the standpoint of International Law … municipal laws are merely facts' (*Certain German interests in Polish Upper Silesia (Germany v. Poland)* (Merits) PCIJ Rep Series A No 7, 19), domestic law may well be applicable law in investment arbitration and, thus, should not be the object of the parties' burden of proof due to the *jura novit curia* principle (Frédéric G Sourgens, Kabir Duggal, and Ian A Laird, *Evidence in International Investment Arbitration* (OUP 2018) 135–46). This is all the more true with regard to international law. Thus, scholars have suggested that legal experts would better serve as co-counsel (Nigel Blackaby and Alex Wilbraham, 'Practical Issues Relating to the Use of Expert Evidence in Investment Treaty Arbitration' (2016) 31 ICSID Review 655; Hodgson and Stewart (n 6) 454–5) or should be disqualified (Alvarez (n 5) 415–8).

16 To the Author's knowledge, investment tribunals have appointed experts, mostly quantum experts, only in few cases, namely *American Manufacturing & Trading, Inc. v. Republic of Zaire*, ICSID Case No. ARB/93/1, Award (21 February 1997) para 7.19); *S.A.R.L. Benvenuti & Bonfant v. People's Republic of the Congo*, ICSID Case No. ARB/77/2, Award (8 August 1980) paras 1.24, 4.77; *CMS Gas Transmission Company v. The Republic of Argentina*, ICSID Case No. ARB/01/8, Award (12 May 2005) paras 50–51; *Enron Corporation and Ponderosa Assets, L.P. v. Argentine Republic*, ICSID Case No. ARB/01/3, Award (22 May 2007) para 38; *Sempra Energy International v. The Argentine Republic*, ICSID Case No. ARB/02/16, Award (28 September 2007) para 47; *Société Ouest Africaine des Bétons Industriels v. Senegal*, ICSID Case No. ARB/82/1, Award (25 February 1988) para 9.06.

17 IBA Rules (n 13) art 5(1); ICSID Arbitration Rules (n 7) arts 38(1), 38(7); UNCITRAL Arbitration Rules (n 9) art 27(2).

18 This may be inferred from a contextual reading of the ICSID Arbitration Rules (n 7) arts 38(1), 38(4), and 38(7) and from the UNCITRAL Arbitration Rules (n 9) art 27(2). It is also explicitly provided for under the IBA Rules (n 13) art 5(5).

be disregarded if the submitting expert is not present during the hearings,[19] notwithstanding the fact that neither the ICSID Arbitration Rules nor the UNCITRAL Arbitration Rules explicitly provide for this effect in cases of the expert's failure to attend to the hearings. However, this practice has been commonly applied by investment tribunals, even explicitly referring to the IBA Rules.[20]

According to Article 5 IBA Rules, the expert report must be filed within a timeframe set by the tribunal. Arbitral practice has usually followed the IBA Rules that require expert reports to be filed at the earliest possible stage of proceedings.[21] The current version of Article 5 ICSID Arbitration Rules establishes the same,[22] while the UNCITRAL Arbitration Rules remain silent on the point.[23]

Neither the IBA Rules nor the ICSID and UNCITRAL Arbitration Rules establish the consequences of late filing of expert reports. According to general rules on international adjudication, as exemplified by Article 56 ICJ Rules

19 IBA Rules (n 13) art 5(5).

20 See, among others, *Discovery Global LLC v. Slovak Republic*, ICSID Case No. ARB/21/51, Procedural Order No. 1 (28 March 2022) para 19.7; *Hela Schwarz GmbH v. People's Republic of China*, ICSID Case No. ARB/17/19, Procedural Order No. 1 (9 March 2018) para 21.6; *Michael Anthony Lee-Chin v. Dominican Republic*, ICSID Case No. UNCT/18/3, Procedural Order No. 1 (23 October 2018) para 17.4; *OOO Manolium Processing v. Republic of Belarus*, UNCITRAL, PCA Case No. 2018–06, Procedural Order No. 1 (17 May 2018) para 40; *Pawlowski AG and Project Sever s.r.o. v. Czech Republic*, ICSID Case No. ARB/17/11, Procedural Order No. 1 (13 February 2018) para 19.2.

21 See, among others, *Beijing Shougang and others v. Mongolia*, UNCITRAL, PCA Case No. 2010–20, Procedural Order No. 1 (2 October 2010) para 41; *Eco Oro Minerals Corp. v. Republic of Colombia*, ICSID Case No. ARB/16/41, Procedural Order No. 1 (30 November 2017) para 18.1; *Gabriel Resources Ltd. and Gabriel Resources (Jersey) v. Romania*, ICSID Case No. ARB/15/31, Procedural Order No. 1 (26 August 2016) para 17; *Lone Pine Resources Inc. v. The Government of Canada*, ICSID Case No. UNCT/15/2, Procedural Order No. 1 (11 March 2015) para 49.

22 'ICSID Arbitration Rules (n 7) art 5(1): 'Supporting documents, including witness statements, expert reports, exhibits and legal authorities, shall be filed together with the request, written submission, observations or communication to which they relate'. It is to be noted that, during the discussion on the amendments to the ICSID Arbitration Rules, the point of the timing of filing the expert reports was not raised specifically. Indeed, the only proposal, which was not adopted, was that of mirroring art 5(1) in art 38 (see ICSID, 'Proposals for amendment of the ICSID Rules' (June 2021) 1 Working Paper #5 para 68 <https://icsid.worldbank.org/resources/rules-amendments> accessed 15 December 2022).

23 The UNCITRAL Arbitration Rules just refer to the obligation to provide a written statement of the expert witness as evidence unless the tribunal decides otherwise (UNCITRAL Arbitration Rules (n 9) art 27(2)).

of Procedure, adjudicators may allow late filing, even with the disagreement of the parties, if they consider the evidence necessary to decide the case. Investment arbitration has however followed a different solution. The arbitral practice has filled the gap in arbitration rules by sanctioning late production with inadmissibility[24] unless 'special circumstances' justifying late filing are demonstrated and the other party has the possibility to submit its observations on the matter.[25]

Article 5 IBA Rules goes on to require that the report includes a 'description of [the expert's] background, qualifications, training and experience'.[26] Such a guideline has not been explicitly adopted by the ICSID or UNCITRAL during the last round of amendments of their arbitration rules, though, again, arbitral tribunals usually conform to it.[27]

Incomplete filing of the above information has been met in arbitral practice with a reduction of the expert's credibility, rather than inadmissibility of the report. This is in line with the general practice in international adjudication where the relevance of a given piece of evidence does not play a role in determining its admissibility.[28] That means that issues concerning the expert's qualification impact on the probative value of the evidence. This occurred in *Yukos*, where the Tribunal allowed the production of an expert

---

24 See, for example, Procedural order No. 1 in *Berkowitz v. Costa Rica*, whereby '[t]he Tribunal shall not admit any [expert] testimony that has not been filed with the written submissions' (*Aaron C. Berkowitz, Brett E. Berkowitz and Trevor B. Berkowitz* (formerly *Spence International Investments and others*) *v. Republic of Costa Rica*, ICSID Case No. UNCT/13/2, Procedural Order No. 1 (26 February 2014) para 19.2).

25 See, for example, *ACP Axos Capital GmbH v. Republic of Kosovo*, ICSID Case No. ARB/15/22, Procedural Order No. 1 (10 February 2016) para 17.2; *Freeport-McMoRan Inc. v. Republic of Peru*, ICSID Case No. ARB/20/8, Procedural Order No. 1 (17 June 2021) para 18.2; *Koch Industries, Inc. and Koch Supply & Trading, LP v. Canada*, ICSID Case No. ARB/20/52, Procedural Order No. 1 (29 June 2021) para 17.3; *Sodexo Pass International SAS v. Hungary*, ICSID Case No. ARB/14/20, Procedural Order No. 1 (17 June 2015) para 17.2.

26 IBA Rules (n 13) art 5(2)(a).

27 One may mention in this sense Procedural order No. 1 in *Resolute Forest*, whereby '[e]ach expert report shall include [...] a statement of qualifications of the expert in the claimed area of expertise' (*Resolute Forest Products Inc. v. Government of Canada*, UNCITRAL, PCA Case No. 2016–13, Procedural Order No. 1 (29 June 2016) para 12.2. Similarly, *Lion Mexico Consolidated L.P. v. United Mexican States*, ICSID Case No. ARB(AF)/15/2, Procedural Order No. 1 (14 October 2016) para 19.3.2; *Menzies Middle East and Africa S.A. and Aviation Handling Services International Ltd. v. Republic of Senegal*, ICSID Case No. ARB/15/21, Procedural Order No. 1 (30 October 2015) para 19.1.2: *Pawlowski AG* (n 20) para 18.6.3).

28 Chester Brown, *A Common Law of International Adjudication* (OUP 2007) 90–92.

report by a non-lawyer on termination of the ECT, but held that the report was not authoritative, thus attributing limited probative value.[29]

The third and last requirement of the expert report under the IBA Rules is the inclusion of a 'statement of the facts upon which [the expert] is basing his or her expert opinions and conclusions'.[30] This includes specifying the documents on which the expert relies. As is apparent, the rationale of such a requirement is to assure the opposing party a fair chance to challenge the substance of the expert's opinion.

This requirement has no place either in the ICSID Arbitration Rules or in the UNCITRAL Arbitration Rules. Moreover, the preparatory works of the amendments to Article 38 ICSID Arbitration Rules imply that such indication is not required.[31]

Again, arbitral practice has supplemented the lack of explicitness in relevant arbitration rules by following the guidance provided by the IBA Rules.[32] The *South American Silver Ltd* arbitration is of particular interest in this regard. There, the Respondent, Bolivia, asked for the production of the transcription of certain handwritten notes, taken by the claimant's expert during discussions with analysts, to aid in the preparation of the expert report. The Claimant objected that such a request had no basis in the procedural rules applicable to the arbitration. The Tribunal found for Respondent, holding that 'the conversations between [the expert] and these four analysts are information upon which [the] expert report relies'.[33] The Tribunal was assisted in reaching this conclusion by the introduction of the report itself, which hinted to the relevance of such notes as a basis for the expert's opinion.[34]

---

29 *Yukos Universal Limited (Isle of Man) v. The Russian Federation*, UNCITRAL, PCA Case No. 2005-04/AA227, Interim Award on Jurisdiction and Admissibility (30 November 2009) para 96.

30 IBA Rules (n 13) art 5(2)(d).

31 'There is no specific form requirement for a witness statement or expert report, other than that it must be in writing, identify the witness or expert, describe the testimony of the witness or expert, and be signed and dated' (ICSID, 'Proposals for amendment of the ICSID Rules' (2 August 2018) 3 Working Paper #1 para 429 <https://icsid.worldbank.org/resources/rules-amendments> accessed 15 December 2022).

32 *BSG Resources Limited, BSG Resources (Guinea) Limited and BSG Resources (Guinea) SÀRL v. Republic of Guinea*, ICSID Case No. ARB/14/22, Procedural Order No. 1 (13 May 2015) para 19.6; *Discovery Global* (n 20) paras 19.4–19.5; *Lion Mexico Consolidated* (n 27) para 19.3.3; *Tennant Energy, LLC v. Government of Canada*, UNCITRAL, PCA Case No. 2018–54, Procedural order No. 1 (24 June 2019) para 10.2.

33 *South American Silver Limited v. Bolivia*, UNCITRAL, PCA Case No. 2013–15, Procedural Order No. 11 (27 May 2014) para 20.

34 ibid para 19.

However, situations of uncertainty are common, and neither the IBA Rules nor the case law provide clear guidance on the issue. Given this context, it seems reasonable to agree with scholars who argue that the relevant criterion should be whether the information in point introduces new facts.[35] This is arguably particularly relevant for scientific expert reports which, for their very nature, may introduce a number of new facts in the proceedings.

3 Tribunal-Appointed Experts

The law of international adjudication acknowledges the inherent power of tribunals to appoint their own experts.[36] This also occurs in investment arbitration. As mentioned above, Article 6 IBA Rules, Article 39 ICSID Arbitration Rules and Article 29 UNCITRAL Arbitration Rules codify such power.

The arbitral practice concerning tribunal-appointed experts is much less common than that of party-appointed experts.[37] This is most likely due to the consideration that the appointment of a tribunal expert would increase the costs of the proceedings, which would ultimately be borne by the parties.[38] Furthermore, even if a tribunal decides not to appoint its own experts, it may still benefit from scientific expertise from other sources, namely *amici curiae* brief. This is perfectly exemplified in the *Philip Morris* case, where the Tribunal found for Respondent with regard to the FET compliance of tobacco control measures, due to evidence on their utility in decreasing smoking provided as *amici* by the World Health Organization, the Secretariat of the Convention on Tobacco Control and the Pan American Health Organization.[39]

Article 39(2) ICSID Arbitration Rules requires the Tribunal to consult with the parties regarding the 'terms of reference' of the experts. According to the

35 Sourgens, Duggal, and Laird (n 15) 227–8.

36 Cesare PR Romano, 'The Role of Experts in International Adjudication' in Société Française pour le Droit International (ed), *Le Droit International Face aux Enjeux Environnementaux* (Pedone 2010) 181; Malcom N Shaw, *Rosenne's Law and Practice of the International Court: 1920–2015*, vol 3 (Brill 2016) 276, 325.

37 See (n 16).

38 Indeed, the IBA Rules, the ICSID Arbitration Rules and the UNCITRAL Arbitration Rules all require the tribunal to consult with the parties as to the fees of the tribunal-appointed expert (IBA Rules (n 13) art 6(1); ICSID Arbitration Rules (n 7) art 39(2); UNCITRAL Arbitration Rules (n 9) art 29(1)).

39 *Philip Morris Brands Sàrl, Philip Morris Products S.A. and Abal Hermanos S.A. v. Oriental Republic of Uruguay*, ICSID Case No. ARB/10/7, Award (8 July 2016) para 391. For an in-depth analysis of the use of scientific experts in *Philip Morris*, see Alvarez (n 5) 414–5.

preparatory works of the new ICSID Arbitration Rules, this means that the expert will have to provide a statement of qualification and disclosure of any impartiality issue.[40] The UNCITRAL Arbitration Rules are more explicit in this regard when compared to ICSID Arbitration Rules. Article 29(2) explicitly refers to the fact that '[t]he expert shall [...] submit to the arbitral tribunal and to the parties a description of his or her qualifications and a statement of his or her impartiality and independence'.[41]

This appears reasonable. Indeed, the qualifications and independence of a tribunal-appointed expert is more sensitive than that of a party-appointed expert. As the *Abaclat* case shows, the relationship between a tribunal-appointed expert and one of the parties may be raised as grounds for 'disqualification' of the expert,[42] similar to what happens to arbitrators.[43] In this sense, the *ad hoc* Committee in *Exxon Mobil* acknowledged that the lack of impartiality of the tribunal-appointed expert may impact on the tribunal's impartiality, though not automatically.[44]

The tribunal-appointed expert report must be provided to the parties, and the expert may be cross-examined by counsels and experts of both parties.[45] Since provisions on party-appointed experts apply *mutatis mutandis* to tribunal-appointed experts,[46] it could be argued that the report must contain an indication of facts, information and methodology on which it is based. Moreover, the ICSID and the UNCITRAL Arbitration Rules follow the same approach as a requirement for parties to disclose to the expert any information he or she needs and refer potential disputes on that to the tribunal.[47]

---

40 ICSID, 'Proposals for Amendment of the ICSID Rules' (March 2019) 1 Working Paper #2 181, paras 254–255 <https://icsid.worldbank.org/resources/rules-amendments> accessed 15 December 2022; Working Paper #3 (n 8) para 100.

41 ICSID Arbitration Rules (n 7) art 29(2).

42 *Abaclat and Others v. Argentine Republic*, ICSID Case No. ARB/07/5, Procedural order No. 15 (20 November 2012) para 14; *Mobil Exploration and Development Inc. Suc. Argentina and Mobil Argentina S.A. v. Argentine Republic*, ICSID Case No. ARB/04/16, Decision on Disqualification of Tribunal Expert (23 March 2015).

43 For the sake of completeness, it should be recalled that recent case law points toward the fact that undisclosed relationships between an arbitrator and party-appointed experts may lead to annulment (*Eiser Infrastructure Limited and Energía Solar Luxembourg S.à r.l. v. Kingdom of Spain*, ICSID Case No. ARB/13/36, Decision on annulment (11 June 2020)).

44 *Mobil Exploration and Development Inc. Suc. Argentina and Mobil Argentina S.A. v. Argentine Republic*, ICSID Case No. ARB/04/16, Decision on Annulment (8 May 2019) para 46.

45 IBA Rules (n 13) art 6(4)-(5); ICSID Arbitration Rules (n 7) art 39(5); UNCITRAL Arbitration Rules (n 9) art 29(4)-(5).

46 ICSID Arbitration Rules (n 7) art 39(6).

47 ibid art 39(4); UNCITRAL Arbitration Rules (n 9) art 29(3).

ICSID and UNCITRAL Arbitration Rules are also similar in recognising the parties' right to make written submissions after the filing of the report and the right to examine the expert during the oral proceedings.[48] This puts tribunal-appointed experts on an equal footing with respect to party-appointed experts, in compliance with the equality of arms principle and the adversarial nature of investment arbitration.[49] It also prevents investment tribunals from using 'phantom experts' like the ICJ.[50] Indeed, using phantom experts in the context of investment arbitration would most likely impact on the credibility of the award for the losing party and may lead to an annulment for manifest excess of power or departure from a fundamental rule of procedure. This corroborates the view that 'the institutional context matters' and that 'caution [is suggested] before assuming that the evidentiary practice (and premises) applicable in the ICJ should be applied to [...] investor-state arbitration'.[51]

4 The Assessment of Evidence Presented by Party-Appointed Experts

The assessment of the probative value of evidence provided by scientific and technical experts involves several challenges for arbitrators, given the fact that expert reports are likely to rely on objective facts, defined best practices,

48 ICSID Arbitration Rules (n 7) art 39(5)-(6); UNCITRAL Arbitration Rules (n 9) art 29(4)-(5).

49 Campbell McLachlan, 'Equality of Parties before International Investment Tribunals (2019) 80 Ann IDI 1; Eve Bain, 'When Some are More Equal than Others: The Need for a More Substantive Conception of "Equality of the Parties" in Investment Arbitration' (2018) YB Intl Inv L & Pol 292.

50 The debate on the use of 'phantom experts' was prompted by the joint dissenting opinion of Judges Al-Khasawneh and Simma in the Pulp Mills case (*Pulp Mills on the River Uruguay (Argentina v. Uruguay)* (Joint dissenting opinion of Judges Al-Khasawneh and Simma) [2010] ICJ Rep 108, para 14), though the use of 'ghost experts' by the ICJ has been common for years, as acknowledged by Former President Jennings (Robert Jennings, 'International Lawyers and the Progressive Development of International Law' in Jerzy Makarczyk (ed), *Theory of International Law at the Threshold of the 21st Century: Essays in Honour of Krzysztof Skubiszewski* (Kluwer 1996) 413, 413), and also not unknown under the guise of 'in-house experts' by the WTO (Chad P Bown, *The WTO Secretariat and the Role of Economics in Panels and Arbitrations* (CUP 2010) 14). Amongst the many voices who participated to such debate, see Lucas C Lima, 'The Debate on The Use of Experts by the International Court of Justice: An Inquiry Through Sociological Lenses' (2020) 34 Temple Int CompLJ. 253; Guillaume Gros, 'Unseen Actors as Unseen Experts: Ghosts in International Adjudication' in Freya Beatens (ed), *Legitimacy of unseen actors in international adjudication* (CUP 2019) 347; Giorgio Gaja, 'Assessing Expert Evidence in the ICJ' (2016) 15 LPICT 409; Mbengue (n 1).

51 Alvarez (n 5) 421–2.

research protocols, or industry standards that arbitrators are unlikely to be familiar with.

Arbitrators bridged potential gaps in knowledge necessary to assess the probative value of experts' evidence by focusing on their role of determining whether states' actions based on scientific or technical knowledge complied with standards of treatment, rather than assessing the 'scientific truth'.[52] For example, in *Chemtura*, the dispute revolved around Canada's ban on the use of a pesticide, of which the investor was a producer, due to alleged environmental and health risks. The investor claimed that such ban was in breach of the FET and constituted expropriation under the NAFTA. To streamline its task, the Tribunal focused on the reasonableness of Canada's process of reviewing the use of the pesticide.[53] The Tribunal found for Respondent because the evidence submitted by the Claimant did not show bad faith, discrimination or other arbitrary conducts by Canada or its reviewing agency, rather than because of proof of the environmental risk allegedly posed by the pesticide – i.e. the underlying scientific issue.[54]

In assessing the probative value of expert evidence, as aptly highlighted by Judge Donoghue, arbitrators have applied so-called 'second-order indicators', which are geared towards assessing facts by probabilities.[55] This appears in line with the wide use of the probabilistic standard of proof of 'preponderance of evidence' in international adjudication in general,[56] and in investment

---

52 Joan E Donoghue, 'Expert Scientific Evidence in a Broader Context' (2018) 9 JIDS 379, 382–3. This consideration echoes Judges Al-Khasawneh and Simma's statement according to which 'the task of a court of justice is not to give a scientific assessment of what has happened, but to evaluate the claims of parties before it and whether such claims are sufficiently well-founded so as to constitute evidence of a breach of a legal obligation' (*Pulp Mills* (n 50) para 4).

53 *Chemtura Corporation v. Government of* Canada, UNCITRAL, PCA Case No 2008–01, Award (2 August 2010) para 137.

54 ibid para 138. For a summary of the decision, see Alain Pellet, 'Police Powers or the State's Right to Regulate: Chemtura v. Canada' in Meg Kinnear and others (eds), *Building International Investment Law: The First 50 Years of ICSID* (Kluwer 2016) 447.

55 Donoghue (n 50) 283–4.

56 On the standard in general, see Chittharanjan F Amerasinghe, *Evidence in International Litigation* (Brill 2005) 241–2; Markus Benzing, 'Evidentiary Issues' in Andreas Zimmermann and others (eds), *The Statute of the International Court of Justice: A Commentary* (3rd edn, OUP 2019) 1371, 1403; Brown (n 28) 100; Mojtaba Kazazi, *Burden of Proof and Related Issues. A Study on Evidence Before International Tribunals* (Brill 1996) 347–50. Such standard has been summarized in the case law of the ICJ as one requiring the establishment of a fact 'on a balance of probabilities' (*Land, Island and Maritime Frontier Dispute* (*El Salvador/Honduras: Nicaragua intervening*) (Merits) [1992] ICJ Rep 506, para 248). On the ICJ case law on the standard of proof, see Gian Maria Farnelli, 'Consistency in the ICJ's Approach to the Standard of Proof: An Appraisal of the Court's Flexibility' (2022) 21 LPICT 98.

arbitration in particular,[57] notwithstanding authoritative scholarly works pointing out that 'scientific fact-finding enunciates "probabilities" while traditional fact-finding methods validate "veracities"'.[58]

Among these 'second-order indicators', the analysis of factors which impinge on an expert's credibility and impartiality is particularly important, as demonstrated in the *Yukos*[59] and *Occidental Petroleum*[60] arbitrations. This consideration is also corroborated by the debate that took place during the amendment of ICSID Arbitration Rules. Some states proposed that Article 38 required party-appointed experts 'to submit a written declaration of independence and impartiality and to disclose their relationships, if any, with the participants in the proceeding'.[59] Such a proposal was not adopted, because concerns as to the independence and impartiality of experts 'go to the credibility of the [...] expert', that is the probative value of experts' evidence, which is for the tribunal to assess.[60] However, a tribunal has to be careful in assessing the probative value of a report by an unqualified expert, as *Enron* demonstrates. There, the Tribunal allowed the submission of an expert report by a non-legal expert and heavily relied on its position for purposes of construing the customary rule on the state of necessity.[61] The *ad hoc* Committee later annulled the award on the ground of manifest excess of powers because, *inter alia*, the Tribunal failed to consider the lack of qualification of the expert in weighing the evidence.[62]

Other relevant 'second-order indicators' appear to be the agreement between the parties' experts,[63] which the tribunal may order to be recorded in

57 Sourgens, Duggal, and Laird (n 15) 80–5. But see Robert Pietrowski, 'Evidence in International Arbitration' (2006) 22 Arb Int'l 373, 379–80.

58 D'Aspremont and Mbengue (n 1) 246. On scientific evidence and related burden of proof issues in international adjudication in general, see Caroline Foster, *Science and the Precautionary Principle in International Courts and Tribunals: Expert Evidence, Burden of Proof and Finality* (CUP 2011) 77 ff.

59 Working Paper #3 (n 8) para 94.

60 ibid para 97.

61 *Enron Corporation* (n 16) paras 300 ff.

62 *Enron Corporation* (n 16) Decision on the Application for Annulment of the Argentine Republic (30 July 2010) paras 374–77. On the issues, see Johannes Hendrik Fahner, *Judicial Deference in International Adjudication. A Comparative Analysis* (Hart 2020) 95–96.

63 See, for example, *Ioan Micula, Viorel Micula, S.C. European Food S.A, S.C. Starmill S.R.L. and S.C. Multipack S.R.L. v. Romania* [I], ICSID Case No. ARB/05/20, Final Award (11 December 2013) para 792; *Sevilla Beheer B.V. and others v. Kingdom of Spain*, ICSID Case No. ARB/16/27, Decision on Jurisdiction, Liability and Principles of Quantum (11 February 2022) para 1001.

writing,[64] and the methodology and sources described in the experts' reports.[65]

As it is apparent, the use of 'second-order indicators' by arbitrators means that tribunals decide scientific and technical issues raised by the parties in investment arbitration exclusively based on each party persuasiveness, leaving little or no room for deference of any party's scientific assessment.[66] This is likely not the case regarding scientific and technical assessments made by the tribunal-appointed experts. Indeed, arbitrators may feel compelled to defer to the tribunal-appointed expert's assessment of scientific or technical facts, that is to attribute to the evidence provided by the expert full probative value. This flows from the consideration that elements impinging on the expert's credibility would most likely be considered by the tribunal before, rather than following, appointment. The risk that a similar situation may impact on the arbitrators' decision-making power has raised some concerns among practitioners and states during the debate over the amendment of ICSID Arbitration Rules,[67] concerns which were cursorily met with the consideration that burden of proof-related issues will remain in the tribunal's power according to Article 36 ICSID Arbitration Rules.[68]

5 Conclusion

This analysis has shown that procedural rules concerning the introduction of scientific and technical evidence *via* experts in investment arbitration still have significant gaps. While the recent development in ICSID Arbitration Rules, as

64 According to the IBA Rules, a tribunal may request the experts to record those points of agreement in writing. (IBA Rules (n 13) art 5(4)). Such guideline has not been adopted neither by the ICSID nor the UNCITRAL.

65 As pointed out by Nigel Blackaby and Alex Wilbraham, '[o]ne of the key qualities required for any technical assertion to be deemed compatible with scientific methodology is that it be independently verifiable or susceptible to peer review' (Blackaby and Wilbraham (n 15) 660).

66 This is in stark contrast with the practice of other international economic law *fora*, with special regard to the WTO Dispute Settlement Body. Some authors have voiced against this practice by investment tribunals, calling for more deference to States' scientific assessment due, inter alia, to tribunals being 'less suited to making a determination regarding scientific facts compared with the government that adopts a measure based on that facts' (Yuka Fukunaga, 'Standard of Review and "Scientific Truths" in the WTO Dispute Settlement System and Investment Arbitration' (2012) 3 JIDS 559, 575). See also Fahner (n 62) 93–96.

67 Working Paper #2 (n 40) para 251; Working Paper #3 (n 8) para 102.

68 Working Paper #3 (n 8) para 102.

well as the ample reference to soft law instruments, like the IBA Rules, must be welcomed, many issues still remain unaddressed. Namely, those concerning requirements for the admissibility of experts' evidence and the assessment of its probative value, given the likely lack of knowledge of the arbitrators as to the methodology and standards applied by the expert.

This is particularly relevant when one considers the practice of not meeting lack of qualification and expertise of a party-appointed expert with inadmissibility. While such practice, arguably stemming from the consideration that arbitrators lack the competence to assess such elements as early as the filing of the report, may appear a sensible one, it also implies that the other party will have to produce evidence to counter it. This also applies in the case of a report drafted by a patently unqualified person, which may lead to annulment, as the *Yukos*[69] and *Enron*[70] disputes demonstrate, and involves additional costs.

A wider use of tribunal-appointed experts, in particular those with scientific backgrounds, from the early stage of proceedings may arguably be instrumental in avoiding the risk of additional costs. Indeed, the tribunal expert might provide guidance also in assessing the qualification of a party-appointed expert, thus allowing the tribunal to assess the relevance of the report and then decide whether to admit its production or not.

However, the appointment of a tribunal expert may pose issues, particularly regarding costs and the distribution of the tribunal's fact-finding power. In this regard, direct regulation by relevant ISDS institutions providing guidelines on the use of tribunal-appointed experts may appear a wise solution, especially considering that scientific expertise is becoming increasingly relevant in investment arbitration, given the possibility of COVID-19 and climate change-related investment litigation in the near future, dealing with highly technical and specialized medical and environmental issues.[71]

69 See (n 28).

70 See (n 62).

71 On the issue in point, see the considerations by Carolina Arlotta, 'The Impact of the COVID-19 Pandemic on Foreign Investment and Investment Arbitration: From Energy Transition Disrupted to the Path Forward to a Greener Future' (2022) 15 JWEL & B 382.

Selected Bibliography

Chapter 1

Acconci, Pia 'Sustainable Development and Investment. Trends in Law-making and Arbitration' in Andrea Gattini, Attila ME Tanzi, and Filippo Fontanelli (eds), *General Principles of Law and International Investment Arbitration* (Brill 2018) 290.

Acconci, Pia 'The Integration of Non-investment Concerns as an Opportunity for the Modernization of International Investment Law: Is a Multilateral Approach Desirable?' in Giorgio Sacerdoti and others (eds), *General Interests of Host States in International Investment Law* (CUP 2014) 165.

Choudhury, Barnali 'International Investment Law and Non-Economic Issues' (2020) 53 Vanderbilt Journal of Transnational Law 1.

Faccio, Sondra *Indirect Expropriation in International Investment Law. Between State Regulatory Powers and Investor Protection* (Editoriale Scientifica 2020).

Henckels, Caroline 'Indirect Expropriation and the Right to Regulate: Revisiting Proportionality Analysis and the Standard of Review in Investor-State Arbitration' (2012) 15 Journal of International Economic Law especially 238.

Katselas, Anna T 'Do Investment Treaties Prescribe a Deferential Standard of Review' (2012) 34 Michigan Journal of International Law 87.

Manciaux, Sébastien 'Big Pharma and Investment Arbitration' (2021) 4 Vietnamese Journal of Legal Sciences 88.

Mistelis Loukas and Giammarco Rao, 'Multilateral Principles in a Bilateral World' (2021) 1 The Italian Review of International and Comparative Law 59.

Ortino, Federico 'The Social Dimension of International Investment Agreements: Drafting A New BIT/MIT Model?' (2005) 7 International Law FORUM du droit international 243.

Puig Sergio and Gregory Shaffer, 'A Breakthrough with the TPP: the Tobacco Carve-out' (2016) 16 Yale Journal Health Policy, Law, and Ethics 327.

Chapter 2

Baetens, Freya 'Protecting Foreign Investment and Public Health Through Arbitral Balancing and Treaty Design', 71 ICLQ (2022) 139.

Bartels Lorand and Federica Paddeu, 'Introduction' in Lorand Bartels and Federica Paddeu (eds), *Exceptions in International Law* (OUP 2020) 1.

Beyer Vincent and Hamed El-Kady, 'Accelerating Substantive International Investment Agreements Reform: Policy Perspectives in Times of a Global Pandemic' in Yulia

Levashova, Pascale Accaoui Lorfing (eds), *Balancing the Protection of Foreign Investors and States Responses in the Post-Pandemic World* (Kluwer 2022) 191.
Gostin, Lawrence O *Public Health Law – Power, Duty, Restraint* (University of California Press 2008).
Henckels, Caroline 'Scope Limitation or Affirmative Defence? The Purpose and Role of Investment Treaty Exception Clauses' in Lorand Bartels and Federica Paddeu (eds), *Exceptions in International Law* (OUP 2020) 363.
Qin, Julia Ya 'Forced Technology Transfer, and the US-China Trade War: Implications for International Economic Law' (2019) 22 Journal International Economic Law 743.
Taylor, Allyn L 'Global Health Law: International Law and Public Health Policy' (2017) International Encyclopedia of Public Health 268.
Vadi, Valentina 'Towards a New Dialectics – Pharmaceutical Patents, Public Health, and Foreign Direct Investments (2015) 5 New York Journal of Intellectual Property and Entertainment Law 1.
Vadi, Valentina *Public Health in International Investment Law and Arbitration* (Routledge 2013).
Viñuales, Jorge E 'Seven Ways of Escaping a Rule: Of Exceptions and Their Avatars in International Law' in Lorand Bartels and Federica Paddeu (eds), *Exceptions in International Law* (OUP 2020) 65.

Chapter 3

AES v. Argentine, ICSID Case No. ARB/02/17, Decision on the Respondent's Proposal to Disqualify All Members of the Tribunal (6 April 2022).
Bernasconi-Osterwalder Nathalie and Sarah Brewin Nyaguthii Maina, 'Commentary: Protecting against Investor–State Claims Amidst COVID-19: A Call to Action For Governments' (*IISD*, April 2020) <www.iisd.org/system/files/publications/investor-state-claims-covid-19.pdf> accessed 13 December 2022.
Case Concerning the Detention of Three Ukrainian Naval Vessels (Ukraine v. Russian Federation), (Provisional Measures, Order of 25 May 2019) ITLOS Reports 2019.
HSH Nordbank AG v. Spain, ICSID Case No. ARB/15/45, Decision on the Second Proposal to Disqualify All Members of the Tribunal (15 December 2020).
ICC, 'ICC Guidance Note on Possible Measures Aimed at Mitigating the Effects of the COVID-19 Pandemic' (9 April 2020) <https://iccwbo.org/publication/icc-guidance-note-on-possible-measures-aimed-at-mitigating-the-effects-of-the-covid-19-pandemic/> accessed 13 December 2022.
ICSID, 'Code of Conduct for Adjudicators in International Investment Disputes' <https://icsid.worldbank.org/resources/code-of-conduct> accessed 2 April 2023.

Roberts Anthea and Taylor St John, 'Complex Designers and Emergent Design: Reforming the Investment Treaty System' (2022) 116 AJIL 96.

UNCITRAL, 'Decisions Adopted by States Members of UNCITRAL in August 2020 in Accordance With the Procedure for Taking Decisions of UNCITRAL During the Coronavirus Disease 2019 (COVID-19) Pandemic' (28 August 2020) A/CN.9/1038.

Waibel Michael (ed), *The Backlash Against Investment Arbitration: Perceptions and Reality* (Kluwer 2010).

Chapter 4

Bonnitcha, Jonathan 'Investment Wars: Contestation and Confusion in Debate About Investment Liberalization' (2019) 22 J Intl Econ L 629.

Casey, Christopher A *Nationals Abroad: Globalization, Individual Rights, and the Making of Modern International Law* (CUP 2020).

Farrell Henry and Abraham L Newman, 'Weaponized Interdependence: How Global Economic Networks Shape State Coercion' (2019) 44 Intl Secur 42.

Lall Sanjaya and Paul Streeten (eds), *Foreign Investment, Transnationals and Developing Countries* (Palgrave Macmillan 1977).

OECD, 'Framework for Screening Foreign Direct Investment into the EU. Assessing Effectiveness and Efficiency' (2022) <www.oecd.org/investment/investment-policy/oecd-eu-fdi-screening-assessment.pdf> accessed 22 September 2023.

Pohl, Jens Hillebrand 'The Impact of Investment Treaty Commitments on the Design and Operation of EU Investment Screening Mechanisms' in Steffen Hindelang and Andreas Moberg (eds), *YSEC Yearbook of Socio-Economic Constitutions 2020: A Common European Law on Investment Screening (CELIS)* (Springer 2021) 725.

Shirlow, Esmé *Judging at the Interface: Deference to State Decision-Making Authority in International Adjudication* (CUP 2021).

Wigell, Mikael, Sören Scholvin, and Mika Aaltola, *Geo-Economics and Power Politics in the 21st Century: The Revival of Economic Statecraft* (Routledge 2018).

Chapter 5

Aiyar, Shekhar, Andrea F Presbitero, and Michele Ruta (eds), *Geoeconomic Fragmentation: The Economic Risks from a Fractured World Economy* (CEPR 2023) 11.

Bassan, Fabio *The Law of Sovereign Wealth Funds* (Elgar 2011).

Chan Zenobia T and Sophie Meunier, 'Behind the Screen: Understanding National Support for a Foreign Investment Screening Mechanism in the European Union' (2022) Rev Int Organ 513.

Hindelang Steffen and Andreas Moberg (eds), YSEC *Yearbook of Socio-Economic Constitutions 2020* (Springer 2021).

Pohl Jens Hillebrand and others (eds), *Weaponising Investment*, vol 1 (Springer 2023).

Pugliese, Sara 'Toward a New EU Strategic Dimension: Common Purchase and Investment Screening Mechanisms as a Means of Crisis Preparedness and Management' (2022) Il Diritto dell'Unione Europea 391.

Roberts, Veronica *Foreign Direct Investment Regulation Guide* (2nd ed, Law Business Research 2022).

Velten, Jens *Screening Foreign Direct Investment in the EU Political Rationale, Legal Limitations, Legislative Options* (Springer 2022).

Wehrlé Frédéric and Joachim Pohl, 'Investment Policies Related to National Security: A Survey of Country Practices' (2016) 3 OECD Working Papers on International Investment <https://doi.org/10.1787/5jlwrrf038nx-en> accessed 5 December 2023.

Xueref-Poviacas Emily and others, 'The Evolving Concept of National Security' in Veronica Roberts (ed), *Foreign Direct Investment Regulation Guide* (Law Business Research Ltd 2022) 23.

Chapter 6

EU Commission, 'Communication from the Commission – Guidance to the Member States Concerning Foreign Direct Investment and Free Movement of Capital from Third Countries, and the Protection of Europe's Strategic Assets, Ahead of the Application of Regulation (EU) 2019/452 (FDI Screening Regulation)' [2020] OJ C099I/1.

EU Commission, 'Report from the Commission to the European Parliament and the Council: Second Annual Report on the screening of foreign direct investments into the Union' COM (2022) 433 final.

French Ministry of Economics, 'Le contrôle des Investissements Étrangers en France en 2021' (March 2022) <https://www.tresor.economie.gouv.fr/Articles/9aa76183-24a8-49ba-9466-179c5b29f99c/files/47b9b032-3d2b-4779-8327-15d3400045ab> accessed 10 October 2023.

German Ministry of Economic Affairs and Climate Action, 'Investment Screening in Germany: Facts & Figures' (2023) <www.bmwk.de/Redaktion/EN/Publikationen/Aussenwirtschaft/investment-screening-in-germany-facts-figures.pdf?__blob=publicationFile&v=6> accessed 23 September 2023.

Judgment of the Court of Justice of the EU of 23 May 2000, Case C-58/99 *Commission v Italy* [2000] ECR I-03811.

Judgment of the Court of Justice of the EU of 26 March 2009, Case C-326/07 *Commission v Italy* [2009] ECR I-02291.
Lai, Keyan 'National Security and FDI Policy Ambiguity: A Commentary' (2021) 4 J Int Bus Policy 496.
Regulation (EU) 2019/452 of the European Parliament and of the Council of 19 March 2019 Establishing a Framework for the Screening of Foreign Direct Investments into the Union [2019] OJ L079I/1.
Schöning Falk and Stefan Kirwitzke, 'The Rise of Foreign Investment Control in Europe and Beyond Under the Impact of COVID-19' (2020) 16 Competition L Int'l 31.
Sottosegretariato di Stato alla Presidenza del Consiglio dei ministri, 'Relazione Concernente l'attività Svolta sulla Base dei Poteri Speciali sugli Assetti Societari nei Settori della Difesa e della Sicurezza Nazionale, Nonché per le Attività di Rilevanza Strategica nei Settori dell'energia, dei Trasporti e delle Comunicazioni – Anno 2021' (2022) DOC LXV, N 4.

Chapter 7

Baetens, Freya 'Protecting Foreign Investment and Public Health Through Arbitral Balancing and Treaty Design' (2022) 71(1) ICLQ 139.
Blanco, Sebastián Mantilla 'Full Protection and Security and the Rule of Law' in August Reinisch and Stephan Schill (eds), *Investment Protection Standards and the Rule of Law* (OUP 2023) 81.
Blanco, Sebastián Mantilla *Full Protection and Security in International Investment Law* (Springer 2019).
Gruszczynski, Lucasz *Regulating Health and Environmental Risks under WTO Law* (OUP 2011).
Herdegen, Matthias *The International Law of Biotechnology* (2nd edn, Elgar 2023).
Kurtz, Jürgen *The WTO and International Investment Law: Converging Systems* (CUP 2016).
Levashova Yulia and Pascale Accaoui Lorfing (eds), *Balancing the Protection of Foreign Investors and States Responses in the Post- Pandemic World* (Kluwer 2022).
Matsushita Mitsuo and others, *The World Trade Organization* (3rd edn, OUP 2015).
Roberts, Anthea 'Clash of Paradigms: Actors and Analogies Shaping the Investment Treaty System' (2013) 107 AJIL 45.
Salacuse, Jeswald *The Law of Investment Treaties* (3rd edn, OUP 2021).

Chapter 8

Besson, Samantha 'Sovereignty, International Law and Democracy' (2011) 22 EJIL 376.

de Brabandere, Eric, Paula B M da Cruz, 'The Role of Proportionality in International Investment Law and Arbitration: A System-Specific Perspective' (2020) 89 Nordic Journal of International Law 471.

Gaukrodger, David 'The Balance Between Investor Protection and the Right to Regulate in Investment Treaties: A Scoping Paper' (2017) 2 OECD Working Papers on International Investment 1.

Hertogen, An 'Letting Lotus Bloom' (2015) 26(4) EJIL 901.

Karl, Joachim 'International Investment Arbitration: A Threat to State Sovereignty' in Wenhua Shan and others (eds), *Redefining Sovereignty in International Economic Law* (Hart Publishing 2008).

Kingsbury Benedict and Stephan Schill, 'Public Law Concepts to Balance Investors' Rights with State Regulatory Actions in the Public Interest – the Concept of Proportionality' in Stephan Schill (ed), *International Investment Law and Comparative Public Law* (OUP 2010).

Levashova, Yulia *The Right of States to Regulate in International Investment Law: The Search for Balance Between Public Interest and Fair and Equitable Treatment* (Kluwer Arbitration 2019).

Ortino, Federico 'The Obligation of Regulatory Stability in the Fair and Equitable Treatment Standard: How Far Have We Come?' (2019) 21(4) Journal of International Economic Law 845.

Ratner, Steven 'Fair and Equitable Treatment and Human Rights: A Moral and Legal Reconciliation' (2022) 25(4) JIEL 568.

Valenti, Mara 'The Protection of General Interests of Host States in the Application of the Fair and Equitable Treatment Standard' in Giorgio Sacerdoti and others (eds), *General Interests of Host States in International Investment Law* (CUP 2014).

Chapter 9

Bücheler, Gebhard *Proportionality in Investor-State Arbitration* (OUP 2015).

De Brabandere, Eric 'States' Reassertion of Control over International Investment Law – (Re)Defining "Fair and Equitabe Treatment" and "Indirect Expropriation"' in Andreas Kulick (ed), *Reassertion of control over the investment treaty regime* (CUP 2017) 304.

Hoffmann, Anne K 'Indirect Expropriation' in August Reinisch (ed), *Standards of investment protection* (OUP 2008).

Paine, Joshua 'Standard of Review: Investment Arbitration' (*Max Planck Encyclopedia of Public International Law*, January 2018) <https://opil.ouplaw.com/view/10.1093/law-mpeipro/e3664.013.3664/law-mpeipro-e3664> accessed 30 October 2019.

Reinisch August and Christoph Schreuer, *International Protection of Investments: The Substantive Standards* (CUP 2020).

Reinisch, August 'Legality of Expropriations' in August Reinisch (ed), *Standards of investment protection* (OUP 2008) 173.

Titi, Catharine 'Police Powers Doctrine and International Investment Law' in Andrea Gattini and others (eds), *General Principles of Law and International Investment Arbitration* (Brill Nijhoff 2018) 323.

Weiner, Allen S 'Indirect Expropriations: The Need for a Taxonomy of "Legitimate" Regulatory Purposes Recurring Themes: Indirect Expropriation in International Law' (2003) 5 Int'l LF D Int'l 166.

Zhu, Ying 'Do Clarified Indirect Expropriation Clauses in International Investment Treaties Preserve Environmental Regulatory Space?' (2019) 60 Harv Int'l LJ 377.

Ziad Roland and Bo Ra Hoebeke, 'Perspectives on Expropriation Claims in a Post-Pandemic World' in Yulia Levashova and Pascale Accaoui Lorfing (eds), *Balancing the Protection of Foreign Investors and States Responses in the Post-Pandemic World* (Wolters Kluwer 2022) 155.

Chapter 10

Arato, Julian, Kathleen Claussen, and Benton J Heath, 'The Perils of Pandemic Exceptionalism' (2020) 114(3) AJIL 627.

Bernasconi-Osterwalder, Nathalie, Sarah Brewin, and Nyaguthii Maina, 'Protecting Against Investor–State Claims Amidst COVID-19: A call to action for governments' (IISD, April 2020) <https://www.iisd.org/articles/protecting-against-investor-state-claims-amidst-covid-19-call-action-governments> accessed 1 August 2022.

Chaisse, Julien 'Both Possible and Improbable: Could COVID-19 Measures Give Rise to Investor-State Disputes?' (2020) 13 Contemporary Asian Arbitration Journal 99.

Inan, Onur 'Can States Successfully Resort to the Customary International Defences against the Possible Claims Arising out of COVID-19 Measures?' (2020) 14 Romanian Arbitration Journal 131.

Joshi, Riddhi 'Force Majeure under the ILC Draft Articles on State Responsibility: Assessing its Viability against COVID-19 Claims' (2020) 24(24) ASIL <https://www.asil.org/insights/volume/24/issue/24/force-majeure-under-ilc-draft-articles-state-responsibility-assessing> accessed 1 August 2022.

Ostrove Michael and others, 'State Defences to Investment Claims Arising from COVID-19' (DLA Piper, 29 April 2020) <https://www.dlapiper.com/fr/france/insights/publications/2020/04/state-defences-to-investment-claims-arising-from-covid-19/> accessed 1 August 2022.

Paddeu Federica and Freya Jephcott, 'COVID-19 and Defences in the Law of State Responsibility: Part I' (17 March 2020) EJIL Talk <https://www.ejiltalk.org/covid-19-and-defences-in-the-law-of-state-responsibility-part-i/> accessed 1 August 2022.

Paddeu Federica and Freya Jephcott, 'COVID-19 and Defences in the Law of State Responsibility: Part II' (17 March 2020) EJIL Talk <https://www.ejiltalk.org/covid-19-and-defences-in-the-law-of-state-responsibility-part-ii/> accessed 1 August 2022.

'Perspectives – COVID-19 & International Investment Protection' (Shearman & Sterling, 14 April 2020) <https://www.shearman.com/Perspectives/2020/04/COVID-19-International-Investment-Protection> accessed 1 August 2022.

Potin, Nathalie 'Lines of Attack and Defences for Foreign Investors and States in Future Investment Disputes Post-Pandemic' (2022) 28(2) International Trade Law and Regulation 90.

Titi, Catherine 'Police Powers Doctrine and International Investment Law' in Andrea Gattini, Attila ME Tanzi, and Filippo Fontanelli (eds), *General Principles of Law and International Investment Arbitration* (Brill 2018) 323.

Chapter 11

Baetens, Freya 'Protecting Foreign Investment and Public Health through Arbitral Balancing and Treaty Design' (2022) 71 ICLQ 139.

Bayrak, Orhan 'Economic Crises and the Fundamental Change of Circumstances in Investment Arbitration' (2020) 35(1–2) ICSID Review 130.

Beechey John and Antony Crockett, 'New Generation of Bilateral Investment Treaties: Consensus or Divergence?' (2008) Contemporary Issues in International Arbitration and Mediation: The Fordham Papers 5.

Burke-White William and Andreas von Staden, 'Investment Protection in Extraordinary Times: The Interpretation and Application of Non-Precluded Measures Provisions in Bilateral Investment Treaties' (2008) 48(2) VaJIntlL 307.

Cristani, Federica 'How the Coronavirus Crisis Challenges International Investment (Customary) Law Rules: Which Role for the Necessity Defense?' (2021) 53 Case Western Reserve JIntlL 89.

Kabra, Ridhi 'Return of the Inconsistent Application of the "Essential Security Interest" Clause in Investment Treaty Arbitration: CC/Devas v India and Deutsche Telekom v India' (2019) 34(3) ICSID Review 723.

Katsikis, Dimitrios '"Necessity" due to COVID-19 as a Defence to International Investment Claims' (2021) 36(1) ICSID Review 46.

Khachvani, David 'Non-Compensable Regulation versus Regulatory Expropriation: Are Climate Change Regulations Compensable?' (2020) 35(1–2) ICSID Review 154.

Kim, Julie 'Balancing Regulatory Interests through an Exceptions Framework under the Right to Regulate Provision in International Investment Agreements' (2018) 50(2) Geo Wash Intl L Rev 289.

Lee, Janice 'Note on COVID-19 and the Police Powers Doctrine: Assessing the Allowable Scope of Regulatory Measures during a Pandemic' (2020) 13(1) Contemp Asia Arb J 229.

Chapter 12

Blackaby Nigel and Alex Wilbraham, 'Practical Issues Relating to the Use of Expert Evidence in Investment Treaty Arbitration' (2016) 31(3) ICSID Review 655.

Faccio, Sondra 'The World Health Organization's Response to the Health Emergency and its Impact on Investment Arbitration and Human Rights Case Law' (2023) 25 International Community Law Review 476.

Gazzini, Tarcisio *Interpretation of International Investment Treaties* (Hart 2016).

Orellana, Marcos A 'The Role of Science in Investment Arbitrations Concerning Public Health and the Environment' (2006) 17(1) Yearb Int Environ Law 48.

Sheargold Elizabeth and Andrew D. Mitchell, 'Public Health in International Investment Law and Arbitration' in Julien Chaisse, Leïla Choukroune, Sufian Jusoh (eds), *Handbook of International Investment Law and Policy* (Springer 2021).

Sulyok, Katalin *Science and Judicial Reasoning. The Legitimacy of International Environmental Adjudication* (CUP 2022).

Viñuales, Jorge E *Foreign Investment and the Environment* (CUP 2012).

Chapter 13

Baetens, Freya 'Protecting Foreign Investment and Public Health through Arbitral Balancing and Treaty Design' (2022) 71 ICLQ 139.

Gaja, Giorgio 'Assessing Expert Evidence in the ICJ' (2016) 15(3) The Law and Practice of International Courts and Tribunals 409.

Kent Avidan and Jamie Trinidad, 'Amicus Curiae Participation in International Proceedings' in Avidan Kent, Nikos Skoutaris, and Jamie Trinidad (eds) *The Future of International Courts* (Routledge 2019).

Kent Avidan and Jamie Trinidad, 'International Law Scholars as Amici Curiae: An Emerging Dialogue (of the Deaf)?' (2016) 29(4) Leiden Journal of International Law 1081.

Kent Avidan and Jamie Trinidad, 'The Management of Third Party Amicus Participation before International Criminal Tribunals: Juggling Effectiveness and Legitimacy' (2017) 17 International Criminal Law Review 728.

Kent, Avidan 'Public Participation as an Evolving Norm: From Rio to Mauritius' in Eric De Brabandere and others (eds), *Public Participation and Foreign Investment Law* (Brill 2021).

Krislov, Samuel 'The Amicus Curiae Brief: From Friendship to Advocacy' (1962) 72 Yale Law Journal 694.

Lima, Lucas Carlos 'Expert Advisor or Non-Voting Adjudicator? The Potential Function of Assessors in Procedure of the International Court of Justice' (2016) 99 Rivista di Diritto Internazionale 1123.

Pauwelyn, Joost 'The Use of Experts in WTO Dispute Settlement (2002) 51(2) ICLQ 325.

Chapter 14

Alvarez, José E 'The Search for Objectivity: The Use of Experts in Philip Morris v Uruguay (2018) 9 JIDS 411.

Cortesi, Giulio Alvaro *Proof and the Burden of Proof in International Investment Law* (Springer 2022).

D'Aspremont Jean and Makane M Mbengue, 'Strategies of Engagement with Scientific Fact-Finding in International Adjudication' (2014) 5 JIDS 240.

de Chazournes, Laurence Boisson 'Introduction: Courts and Tribunals and the Treatment of Scientific Issues' (2012) 3 JIDS 479.

Fukunaga, Yuka 'Standard of Review and "Scientific Truths" in the WTO Dispute Settlement System and Investment Arbitration' (2012) 3 JIDS 559.

Hodgson Mélida and Melissa Stewart, 'Experts in Investor-State Arbitration: The Tribunal as Gatekeeper' (2018) 9 JIDS 453.

Mbengue, Makane M 'Scientific Fact-finding at the International Court of Justice: An Appraisal in the Aftermath of the Whaling Case' (2016) 29 LJIL 529.

Neuhaus, Joseph E, Andrew J Finn, and David S Blackman, 'The 2020 IBA Rules on the Taking of Evidence in International Arbitration: A History and Discussion of the 2020 Revisions' in Amy C Kläsener, Martin Magál and Joseph E Neuhaus (eds), *The Guide to Evidence in International Arbitration* (Law Business Research 2021) 20.

Romano, Cesare PR 'The Role of Experts in International Adjudication' in Société Française pour le Droit International (ed), *Le droit international face aux enjeux environnementaux* (Pedone 2010) 181.

Sourgens, Frédéric G, Kabir Duggal, and Ian A Laird, *Evidence in International Investment Arbitration* (OUP 2018).

Index

Printed in the United States
by Baker & Taylor Publisher Services